THE PROFESSIONAL

LANDSCAPER'S HANDBOOK

EVERYTHING YOU NEED TO KNOW TO START & RUN YOUR OWN LANDSCAPING or LAWN CARE BUSINESS

GREG MICHAELS

≋ american river press

Published by American River Press®, Berkeley, California,
United States.

The Professional Landscaper's Handbook: Everything
You Need to Know to Start and Run Your Own
Landscaping or Lawn Care Business

ISBN: 978-0-9841838-2-1

Table of Contents

Chapter 5: Landscape Plant Management 73

Acknowledgements

Many thanks to Don Shor, Advanced California Certified Nursery Professional and owner of Redwood Barn Nursery in Davis, CA for proofreading several drafts of this book. Many improvements and corrections were added through his efforts. I'm grateful Don took this project on and that I had the opportunity to learn from him. Included below is a partial list of individuals and organizations that also contributed to this book. I extend my sincere thanks to each of them.

Larry Costello, environmental horticulture advisor for the University of California Cooperative Extension, proofread and provided editorial suggestions for the Landscape Plant Management, Soil, and Pruning chapters. Turfgrass specialist Ali Harivandi of the University of California Cooperative Extension proofread and provided editorial guidance for the Turfgrass Management chapter. I'm grateful and indebted to both Larry and Ali for lending their expertise; their suggestions improved the text.

Landscape architect Jess Stryker (irrigationtutorials.com) proofread and provided editorial suggestions for the Irrigation System Repair chapter. Sarah Wikander of Irrigation Equipment Company proofread a draft of the Irrigation System Repair chapter. Micah Charlot of Irrigation Equipment Company contributed technical irrigation information. Brad and Frank of JB's Power Equipment proofread a draft of the Equipment and Supplies chapter. UC horticulture associate Katherine Jones provided suggestions for the Pruning Fruit Trees chapter.

Ron Fujie, CPA, proofread and provided useful editorial feedback on the tax, bookkeeping, and other small business information. Tony Delevati, CPA, proofread an early draft of the accounting and tax chapters. Copyeditor Ralph Dranow proofread two early drafts of this book.

Sydney Park Brown facilitated the permissions procedure to reproduce the University of Florida IFAS Extension article entitled, *Considerations for Developing a Lawn and Landscape Maintenance Contract*.

James R. Huston, author of *How To Price Landscape & Irrigation Projects*, gave his consent for me to write about the estimating/bidding system he calls the Lawn Maintenance Package Approach. Huston's book is helping many green industry professionals run their businesses.

The Irrigation Association granted permission to reproduce the tables on species factors, density factors, and microclimate factors and the accompanying footnotes from their publication *Landscape Irrigation Scheduling and Water Management*.

Lance Elliot of Hunter Industries facilitated the permissions procedure to reproduce the selected irrigation factor tables from *Irrigation Notes: Scheduling Irrigation* (LIT-088).

Echo Marketing Services provided the image of the Echo PE-280 edger and granted permission to reproduce it.

The following individuals also helped facilitate the use of proprietary material: Larry Costello of University of California Cooperative Extension; Michelle Johnson of Pearson Education; Bob MacArthur of Grounds Maintenance Magazine; Kathy Ashmore of the International Society of Arboriculture; Diana J. Hagan EDIS Librarian IFAS extension University of Florida; Bill Darlington, Scott McKee and Jim West of Soil and Plant Laboratory; John Dunn and Brad Fresenburg of the University of Missouri; Julie Saare-Edmonds of the California Department of Water Resources; Colleen Rodriguez of the University of Colorado Cooperative Extension; Kathleen Combs of API; Gina Harps of OSHA; Charlie Melendez of Storm Manufacturing Group Inc., David Dugan of Oregon® Blount; Marcella McTaggart and Gerri Silva of the El Dorado County Environmental Management Department; the staff at the Outdoor Power Equipment Institute; and last but not least, landscaping author Robert Kourik.

Dan Young formatted the references. Daniel R. and Gabriel H. generously provided feedback. Shanti xviiiTHE PROFESSIONAL LANDSCAPER'S HANDBOOK

S., Jing Z., F. Watson, and Kate H. also provided helpful feedback.

Special thanks to a few of the clients I've had over the years, including June, Dave and Melinda, Bob W., Richard S., Paul and Marie, Steve H., Mary B., Suzanne S., Mary M., and Janet S.

Warning-Disclaimer

This book provides information on starting and running a landscape management business. It is sold with the understanding that the publisher and author are not engaged in rendering legal, accounting, or other professional services. If legal or other expert assistance is required, the services of a competent professional should be sought.

It is not the purpose of this book to reprint all of the information that is available to landscape management professionals, but only to complement and supplement other texts. You are urged to read all of the available material, learn as much as possible about landscape management and small business, and tailor the information to your needs. For more information, see the many resources in the appendix.

Every effort has been made to make this handbook as complete and accurate as possible. However, there may be mistakes, both typographical and in content. Therefore, this text should be used only as a general guide and not as the ultimate source of landscape management or small business information. Furthermore, this handbook contains information on landscape management and small business that is current only up to the printing date.

The author and publisher shall have neither liability nor responsibility to any person or entity with respect to any loss or damage caused, or alleged to have been caused, directly or indirectly, by the information contained in this book. Further, no warranty may be created or extended by promotional materials.

The mention of a specific trademark, company, or organization is not intended to imply any endorsement by or affiliation with that entity. Reference to an organization or website does not necessarily mean that the author or the publisher endorses the information the organization or website provides. The mention or photograph of a product is for instructional and informational purposes only and does not constitute an endorsement. Readers are advised to conduct their own research to determine which products best suit their needs.

The fact that some product marks or names in this text do not bear a trademark symbol does not mean that the product mark or name is not registered as a trademark or trade name. All trademarked names mentioned are the property of their owners.

Preface

Preface to the 2019 minor update. A few years have passed since PLH was first released, and I'm grateful the book has been well received by the landscaping community. When I entered this field in the '90s, I started to build my own landscaping business with little more than drive, determination, and the right customer service mindset. But I quickly came to see that a lot of specialized knowledge was also needed. I searched for a detailed, comprehensive resource that would teach me the trade. I found a few good books, but none that answered most of my basic questions.

It became clear to me that many landscapers were plying their trade without adequate knowledge, as evidenced by less-than-professional trade practices and off-the-cuff bidding practices. I realized that the average professional landscaper needed a well-researched handbook that covered both landscape management and small business. I thought the ideal book would also contain enough detailed trade information that it could serve as an in-field reference. When I set out to create such a book, I didn't realize the amount of work it would require or how many years it would take, but I eventually got it done, and I'm satisfied with the result. My hope is that PLH continues to help new landscapers quickly get up to speed and help established businesses increase profitability. The research-based information in PLH will give you an edge over much of the competition.

The few changes for 2019 include minor updates to the tax and bookkeeping chapters. None of these updates were necessary since you are always directed to IRS resources for the most current information. Thank you again to all those who have purchased and read PLH. It's my genuine wish that it helps you succeed in your business.

Original preface. This is a handbook of landscape management and small business practices for landscaping and lawn care professionals. This book was written for new landscapers seeking a practical introduction to the trade and for existing professionals who want a concise overview of a broad range of topics. The handbook focuses on practices used in residential maintenance, though many of the techniques are used in all areas of landscape management.

Comments on the Text

Coverage. The majority of the handbook covers landscape management practices. Each topic is treated broadly as an introductory overview, but includes details and technical information useful to professionals. Basic concepts are explained in order to help newcomers understand the rationale or scientific basis of the practices. Naturally, when starting out, it is helpful to keep business tasks as simple as possible. For this reason, the text emphasizes the fundamentals of running a small business: pricing, bookkeeping, and taxes.

Common practices and reference information. The handbook covers common landscape management and business practices, though it also includes less common information that is useful for professionals. For example, professionals can benefit from understanding how to fertilize based on recommendations given in terms of pounds of nitrogen per 1000 square feet, even if most fertilizer is applied according to the product label.

Technical and non-technical approaches. An introduction to several technical topics is provided for those who are interested. Whenever possible, simple and acceptable alternatives to technical approaches are included. For example, before discussing irrigation scheduling equations, the text covers irrigation rules of thumb, which can be used as a stand-alone approach to scheduling.

Environmental considerations. The handbook includes instruction on water conservation techniques and responsible fertilizer use. Note that professional turfgrass management practices integrate weed-reduction strategies and the minimization of pesticide use. Therefore, many of the practices presented here also serve as foundations for organic lawn care. With the use of suitable fertilizers and pest control strategies, readers can use the information in this book to run an organic landscape management service.

Cross references. Cross references to related topics have been included in the text. Whenever possible, the cross reference's page number has been provided for ease of use. Selected source citations have also been included. Note that citations point the reader to where information was obtained for this book, not necessarily to the original author or researcher of the information.

Regional differences. The book is meant to be suitable for all regions, though there may be regional differences in horticultural practices or business requirements that are not covered here. It is assumed that readers will complement the book's instruction with information specific to their region. Note that some landscaping professionals may use acceptable methods that differ from the ones described here. The practices in this handbook are not presented as the only correct ones.

References for further reading. While this handbook is a stand-alone resource, occasionally readers are directed to outside sources for more detailed coverage. Note that web addresses are current at the time of printing. If a web address no longer works, search for the publication from the listed website's home page.

Terms. The terms *landscaping, gardening, landscape maintenance*, and *landscape management* are used interchangeably in this book. Note that the term *landscaping* is also used to refer to landscape construction or installation, which is not the subject of this book.

About the Author

Greg Michaels has over ten years experience running his own landscape management business in California's Sacramento Valley and San Francisco Bay Area.

Introduction

Those unfamiliar with landscape management might think that professional landscaping requires no more knowledge than is needed to operate lawn mowers, grass trimmers, hedge clippers, and the various other tools of the trade. The apparent simplicity of the work leads some enterprising individuals to purchase equipment, advertise landscaping services to the public, and try to figure things out as they go along. In fact, this is how I got started in the trade some years ago.

An independent spirit is an essential trait for the self-employed landscaper. However, knowledge of plant biology, soil science, landscape horticulture, and turfgrass management—as well as many business procedures—is also required. These are not subjects that can be figured out correctly for oneself; at least not without considerable research and some period of trial-and-error. Unfortunately, practicing landscaping without adequate instruction can be detrimental to landscapes, property owners, and the environment.

Entering the business without suitable instruction also compromises new business owners themselves. For example, without an understanding of sound job pricing, new business owners have little choice but to try to learn what other landscapers charge and to bid with those prices in mind. As a result, many new landscapers underprice their services and undermine their chances of success.

A conscientious newcomer can learn the trade through a two- or four-year university horticulture program, by working for an established landscape management company, or by joining trade associations and reading books on related topics. This handbook provides a practical introduction to a broad range of topics in small business and landscape management.

The Purpose of This Handbook

Newcomers to residential landscaping need a comprehensive introduction to the trade—an information toolkit that includes instruction on small-business procedures as well as landscape management practices. *The Professional Landscaper's Handbook* has been designed to meet this need, distilling some of the vast amount of information required by self-employed landscapers into a concise handbook. It compiles essential information from the subjects of turfgrass management, landscape plant management, soil science, pruning, irrigation system repair, business start-up, job pricing, bookkeeping, and taxes, among others.

The Benefits of This Handbook

This book will help readers bypass the trial-and-error school of landscaping and quickly get up to speed in their own legal, profitable, horticulturally informed landscape management business. Experienced landscapers can use this book as a convenient single-volume resource for a broad range of professional practices. It also provides clear explanations of a number of technical topics, including evapotranspiration-based irrigation scheduling and calculating an accurate hourly billing rate. The detailed estimating system presented in Chapter 11 should help both new and experienced landscapers increase profitability.

How The Handbook Is Organized

Part I: Business Start-up

Part I is a guide to starting a landscape management business. Chapter 1 introduces legal requirements, including registering a business name, getting a business license, purchasing insurance, and so on. Chapter 2 discusses some of the tools of the trade, including power equipment, hand tools, office supplies, and computer software.

Part II: Landscape Management

Part II is the largest section of the book. It provides instruction on a range of landscape management topics, including safety, turfgrass management, landscape plant management, soil, pruning, irrigation system repair, and more.

Part III: Business Management

Part III covers selected business topics, including calculating an accurate hourly rate, a sample maintenance contract, employer requirements, bookkeeping, and an overview of tax preparation for a small, service-based business.

This book can be read cover to cover or used as a reference. Topics are designed to stand alone, though cross-references to related topics are provided. The appendixes in Part IV include resources, references, and a detailed index. See the Table of Contents for a list of topics.

Part I

Business
Start-up

Part I

Part I covers the legal requirements of starting a landscaping business and introduces some of the tools and supplies used in the trade.

Starting a Landscape Management Business

To create a legitimate small business, you must meet a few legal requirements, which involves completing some simple paperwork. Once these administrative tasks are complete, your business will have a solid legal foundation to build on. This chapter divides the process of starting a small business into six steps and introduces some of the choices available to you.

1. Choose a Legal Structure

Before starting your business, you must decide on your business's legal structure. Some common legal entities are the sole proprietorship, partnership, limited liability company (LLC), S corporation, and standard corporation. Each legal structure places different requirements and responsibilities on the business owner. The legal structure affects taxes, record keeping, personal risk, and more.

The majority of small businesses are sole proprietorships. For tax and legal purposes, the owner and the business are the same in a sole proprietorship. One disadvantage of this structure is that there is no separation between the owner's business assets and personal assets. In other words, the owner's personal assets are at risk if

there is a business debt or lawsuit. In contrast, some business structures, such as a corporation or LLC, can protect the owner's personal assets if there is a business debt or lawsuit. However, even incorporation may not protect the personal assets of an owner-operator. If you are interested in forming a corporation or LLC, talk with a certified public accountant or tax lawyer to see if these structures are a good match for your business.

Sole proprietorship has many advantages, the most notable being its simplicity—you don't need to do anything special to claim sole proprietor status; just declare it on your business license application and tax forms. There are no legal requirements associated with sole proprietorship apart from record keeping and income tax payment (there are more if you resell products or hire employees). And as a sole proprietor, you don't have to share control of your business with anyone else: you make the decisions.

A partnership is a legal business structure in which two or more parties go into business together. Roughly speaking, each person contributes to the business in one form or another, and each expects a share of the profit or loss. The partners, to a large extent, determine their individual contributions and share of the profit. If an agreement between partners is put into writing, it is legally binding. If an agreement is not put into writing, in most states the partners are still subject to the Uniform Partnership Act (UPA) or the Revised Uniform Partnership Act (RUPA), which says that each partner is entitled to an equal share in the profits and an equal say in the management of the business (Steingold 2005). Whatever the partnership agreement, each owner pays taxes on the amount earned in the business in a similar way to sole proprietors.

Each owner in a partnership is responsible for any business debts. For example, if your partner decides to buy a $3000 lawn tractor with the business credit card, you are equally responsible for paying for it. Similarly, if one partner injures someone or damages property while running the business, both owners are liable.

Business partnerships are notorious for creating conflict. Often partners don't clearly define their individual business obligations and entitlements. Even with a clear written agreement, the nature of the relationship and the involvement of labor and money tend to generate problems. Keep in mind that small business management is sometimes more effective with one owner than two. For more information, see *Selecting the Legal Structure for Your Business* on the IRS website at http://www.irs.gov, or consult one of the small business books listed in appendix A.

2. Choose a Business Name

Your business name will be used in advertising, telephone greetings, signage, and business forms. It makes an immediate impression on potential clients, influencing which clients call you and the number of calls you receive. Choose a name that presents a business image that your targeted clients will feel comfortable with and that will continue to reflect your business as it grows.

There is nothing wrong with using the term *landscaping* in your business name; however, this may increase the number of calls you receive from people seeking landscape installation, which is the

work of landscape contractors. Note that it is illegal to represent yourself as a landscape contractor if you are not one. Various terms can be substituted for *landscaping*, such as *gardening, landscape gardening, landscape maintenance*, or *landscape management*. Once you choose a business name, you need to investigate if the name is already being used by another business; this is explained next.

3. File for a Fictitious Business Name

To do business under a name other than your own, you have to file for a fictitious business name (FBN), also known as an assumed name or a DBA (doing business as) name. Fictitious business names are filed with your county, usually the County Clerk Recorder or County Registrar's Office. Call the appropriate office and request to have a fictitious business name form mailed to you.

Search the county records to see if the name you have chosen is already being used by another business. Some counties have a database that can be accessed through the internet. Don't assume that the county will check their files to see if your chosen business name is available. And avoid using names or descriptive terms that are already in use. For example, if you want to use the name Rock Creek Landscape Maintenance and another business in your county is already using the name Rock Creek Lawn Care, avoid using "rock creek" entirely—your business name must be unique to avoid customer confusion. If you do business under a business name that is already in use, you may have to give it up later, or worse, you may be sued by the business already using the name.

In addition to searching the county records, check the ads for local gardeners and landscapers at http://www.craigslist.org. Also scan local newspapers and phone books; the city or county library will have these publications. Note that there are often several phone book publishers for each area, and their phone books will have different ads.

If the county records and local publications show no other business using your business name, you

Do You Need an Employer ID Number?

If you plan to hire employees, you will need an Employer Identification Number (EIN), also known as a Federal Tax Identification Number. The EIN is like a social security number for your business. It is used on your business license and tax forms, among other places. You can request Form SS-4 *Application for Employer Identification Number* by calling the IRS at 1-800-TAX-FORM (1-800-829-3676), or you can download it from the IRS website at http://www.irs.gov.

If you don't intend to hire employees and your business is a sole proprietorship (or a one person LLC not taxed as a corporation), you can use your social security number instead of an EIN. You can always apply for an EIN later if you decide to hire employees. However, you may still want to get an EIN to maintain a distinction between your business and personal affairs (Steingold 2005). In addition to the federal EIN, you'll also need a state EIN. Also see "Employer Identification Number" on page 207.

can probably use it without running into legal complications. For example, if you are the only Dan's Gardening in your county, you are not likely to run into legal complications with a different Dan's Gardening on the other side of the country, or even 100 miles away. That's because your businesses serve different areas, so there is little risk of customer confusion. However, exceptions exist, and we look at these here.

The business name you want may already be in use by a state-wide or nation-wide business, possibly a franchise. To be safe, you can expand your search to the state level by contacting the Corporations Commissioner or other state office where corporations and LLCs register their fictitious business names. This can help you determine if there are landscape-oriented companies or franchises using a particular business name in your state.

An even more comprehensive search involves checking the federal trademark register, where national companies register their business names. Some public libraries have federal trademark registers for you to search, or you can search online at the U.S. Patent and Trademark Office (USPTO) website at http://www.uspto.gov. On the USPTO site, find the Trademark Electronic Search System (TESS). Even an online federal trademark search,

however, is not exhaustive. For more information on conducting a statewide or federal name search, consult a specialized book such as Peri Pakroo's *The Small Business Start-Up Kit* or Stephen Elias's *Trademark: Legal Care for Your Business & Product Name,* available at many public libraries.

The internet can complicate name selection even for small service-based businesses that serve different regions. For example, if you decide to put up an informational website that describes your services and provides seasonal gardening tips, you may find yourself in competition with another business of the same name in another part of the country, or even a different country. If that business can prove that it owns the trademark of the business name, you may be forced to change your business name (Pakroo 2004). You can search for domain names at domain registration websites.

Once you return the FBN form to the County Registrar's Office with your payment (approximately $30), the clerk will stamp it with the county seal and return it to you. You must then publicly announce the fictitious business name by running it in a newspaper for a specified amount of time. The county will have a list of newspapers that perform this service; call several papers because prices can vary greatly.

After the newspaper runs the ad, it will return the proof of publication to the County Registrar's Office and send you a copy; confirm that the newspaper will do this for you. Once you have the proof of publication, you can advertise, open a business checking account, and conduct other business activities using your business name. Note that FBN registration expires after a period of time, usually five years. Re-register before the expiration date to maintain your FBN.

4. Get a Business License

After filing for a fictitious business name, request a business license application from your city government offices. If the city does not handle business licenses, you may be redirected to a county or state agency. The license is inexpensive, and the city will mail a renewal form every year with renewal fees; renewal may be more frequent, depending on where you live. If you plan to work in several cities, you may need a business license from each city. Call the business office of the city in question to find out.

Along with the application, you may be sent information on additional requirements for landscape gardeners, such as pest control applicator's licensing. If you plan to use herbicides, insecticides, or fungicides, you must become certified by the agency in your state that oversees the commercial use of these products. For more information, see "Pest Control Applicator's Licensing" on page 70.

5. Open a Separate Bank Account

Once you have a fictitious business name, you can open a checking account in your business name; this will allow you to cash checks written to your business name. Most small business owners open a business checking account. The minor drawbacks of a business checking account are that it costs slightly more than a regular checking account and it provides extra services that you may not need. In addition, the minimum balance you must keep in the business account to avoid monthly fees is usually higher than a personal account.

Another option is to open a personal checking account and request that a DBA name be attached to the account. DBA stands for "doing business as". For example, Dan Smith might open a personal checking account for his gardening business and request that the DBA "Dan's Gardening" be attached to the account. Note that not all banks allow DBAs with personal checking accounts.

Do not use one bank account for business and personal use. Having a checking account designated for business use will help you keep your business and personal finances distinct. If you are ever audited, the IRS may ask to see the statements for your business checking account. If you have only one checking account for business and personal use, the IRS could consider personal deposits to be business income that you've been hiding, and they could subject you to tax and penalties on the amount in question. See "Bank Account" on page 214 for more information.

6. Comply With Zoning Ordinances

Most residential landscapers operate their businesses from home. Before investing in start-up supplies, find out the zoning ordinances and private land use restrictions for your residence. Zoning ordinances exist to regulate construction and land use in a city. Broadly speaking, some areas of a city are designated for residential use, some for commercial use, and some for a mix of both. Activities associated with manufacturing, for example, would violate a zoning ordinance if they took place in an area of single-family homes.

In residential areas, zoning ordinances primarily serve to maintain the character of a neighborhood. Some residential zoning ordinances allow home-based businesses, others do not, and some allow them with restrictions. Restrictions may affect your business' vehicle and foot traffic, on-street parking, power equipment operation hours, number of employees, or other aspects of your business.

If a business is in violation of a zoning ordinance, city officials may send a letter telling the business

Do You Need a Seller's Permit?

A seller's permit is a state-issued permit that allows you to buy goods wholesale and resell them. You pass any required sales tax on to the client at the time of sale. Once you have a sales permit, you must file periodic sales and use tax returns and pay any accumulated sales tax to the sales tax authority in your state. A few states do not require resellers to get a seller's permit.

Plants, bark, fertilizer, sprinklers, rain sensors, and irrigation controllers are just some of the supplies landscapers can resell. However, reselling materials creates additional bookkeeping and tax work. Depending on your business, the potential profits may not be worth the extra effort. Landscape contractors typically sell enough landscape materials and devices to warrant getting a seller's permit. But businesses performing only residential landscape management often purchase minimal materials to profit from through resale.

The decision to get a seller's permit does not need to be made right away. You can avoid getting a seller's permit by purchasing materials for clients as needed and charging them the amount you paid. In this way, you pay the sales tax when you purchase the item, and the client reimburses you. Purchases made this way are considered "supplies" and are deducted as business expenses at tax time. For more information, see "Supplies" on page 227.

owner to make changes. Further violations can result in fines, business closure, or even criminal prosecution. Contact your city's Zoning and Planning Department to learn the zoning ordinances for your residence. If you think you have been wrongly charged with a zoning violation, you can take up the matter with the city or with the zoning board itself.

Homes, condos, and co-op units can also be subject to private restrictions, which will be listed on the leases for these properties. Housing associations can also provide information on private restrictions.

Most of your business activity will take place away from your residence. However, loading and unloading your truck, cleaning and repairing tools, and storing supplies—not to mention the coming and going of employees if you have them—are just a few of the activities that can attract neighbors' attention. Find out what business activities your zoning ordinances allow, and avoid or be discreet about activities that are likely to raise concern.

Health Insurance

You are not legally required to have medical insurance, and it is beyond our purposes to discuss health insurance in detail. However, it's important to know that going without medical insurance puts your health and finances at risk. If you need medical attention and don't have insurance, you may still be able to receive treatment at a hospital. But if you receive treatment and don't have insurance, you will have to pay out of pocket, and it can be expensive. An anecdote illustrates this point: A local landscape gardener broke his ankle on the job. When he was finished with medical treatment, his medical expenses totaled over $15,000. Consider medical insurance a necessary expense.

Business Insurance

Apart from workers' compensation insurance (if you hire employees) and vehicle insurance, you may not be required to buy additional business insurance; however, it is in your best interest to

Landscape Construction

Landscape contractors install irrigation systems, lawns, plants, fences, decks, brickwork, and other landscape features. These professionals have a state contractor's license that certifies they have sufficient knowledge, experience, insurance, and bonding to install permanent landscape features. Clients have certain rights when they hire a landscape contractor that they do not have when hiring a non-contractor. You will undoubtedly have opportunities to do landscape construction—the question is, should you?

The first thing to consider is the law in your state. For instance, in California, city permits are required for the installation of many landscape features, and cities only provide permits to licensed contractors or the homeowner. If the job does not require a permit—laying mulch, for example—non-contractors can do the work, provided they do not charge more than $500 for materials and labor combined. Contact the Planning and Building department of your city government offices to learn the requirements for your area.

Installation of landscape features requires specialized knowledge and training. And numerous safety measures need to be taken to avoid causing property damage or injury to yourself or others. Contractors also face increased financial risk. If the job is not done right, it must be corrected, or the contractor could face legal consequences. To learn how to become a licensed landscape contractor in your state, call your state's contractors license board or visit their website. Phone numbers can be found in the State Government Offices section of your phone book. Most states require several years of experience in the field. You must pass an examination and fulfill certain requirements.

do so. Remember, as a sole proprietor, your business *and* personal assets are at risk if there is a lawsuit against your business. The two main forms of business insurance are property insurance and liability insurance.

Property Insurance

Property insurance includes coverage for all forms of business property, from equipment to buildings. If you rent a commercial space to run your business, the terms of your lease may require you to insure the building. If you are not required to insure the building, it is still advisable to get a renter's commercial policy to protect yourself against any damage to the rented space caused by you or your employees.

You may choose not to get property coverage if you don't rent a commercial space, and if you are willing to replace your business equipment out of pocket in the event of theft or other loss. Before you decide on "self insurance" for your business equipment, keep in mind that most landscapers have a story to tell about having equipment stolen. Without insurance or emergency funds, one theft can strain your business resources, if not put you out of business. If you insure your business property, get coverage that will pay the amount it will cost to replace the items, not just their current value.

Note that your homeowner's insurance policy may not cover damage or loss of business property (Steingold 2005). For example, if you store your equipment in the garage and it is stolen, your homeowner's policy may not cover the loss. However, by adding the appropriate riders (additional coverage) to your existing homeowner policy, your business property will be covered. While these riders are generally inexpensive, it may be even less expensive to get a policy designed to cover both your home and home-based business. With these policies, your business property is covered whether you are at home or on the job (Steingold 2005).

Liability Insurance

General liability insurance is all the business insurance some landscape gardeners need. General liability policies cover personal injuries and property damage sustained by others as a result of your actions on the job. For example, if you remove a tree limb and it damages a car, your liability insurance would keep you from having to pay out of pocket for the repair.

Your policy should include coverage for herbicide- and pesticide-related damages if you plan to apply these chemicals as a part of your service. Tree work also requires additional coverage. And if you intend to hire employees, you will also need workers' compensation insurance. See the chapter "Employer Requirements" on page 207 for more information. Note that general liability insurance does not serve as vehicle insurance.

Vehicle Insurance

Vehicle damages that you cause while on the job may not be covered by your standard vehicle insurance policy. To ensure coverage, inform your vehicle insurance agent that your vehicle will be used for business. If you have employees who will be using their own vehicles on the job, you will need Non-Owned Auto Liability Insurance. This insurance protects you in the event that an employee causes injury or damage with his or her own vehicle while on the job. Note that employees are not protected by Non-Owned Liability and still require their own auto insurance (Kamoroff 2005).

Insurance Agents

The insurance coverage discussed above is intended to serve as food for thought. Your agent will determine your business insurance needs. If possible, find an agent who works with other landscapers so she is already familiar with the coverage needed. A good agent will ask you many questions before writing up your policy. Think twice about working with an agent who does not inquire into the specifics of your business. And ask your agent questions so you have a working understanding of what your insurance covers.

The deductible is the part of the insurance claim that must be paid by the insured before the insurer will cover expenses. This means that if you need to make a claim, you will need to pay up to the amount of the deductible. Accepting a higher deductible can lower your premiums.

Additional Considerations

- Before using your vehicle for business, set up a mileage logbook to keep track of your business mileage. For more information, see "Mileage Logbook" on page 221 and "Car and Truck Expenses" on page 225.

- Cities have noise ordinances that state the acceptable hours of power equipment operation. Some cities place additional restrictions on power equipment use. Call the business number of your local police department to find out the ordinances for landscape power equipment use in your city.

Equipment and Supplies

This chapter introduces some of the equipment and supplies used in landscape management. Product research can be done online or through lawn mower/small engine repair shops and home-and-garden centers. Online forums for professionals are also a good place to get opinions on tools of the trade. See "Online Landscaping Forums" on page 238 for a list.

When researching power equipment, keep in mind that commercial-grade equipment is more powerful and durable than homeowner-grade equipment. Money saved by investing in inferior equipment invariably results in more money lost to downtime and more money spent on equipment repairs. In the long run, commercial-grade equipment is often less expensive than homeowner-grade equipment because it lasts longer.

Note: Start-up expenses are business expenses you incur before opening your doors for business. Deducting start-up expenses for tax purposes requires special knowledge and extra tax work. By familiarizing yourself with some of these rules, you may be able to avoid certain tax complications. For more information, see "Start-up Expenses" on page 227.

Commercial Walk-Behind Mowers

Commercial mowers are built to provide years of daily use. Compared to homeowner models, the engines last longer; the levers and cables are stronger; the gas tanks and air filters are larger; and the self-propelling mechanisms are variable-speed, ranging from slow to a fast walking pace. Below are a few of the more common features available on commercial rotary mowers.

- *Mulching mechanism.* A mulching or grass-recycling mechanism cuts grass clippings into fine pieces and deposits them onto the lawn surface. The clippings are not noticeable and quickly decompose, returning nutrients and organic matter to the soil. Mulching is a beneficial lawn management practice when performed correctly. See "Mulching vs. Bagging" on page 43 for more information.

- *Self-propelling mechanism.* Most commercial mowers come with a variable-speed, self-propelling mechanism. This and a mulching mechanism are essential features for a walk-behind mower.

- *Operator presence control (OPC).* OPC is sometimes called an engine kill lever. OPC shuts off the engine or stops the blade when the user steps

Commercial mowers are built to handle years of daily use. Recycling features and self-propelling mechanisms are common. Toro is the manufacturer of the mower shown here.

away from the mower. This is an important safety feature that is standard on all mowers.

Purchase a mower with a deck that is at least 21 inches wide, and purchase at least one additional mower blade so you can replace a dull one with a sharp one as needed. You can expect to pay between $500 and $1200 on a standard-sized, walk-behind rotary lawn mower. Mower shops sometimes sell used commercial mowers. In general, new equipment is a better investment, though a used mower without many hours of use on it can be a reasonable choice if cost is a limiting factor. Consider purchasing a separate mower for high-end accounts. See "Minimizing the Spread of Weeds" on page 44 for details.

Mid-size walk-behind mowers have wider decks (32" or 36") and larger engines than standard walk-behinds. Riding mowers and zero turn radius (ZTR) mowers are less common in residential maintenance though some gardeners use them. Some residential lawns cannot be accessed with riding mowers. Note that a number of manufacturers produce propane-powered mowers, which produce lower emissions. Recently more landscaping companies have begun to use this technology, though it is not yet popular.

Other Power Equipment

Many commercial power tools, such as grass trimmers and hedge clippers, are powered by two-cycle engines, also called two-stroke engines. Two-cycle engines run on a mixture of gas and oil called two-cycle mix, which serves as fuel and lubrication for the engine; there is no engine oil to change. Two-cycle mix comes in different ratios, and each tool is designed to run on a specific mix, the most common being 50:1. Two-cycle engines are durable and low maintenance. They have a high power-to-weight ratio and can be operated in different positions.

The four-cycle or mini four-stroke engine runs on straight gas and boasts low emissions and quieter operation. Some four-cycle engines run on a gas/oil mix. Unlike two-cycle engines, most four-cycles need regular oil changes. Four-cycle engines tend to be a little heavier and more expensive than two cycle engines, and they may require periodic valve adjustments.

As you research power equipment, consider models with a built-in vibration-reduction system. These will be easier on the hands during extended use. And choose brands that are popular among professionals. Some brands are only available through dealers who also service the tools.

Leaf Blowers

Leaf blowers are available in backpack or handheld models. Backpack models are the more powerful of the two, making them a good choice for clearing the pavement of large properties and parking lots. Handheld blowers have enough power to service most small to mid-size residential accounts. They are also less expensive than backpack blowers and take up less space. Another advantage of handheld blowers is that they can be started and stopped several times at a property without having to be put on and taken off each time.

Check with your city before purchasing a leaf blower—some cities have ordinances that restrict or ban their use. Consider purchasing a blower with a low decibel (noise) rating, and practice responsible blower use. See "Leaf Blower Use Guidelines" on page 26 for more information.

Grass Trimmers

Grass trimmers, sometimes called line edgers or "weed whackers", spin short sections of nylon line at high speeds. Trimmers are available with a straight or curved shaft. A high-powered, straight-shaft model is a good choice for clearing extensive brush and weeds. Many professionals prefer the longer reach of straight-shaft models. Straight-shaft trimmers have either a steel cable drive shaft or a solid-steel drive shaft. A solid-steel drive shaft is a good choice if you want the option of adding a blade attachment, which enables you to use the trimmer as a brush cutter.

The head of the trimmer is the component that holds the trimmer line and spins. Different types of heads require different methods of replacing trimmer line once it wears out. With a fixed-line head, short sections of pre-cut line are manually inserted into the head. Bump-feed or tap-advance heads are tapped on the ground during operation to lengthen the spooled line. One potential problem with spooled line is that it can occasionally "weld" to itself, preventing the line from advancing. This can usually be avoided with consistent line advancement.

Trimmers with larger engines allow you to use thicker nylon line (0.095 and up), which lasts longer. Dealers sometimes have demonstration trimmers you can try out. See "Lawn Edgers" for more information.

Hedge Clippers

Gas-powered hedge clippers are available in short-reach or long-reach models. Short-reach models provide good control and maneuverability because the cutting bar remains close to the user. However, these models can be tiring during extended use because the weight of the engine must be held in front of the body. And since the engine is near the face during operation, the user tends to breathe exhaust.

Short-reach power clippers are available with single-sided or double-sided cutting bars that are between 20" and 40" in length. Double-sided cutting bars employ the user's natural back-and-forth

Walk behind edgers provide a straight and consistent cut. They are designed to be used on lawns that have a mowstrip. Power Trim is the manufacturer of the edger shown here.

cutting motion. Single-sided bars have longer teeth and cut more vegetation with a single sweep. Single-sided bars can be fitted with an accessory called a collector or deflector shield, which attaches to the bar and sweeps clippings off of shrubs and hedges.

Long-reach hedge clippers have the cutting bar mounted on the end of a shaft. Depending on the model, the shaft extends the cutting bar 20 to 60 inches away from the forward arm. In addition to providing longer reach, the shaft reduces user fatigue by balancing the tool and keeps the engine farther from the user's face. Some pole clippers come with an articulating cutting bar. With the cutting bar set at an angle, the user can trim the tops of some hedges without a ladder and trim groundcovers without bending down.

Lawn Edgers

There are three main types of power lawn edgers. The three-wheeled walk-behind edger is designed to be used with a mowstrip, which many properties do not have. These edgers have powerful, long-lasting engines and cut with a vertically rotating blade, which gives a straight, consistent edge. The drawbacks of this type of edger are its size and limited maneuverability.

The second type of edger is the grass trimmer. Grass trimmers can be used to trim grass around buildings, sprinkler heads, paving stones, and the

Stick edgers look like grass trimmers except that they have a lawn edger mounted on the end. The tool is maneuverable and takes up minimal storage space. The edger head of Echo model PE-280 is shown here.

edge of planting areas. Since these features are so common, some professionals use a grass trimmer for all edging, rather than switch to a different tool to edge sidewalks and walkways. Compared to blade edgers, grass trimmers create an inconsistent edge and a wider gap between walkways and the lawn. Gaps encourage weed seeds to germinate by exposing soil to sunlight.

Grass trimmers should not be used to trim around young trees growing in turfgrass because the nylon line can easily cut into the bark. Cuts through the bark can stunt a tree's growth and lead to disease; completely girdling a trunk with trimmer line can kill a tree. Reciprocating edgers cut with scissor-action and pose less risk to trees, but they can still damage the bark of young trees if the metal head bumps the trunk. For more information, see "Protecting Trees and Shrubs" on page 40.

Stick edgers look like grass trimmers, except that instead of a trimmer head, they have a stabilizing wheel and vertically rotating blade mounted on the end. This design solves some of the maneuverability problems of walk-behind edgers while maintaining a straight, consistent cut. A minor drawback of the stick edger is that the blade can wear out a little faster than the blade on a walk-behind edger.

Chainsaws

You do not need to own or operate a chainsaw to perform residential landscape management. A manual pruning saw can usually be substituted for a chainsaw, and manual saws have the advantage of being safer, lighter, and lower maintenance.

Chainsaw use requires training and safety gear to minimize the risk of injury to yourself or others. With that said, a chainsaw can allow you to competitively bid landscape clean-ups that might be too labor intensive with manual tools. A saw with a 12" to 16" bar is adequate for most residential work.

Chainsaw use requires a commitment to safety. Plan to take a chainsaw safety course before operating a chainsaw. Dealers can give you a few pointers, but it is not their job to provide safety instruction. Read the operator's manual that comes with your saw; if you rent a saw, ask to borrow the manual. Note that even when all safety precautions are taken, accidents with this tool can result in serious or fatal injury.

Steel-toed footwear, heavy non-slip gloves, non-fogging goggles, an approved hard hat (logger's helmet) with built-in brush guard, hearing protectors, and chainsaw chaps are some of the recommended chainsaw safety gear. A saw tip protector and a low-kickback saw chain can reduce kickback. Remember, chainsaw manufacturers design safety products for a reason. No one is immune from an unexpected kickback or a moment of inattentiveness. Proper training and safety gear are necessary precautions. For more information, see "Chainsaw Safety" on page 27.

Chainsaws require more frequent maintenance than other power equipment. Be prepared to spend time sharpening and adjusting the chain, cleaning the guide bar, refilling the chain oil reservoir, and cleaning the air filter. You will need filing tools such as a bar groove cleaning tool, a depth gauge, and round and flat files. A bar-mounted filing tool can help you maintain the proper sharpening angle. Consider purchasing a spare chain to replace a dull one while on the job and a non-metal wedge to take pressure off the bar if it becomes pinched in a branch.

Chain tension needs to be checked regularly. Chain adjustment involves loosening the chain brake nuts, adjusting the chain tensioner, and retightening the chain brake nuts. Some chainsaws come with a manual chain adjuster, which allows the user to tighten or loosen the chain without a tool.

Power Pole Pruners

Power pole pruners, also called power pole saws, operate a small chainsaw at the end of a pole, extending the saw's reach approximately 10 to 16 feet from the ground. Like manual pole saws, these tools reduce the need to climb and reposition a ladder. However, they are not always the best for making good pruning cuts because the length of the shaft can make it difficult to precisely place the cutting head. For this reason, an orchard ladder and a manual pruning saw are still needed in many cases.

A power pole pruner can be time-saving and cost-effective; however, if the user lacks an understanding of correct pruning practices, this tool may simply be used to make bad cuts more quickly. If you are new to pruning, a manual pruning saw and a pair of high-quality hand pruners are good tools to learn with. Many experienced landscapers prefer manual pruning tools.

Back-Up Equipment

Consider purchasing back-up tools for the power equipment you use frequently. That way, if a tool fails, your work pace won't slow down, and you won't have to ask the shop to repair the tool quickly. Since landscape power equipment is generally durable and trouble-free, back-up tools often remain in storage for long periods. If you don't plan to use a back-up tool for more than one month, prepare the tool for storage as described below.

Winterizing Equipment

If you plan to store a piece of power equipment for longer than one month, you will need to prepare the tool for storage, sometimes called winterizing a tool. Some of the more common tool winterization tasks are described here. Consult your operator's manual for definitive information and follow your manual's recommendations if they conflict with guidelines provided here. When working on equipment, follow all safety precautions recommended by the product's manufacturer.

Typical tool winterization tasks include replacing filters and worn belts; inspecting the fuel cap gasket for wear; sharpening or replacing blades; tightening nuts and fasteners; applying lightweight machine oil to cutting teeth; and lubricating per the manufacturer's instructions. Tools should be stored in a dry, secure, ventilated place, away from children and sources of open flame.

Before storing a piece of power equipment, it is important to protect the tool's fuel system. After about a month of storage in a container, gasoline can start to go bad (oxidize), plugging up fuel lines with a gummy residue. Old gasoline can also do other damage, such as dissolve the finely machined parts of a carburetor or fuel pump (Donahue 2002).

Gasoline stabilizer will help to protect fuel system components for about one year. Failure to use a stabilizer can result in starting difficulty, damage to components, and reduced tool life. For best results, mix the stabilizer with a can of fresh gasoline, fill the tool's fuel tank, and run the tool for several minutes to circulate the stabilizer through the fuel system.

Expert opinions differ on the correct winterization procedure for two-cycle tools. Some equipment maintenance experts recommend draining all gas from the fuel system. This method is described below. Others say emptying the fuel system does not ensure that all gas has been removed from the lines and carburetor. They argue that even a small amount of gas in the system can cause problems, and that a dry fuel system can cause gaskets to crack. These experts recommend using gasoline stabilizer with two-cycle tools.

If you choose to winterize the fuel system of a two-cycle tool by draining the gas, follow these guidelines: Allow the engine to cool off if it was recently in operation, then empty the tool's fuel tank into an approved container or into the tank of another tool that uses the same gas/oil mix. If the tool has a primer or purge bulb on the carburetor, repeatedly press it to clear fuel from the lines. Start the tool and run it until it dies, then attempt a restart to be sure no gas/oil mix remains.

Engine components must remain lubricated during storage. The standard procedure is to remove the tool's spark plug and pour in one tablespoon of motor oil. Use the same weight of oil required by the engine. For two-stroke engines, use two-stroke oil. For its two-cycle products, power equipment manufacturer Echo recommends $1/4$ ounce of fresh, clean two-stroke engine oil (Echo 2006) ($1 1/2$ teaspoons = $1/4$ ounce, approximately).

Distribute the oil by pulling the starter cord slowly several times. After several pulls, release the starter cord when the piston reaches the highest point, as seen through the spark plug hole. Replace the spark plug, but leave the spark plug wire disconnected. Note that some landscapers use aerosol fogging oil instead of engine oil to keep engine components lubricated during storage.

Hand Tools

High-quality hand tools can be relatively expensive, but they last longer and perform better than poorly made tools. Cheap hand tools frequently break or fail to perform adequately. For example, inexpensive loppers or hand pruners are worthless if the stamped-metal blade flexes and you are unable to make a clean cut. Money spent to replace a cheap tool could have been spent on a reliable tool to begin with. The following is a list of some common landscaping tools.

Lawn rake: A lawn rake is a wide rake that is used mostly in the fall to clear leaves and debris off lawns before mowing. Plastic models are light and affordable but can break with heavy use. A mid-size rake is also useful.

Narrow rake: Narrow-headed rakes are useful for flower and perennial beds.

Spade: Spades, also called round-point shovels, are available with a fiberglass, wood, or metal handle. An inexpensive wood-handled spade will suffice for the occasional planting.

Drain spade shovel: With a short handle and a narrow-nose, drain spade shovels are useful for many tasks, including sprinkler repair, planting, and yard clean-ups.

Hand trowel: Trowels are used to plant bulbs and annual flowers. Cheap trowels bend.

Rough-surface push broom: Clearing debris from streets and walkways is a common task. Stiff bristle brooms work well on asphalt. Purchase a wide model with metal supports that secure the handle to the head.

Two-way action hoe: This tool is sometimes called a hula hoe. Its blade slides beneath the soil, cutting the upper portion of a weed's roots; most weeds cut this way will regrow. This tool is good for weeding closely planted beds or areas where a grass trimmer might pose a risk, such as an island in the middle of a busy street. A drawback to the hula hoe is that it cuts through the soil surface. Disturbing the soil in this way can encourage dormant weed seeds to sprout.

Loppers: Purchase loppers with a drop-forged metal cutting head. Drop-forged metal is strong because it is hammered into shape. Lower quality loppers contain stamped metal, which flexes and causes cutting problems.

Pruning saw: This saw cuts on the pull stroke and can be used to quickly remove large branches. Approximately 13 inches is a good blade length. A holster is useful for non-folding models.

Felco # 8 bypass pruners.

Bypass hand pruners with holster: Hand pruners, or secateurs, are used to prune trees, shrubs, and perennials. Bypass pruners are a better choice than anvil-type pruners for most pruning. Anvil pruners press a cutting blade onto a flat surface; they are useful for larger stems, woody stems, and dead wood, but they may cause unnecessary damage to tender stems. Bypass pruners are one of the most frequently used tools by skilled landscapers, so it is important to purchase a high-quality pair. Expect to pay over $60 for high-quality bypass pruners.

Pole pruners/pole saw: Pole pruners are used to prune fruit trees and to perform other miscellaneous tree work. Arborist supply stores carry professional-grade equipment. Choose a pruner head that is made of forged metal and has a cutting capacity of 1 3/4 inches. A fiberglass pole fitted with an aluminum adapter allows you to switch the pruner head to a saw head (see photo).

Extension pruners: An extension pruner, also called a long-reach pruner, is like a hand pruner on the end of an extendable pole. It is used to cut shoots up to 1/2 inch in diameter that are high in a canopy. This tool can break if it is used to cut branches that are too large or too hard.

Orchard ladder: Orchard ladders, also called tripod ladders, have a wide base and provide greater stability on soil than other ladders. The single support pole can be placed in areas of congested growth, giving the user close access to tall shrubs and hedges (see photo, page 145). Some models are available with an adjustable support pole, which enables the ladder to be used on slopes. Ladders taller than 10 feet put more in reach, but they are also unwieldy and present storage problems.

Hori-Hori Weeder Knife: This Japanese tool is good for planting annuals and weeding. Many other types of hand weeders are available. Forked-tip weeding tools are good for removing weeds that have taproots, such as dandelion.

Stake pounder: This tool is designed to drive tree stakes into the ground. A sledge hammer can substitute for the occasional tree staking.

Nitrile-coated, rubber-coated, or leather gloves: Inexpensive gloves are usually adequate, though they wear out quickly. Note that thorn punctures can cause sporotrichosis; see page 35 for more information.

Wire stripper and lineman's pliers: These tools are used to make irrigation field-wiring splices. Lineman's pliers are also called combination pliers.

Fertilizer spreader: A handheld broadcast fertilizer spreader is large enough for many small to mid-size residential properties. Some models are designed to be supported by the forearm. For larger turf areas, you will need a walk-behind broadcast spreader with a hopper that can hold at least 30 pounds of fertilizer. Drop spreaders apply fertilizer more slowly than broadcast spreaders, and they require more careful use to apply fertilizer evenly.

Multimeter or volt/ohm meter (VOM): This device measures electrical voltage, current, and resistance. In landscaping, a multimeter is used to troubleshoot electrical irrigation system components. See "Volt/Ohm Meter" on page 168. Multimeters are available in analog or digital models. Digital multimeters are abbreviated DMM.

Stub remover or riser extractor: Riser extractors are used to unscrew threaded sprinkler risers from in-ground couplers.

Gas container: Only use containers approved to store gasoline. Purchase a no-spill model. Some two-cycle mix containers are made to be used with a five-gallon container.

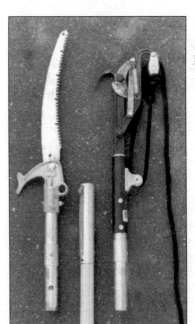

A fiberglass pole with saw and pole-pruner attachment heads. The pruner head should be made of forged metal. Corona is the manufacturer of the pruner head shown here (model 1600).

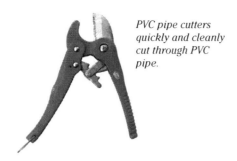

PVC pipe cutters quickly and cleanly cut through PVC pipe.

PVC pipe cutter: This tool cleanly cuts polyethylene risers and PVC pipe. It can be used in tight spaces.

Blade balancer: This inexpensive device is used to check the balance of a mower blade.

Bench grinder or medium-coarse mill file: A bench grinder can be used to sharpen mower blades. Do not use a bench grinder or mill file to sharpen hand pruners and loppers; use only a fine-grit sharpening stone on these tools.

Digital camera: A digital camera can be used to photograph landscape features during a site inspection, to take before-and-after photos of clean-ups, or to document automobile or other accidents.

Safety Equipment

Safety cones and safety vest: Safety cones warn drivers that you are engaged in loading/unloading or other short-duration work near your truck. Twenty-eight-inch cones with reflective tape provide the best visibility. Smaller cones have the advantage of being more compact. Contact your city's office of transportation to learn the proper placement of safety cones for short-duration maintenance work.

Wearing high visibility reflective apparel (e.g., a bright orange safety vest with built-in reflective material) makes it easier for drivers to see you while you work near streets and in parking lots. Safety vests should meet current American National Standards Institute (ANSI) standards.

Fire extinguisher: There are different classes of fire, and each class requires a specific type of fire extinguisher. Class A fires involve wood, paper,

trash, or plastics. Class B fires involve flammable liquids, such as gasoline, petroleum oil, propane, and butane. Class C fires involve electrical equipment. Purchase an ABC-type (multipurpose), dry-chemical fire extinguisher to keep in your truck; consider keeping another one where you store your tools. Fire extinguishers should be inspected monthly for proper placement and pressure. They must also be inspected and serviced annually by a fire-equipment professional.

Type III first aid kit: First aid kits for the workplace are subject to ANSI standards. Type III (mobile outdoor) first aid kits are suitable for construction and landscaping. These kits are portable and designed to be resistant to moisture, corrosion, and impact. They have a handle and can be mounted in a fixed position. Keep a Type III first aid kit in your truck. When searching online, look for logger's/landscaper's first aid kits. Include a first aid manual and a list of emergency phone numbers in your first aid kit.

Eye protection: Wear eye protection whenever you operate power equipment. Use the protective gear recommended in the operator's manual of the tool you are using. The eye protection gear must meet ANSI standards, currently Z87.1-2003.

Hearing protectors: It is essential to wear hearing protectors whenever you operate power equipment. Foam earplugs get dirty quickly, and time and attention are required to properly insert them into the ear. Motivation to fit them properly can fade amidst the demands of the work day. Soft rubber earplugs are easier to use, but have similar drawbacks to foam ones. Over-the-ear hearing protectors (earmuffs) are easy to put on and take off: something that needs to be done many times a day. Hearing protectors must meet current ANSI standards. See "Hearing Protection" on page 28 for more information.

Dust masks: Dust masks can be worn during leaf blower operation. They do not protect the lungs against chemicals, such as herbicides.

Steel-toed boots: Steel-toed work boots help to protect the feet in the event of a lawn mower accident.

Adequate hearing protection should be worn whenever you operate power equipment. Maintenance workers who go without hearing protection risk permanent hearing damage. Husqvarna is the manufacturer of the protectors shown here.

Back brace: In addition to practicing good body mechanics while lifting—such as bending at the knees and keeping the back straight—using a back brace will help protect your back when digging or lifting.

Respirator: A respirator should be worn when applying chemical garden products that require the use of a respirator. According to OSHA, "the appropriate respirator will depend on the contaminant(s) to which you are exposed and the protection factor (PF) required. Required respirators must be NIOSH-approved and medical evaluation and training must be provided before use." Be certain that the cartridges/filters match the contaminants, and replace the cartridges according to the manufacturer's recommendations. Note: This book does not discuss the use of chemical garden products. Additional training and certification is required to work with these substances. For more information, see "Pest Control Applicator's Licensing" on page 70.

Chemical-resistant gloves: Chemical-resistant gloves should be worn when you work with chemical garden products. The label of the gloves should state that the gloves are safe for use with the chemicals you intend to use.

Start-up Supplies

Burlap or nylon tarps: Burlap or nylon 5' x 5' tarps are ideal for toting debris. They are inexpensive and available at many small engine repair shops and arborist supply stores.

Steel wool and lightweight machine oil: Steel wool is good for cleaning manual pruning tools, such as hand pruners and loppers. To keep pruning tools rust-free, apply lightweight oil to the blades after cleaning.

PVC cement: PVC cement is used in sprinkler-pipe repairs. There are different PVC cements for different sizes and grades of PVC pipe, and for different conditions. See "PVC Cements" on page 158 for more information. Some brands are marketed as containing low amounts of volatile organic compounds (low VOC).

PTFE tape: PTFE tape is more commonly known as Teflon tape. This non-sticky tape is used to seal the fitting of threaded sprinkler parts.

Miscellaneous irrigation system parts: Some frequently used parts include drip tubing and couplers ($1/4$" and $1/2$"), compression couplers and "T"s ($1/2$" and $3/4$"), poly cut-off risers, adjustable-radius spray heads, and waterproof wire connectors.

Two-cycle mix: Two-cycle mix is added to the gasoline used in two-cycle power equipment. Use the mix ratio recommended for your tools; 50:1 is a common ratio.

Office Supplies

Scheduling jobs, writing estimates, creating invoices, and documenting income and expenses are a few common business management activities. A low-tech approach to these tasks is to manually fill out pre-ruled forms. Business forms can be found in some small-business books and in office supply stores. Some forms can be drafted in a spreadsheet or word processing program. The following is a partial list of forms and office supplies.

Call sheet: Keep copies of this sheet near your business phone to write down clients' names, phone numbers, and addresses. Recording calls on random pieces of paper or in a planner will make retrieving client contact information at a later date more difficult. A call sheet that you can photocopy is included on page page 242.

Invoices: An invoice is a bill left for a client at the end of a job or maintenance cycle. Most store-bought invoice pads create a carbonless copy of the invoice. Invoices can double as receipts; simply write "paid" on the form, the payment type, the check number, and the date of payment. See "Income Records" on page 215 for more information. An invoice that you can photocopy is included on page page 242.

Mileage logbook: A mileage logbook is used to record vehicle mileage associated with the business use of your vehicle. Any notebook can serve as a mileage logbook. Consider purchasing a notebook that will fit in your vehicle's glove box. For more information, see "Mileage Logbook" on page 221 and "Car and Truck Expenses" on page 225.

Business cards: Business cards are an inexpensive marketing tool. They can be handed to a potential client during a bid or attached to bid proposals for commercial properties. Some internet-based businesses offer business cards for free (not including the cost of shipping). You can also design and print your own cards using templates available on the internet.

Clip board: A clip board can be used to write up invoices or to take notes during a site inspection. Some models fold open and contain storage space for forms, business cards, and other supplies.

Ledgers: These are notebooks of pre-ruled paper that are used to record financial information. Unless you use accounting software, you will need an income ledger and an expenditure ledger. See the Bookkeeping chapter for more information.

Planner: The use of a planner or datebook is an effective, low-tech way to schedule jobs and managerial tasks.

File folders: File folders are used to store business receipts. Use a separate folder for each category of expense. A half-size (two-drawer) file cabinet is adequate for most new landscapers. Manila envelopes can be used as an alternative to folders. Record keeping is covered in the Bookkeeping chapter.

Rubber stamps: A rubber stamp used to personalize forms should include your business name, business address, and phone number. A stamp used to endorse checks should include the name of your bank, the name on the account, and the account number.

Miscellaneous office supplies: Some miscellaneous supplies include postage, legal-size envelopes, mailing labels, folders, and calculators (one for the office and one for the truck).

Computer and Software

This book contains references to websites, though none of the information presented here requires you to own a computer to run your business. You will need a computer if you intend to use accounting, estimating, or scheduling software, or access the internet.

Internet: The internet can be used to research products and horticultural information, to download government forms and publications, and to exchange ideas in online forums. Email is a convenient way to communicate with clients; see "Client Communication and Email" on page 205.

Accounting software: Software simplifies much of the complex work associated with maintaining ledgers and generating financial reports. Accounting software can improve the accuracy and organization of your business's financial information. See "Accounting Software" on page 221 for more information.

Business management software: Landscape management business software is designed to simplify common business tasks, such as billing, scheduling, and job costing. See "Scheduling and Billing Software" on page 238 for a list of some of the products available.

Part II

Landscape Management

Part II

Part II is a practical introduction to landscape management. Chapters include safety, turfgrass management, landscape plant management, soil, pruning, and irrigation system repair.

Safety

To highlight the importance of safety instruction, consider that each year in the U.S., tens of thousands of people are treated in emergency rooms for lawn mower-related injuries. This chapter introduces safe work practices that will help you reduce the risk of injuring yourself or others while on the job.

Power equipment manufacturers include operator's manuals with their products. These guides contain important safety and maintenance information that users must be aware of. If you are missing a manual for a tool, call the manufacturer to request a replacement, or download the manual from the manufacturer's website.

Important: *The safety instruction provided here is meant to serve as general guidance only—it is not intended to be complete or to substitute for medical information or the information in your equipment operator's manuals.*

Power Equipment Safety

The Outdoor Power Equipment Institute, Inc. (OPEI; http://www.opei.org) suggests the following eight basic rules for outdoor power equipment safety:

1. Know how to operate the equipment. Read the operator's manual before using any power equipment. Know where the controls are and what they do. Follow the safety instructions.

2. Dress properly for the job. Wear long pants, close-fitting clothes, sturdy shoes, and safety glasses. Don't wear anything that could get caught in moving parts (e.g., loose jewelry or clothing; be careful of long hair).

3. Handle gas carefully. Fill up a [tool's gas tank] before you start [the tool], while the engine is cold. Don't spill when you fill. Store gas in an approved container, [and store the container] in a cool, ventilated area. Never smoke around gasoline.

4. Clear the area before you start. Pick up rocks, twigs, cans, golf balls, or anything that could be thrown by mowing equipment.

5. Keep children and pets away from the area until you are finished. Never allow children to operate a mower. And never carry children as passengers on a riding mower.

6. Operate equipment carefully and follow recommended procedures. Always turn off the engine and disconnect the spark plug wire before attempting to unclog or work on outdoor power equipment. When leaving equipment unattended, turn off the engine and remove the key.

7. Keep hands and feet away from moving parts. Never work on equipment while it is running. Never remove or tamper with safety devices and labels.

8. Wear hearing protection. [When working with power equipment] wear hearing protec-

tion, such as special earmuffs, to prevent potentially damaging sounds from reaching your ears without eliminating the sounds you will *need* to hear. Protect your ears from sounds that are too *loud* and too *close* for too long (OPEI 2005; reproduced with permission).

These eight rules provide a basic orientation to power equipment safety. Here are some safety guidelines for specific tools.

Refueling Precaution: *Gasoline spilled on a hot engine can ignite. To reduce the risk of igniting gasoline vapor, let power equipment cool down before refueling, and restart at least ten feet from where you refueled.*

Grass Trimmer Safety

Grass trimmers can send rocks and debris flying in unpredictable directions, so it is important to wear adequate eye protection every time you operate your grass trimmer. Many maintenance workers only wear sunglasses, but these do not provide enough protection—rocks and debris can still fly in at an angle and reach the eye. Safety glasses with side protection are a better choice than sunglasses, but still leave room for flying debris. Manufacturers recommend safety goggles and often include an OSHA-approved pair with their grass trimmers. A high-impact polycarbonate full-protection face shield can help protect the face from flying debris. Follow the guidelines in your operator's manual.

When operating your trimmer, take measures to protect the people, pets, and property around you. Shut off the engine when a person or pet approaches (within 50 feet) or is in the range of flying debris. To do this, you must regularly pause your work and scan the area. Remember, the people around you are not wearing protective equipment. In general, bystanders are not aware of the dangers associated with this tool. Consider advising clients, neighbors, or others in the vicinity to stay out of the area while the tool is in operation. Even if you provide this warning, you should still regularly check to see if others are in the area.

Keep in mind that small rocks thrown by a grass trimmer can chip car paint, crack a house window, and cause other property damage. For more information, see "Hearing Protection" on page 28 and "Protecting Trees and Shrubs" on page 40.

Lawn Mower Safety

Despite the mower deck, which encloses the blade, a lawn mower can project objects with great force and at unpredictable angles. Always wear adequate eye protection while mowing. Toys, wood, rocks, and other objects hidden in overgrown grass can damage the mower blade and become projectiles. Inspect the mowing area and clear it of objects before mowing. If the mower hits something and vibrates oddly afterward, shut off the engine, disconnect the spark plug wire, and inspect the blade. A blade that is out of balance or warped should be replaced to avoid damaging the mower.

Operate walk-behind rotary mowers across the face of sloped areas, not up and down. (Riding mowers have unique operation and safety rules, not included here.) Start at the top of sloped areas and work your way down. Use caution when pulling a mower toward you: it is possible to slip and have the mower move over your foot or leg. Wear steel-toed boots on the job to minimize damage to the feet in the event of a lawn mower or other power equipment accident.

Always disconnect the spark plug wire and secure it away from the spark plug before tilting the mower on its side or before putting your hand near the blade. Do not disconnect your mower's engine-kill lever, and do not operate your mower without a bag or mulching plug. Follow the refueling guidelines mentioned previously. See "Hearing Protection" on page 28 for related information.

Leaf Blower Use Guidelines

In addition to following your leaf blower's operating instructions, it is also important to use your leaf blower responsibly. Responsible leaf blower use includes the following practices:

- When a person approaches the area you are blowing (within 50 feet)—on foot or in a vehicle—turn off your blower until the person passes. At times it may be acceptable to let the tool idle until the person passes. Never aim a blower at people or pets.

- Do not blow debris into the street. Scattering debris in this way is unprofessional, and it can cause drivers to react unpredictably. And wet leaves scattered onto a roadway can create a slippery surface. If you must blow some debris into the street to effectively manage a property, sweep it into a pile, and remove it when you are finished. Debris left in the street can wind up in storm drains or on neighbors' properties.

- To minimize noise, use the lowest throttle necessary for the job.

- Follow the noise ordinances for leaf blower use in your city. Avoid using blowers in the early morning or late in the day.

- Do not operate more than one blower at time in a given location.

- Ensure that the blower's muffler, air intakes, and air filter are in good operating condition.

- Do not blow near open windows or doors.

- Wet dusty areas before blowing.

- Do not blow areas that will produce a lot of dust, such as areas of dry, bare dirt or areas containing gravel dust.

- Protect your lungs by wearing a dust mask in dusty conditions.

- Use rakes and brooms if they will clear an area more effectively than blowing.

The Outdoor Power Equipment Institute (http://www.opei.org) has an online publication entitled *Leaf Blowers: A Guide To Safe & Courteous Use*, which includes other useful suggestions.

Chainsaw Safety

In general, a chainsaw is not an essential tool in residential landscape management. If you choose to use one, get the necessary training. Before operating a chainsaw, you are strongly encouraged to take a chainsaw safety training course.

An informative article entitled "General Safety Precautions for Use of Chainsaws" can be found on the Oregon®, Blount website at http://www.oregonchain.com/pro/service/technical_safety_info.htm. See "Chainsaws" on page 16 for a partial list of recommended safety gear. The following guidelines are not intended to be complete. They are provided only to call your attention to a few common chainsaw safety precautions.

The following information has been reproduced with permission from an OSHA Quick Card entitled Chainsaw Safety Tips (HA 3269-1 0N-05). OSHA Quick Cards present a few practical safety guidelines; they are not intended to present complete safety information.

Operating a chainsaw is inherently hazardous. Potential injuries can be minimized by using proper personal protective equipment and safe operating procedures.

Before Starting a Chainsaw

- Check controls, chain tension, and all bolts and handles to ensure that they are functioning properly and that they are adjusted according to the manufacturer's instructions.

- Make sure that the chain is sharp and the lubrication reservoir is full.

- Start the saw on the ground or on another firm support. Drop starting is never allowed.

- Start the saw at least 10 feet from the fueling area, with the chain's brake engaged.

Fueling a Chainsaw

- Use approved containers for transporting fuel to the saw.

- Dispense fuel at least 10 feet away from any sources of ignition when performing construction activities. No smoking during fueling.

- Use a funnel or a flexible hose when pouring fuel into the saw.

- Never attempt to fuel a running or HOT saw.

Chainsaw Safety

- Clear away dirt, debris, small tree limbs and rocks from the saw's chain path. Look for nails, spikes, or other metal in the tree before cutting.

- Shut off the saw or engage its chain brake when carrying the saw on rough or uneven terrain.

- Keep your hands on the saw's handles, and maintain secure footing while operating the saw.

- Proper personal protective equipment must be worn when operating the saw. [This equipment] includes hand, foot, leg, eye, face, hearing and head protection.

- Do not wear loose-fitting clothing.

- Be careful that the trunk or tree limbs will not bind against the saw.

- Watch for branches [that are]under tension; they may spring out when cut.

- Gasoline-powered chainsaws must be equipped with a protective device that minimizes chainsaw kickback.

- Be cautious of saw kick-back. To avoid kickback, do not saw with the tip. If [the saw has a tip guard, keep the tip guard in place.] (OSHA)

Kickback is a particularly dangerous chainsaw hazard. According to Oregon®, Blount Inc. (2009),

Kickback may occur when the moving chain at the nose or tip of the guide bar touches an object, or when the wood closes in and pinches the saw chain in the cut. Tip or bar nose contact can, in some cases, cause a lightning-fast reverse reaction, kicking the guide bar up and back toward the operator. Pinching the cutting chain along the top of the guide bar may push the guide bar rapidly toward the operator. Either of these reactions may cause you to lose control of the saw, which could result in serious personal injury to yourself or to bystanders (http://www.oregonchain.com/pro/service/kickback.htm).

Precautions against kickback include maintaining a firm grip on the saw with both hands; standing to the side of the saw; not operating the saw overhead; using a low-kickback saw chain; and wearing chainsaw safety gear. Never operate a chainsaw from a ladder or in a tree without appropriate training.

Hearing Protection

Common sense dictates the use of hearing protectors whenever you operate power equipment. You may not think you are affected by loud noises, but problems can develop over time and may not become apparent until months or even years later. Noise induced hearing loss (NIHL) is only one of the potential risks. For example, a disorder called tinnitus can be caused by prolonged exposure to loud noise and may not develop until later in life, years after the damaging noise exposure. A person who has tinnitus may experience ringing or hissing in the ears that does not go away. The consistent use of hearing protectors will reduce your risk of developing hearing disorders. Regardless, you should have your hearing checked regularly by a doctor.

Over-the-ear hearing protectors (earmuffs) are easy to put on and take off—something that needs to be done many times throughout the day. Foam or rubber earplugs require more time and care to use correctly, and the motivation to insert them properly into the ear can fade over the course of the day. Depending on the level and duration of noise exposure, OSHA may require employees who operate power equipment to wear hearing protectors.

Safety and OSHA

The Occupational Safety and Health Administration (OSHA) is a division of the United States Department of Labor that regulates workplace safety. If you hire employees, you must comply with OSHA to ensure a safe working environment (see "OSHA Requirements" on page 208). OSHA is a good source of information on safe work practices. See OSHA's Landscape and Horticultural Services webpage for important safety information that all landscapers should be aware of. To find this page, go to OSHA's home page at http://www.osha.gov and search for "landscape" in the A-Z index. The direct address for the page is http://www.osha.gov/SLTC/landscaping/index.html. OSHA can also be reached by phone at 1-800-321-OSHA (6742).

Eye Protection

Wear eye protection whenever you operate power equipment. The recommended eye protection will be listed in your equipment operator's manuals. Safety glasses are a standard piece of personal protective equipment. High-impact safety goggles provide better protection when working with certain tools (e.g., grass trimmers). Eye protection is also appropriate when using many hand tools. For example, when using pole pruners, branches can fall straight down toward you. Eye protection must meet the latest American National Standards Institute (ANSI) standards, currently Z87.1-2003.

Safety glasses or goggles also protect the eyes from other hazards. For example, when some plants are cut, they excrete liquid that can splash into the eyes, causing irritation or injury (see "Dangerous Plants" on page 31). When safety glasses are not needed, sunglasses with UVA/UVB protection will shield the eyes from the sun's harmful rays.

Power Equipment Fire Safety

Use fire safety practices when working in areas of dry grass or brush. If a lawn mower blade, metal grass trimmer wire, or brush cutter blade strikes a rock, it can create a spark, which can ignite dry grass. Hot mufflers or faulty spark arresters can also ignite dry grass. Use extra caution when operating power equipment in developed areas that are near wildlands, known as wildland-urban interface (WUI) areas.

Contact your city or county fire department to learn the laws and guidelines specific to your area. The following fire safety guidelines have been reproduced with permission from the website of the Air Quality Management District of El Dorado County, California.

- Restrict lawn mowing and equipment use to the cooler morning hours when lower temperatures and higher humidity reduce the risk of starting a wildfire.

- Do not smoke while refueling or adjusting an engine.

- Stop the engine and wait several minutes before refueling.

- Set a hot engine on bare ground, a log, or stump—never on dry forest materials.

- Avoid fuel overflow spill by not filling equipment gas tanks to the top.

- [After refueling and before starting the engine,] move 10-15 feet from the fueling spot, away from gasoline vapors.

- Be sure spilled gasoline is dried-up before starting [a tool].

- Check [the tool] for leaks, and clean oil, dirt, and fine flammables from metal parts (*continued*).

- Keep the tool's fire prevention exhaust system in place, and clear away any carbon accumulation.

- Inspect and clean the spark arrestor screen before each operation.

- Don't leave the engine idling unattended.

- Keep an approved fire extinguisher and shovel within 25 feet of operation.

- Know where the nearest phone is and who to call for help.

- Check for smoldering embers before leaving the area.

On-the-Job Safety

Paying attention to your surroundings and the task at hand can help prevent accidents. For example, when clearing debris from the street in front of a residence, it's easy to assume that drivers see you, when they may not. Even failing to notice unevenness in the turf you are mowing can result in an accident. Landscape architect Jess Stryker sums it up this way: "Your brain is the best safety device you have—don't start work without it!"

Below are some general on-the-job safety considerations. More comprehensive coverage of landscape hazards and safety practices can be found on the OSHA website at http://www.osha.gov/SLTC/landscaping/index.html.

Private Property

Private property trespassing laws vary from state to state. By nature of your work agreement, it is reasonable to assume that the homeowner, tenant, or property manager has granted consent for you to enter the yard at the scheduled work times. Regardless, do not enter a locked yard without permission from the owner. If it is a rental property, do not enter a locked yard without permission from the property manager and the tenant. If a gate is locked, get the owner or tenant to open it for you. If the owner or tenant is not home, skip that area of the yard.

Underground Utilities

Public utility lines, such as gas, electric, water, and telecom lines, are sometimes buried beneath the street, though they may be buried beneath sidewalks or on private property. Digging into a power line can result in power outages, as well as personal injury or death.

Before digging on public or private property, you are legally required to contact local utility companies to notify them of your intention to dig. Once they have been notified, the utility companies will send out people to mark any buried utilities in the area.

Since there can be several utility companies that require notice before a dig, state's have "one call" phone numbers to simplify the notification process. In 2007, the FCC designated the three-digit telephone number "811" as the national call-before-you-dig number. Call 811 at least several days in advance of beginning the work. You can find more information at http://www.call811.com. Note that if you damage a utility, you may be responsible for repair costs and penalties.

Electrical Safety

Potential electrical hazards on the job include buried or overhead power lines, wall outlets, irrigation controllers, and lightning. Always assume that electrical wires are energized and unsafe to touch, even if the wire is on the ground or is insulated. Use caution when moving pipes, tools, or ladders near overhead power lines—electricity can arc from a power line to nearby equipment. In other words, electrical current can contact equipment even if the equipment is not in direct contact with the power line.

The "10-foot rule" is to maintain a distance of at least 10 feet (3 meters) from overhead wires at all times. The 10-foot rule applies to your body and to materials and equipment. You are legally required to contact the electric company if you will be working less than 10 feet from a power line. Note that some equipment manufacturers recommend keeping tools farther than 10 feet from power lines. If a client asks you to remove branches that are near a power line, advise the client to hire a licensed tree care company for the job.

Pesticide Safety

Many pesticides are toxic substances that can cause serious health and environmental damage if handled improperly. For this reason, the commercial use of pesticides requires training and certification, as approved by the state agency that oversees the application of these materials. It is against the law to apply pesticides commercially without certification. This means that without certification, landscaping professionals cannot apply any pest control product. This book does not cover the use of pesticides (insecticides, herbicides, and fungicides). Get the required training and certification if you intend to work with these substances.

To locate the state agency in charge of pesticide applicator licensing, see the website of the National Pesticide Information Center at http://npic.orst. edu/state1.htm, or call 1-800-858-7378. For more information, see "Pest Control Applicator's Licensing" on page 70.

Dangerous Plants

Landscaping can expose a person to a variety of plants that can cause adverse reactions ranging from skin irritation to life-threatening illness. Not all individuals react the same to plant allergens; some may be unaffected by a particular allergen, while others may be strongly affected. Certain individuals can experience anaphylaxis upon contact with plant or insect allergens. Anaphylaxis is a life-threatening allergic reaction involving the entire body—it requires immediate medical attention. Those at risk for anaphylaxis should be under the care of a physician and may need to carry emergency medication with them at all times.

A few of the more common plants that can cause painful or dangerous reactions in humans are mentioned here. Online research will turn up many articles and photographs that can help you identify these plants.

Contact with any part of a poison oak (Toxicodendron diversilobum), poison ivy (Toxicodendron radicans), or poison sumac (Toxicodendron vernix) plant can lead to moderate to severe skin inflammation in the majority of people, though some individuals are not affected. It is important to be able to identify these plants in order to avoid them.

Briefly, poison oak and poison ivy may grow as shrubs or vines, and they have leaves that come in clusters of three. Poison sumac is a woody shrub or small tree with red leaf stems that contain 7 to 13 leaflets. All these plants have leaves that may be green, red, yellow, orange, or multicolored. They produce small greenish- or greyish-white berries in late summer and drop their leaves in winter. Even when leafless, the stems can cause skin inflammation. The absence of thorns on these plants helps distinguish them from wild berry plants or brambles.

If you must work near poison oak, poison ivy, or poison sumac, wear a long-sleeve shirt, long pants, a hat, and gloves, and wash your clothing after contact. Washing the skin soon after contact can sometimes avert or lessen the reaction. Once the irritant penetrates the skin, it can't be removed. Before washing up, don't touch your eyes, face, or other body parts. Products that block the effects of these plants are available, but they must be applied to the skin before exposure to the irritant.

Stinging nettle (Urtica dioica) is a 3- to 7-foot-tall perennial with tiny needles that cause a painful or itching reaction that can last from a few minutes to over a week. Some individuals can have a severe allergic reaction that requires immediate medical treatment. Stinging nettle is another plant that is important to be able to identify in order to avoid it or remove it with caution. Wear long pants, a long-sleeve shirt, and gloves when working near nettle.

Euphorbia is a genus of over 2000 plants consisting of annual weeds, perennials, succulents, shrubs, and trees. When cut or damaged, euphorbias exude a white, sticky substance called latex that is caustic and poisonous. Latex can cause mild to severe irritation upon contact with the skin, and burning pain or even vision impairment upon contact with the eyes. Latex-induced eye injuries require prompt medical treatment. For these reasons, it is important to wear eye protection, long pants, a long-sleeve shirt, and gloves when working with Euphorbias. To be on the safe side, wear eye protection when working with any plant that exudes liquid from cuts.

Oldeander (Nerium oleander) is a common shrub and one of the most poisonous plants known. Its close relative, yellow oleander (Thevetia peruviana), is also poisonous. All parts of oleander are toxic, including its sap. Oleander sap can cause severe eye irritation that may require medical treatment. Wear suitable eye protection when working with oleander and dispose of clippings responsibly so that pets or livestock don't eat the leaves.

Insects

The bites and stings of insects found in landscapes can cause a variety of painful reactions, though these are rarely fatal; however, people who are allergic to insect stings can have serious, even life-threatening reactions. While many insects serve a useful role in the landscape by keeping harmful insect populations in check, they can also, at times, be a nuisance to work near.

Wasps. Paper wasps are long and slender, with distinctive narrow waists. They are alarmed by activity near their nests, which are commonly found in doorways and eaves. If you rile up these insects with power equipment or hurried activity, turn off the equipment and step back from their nests. Once they calm down, move more slowly and, if possible, don't operate power tools near their nests.

It is not unusual to find paper wasps nested in ornamental vines growing up the side of a building. Trimming takes on an added dimension when these insects are present. Before turning to a pest control service, research can sometimes reveal non-toxic ways to work around problems. For instance, if cold weather is not far off, you might postpone trimming until some wasps die out for the year. And wasps may be slower in the colder, early-morning hours. Use caution when trimming or removing Pampas Grass, a large, dense, mounded grass, which yellow jackets and hornets sometimes nest in.

Yellow jackets are a more aggressive type of wasp and can be more problematic to work near. In general, it is best to avoid killing predatory insects because they kill plant-damaging insects—in other words, they're good for the landscape. If they are a nuisance or threaten to sting, controls may be necessary. Local mosquito and vector control associations may be able to remove nests. In some cases, you may need to call a pest control service.

Africanized bees. Africanized honey bees, also known as killer bees, were first detected in the U.S. in 1990. These insects slowly made their way up from South America and are now established in some southern regions of the United States. The sting of Africanized bees is roughly equivalent to that of European honey bees. However, Africanized bees pose more of a threat to humans and animals because they attack en masse, sometimes hundreds at a time. True to their nickname, an attack can have potentially life-threatening consequences. Compared to European honey bees, Africanized bees are less particular about where they build their hives, and they defend their hives more aggressively. They can be disturbed by loud noises, such as power equipment. If you are attacked by Africanized bees, find shelter quickly and protect your eyes and face. Most attacks are not fatal. And many regions of the country are still not affected. Even in colonized regions, your chances of encountering Africanized bees are slim.

Spiders. All spiders have poisonous bites, but most are not capable of causing serious harm to humans. Brown recluse (violin spider) or black widow spider bites, among others, can cause a variety of painful reactions in humans, even death, though fatalities are rare. If you are bitten by a dangerous spider, seek medical attention. To reduce your chances of being bitten, wear gloves when cleaning out woodpiles and avoid crawling beneath houses.

Ticks. Ticks are parasites that can attach to the skin during outdoor activity. These tiny insects can spread infectious diseases such as Rocky Mountain spotted fever and Lyme disease, among others. Ticks can drop from overhead growth or latch onto you as you pass through tall grass and other growth. When working in these conditions, check yourself for ticks occasionally throughout the workday. The hiker's trick of tucking your pants into your socks will help keep ticks off your legs. Wearing light-colored clothing can make it easier to spot ticks. EPA-registered insect repellents, such as those containing DEET, can help keep ticks away. At the end of the day, inspect your skin, hair, and clothes for ticks before entering your vehicle or house.

Do not use anecdotal methods of removing ticks. If you find a tick on your skin, use tweezers and slowly pull up on it until it lets go. Do not grab the tick's body with your fingers and do not twist or rock the tick as you lift. If you cannot remove the tick, or parts of it remain in the skin, see your doctor. Once the tick is out, disinfect the area with rubbing alcohol. If you notice redness, rash, blisters, swelling, headache, fever, itching, muscle or joint pain, fatigue, or other symptoms, contact your doctor. If you are pregnant or nursing, contact your doctor if you think you may have been exposed to ticks.

Mosquitoes. The West Nile Virus has been in the US since 1999 and primarily spreads to humans through mosquito bite. According to the U.S. Food and Drug Administration (2007), "In humans, the virus often causes only a mild infection—characterized by fever, headache, tiredness, aches, and rash—that clears up without further treatment. But some patients develop severe infections resulting in neurological disease and even death."

In addition to wearing long pants and a long-sleeved shirt, the use of an EPA-registered insect repellent will reduce your exposure to mosquito bites. Spray insect repellent on exposed skin and on the outside of clothing; do not spray it on skin that will be covered by clothing. Keep insect repellent away from your mouth and eyes, and wash skin and clothes with soap and water after use.

A strategy to reduce mosquito activity in a landscape is to eliminate areas of standing water where mosquitoes breed. For some clients this may mean retiring their bird bath or draining a small pond; others may opt to kill mosquito larvae with nontoxic larvicides containing Bti (*Bacillus thuringien-*

sis). Another option is to stock small ponds with mosquito fish (Gambusia affinis) (Eldridge 1998).

Refilling Portable Gas Containers

The standard precaution when refueling is, "Don't spill when you fill." A number of other safe refueling practices should also be followed. Note that, in addition to open flame, static electricity can ignite gasoline vapors. According to the American Petroleum Institute (API),

> Static electricity-related incidents at retail gasoline outlets are extremely unusual, but the potential for them to happen appears to be highest during cool or cold and dry climate conditions. In rare circumstances, these static-related incidents have resulted in a brief flash fire occurring at the fill point. Consumers can take steps to minimize these and other potential fueling hazards by following safe refueling procedures all year long (API 2006).

The API article *Staying Safe at the Pump*, available at http://www.api.org, contains a complete list of API refueling safety guidelines. Selected guidelines have been reproduced here.

- Do not light matches or lighters and do not smoke while refueling at the pump or when using gasoline anywhere else.

- Do not re-enter your vehicle during refueling. If you cannot avoid re-entering your vehicle, discharge any static build-up *before* reaching for the nozzle by touching something metal with a bare hand—such as the vehicle door—away from the nozzle.

- In the unlikely event a static-caused fire occurs when refueling, leave the nozzle in the fill pipe and back away from the vehicle. Notify the station attendant immediately (continued, next page).

Portable Containers

- When dispensing gasoline into a container, use only an approved portable container and place it on the ground to avoid a possible static electricity ignition of fuel vapors. [Never fill containers while they are inside a vehicle, a car trunk, a pickup truck bed, or a trailer.]

- When filling a portable container, manually control the nozzle valve throughout the filling process. Fill a portable container slowly to decrease the chance of static electricity buildup and to minimize spilling or splattering. Keep the nozzle in contact with the rim of the container opening while refueling.

- Fill containers no more than 95 percent full to allow for expansion.

- Place the cap tightly on the container after filling—do not use containers that do not seal properly.

- If gasoline spills on the container, make sure that it has evaporated before you place the container in your vehicle. Report spills to the attendant.

- When transporting gasoline in a portable container, make sure [the container] is secured against tipping and sliding, and never leave it in direct sunlight or in the trunk of a car (API 2006).

Health Considerations

General conditioning through weight training and cardiovascular exercise will help you prevent injuries and increase strength and endurance. Proper body mechanics, such as bending at the knees and keeping the back straight while lifting, also reduce the risk of injury. This topic looks at a few ailments and provides strategies to prevent them. The following information is not intended to serve as medical advice. If you have health concerns or questions, consult with your doctor.

Medical Check-up

Get a medical checkup before beginning work in landscape management. Ask your doctor if you are up to date on your tetanus ("lockjaw") vaccine. Tetanus is a disease that can infect the body through cuts, and the bacterium that causes it is found in soil. Booster tetanus vaccines are needed every ten years.

If you are unsure if have an allergic reaction to insect bites, mention this to the doctor. Ask how often you should schedule check-ups, and ask what self-examinations you should do on a regular basis. Visit your doctor for a physical exam at least once a year.

Dehydration and Overheating

It is easy to become dehydrated working outdoors, particularly during the summer months. Symptoms of dehydration include light-headedness, mental confusion, and diarrhea, among others. Prolonged dehydration in a hot environment can cause excessive sweating, fatigue, and collapse, which are symptoms of *heat exhaustion*. A similar condition called *heatstroke* is life-threatening and can come on quickly, without warning signs; common symptoms include increased heartbeat and body temperature. Untreated heatstroke can lead to permanent bodily damage, even death. Heatstroke requires immediate medical attention.

To prevent these conditions, use common sense and drink at least one tall glass of water each hour. If you can drink more, do so. On hot days, make it a goal to drink one gallon of water or more while on the job. If you feel the heat getting to you, take a break or call it a day. Pushing your limits can put you at risk for more serious problems.

Sun Protection

Working outdoors for a number of years without sun protection can cause premature wrinkling of the skin. Prolonged sun exposure also increases your risk for sunburn and various types of skin cancer. While people with light complexions are most at risk for sunburn and skin cancer, everyone, including dark-skinned people, can be harmed by the sun's ultraviolet (UV) rays.

To reduce your sun exposure, wear a hat, long pants, a long-sleeved shirt, and sunblock while on the job. A short-sleeved shirt and sunblock on the forearms will also work. Clothing should be tightly woven so that it blocks out sunlight. Once a month, conduct a self-exam of your skin. If you notice areas of skin discoloration or changes in density or texture, especially in or around skin moles, consult a doctor. Skin cancer that is detected early can usually be treated successfully.

To protect yourself from the sun's UV rays, use a UVA/UVB sunblock with a sun protection factor (SPF) of at least 15 (30 or higher is better). Different brands may use different chemicals to provide UV protection. If one brand irritates your skin, try a product with a different active ingredient. Some spray-on products are clear and won't give your skin a pasty appearance.

Apply sunblock at least 30 minutes before beginning work to avoid sweating it off. Cover large areas such as your forearms and the back of your neck, as well as smaller areas such as the tops of your hands, your nose, and the tops of your ears. A broad-brimmed hat provides good sun protection, but it can't be worn with ear muffs. A baseball cap, hearing protectors, and sunblock are an effective combination. Sunglasses with UVA/UVB protection help shield the eyes from sun overexposure.

Sporotrichosis

Working with thorny plants, sphagnum peat moss, hay, or soil can increase your exposure to a fungus called Sporothrix schenckii, which can enter the body primarily through skin abrasions or punctures. This fungus can cause a disease called Sporotrichosis, sometimes called rose thorn disease or rose handler's disease.

The first symptom is usually a firm bump on the skin—possibly red, pink, or purple—that may progress to an open sore that drains clear fluid. New nodules can form over time, and the fungus can spread along the lymph nodes or, in rare cases, infect other areas of the body. It generally does not spread from person to person. This disease should be evaluated and treated by a doctor. Wearing leather or nitrile-coated gloves will help to protect your hands when you work with thorny plants, soil, or soil amendments.

Hand-Arm Vibration Syndrome

Previously called "vibration white finger", hand-arm vibration syndrome (HAVS) is a condition in which the blood vessels in the hand constrict, causing symptoms in the fingers, such as numbness, tingling, loss of sensitivity, discoloration (whiteness, blueness, or redness), discomfort, and pain. HAVS is a form of Raynaud's phenomenon that may be caused by frequent and repeated use of vibrating power tools. The disease is potentially disabling, so consult a doctor if you experience any of these symptoms.

Carpal Tunnel Syndrome

The nerves that control sensation in your fingers travel through a small area of bone and ligament in your wrist known as the carpal tunnel. Inflammation of these nerves can lead to hand pain known as carpal tunnel syndrome (CTS). Symptoms include numbness or prickling sensations in the fingers or hand. For those affected, CTS can become a chronic problem, making it difficult for them to use the hands for many activities. The cause of carpal tunnel syndrome is not always known. Repetitive motion and heavy use of the hands and wrists may be contributing factors. Consult your doctor if you experience any symptoms. The following guidelines can help you prevent carpal tunnel syndrome.

- Keep your wrists straight during work activities, particularly when working with power equipment or performing repetitive tasks such as pruning or raking. A bent wrist puts extra pressure on the nerves in the wrist.

- Keep your body conditioned. This will help you maintain good posture and keep your wrists straight.

- Take breaks when working with power equipment and alternate with another activity.

- Consider purchasing tools with a built-in vibration-reduction system. Vibration-reducing gloves are also available.

Turfgrass Management

This chapter is a practical introduction to turfgrass management. The emphasis is on mowing, fertilization, irrigation, and aeration. These tasks are fairly straightforward, but if they are performed incorrectly, lawns can experience reduced drought tolerance, an increase in weeds, general decline, or worse. This chapter looks at management techniques that help lawns fend off drought-like conditions, weeds, and disease. It also includes suggestions to help you work efficiently and provide professional-looking results.

Turfgrass Basics

Lawns consist of thousands of grass plants growing closely together. Some lawns consist of one grass type, others are a mix of grass types. Grass types, or species, differ in their tolerance of heat, drought, shade, cold, and wear, as well as in their nitrogen requirements and resistance to insects and disease, among other factors. Turfgrasses are broadly classified as either cool-season or warm-season.

Cool-Season Grasses

Cool-season grasses—such as Kentucky bluegrass, ryegrass, bentgrass, and the fescues (tall fescue, red fescue, etc.)—produce the greatest shoot and root growth in the milder temperatures of spring and fall. They do best in climates that are mild for most of the growing season, such as northern regions of the U.S. and cooler coastal regions.

In regions with long, hot summers, cool-season grasses tend to show signs of stress and may yellow or go semi-dormant during extreme heat, even turning brown if drought-stressed. With irrigation, they will usually come back to life in the fall. Cool-season grasses can remain green in regions with long, hot summers, but they require more irrigation than warm-season grasses to achieve this. In areas where the ground does not freeze, cool-season grasses will remain green through the winter.

Warm-Season Grasses

Warm-season grasses—such as St. Augustine grass, zoysia, bermuda grass, and native grasses such as buffalo and blue grama—produce the greatest shoot and root growth during summer. Warm-season grasses are more common in areas of the south and other areas of the country where summers are hot and winters are mild.

Warm-season grasses tend to grow vigorously, often spreading into places they are not wanted. They also develop thatch more quickly than cool-season grasses. These grasses go dormant as temperatures drop for the year and resume growth when temperatures warm. Some warm-season grasses maintain color in winter; others turn brown in winter and turn green again in spring. In generally frost-free areas, warm-season grasses that turn brown can be overseeded in the fall with a cool-season variety, usually annual or perennial ryegrass, that will keep the lawn green through the winter.

Grass and Environment

It is common to encounter grass types that are not suited to their environment. Familiarity with the broad distinctions between grass types can help you tell the difference between a turfgrass problem that requires action and one that can't be prevented. For example, if you live in an area with hot summers and need to care for a bentgrass lawn, you won't be surprised when the appearance of this cool-season grass deteriorates during the summer.

In general, warm-season grasses are better adapted to heat and wear, and cool-season grasses are better adapted to cooler temperatures and shade, though there are exceptions; for example, tall fescue is a durable cool-season grass that does reasonably well in heat and drought stress.

Occasionally a lawn is poorly suited to a landscape and extra efforts are needed to keep the turf in acceptable condition. In these circumstances, it may save time and resources to replace the lawn with a better adapted grass type. Sometimes changes in the landscape can create unfavorable conditions for the lawn. For example, the construction of a building or the growth of a tree can shade turf areas that previously received direct sunlight, and the lawn can suffer as a result. This might be corrected by replacing the lawn with a more shade-tolerant grass, such as the fine fescues (cool-season), or the Palmetto, Seville, or Bitterblue varieties of St. Augustine grass (warm-season).

It is usually enough to learn the names of common grass types in a region and become familiar with their unique maintenance requirements and common problems. Note that a great deal of testing and selection goes on for new varieties that withstand heat, retain color, and so on. You may want to keep up to date on what's available. In the West, tall fescue and its dwarf varieties have become increasingly popular because of their climate flexibility, disease resistance, and low maintenance.

Growth Habit

Grasses are broadly divided into one of two types of growth habit: clumping or spreading. This distinction refers to how a grass grows and expands its territory. Tall fescue and its dwarf varieties are clump-forming grasses: where you plant them is where they stay. Clump-forming grasses spread out slowly, if at all, so they are seeded at a relatively high rate to make a dense stand.

Clump-forming grasses typically do not fill in bare turf areas, so if a patch of grass is killed, additional seed of the same grass type is needed to repair the turf. Lawns that are primarily clump-forming grasses benefit from overseeding every few years to maintain density. To address the drawbacks of clump-forming grasses, turf seed mixes are often blended with a small percentage of spreading grass seed, such as Kentucky bluegrass seed.

Spreading grasses expand their territory through runners, which are stems that spread out and become new grass plants. Runners on the surface of the soil are called stolons; runners below the soil, parallel to the surface, are called rhizomes. Spreading grasses may spread by stolons, rhizomes, or both. Because spreading grasses fill in bare turf areas, they are seeded at a lower rate than clump-forming grasses.

Bluegrass and creeping red fescue spread moderately, filling in bare turf areas from longer rhizomes. Bermuda grass and other subtropical grasses spread quickly, often by rhizomes and stolons. Note that spreading grasses can grow outside of their allotted territory and become invasive.

Edging

Edging is the practice of trimming the grass growing at the edge of a lawn. It is usually the first task performed during a lawn maintenance visit. Edging scatters leaves, debris, and grass clippings onto walkways and driveways. By edging first, these clippings can be picked up by the mower. If edging throws excessive debris onto walkways, the debris can be blown or swept onto the lawn before mowing.

The preferred edging tool for walkways, driveways, and mow strips is a blade edger: either a stick edger or a walk-behind edger (See "Lawn Edgers" on page 15). These tools provide a straight, consistent edge. Grass trimmers create an edge that is slightly uneven, though this is less of a concern on some properties.

Edging creates a narrow gap between the lawn and sidewalks, mowstrips, and driveways. Keep this gap as narrow as possible. Gaps expose soil to sunlight and encourage weed seeds to germinate. It is common for weeds to gain a foothold in the gap and spread to other areas of the lawn. Grass trimmers create a wider gap than blade edgers. This is another reason to use a blade edger along walkways and driveways. When edging, keep the blade of the edger vertical; edging at an angle can expose more soil to sunlight. Clients interested in organic lawn care may wish to forego edging if a manicured lawn is not a priority.

Grass trimmers are used to edge grass growing near walls, fences, and house siding. Use care when trimming near these features because trimmer line can mark and damage wood. Products are available that can be installed at the base of wood fences and fenceposts to protect them. Reciprocating grass trimmers are less likely to damage fenceposts.

Most irrigation systems use 4-inch pop-up spray heads, impact-drive sprinklers, or rotors. When the irrigation system is on, the sprinkler nozzles rise on a stem that provides the necessary clearance above the grass. Mowing is usually enough to keep the grass from obstructing these sprinklers. Edge around these sprinklers with a grass trimmer as necessary.

If the system does not use pop-up sprinklers, or uses brass pop-ups that only provide $1^1/_2$ inch of clearance, edge around the sprinklers as needed to keep them clear. Note that it is best to avoid creating circles of low-trimmed grass around sprinkler heads because this can expose soil and encourage weeds. It also draws attention to the sprinklers, which should remain as inconspicuous as possible.

Finally, use your grass trimmer to cut any weeds growing through gaps in the walkways and driveway. Weeds growing in these areas are particularly unsightly, and clients appreciate this attention to detail.

Blade edgers provide a straight, consistent lawn edge. They also create a smaller gap between the lawn and mowstrips or walkways than line trimmers.

For tap-advance grass trimmers, advance the trimmer line regularly by tapping the line advance button on firm soil. This will help prevent the line from "welding" to itself and will help maintain cutting power. Tapping the line-advance button on concrete will wear out the button more quickly.

Protecting Trees and Shrubs

Use care to avoid contacting the bark of trees and shrubs with your mower or grass trimmer. A mower or grass trimmer can easily cut through a tree's bark and damage the cambium layer, which is a layer of growth cells just beneath the bark. Cuts in the cambium layer can stunt a tree's growth. Completely girdling a trunk with trimmer line can kill a tree. Damaged bark can also become an entry point for disease. Young trees are particularly susceptible to power equipment damage because their bark is tender. Mature trees can also be damaged and are at greatest risk during the spring and early summer.

One way to protect a tree growing in turf from power equipment damage is to remove the turf two or more feet around the trunk, and fill the area with mulch to a depth of 2 to 4 inches (maximum). The mulched area eliminates the need for grass trimming around the trunk and keeps power equipment at a safe distance. Mulched areas have also been shown to help young trees develop more quickly by reducing competition from turfgrass. Keep mulch away from the base of trunks because it can trap moisture there and lead to disease. For more information, see "Mulching Landscape Plants" on page 79.

A drawback to cleared turf areas around trees is that they can become a site of weed seed germination if the mulch becomes thin. Preemergent or post-emergent herbicides are sometimes applied to cleared areas instead of mulch. A problem with this approach is that weeds can quickly take root in the bare soil and invade the grass if this task is not tended to regularly.

Protective staking, which is described on page 78, prevents mowers from accessing the area near a tree's trunk. Some drawbacks to protective staking are that grass trimming around the trunk must be done by hand, and the grass around the stakes must be trimmed. Another alternative is to install tree guards around the base of trees. Tree guards help protect the bark from trimmer line, though a ding with a mower can still damage tender bark.

Leaf Blowing/Sweeping

Edging scatters grass clippings and leaves onto walkways. Moderate amounts of leaves on walkways can be blown or swept onto the lawn before mowing. Be sure to blow any small leaves out of the gap between the lawn edge and walkways. A clean edge, free of debris, gives a professional look. Large amounts of leaves may need to be raked or blown off the lawn before mowing. If there are minimal leaves, blowing may not be necessary before mowing.

Mowing scatters grass clippings onto walkways, though much less than edging. A brief blowing after mowing casts any remaining clippings onto the lawn. The lawn should show no sign of clippings or debris when you are finished. Any remaining debris on walkways can be blown into a general area, swept into a pile with a push broom, and removed.

Sweep leaves and grass clippings out of street gutters at the end of each maintenance visit. This keeps gutters clear and reduces the amount of potential pollutants that can wind up in local waterways. Never sweep debris into storm drains. See "Using Fertilizers Responsibly" on page 53 for more information.

In some situations, sweeping or raking clears an area faster than blowing. For example, wet leaves or large volumes of leaves are sometimes easier to clear from a lawn with a rake than a blower. Finally, follow the guidelines for responsible leaf blower use, as described page 26.

Mowing

Turfgrasses are stressed by mowing, but they tolerate it well because they have growth points (meristematic tissue) at their base, near the soil surface; the growth points are not at the tips of shoots as they are on most plants. In addition, turfgrasses respond to lower cutting heights by increasing in density. The denser leaf area helps grasses tolerate foot traffic.

While turfgrasses are well-suited to mowing, incorrect mowing practices can encourage weeds, disease, drought stress, and general decline. The following mowing guidelines will help you avoid these problems.

General Mowing Guidelines

In general, mowing should be done when the grass is dry. Mowing a wet lawn can cause clumps of wet grass to drop onto the lawn, and it increases the risk of spreading fungal diseases (if present) from one area of turf to another. Mowing a wet lawn can also contribute to soil compaction. See "Mowing and Compaction" on the next page for more information.

When using a walk-behind rotary mower on slopes, start at the top of the slope and work your way down. Cut across the face of slopes, never up and down. Riding mowers are operated up and down slopes, not across. When turning a walk-behind mower on a slope, avoid tipping the mower, and don't let the mower wheels dig into and damage the turf. See "Lawn Mower Safety" on page 26 for more information.

Mowing Patterns

Turf managers for professional sports organizations mow playing fields in a way that gives the turf light and dark green stripes. This technique is called striping, and it is created as reel mowers move over the turf, causing grass blades to bend; alternating the direction of mowing creates the striping effect. Your lawns will not, and should not, have the look of a major league baseball field, but some attention should still be paid to mowing patterns.

Begin mowing by making one or two passes along the perimeter of the lawn to ensure complete coverage of the edges. Mow the rest of the lawn in a back and forth pattern. For a uniform look, use the same mowing pattern for all lawn areas. Change the mowing pattern regularly.

Grass blades bend slightly as the mower passes over, and this bending can make for a slightly uneven cut. To eliminate most of the unevenness, you can make a second pass with the mower at a 90 degree angle to the first. This optional practice is called double cutting. The obvious drawbacks of double cutting are that it takes more time and requires more equipment use. Consider double cutting at select houses in the spring when lawns are growing quickly. Dense, healthy lawns are the best candidates for this technique.

Keep Mower Blades Sharp

A sharp mower blade makes a clean cut and reduces stress to the grass. A dull mower blade creates jaggedly cut grass blades that give the lawn an unsightly brown or white cast. Grass that is cut with a dull mower blade also loses more water and is forced to draw on more of its energy reserves to recover; this makes the turf more susceptible to drought stress and disease.

Always disconnect the mower's spark plug wire and secure it away from the spark plug before checking the mower blade. Check the blade's sharpness once a day. Keep spare, sharpened blades on hand, and replace dull blades as necessary.

Mowing and Compaction

To grow and function, plant roots need the small amounts of air that exist in the gaps between soil particles. Heavy foot traffic or equipment use can cause soil particles to pack tightly together and dispel air. This soil compaction makes it difficult for plant roots to grow and take in nutrients, and a plant's health can decline as a result. Turfgrass tends to suffer from soil compaction more than other landscape plants because it typically receives more foot traffic and equipment use than other landscape areas.

Consistently mowing in the same pattern can cause ruts to form in the lawn. This looks bad and weakens the health of the grass in the ruts. To avoid this, vary the mowing pattern on a regular basis. If ruts form, begin mowing in a different direction and in time the ruts should disappear.

Lawn mowers can leave tracks, which affect the finished look of a lawn. This lawn is beginning to develop ruts from consistent back and forth mowing. The whitish color of the turf is a possible indication of a dull mower blade.

Mowing when the soil is wet from rain or irrigation may contribute to soil compaction and leave tracks in the turf. At times, you may need to mow when the soil is wet, just do it as little as necessary. In the growing season, set irrigation controllers to operate on non-maintenance days. For more information on soil compaction, see "Soil Compaction and Aeration" on page 66 and "Soil Structure" on page 97.

Cutting Height

Cutting height is the height of the grass immediately after mowing. Each variety of grass has its own ideal cutting height (see table 1). In general, cutting the grass at the higher end of its recommended range is better for the grass because it enables the grass to produce more energy, it promotes deeper root growth, and it reduces competition from weeds. Taller heights are particularly important for cool-season grasses in summer. The following information will help you make cutting-height decisions.

- Reduce a lawn's height by no more than one-third at each mowing to lessen the risk of damaging or killing the turf. For instance, if an overgrown lawn is 4 or 5 inches tall, gradually bring it down to its recommended height over several weeks. Similarly, if you will be maintaining a lawn at a 2-inch cutting height, cut the grass before it reaches 3 inches. Cutting more than 40 percent of tissue in a single mowing can cause root growth to stop for days or even weeks (Christians 2004). The

one-third rule is particularly important during summer. Note that if you maintain a lawn at a low cutting height, you need to mow frequently to avoid breaking the one-third rule. If you intend to mow once per week, choose a cutting height that allows you to reduce the lawn's height no more than one-third at each mowing.

- A taller cutting height promotes deeper roots and more root mass, which can help a lawn withstand heat and moisture stress. A taller cutting height also helps to shade the soil, resulting in cooler soil temperature and reduced evaporation from the soil surface (Sachs and Luff 2002).

- After mowing, turfgrass draws on energy reserves to regrow leaves. Cutting a lawn too low over an extended period can cause the grass to use up its energy reserves, increasing the risk of disease and general decline. Low cutting heights also reduce the grass's potential to produce energy. Photosynthesis—the process plants use to make energy—takes place in leaves. Low cutting heights significantly reduce the leaf surface area. At low cutting heights, the grass produces less energy, and its health can decline as a result. Mowing at the recommended height causes minimal stress to the grass. In short, don't try to make a residential lawn look like a putting green.

- Some grasses, such as bentgrass and hybrid bermuda, can be maintained at low cutting heights (less than 1") , but this is not often practical in weekly residential maintenance. At low cutting heights, the incidence of pests and drought stress can increase, and cutting frequency may need to increase. Low cutting heights may also cause rotary mowers to scalp the turf, stressing the grass and exposing areas of soil.

- Cut grass at the higher end of its recommended cutting height range in shaded areas. Grass benefits from having extra leaf area in lower light conditions. Note also that certain shade-adapted species, such as creeping red fescue, have higher growth points than other grasses.

- Weeds require light to grow, and weed seeds require sunlight to germinate. A dense turf canopy shades the soil surface and, in doing so, plays an important role in weed suppression. Cutting a lawn too low can reduce this protective canopy and encourage dormant weed seeds to germinate. On the other hand, a lawn that is cut too tall can become thin. To promote weed suppression, cut lawns at the higher end of their recommended cutting height range. With this practice, you can reduce and sometimes even eliminate the need for herbicides.

Mulching vs. Bagging

Lawn mower mulching (recycling) mechanisms cut grass clippings into tiny pieces and deposit them onto the lawn. Clippings returned to the soil can reduce a lawn's supplemental nitrogen needs by 20 percent or more. Clippings also return potassium and phosphorus to the soil. And clippings serve as food for earthworms and microorganisms, which have beneficial effects on soil structure and fertility. The obvious benefit of mulching is that you don't need to spend time and resources disposing of clippings. Note that grass clippings do not contribute to the buildup of thatch if the lawn is properly mowed with a mulching mower. Thatch is explained on page 66.

Owing to its many benefits, mulching is usually preferable to bagging. Bagging grass clippings is recommended in the following circumstances.

Bag grass clippings:

- When the grass is growing too rapidly for the mower's mulching mechanism to process. The lawn should show no signs of clippings when the mower is mulching well.

- When the grass shows signs of disease. Diseased clippings can spread disease to other turf areas.

- When the lawn contains weeds that are producing seed heads. Bagging clippings when weeds go to seed can help prevent the weeds' spread.

- When the grass is wet and prone to clumping. Clumps drop onto the lawn and can smother and kill patches of grass.

Table 1. Turfgrass Cutting Heights*

Cutting Height of Cool-Season Grasses	
Bentgrass:	0.5 to 1 inch
Fescue, Fine:	2 to 3 inches
Fescue, Tall:	2 to 3 inches
Kentucky Bluegrass:	1.5 to 2.5 inches
Ryegrass:	1.5 to 2.5 inches

Cutting Height of Warm-Season Grasses	
Bahia:	3 to 4 inches
Bermuda	0.75 to 1.5 inches
Blue grama:	2 to 3 inches
Buffalo:	1 to 3+ inches
Centipede:	1.5 to 2.5 inches
St. Augustine (standard):	3.5 to 4 inches
(semi-dwarf)**:	2 to 2.5 inches
Zoysia:	0.5 to 1.5 inches

*These are general recommendations for residential lawns. Note that cutting height recommendations can vary regionally or by cultivar. Consult with local experts for regional recommendations. If you know the cultivar (e.g., St. Augustine 'Seville'), research the recommended cutting height for that cultivar. **The recommendations for St. Augustine grass are from the University of Florida (Trenholm, Cisar, and Unruh 2006).

- When there are excessive leaves on a lawn. Mulching mechanisms can process a limited amount of leaf material at one time.

Clippings can be taken to a municipal composting facility or transfer station. Never dump yard debris in empty lots or alleys, or on public land; this creates a health hazard and it is against the law. Contact your city's solid waste management offices to learn the yard debris policies in your area.

Minimizing the Spread of Weeds

Weed seeds and the seeds and stolons of invasive grasses can stick to the mower and drop onto other turf areas, where they may eventually germinate. This is a common way that weeds and invasive grasses spread within a landscape and between landscapes. Most broadleaf weeds growing in turf can be managed effectively with mechanical methods or broadleaf weed controls. But once invasive grasses such as common Bermuda or bentgrass have breached a lawn, they can be difficult to control.

Invasive grasses can usually be identified by the difference in color or texture between the invader and the desirable grass species. But it is not so easy to see the extent of an infestation because invasive grasses have runners that spread throughout the lawn.

A strategy to minimize the spread of weeds is to clean the mower with a leaf blower at the end of each maintenance visit. (Hosing off a mower can cause some components to rust.) You can also disconnect the spark plug wire, secure it away from the spark plug, and clean the underside of the deck. Products are available that can be sprayed on the underside of the mower deck to minimize the adhesion of grass clippings.

Thoroughly cleaning the mower after servicing each account tends to require more time and effort than is practical. If you have the space and resources, consider purchasing separate equipment designated for use on lawns containing invasive grasses.

Turfgrass Fertilizers

Fertilization is one of the primary practices landscape managers use to keep turfgrass healthy and attractive. Proper fertilization improves a lawn's density, color, drought tolerance, and disease resistance. Improper fertilization can reduce a lawn's drought tolerance and increase its susceptibility to disease.

Turfgrass fertilization requires an understanding of turfgrass nutrient requirements and turfgrass fertilizers. This topic introduces the primary nutrient requirements for turfgrass and the unique performance characteristics of various fertilizer compounds.

Complete Fertilizers

Plants need 17 elements to grow and function. Plants get carbon, hydrogen, and oxygen from the air and water. The mineral nutrients found in fertilizers are categorized as either macronutrients or micronutrients. Of the macronutrients, nitrogen, phosphorus, potassium are considered primary nutrients because they are used in the greatest quantities by plants. The primary nutrients are the nutrients landscapers work with most frequently.

Calcium, magnesium, and sulfur are considered secondary macronutrients. The micronutrients boron, manganese, iron, zinc, nickel, copper, chlorine, and molybdenum are used by plants in much smaller quantities than macronutrients, but they are just as important for plant health. Micronutrient deficiencies are rare in turfgrass.

A fertilizer that contains nitrogen (N), phosphorus (P), and potassium (K) is called a complete fertilizer. Many complete fertilizers also contain secondary nutrients and micronutrients. Complete fertilizers come in different formulas, or grades (ratios of N-P-K), to meet different fertilization objectives or to meet the unique nutrient requirements of certain plants. In general, turfgrass does not require a specific fertilizer grade.

The guaranteed analysis on a fertilizer label lists the nutrients in the product. The fertilizer grade highlights the guaranteed analysis for nitrogen (N), available phosphate (P_2O_5), and soluble potash (K_2O). Available phosphate is the compound used in fertilizers to supply phosphorus (P); soluble potash is the compound used in fertilizers to supply potassium (K). The grade is printed on the product label as three numbers separated by dashes, representing $N–P_2O_5–K_2O$ (more commonly written as N-P-K). To illustrate, a fertilizer with a grade of 16-6-8 contains 16 percent nitrogen, 6 percent available phosphate, and 8 percent soluble potash by weight.

Nitrogen

Of the nutrients contained in fertilizer, nitrogen has the strongest influence on turfgrass growth and color. Nitrogen also helps turfgrass resist pests, mend damage, and remain dense. Because nitrogen is used in relatively large quantities by plants, many forms of nitrogen fertilizer have been developed for use in landscapes.

Categories of nitrogen used in turf fertilization include natural organic, synthetic inorganic, synthetic organic, and coated or controlled-release. A relatively new form of nitrogen is stabilized nitrogen. Note that turfgrass can only use nitrogen in the nitrate (NO_3^-) or ammonium (NH_4^+) forms. Other nitrogen forms must convert to nitrate or ammonium before grass can use them.

Nitrogen types vary in how quickly they become available to plants, how long they remain effective, and how easily they leach through the soil or volatilize to the atmosphere. Understanding the characteristics of the different nitrogen types can help you select a fertilizer that is appropriate for the grass type, the landscape, and the season.

Natural Organic Nitrogen

Natural organic nitrogen sources have a carbon structure and originate from a living source. Blood meal, bone meal, cow manure, and chicken manure are examples. Even grass clippings provide lawns with organic material that will break down and convert to nutrients the lawn can use. Natural organic fertilizers contain many nutrients, though the nutrients tend to be in lower concentrations than those in synthetic fertilizers.

Natural organics are a water-insoluble form of nitrogen (WIN). They require the activity of soil microorganisms to convert the nutrients to forms plants can use. Microorganism activity is strongly influenced by a soil's temperature, moisture, and fertility. Natural organic fertilizers tend to release nutrients more slowly than synthetic fertilizers, and they can be less effective under some conditions, such as low soil temperatures.

Owing to their carbon structure, natural organic fertilizers serve as a food source for soil microorganisms that support soil fertility. And the slow release rate of these products gives them a low nitrogen burn potential on turf. Many brands of granulated natural organic fertilizers are available.

Synthetic Inorganic Nitrogen

Synthetic inorganic nitrogen types are manufactured and do not have a carbon structure. Ammonium nitrate, calcium nitrate, and potassium nitrate are examples of this type—each contains a high percentage of nitrate nitrogen. Nitrogen in the nitrate form is highly water soluble and readily available to plant roots. It is often included in a turf fertilizer mix to provide an immediate growth boost and a quick greening of the grass. It is also one of the nitrogen types used to feed the grass in the fall, and sometimes winter, when soil temperatures drop. Nitrate has a relatively short period of effectiveness, usually four to six weeks.

Fertilizers are salts; applied in excess they can burn plant roots and cause browning of leaves. Nitrate can cause nitrogen burn to turfgrass if it is applied at rates higher than 1 pound per 1000 square feet. The risk of nitrogen burn is greatest in hot weather; therefore, nitrate sources are typically not applied in summer. And because nitrate is soluble, excess rain or irrigation can cause nitrogen runoff or leaching. In general, turfgrass' dense, fibrous root system uses nitrogen efficiently. For more information, see "Using Fertilizers Responsibly" on page 53.

Ammonium is another synthetic inorganic form of nitrogen. Nitrogen in ammonium form is water soluble and can cause nitrogen burn if applied in excess. Like nitrate, ammonium should not be applied at rates higher than 1 pound per 1000 square feet of turf. Ammonium forms of nitrogen (including ammonium-based fertilizers, such as urea, described next) can volatilize, converting to ammonia gas and escaping to the atmosphere. To help prevent this, fertilizers containing ammonium should be watered-in immediately after application. Uptake by grass roots can begin in about one week. Ammonium's period of effectiveness is roughly the same as that of nitrate.

A form of ammonium called ammonium sulfate (21-0-0) is ammonium combined with sulfur. Because of its sulfur source, it can reduce a soil's pH. Ammonium nitrate can also have an acidifying effect on soil. Soil pH is covered on page 105.

Synthetic Organic Nitrogen

Synthetic organic forms of nitrogen are either water-soluble or water-insoluble. Urea (46-0-0) is an example of a water-soluble synthetic organic. Urea has some of the same characteristics as the synthetic inorganics: it is readily available to plants, it is effective in cooler soil temperatures, and it lasts about four to six weeks.

If applied in excess, urea can cause nitrogen burn to turf. Note that urea must be watered-in properly after application. Under-watering can promote volatilization; overwatering can cause nitrogen to leach below the root zone. Urea is economical. This is one reason it is often included in a nitrogen mix.

Ureaformaldehydes (Ureaform or UF, 38-0-0) and methylene urea (MU, 39-0-0) are synthetic organic nitrogen forms that are classed as water-insoluble, though they have limited solubility. They are produced by putting urea through chemical reactions. Their limited solubility slows the release of nitrogen, resulting in a longer-lasting feeding. Ureaform can continue to release nitrogen for 10 to 30 weeks or longer. Methylene urea can release nitrogen for 7 to 9 weeks.

Nitrogen release in the water-insoluble synthetic organics is primarily determined by microbial activity. This makes water-insoluble synthetic organics less effective in cold soils. Factors that affect microbial activity, such as soil pH, soil temperature, and soil moisture, indirectly influence the release rate.

Isobutylidene diurea (IBDU, 31-0-0) is another synthetic organic. It releases nitrogen when wet, though it does so slowly because it is mostly water insoluble. IBDU's nitrogen release is not dependent on microbial activity, so IBDU remains effective at relatively low temperatures. For this reason, IBDU is sometimes used during cooler times of year. The residual activity of IBDU is from 10 to 16 weeks.

Coated Nitrogen

Urea is used in coated products, such as sulfur-coated urea (SCU). A sulfur coating around the urea particle slows the nitrogen release rate. Thicker coatings provide a slower release rate. Some products have an uneven sulfur coating, which provides some slow nitrogen release and some fast nitrogen release.

The release of nitrogen from SCU products is dependent on moisture. Some SCU products also require the activity of microorganisms to release nitrogen; therefore, soil temperature can also affect the release rate. SCU products range from 22 to 38 percent nitrogen and have a residual activity of 10 to 15 weeks.

Polymer-coated fertilizer (PCF) products coat fertilizer with a resin that is semipermeable to water. These products provide a uniform and controlled release of nitrogen over an extended period of time. PCFs are sometimes used in spring and summer applications for their gradual availability of nitrogen and low burn potential.

Stabilized Nitrogen

Stabilized nitrogen technology (SNT) is a more recent development. The extended effectiveness of stabilized nitrogen is not the result of coatings or polymers. Instead, stabilized nitrogen products "have been amended with an additive that reduces the rate of transformation of fertilizer compounds, resulting in extended time of availability in the soil" (AAPFCO 2006). Stabilized nitrogen products minimize nitrogen loss to the soil and atmosphere; as a result, nitrogen stays in a plant-available form. These products are not dependent on weather or microbial activity, so they perform in a variety of climates. Another advantage is that these products cannot be damaged by mowing, as coated products can.

Phosphorus

The second number on a bag of complete fertilizer refers to the percentage by weight of available phosphate (P_2O_5), which is used in fertilizers to supply phosphorus (P). Phosphorus serves many purposes in plant functioning. In particular it is needed for root development, and it is essential for plants during their establishment period.

Soil phosphorus deficiencies are rare but can be detected with a soil test, which should be performed every few years for turfgrass areas. Local certified nursery professionals or university extension agents will know if the majority of lawns in the area have adequate soil levels of phosphorus. Sometimes a soil with excessively high (alkaline) or low (acidic) pH will make phosphorus unavailable, in which case the pH should be corrected, if possible. Soil pH and soil testing are covered in the Soil chapter, on page 97.

If a soil is phosphorus deficient, a phosphate fertilizer should be incorporated into the soil before planting. Phosphorus applied to the soil surface tends to remain in the top 2 to 3 inches of soil and will not be accessible to deeper roots. (However, a high rate of phosphorus is often applied to the soil surface when establishing a new lawn from seed.) If established turf areas are not phosphorus deficient, use a product that contains a low phosphorus rate or no phosphorus (e.g., 16-0-8). High rates of phosphorus fertilizer on established turf can promote the germination of crabgrass, annual bluegrass, and other weeds.

The inorganic phosphorus used in fertilizers does not readily leach through the soil as some forms of nitrogen do; however, runoff can still cause phosphorus to enter local waterways, where it can promote excessive algae formation. See "Using Fertilizers Responsibly" on page 53 for more information. Minnesota has a law that bans the use of phosphorus fertilizer on established lawns, with some exceptions. Check local regulations to learn the laws governing phosphorus fertilizer use in your area.

Some common phosphate fertilizers are superphosphate (0-20-0), concentrated superphosphate (a.k.a. triple superphosphate; 0-40-0), ammonium phosphate (16-20-0), and diammonium phosphate (18-46-0). The ammonium forms are highly water soluble, and they are also sources of nitrogen.

Potassium

The third number on a bag of complete fertilizer refers to the percentage by weight of soluble potash (K_2O), which is used in fertilizers to supply potassium (K). Potassium is said to influence the drought tolerance and disease resistance of turfgrasses (Landschoot 2003). It is also associated with turf durability and stress tolerance. Potassium is second only to nitrogen in the amount needed for turfgrass growth.

A soil test conducted by a lab will reveal any signs of potassium deficiency and will include fertilizer recommendations. Phosphorus and potassium both move little in the soil, so tests for these nutrients will remain valid for several years (Rosen, Horgan, and Mugaas 2006).

Sandy soils tend to leach potassium more quickly than other soil types. The high permeability of sandy soil is often countered through smaller, more frequent fertilizer applications. Grass clippings are a valuable source of potassium. Lawns where grass clippings are bagged will require more potassium supplementation than where clippings are returned to the soil with a mulching mower.

Some common potassium fertilizers are potassium chloride (muriate of potash; 0-0-60) and potassium sulfate (sulfate of potash; 0-0-50). Natural materials used as potassium sources include kelp and greensand. Lawn fertilizers labeled as "winterizers" contain a relatively high percentage of soluble potash. They are sometimes applied in the fall to help grass through the winter.

Selecting a Fertilizer

Considerations for selecting a turfgrass fertilizer include soil test results, the grass species, the soil type, the time of year, the frequency of fertilization, and cost. Ideally a soil test will be performed for a property's turfgrass and ornamental areas before fertilization. Soil testing is the most accurate way to determine phosphorus and potassium requirements. The test results for these nutrients should remain reasonably accurate for several years. Subsequent testing should be performed once every three to four years. See Soil Tests on page 108 for more information.

Unless a soil test indicates a deficiency, use a turfgrass fertilizer containing a low percentage of phosphorus. If a soil test shows that phosphorus and potassium levels are high, a product with no phosphorus and no potassium can be used (Taylor, Rosen, and White 1990). In regions that prohibit the used of phosphorus fertilizer on lawns, use a product containing no phosphorus.

Most complete lawn fertilizers contain a mix of nitrogen sources, providing some rapid and some prolonged release of nitrogen. The guaranteed analysis shows how much of each nitrogen type the product contains. For example, in a complete fertilizer with a grade of 25-6-3, the 25 percent nitrogen may represent 18 percent urea, 6 percent ammonium, and 1 percent nitrate. Keep in mind that the more nitrate, ammonium, or non-coated urea the fertilizer contains, the more caution should be used to avoid burning the lawn.

Products that contain a moderate to high amount of slow-release nitrogen supply nutrients for several months and reduce the risk of nitrogen burn. This makes slow-release products a good choice for spring and summer applications. When fertilizing turfgrass growing on sandy soil, it is important to use a fertilizer that contains 30 to 50 percent slow-release nitrogen to reduce the risk of nitrogen leaching. A product contains 50 percent slow-release nitrogen if half of its nitrogen content is from slow-release forms. On fertilizer labels, slow-release forms may be listed as natural organic, water-insoluble (WIN), or coated urea.

Products that contain little or no slow-release nitrogen are relatively inexpensive and can be used without significant risk (on soil types other than sandy soil), provided you do not apply more than the maximum nitrogen amount, as described later. Late fall applications typically require the use of products that contain a lower percentage of slow-release nitrogen. See "Late fall" on page 50 for more information.

Fertilizers marketed as "winterizer" are products with a relatively high level of potassium (e.g., 22-4-22). They are designed to be applied in the fall to help turfgrass through the winter. Note that the availability of micronutrients can be influenced by soil pH. For more information, see "Soil pH" on page 105.

Turfgrass Fertilization Programs

Choosing a fertilizer is only one step in developing a turfgrass fertilization program. You must also determine the timing and frequency of fertilization and the amount of fertilizer to use at each application. General guidelines for cool-season and warm-season grasses are presented later. We start by looking at the importance of nitrogen in a turfgrass fertilization program.

Nitrogen Fertilization

Turfgrass fertilization programs typically center around the application of nitrogen. This is because nitrogen has the greatest effect on turfgrass growth and color and poses the greatest risk of damaging turf If applied in excess. The aim of nitrogen fertilization is to apply enough of the nutrient to improve grass health and appearance, but not so much as to cause problems associated with excess nitrogen. These problems include excess top growth, root growth inhibition, depletion of carbohydrate supply, susceptibility to disease, increased thatch, and nitrogen burn.

Pounds of Nitrogen/Actual Nitrogen

When turfgrass experts recommend nitrogen rates for turfgrass, it is usually in terms of *pounds of nitrogen* (also stated as *pounds of actual nitrogen*) per 1000 square feet. This enables turfgrass managers to apply the recommended nitrogen amount, regardless of the fertilizer's nitrogen analysis. For example, using some simple calculations, a turfgrass manager can determine how much fertilizer is needed to apply 1 pound of nitrogen using 16-6-8, 22-4-22, 46-0-0, or any other suitable fertilizer grade.

Fertilizer calculations are covered on page 51. The following calculation is presented only to illustrate the term *pounds of nitrogen*: To determine how many pounds of nitrogen (how much actual nitrogen) fertilizer bag contains, divide the weight of the bag by the percentage of nitrogen listed in the analysis. For example, a 100-pound bag of a 26-0-3 fertilizer contains 26 pounds of actual nitrogen (100 lbs. x 0.26 = 26). A 50-pound bag of 26-0-3 contains 13 pounds of actual nitrogen (50 lbs. x 0.26 = 13).

Maximum Nitrogen Amount

As a general rule, apply no more than 1 pound of nitrogen per 1000 square feet of turf in a single application. Rates higher than 1 pound per 1000 square feet put the turf at greater risk for nitrogen burn. With slow-release forms of nitrogen, it may be possible to apply 1 1/2 pounds per 1000 square feet without risk, though 1 pound is still recommended.

Fertilizers are salts and, as such, they can draw water from the surrounding soil. If applied in excess, fertilizer salts can damage plant roots or make it difficult for plants to extract water from the soil. This can dehydrate and possibly kill the plants. Nitrogen applied at the correct rate poses little risk of nitrogen burn. Note that most ornamental trees and shrubs can tolerate higher rates of nitrogen than turfgrass. This has consequences for the fertilization of trees and shrubs growing in turfgrass. See "Fertilizer Application Methods" on page 84 for more information.

Cool-Season Turfgrass Fertilization

Cool-season grasses produce the most root and shoot growth in spring and fall. High summer temperatures stress cool-season grasses and cause them to go dormant or grow slowly; therefore, these grasses are usually not fertilized in mid-summer.

This topic presents a general fertilization program for cool-season turfgrass. These guidelines should be adjusted based on the unique site characteristics, including the grass type, maintenance level, length of the growing season, soil type, turf use, and cultural practices, such as clipping removal. See the note at the end of the discussion for a recommendation specific to California.

Spring. Spring fertilization of cool-season grasses requires lower rates of nitrogen than fall fertilization. In the spring, cool-season lawns grow rapidly. A high rate of nitrogen applied at this time generally has a positive effect on the turf's appearance—but at too high a cost to the grass's health. High rates of nitrogen in the spring promote excessive top growth and deplete the grass's energy reserves.

When the grass's energy reserves are low, the grass is more susceptible to heat and drought stress. And because excessive top growth is succulent, the grass is more susceptible to disease. Some turf specialists go so far as to recommend no nitrogen applications in spring for these reasons, though most maintenance professionals apply low rates of nitrogen in the spring.

The goal of spring fertilization of cool-season grasses is to provide just enough nitrogen to prevent the grass from becoming chlorotic (Christians 2004). Chlorosis is a yellowing of leaves. It is associated with reduced photosynthesis/reduced energy (carbohydrate) production. Applications of 1/2 to 3/4 pound of nitrogen per 1000 square feet are usually enough to prevent chlorosis. Higher rates increase the risk of promoting succulent top growth and depleting energy reserves. In some cases, higher or lower rates may be required. Total nitrogen applications for spring and early summer should not exceed 1 1/2 pounds per 1000 square feet unless special circumstances warrant the application of a higher rate (Christians 2004).

Late summer/fall. Late summer fertilization is the most important for cool-season grasses because it helps the grass recover from drought and heat-related injuries sustained during mid-summer (Landschoot 2003). Nitrogen applied in late summer/early fall (late August to September) will stimulate shoot growth, but not as much as spring applications; therefore, higher rates can be used in late summer and fall (up to 1 lb. N/1000 sq. ft. at each application).

In late summer, grass plants begin storing energy reserves for winter. The carbohydrates stored at this time will also be used for spring growth. Note that the appearance of many cool-season grasses deteriorates in the winter. With fall fertilization, cool-season lawns in mild-winter regions will look better through the fall and winter and have larger energy reserves to draw on for their spring growth.

Late fall. Late fall fertilization, once the turf stops growing, helps the grass produce and store energy that will be used the following spring. In some cases, late fall fertilization is a good substitute for an early spring application because it avoids the risks associated with excessive spring nitrogen applications. Up to $1\frac{1}{2}$ pounds of nitrogen per 1000 square feet can be used (Christians 2004).

Late fall fertilization is an optional practice. When it is performed, it is generally in November, though the application time may be earlier in some regions. Avoid late fall applications when the ground is frozen. Most of the nitrogen should be from fast-acting (soluble) sources; up to approximately 25 percent can be slow-release (Rieke 1998).

California. According to Ali Harivandi, turfgrass specialist at the University of California Cooperative Extension, the previous discussion of fertilization of cool-season grasses is not applicable to all regions of California. He recommends fertilizing cool-season grasses in California with approximately 2 pounds of nitrogen in the spring and 2 pounds in the fall; that is, 1 pound of nitrogen per 1000 square feet at approximately March 1, April 15, September 15, and October 15. No nitrogen is applied in the summer or winter. Any additional nitrogen applied in the fall can be leached with rain and lead to pollution (Harivandi 2011).

Winter. For high-maintenance cool-season lawns in mild-winter regions, you can fertilize in January with a fertilizer that contains 6 to 8 percent nitrate nitrogen. This will help maintain grass color during the winter and promote early greening in spring. Nitrate is soluble and cool-season grasses can take it up even in cooler soil temperatures. Do not apply fertilizer when excessive rainfall is expected. Winter fertilization is an optional practice.

Warm-Season Turfgrass Fertilization

Warm-season grasses become active in late spring and grow throughout the summer. In the fall, as temperatures cool for the year, these grasses go dormant. Some varieties turn brown during dormancy and turn green again in spring.

The goal of a fertilization program for warm-season grass is to sustain the grass throughout its growing season. Fertilization begins in late spring as the grass begins to grow. Note that fertilization too early in the spring can encourage the germination of weed seeds. Subsequent fertilizations are made throughout the growing season, at intervals based on the climate, the grass type, the maintenance level, and the percentage of slow-release nitrogen in the fertilizer.

See table 2 for nitrogen recommendations for common grass types. In general, high-maintenance warm-season lawns can be fertilized at $1/2$ to 1 pound of nitrogen per 1000 square feet, each month of the growing season. Low to moderate maintenance lawns can be fertilized two to three times a year, usually early and late summer. Intense heat can stress warm-season grasses, especially if they do not receive enough water, so fertilization is usually avoided during the highest temperatures of the year. Fertilize warm-season grasses no later than one month before they go dormant.

Annual Nitrogen Requirements by Grass Type

Table 2 shows the annual nitrogen requirements of common grass types. You must decide the annual nitrogen amount to apply within the recommended range, based on the maintenance level and other factors. To illustrate: Kentucky bluegrass has an annual nitrogen requirement of 2 to 6 pounds per 1000 square feet; therefore, it requires multiple applications (of $1/2$ to 1 lb. N/1000 sq. ft.) made at appropriate times throughout the year. Centipedegrass has an annual nitrogen requirement of 1 to 2 pounds per 1000 square feet. A low-maintenance lawn of centipedegrass may require only one fertilization a year. Note that you can often get acceptable quality turf with the minimum annual nitrogen rate.

Table 2. Annual Nitrogen Requirements by Grass Type*

Nitrogen Needs of Cool-Season Grasses

Bentgrass: 2-6 lbs. per 1000 ft²/year
Fine fescue: 2 lbs. per 1000 ft²/year
Kentucky bluegrass: 2-6 lbs./1000 ft²/yr
Ryegrass: 2-6 lbs. per 1000 ft²/year
Tall fescue: 2-6 lbs. per 1000 ft²/year

Nitrogen Needs of Warm-Season Grasses

Bahia: 1-4 lbs. per 1000 ft²/year
Bermuda, common: 2-6 lbs./1000 ft²/yr
Bermuda, hybrid: 4-6 lbs./1000 ft²/yr
Buffalo: 0.5-2 lbs. per 1000 ft²/year
Centipede: 1-2 lbs. per 1000 ft²/year
St. Augustine: 3-5 lbs. per 1000 ft²/year
Zoysia: 2-3 lbs. per 1000 ft²/year

*Local extension service agents and certified nursery professionals will have the most specific regional information.

Factors that Influence Nitrogen Requirements

Here are some factors to consider when choosing an annual nitrogen amount for turfgrass.

Length of the growing season. If summers are long and winters are mild in the region, consider using the higher end of the nitrogen range. If the growing season is short and winters are cold in the region, consider using the lower end of the nitrogen range (Walheim 1998). In regions with a long growing season, it may be acceptable to use a higher annual rate than is recommended in table 2.

Maintenance level. High-maintenance lawns may require the higher end of the nitrogen range; low-maintenance lawns can be fertilized at the lower end of the range. Turfgrass can often remain healthy and look acceptable with as little as 1 to 2 pounds of nitrogen per 1000 square feet per year.

Mulching. Clippings returned to the lawn can meet approximately 20 percent or more of a lawn's ni-

trogen needs. When clippings are removed, more supplemental nitrogen is needed.

Soil conditions. Infertile soils require more nutrient supplementation than fertile soils. Soils with nutrient-rich organic matter naturally supply more nitrogen to plants. See "Organic Matter" on page 100 for more information.

Degree of turf use. Nitrogen will help maintain or restore turfgrass health and density on lawns that receive extensive foot traffic.

Shade. Shaded lawns require less nitrogen than lawns growing in full sun. Fertilize shaded lawns at the lower end of their recommended range.

Calculating the Fertilizer Amount

Once you have chosen a fertilization program and decided how many pounds of nitrogen to apply to 1000 square feet of turf in the current application, the next step is to calculate the fertilizer amount. This is divided into three steps:

Step 1: Calculate the square feet of the lawn area to be fertilized, as explained in the upcoming topic Turfgrass Area Calculations.

Step 2: Determine the number of pounds of fertilizer required to apply the desired pounds of nitrogen per 1000 square feet. (The nitrogen rate should be no more than 1 pound per 1000 square feet.) This is calculated as follows:

Divide the desired pounds of nitrogen per 1000 square feet by the percentage of nitrogen in the product.

For example, to apply 1 pound of nitrogen per 1000 square feet using a 16-6-8 fertilizer, the calculation is as follows: Divide 1 by 16% (1 ÷ 0.16 = 6.25). You need to apply 6.25 pounds of 16-6-8 to apply 1 pound of nitrogen to 1000 square feet of turf. Another example: To determine the number of pounds of 16-6-8 required to apply 1/2 pound of nitrogen per 1000 square feet, divide 0.5 by 16% (0.5 ÷ 0.16 = 3.125 lbs. of 16-6-8).

Step 3: Determine the pounds of fertilizer needed for the entire lawn, as follows:

Divide the square feet of the lawn by 1000, then multiply the result by the pounds of fertilizer mix required per 1000 square feet (as calculated in step 2).

For example, if the lawn is 2500 square feet, the calculation is as follows: 2500 ÷ 1000 = 2.5; 2.5 x 6.25 pounds (from the example in step 2) = 15.63. It takes roughly 15 1/2 pounds of 16-6-8 to apply 1 pound of nitrogen to 2500 square feet of turf.

Turfgrass Area Calculations

To apply the correct amount of fertilizer, you need to know the square feet of the fertilization area. Determining the square feet of a landscape area involves taking measurements and using simple formulas, which are included below. Note that irregular turf areas can sometimes be broken down into simpler shapes.

The following is a simple, though inexact, measuring technique: Start by measuring the distance between your rear heel and front toe in a natural walking gait. Then walk the fertilization area and count your paces. Use the appropriate formula to calculate the area's square feet. For example, if your walking gait is 2 1/2 feet and a lawn area is 10 paces by 20 paces, you would calculate the lawn's square feet as follows: (10 paces x 2.5 feet) x (20 paces x 2.5 feet) = 1250 square feet.

Measuring tape provides the most precise measurement. Tape length should be at least 100 feet. In general, fiberglass measuring tape is durable and trouble-free. A measuring wheel (surveyor's wheel) is more expensive than measuring tape and less precise, though it is adequate for lawn areas. Wheel size should be at least 10 inches; 14 to 16 inches is preferable. Larger wheels are suitable for playing fields and commercial properties. A few area formulas are included here.

Squares and rectangles: Area = L (length) x W (width)

Circle: Area = $3.14 \times r^2$ (radius squared, or r x r) The radius of a circle is the distance from the center to the circumference. The radius is half the diameter.

Oval: Area = (L x W) x 0.8 That is, area = (length x width) x 0.8

Triangle: Area = (B x H) ÷ 2 That is, area = length of base x length of height ÷ 2. For acute triangles, the base is the longest side and the height is the widest point.

Unusual shapes: To determine the area of unusually shaped lawns (see diagram), start by measuring the length line, which is the distance between points A and B. Divide the length line into equal sections, as shown for points C through H, and measure the length of these offset lines. Use as many or few offset lines as necessary. Use the same interval between each offset line (e.g., 10 feet). The formula is as follows:

Area = (C + D + E + F + G + H) x distance between offset lines.

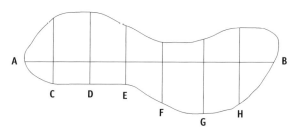

Example: C = 15 ft., D = 18 ft., E = 14 ft., F = 15 ft., G = 19 ft., H = 22 ft.
Distance between lines = 10 feet.
Area = (15 + 18 + 14 + 15 + 19 + 22) x 10 = 1030 square feet.

Acres: To calculate the fertilizer amount for one acre, multiply the amount per 1000 square feet by 43.6 (there are 43,560 square feet in an acre). For example, if you know that you need to apply 6.25 pounds of 16-6-8 per 1000 square feet to apply 1 pound of nitrogen, you would calculate the amount of 16-6-8 to apply to an acre as follows: 6.25 x 43.6 = 272.50 pounds per acre.

Applying Fertilizer

Fertilizer can be applied with a drop spreader (also called a gravity spreader) or a broadcast spreader (also called a centrifugal spreader). Drop spreaders apply fertilizer to the area directly beneath the path of the spreader. They apply fertilizer slowly and require careful use to avoid uneven application. Broadcast spreaders cast fertilizer in a wider swath, covering larger turf areas more quickly; overlap between passes is also easier, reducing the chances of uneven coverage. Care must be used with broadcast spreaders to avoid casting fertilizer or seed into flower beds or other non-turf areas.

Handheld broadcast spreaders are useful for small and medium-sized turf areas. Walk-behind broadcast spreaders have a large hopper that can hold at least 30 pounds of fertilizer. They can also be used to apply soil conditioners or granular pesticides. Fertilizer labels list common spreader models and provide the recommended spreader settings. If you don't see your spreader listed and don't know what model is comparable to yours, call the fertilizer manufacturer for advice.

Walk-behind broadcast spreaders need to be calibrated yearly to ensure accurate application rates. Follow the calibration instructions that come with your model. Though it is not ideal, you can apply fertilizer with an uncalibrated broadcast spreader as follows: fill the hopper with the amount of product needed to cover the area, set the spreader on the lowest setting, then walk the area until all the fertilizer has been applied. For uniform coverage, always apply turfgrass fertilizers in two directions: make one complete pass over the turf area, then another complete pass at a 90 degree angle to first.

If fertilizer spills onto turf it can cause nitrogen burn and uneven growth and color. Even so, some experts recommend filling and washing spreaders over turf areas because it reduces the risk of fertilizer winding up in storm drains. Other experts recommend filling spreaders over hard surfaces so spills can be cleaned up easily. Never hose off spreaders over hard surfaces.

Begin by fertilizing the outer edge of the lawn. Fertilize the rest of the lawn in back and forth passes, closing the spreader at the end of each pass. When you are finished, sweep or blow stray fertilizer off walkways and onto the lawn. If you hose off empty spreaders, do it over lawn areas.

Using Fertilizers Responsibly

Responsible fertilizer use begins with understanding the potential effects fertilizers can have on the environment. Some of the nutrients in fertilizers can leach through the soil into groundwater or flow into storm drains with water runoff and enter streams and lakes. This is a form of pollution called nonpoint source (NPS) pollution. Under certain conditions, some of the nutrients in complete fertilizers, specifically nitrogen and phosphorus, can contribute to what is called eutrophication.

According to the U.S. Geological Survey, eutrophication is "a process whereby water bodies, such as lakes, estuaries, or slow-moving streams receive excess nutrients that stimulate excessive plant growth (algae, periphyton attached algae, and nuisance plants/weeds)." This growth reduces the oxygen levels in the water. Reduced oxygen levels can kill fish and other aquatic life.

Healthy turfgrass uses nitrogen efficiently. However, excessive rain or irrigation can cause soluble nitrogen to leach through the soil to the water table. To help prevent this, irrigate properly after fertilizing, do not fertilize before heavy rains, and do not apply fertilizer to frozen soils. Sandy soil is particularly prone to leaching. When fertilizing turf on sandy soil, make smaller, more frequent applications and use products that contain 30 to 50 percent slow-release nitrogen.

The general recommendation for phosphorus (phosphate) fertilizer is to apply it only when the soil is deficient, as indicated by soil test results. Many turf fertilizers contain a low percentage of phosphorus. In general, when phosphorus fertilizer is applied to lawns, the phosphorus quickly binds to soil particles and does not leach through the soil. When applying phosphorus fertilizer to the surface of bare soil, reduce the risk of runoff by lightly tilling the granules into the soil and avoiding excessive irrigation. Responsible fertilizer use also includes the following practices:

- Get a soil test for turf and ornamental areas every 3 to 4 years.

- Use slow- or controlled-release fertilizers to minimize the risk of nitrogen leaching.

- Follow the directions and precautions printed on the fertilizer label.

- Fill fertilizer spreaders over turf areas, and clean up spills immediately to avoid burning the lawn. Alternatively, fill spreaders over paved areas, where spills can be swept up.

- After fertilizing, sweep or blow stray fertilizer granules off paved areas and onto the lawn.

- Use caution when applying fertilizer near water sources, such as rivers, streams, and lakes. Some experts recommend not fertilizing within 10 feet of a natural water source.

- Do not fertilize when paved areas that surround the fertilization area are wet.

- Apply $1/4$ to $1/2$ inch of water to the turf after fertilization. Avoid excess irrigation after fertilization, and do not fertilize when heavy rains are expected.

Clear Debris From Street Gutters

Plant residues, such as leaves and grass clippings, contain soluble phosphorus, which can cause nutrient pollution in local waterways. To help prevent surface runoff of phosphorus, sweep grass clippings and debris out of street gutters at the end of each maintenance visit. Never sweep grass clippings or debris into storm drains.

Final Fertilizing Guidelines

- Water the lawn a few days before fertilizing. The soil should be moist, though the grass blades should be dry when fertilizer is applied. Water immediately after fertilizing. This will begin to break

down the fertilizer and deliver it to the roots. It will also minimize the risk of foliar burn, which can occur if soluble forms of nitrogen remain in contact with grass blades. One-quarter to one-half inch of water is enough. Set the controller to run through a cycle of the program assigned to the lawns.

- Mulching grass clippings can reduce a lawn's annual supplemental nitrogen needs by roughly 1 to 2 pounds per 1000 square feet. This can equate to a 20 percent savings or more.

- Apply lawn fertilizer evenly to reduce the risk of uneven lawn growth and greening. Make two complete passes over the turf, one 90 degrees to the other. Some fertilizer labels include spreader settings for two passes.

- Use caution when applying fertilizers that contain iron. Iron will stain wet concrete areas. Do not fertilize when walkways are wet, and sweep or blow stray fertilizer granules off walkways and onto the lawn. Use extra caution around swimming pools, as staining can be extensive and clean-up is expensive.

- "Weed-and-feed" products contain both fertilizer and a broadleaf herbicide; they are designed to fertilize the lawn and, at the same time, kill broadleaf weeds growing in the lawn. Some weed-and-feed products (and broadleaf herbicides) may damage St. Augustine grass. Weed-and-feed will also damage new seedlings and may harm certain species of shallow-rooted trees (e.g., birch, magnolia) growing in or near the lawn. The weed-and-feed product label will include a list of plants to avoid. Note that weed-and-feed products are designed to be broadcast, and it is usually not necessary to cover the turf with herbicide in this way. You need a pest control applicator's license to apply weed-and-feed products commercially; see page 70 for more information.

- The root zones of trees, shrubs, and turfgrass often overlap in landscapes. Fertilizer applied to the turf will also be taken up by nearby trees and shrubs. Many established landscape plants growing in turfgrass receive enough nutrients from the turfgrass fertilization program. If these plants require more than 1 pound of nitrogen per 1000 square feet, use split applications or a drill hole method to avoid burning the grass. For more information see "Surface Application" on page 84.

- Palm trees and palm shrubs have unique fertilizer requirements and may be harmed by the wrong fertilizer type. For instance, the high ratio of N to K and the lack of magnesium (Mg) in most turf fertilizers can induce K or Mg deficiency in palms. Potassium deficiency can kill a palm. For this reason, experts recommend that turfgrass growing within 50 feet of a palm be fertilized with a properly formulated palm maintenance fertilizer (Broschat 2008). See "Fertilizing Palms" on page 82 for guidelines.

Irrigating Turfgrass

Water conservation is an important practice in communities across the United States. The goal in watering landscape plants, including turfgrass, is to apply the amount needed to achieve acceptable results. This maintains landscapes, conserves a limited resource, and keeps clients' water bills reasonable.

Irrigation scheduling is the practice of determining the frequency and duration of irrigation for a particular landscape. General recommendations, such as "Water the lawn at each property for 20 minutes, three days a week", can sometimes produce acceptable results, but they can also be inaccurate, resulting in water waste, shallow rooting, an increase in weeds, and stressed turf. Accurate irrigation scheduling takes into account a property's soil, grass type, irrigation system, slopes, and microclimates.

Turf Irrigation Guidelines

Efficient irrigation can be achieved with scheduling equations, which are described shortly. Several rules of thumb are also commonly used to schedule irrigation for turf; they are included here.

Apply approximately 1 inch of water per week. The general rule is that most grasses need 1 to 1 1/2 inches of water per week during the growing season. In regions with hot, dry summers, some grasses may require more water during the warmest times of year (2" a week is not uncommon). The 1 to 1 1/2 inches may need to be divided into two or more applications, depending on the soil type, to avoid runoff or deep percolation through the soil. Note that warm-season grasses can survive with less water than cool-season grasses.

Water deeply and infrequently. Deep watering encourages deep root growth, which promotes a healthy, drought-tolerant lawn. The upper portions of the soil dry out first, so a deeply rooted lawn will have access to moisture longer than a shallow rooted lawn. Deep watering also discourages the growth of many shallow-rooted weeds. In contrast, shallow watering encourages shallow root growth, which creates a weaker, less drought-tolerant lawn. Water should reach all or much of a plant's root zone at each irrigation. For turfgrass, this means water should penetrate 6 to 8 inches deep at each irrigation.

It is also important to water established turfgrass infrequently. To function, plant roots need oxygen that is present in the space between soil particles. When a soil is saturated with water, it contains no space for oxygen, and plant roots cannot function. By allowing enough time to pass between irrigations, excess water drains from the soil, leaving space in the soil for oxygen. Simply put, let lawns dry out a little between irrigations.

Use visual indicators. You should be able to see your footprints on a lawn that has dried out slightly and is ready for water. If you don't see your footprints, consider extending the time between irrigations. Grass color is another indication of a lawn's need for water. Lawns experiencing moisture stress tend to appear bluish-grey. Grass blades can also bend or curl when a lawn needs water.

Water in the morning. During the heat of summer in desert-like environments, such as parts of the west and southwest, evaporation can cause irrigation systems to lose up to 50 percent of the water applied. One way to reduce evaporative water loss is to program irrigation controllers (timers) to run

Delaying Spring Irrigation

Many homeowners and landscape professionals begin irrigating turfgrass as soon as it starts growing in the spring. Turfgrass specialists Brad Fresenburg and John Dunn of the University of Missouri suggest a different approach. They recommend delaying spring irrigation until drier conditions cause "obvious turf wilt that lasts for more than one day." Allowing the soil to dry slightly and the grass to wilt some during the spring helps the grass develop a deeper root system, which reduces the need for summer irrigation and helps the grass withstand drought. It is said that this moderate wilting in springtime will not damage the lawn (University of Missouri Extension *Home Lawn Watering Guide*, 2004). If you use this technique, inform your clients so they know what to expect.

in the early morning. A start time before 8 a.m. will allow water to soak in before the higher temperatures of midday. Water pressure is also greatest in the early morning hours. Note that irrigation systems run too early in the morning may disturb clients. Unless it is necessary, evening irrigation should be avoided because lawns that remain wet at night may be more susceptible to fungal disease.

Water at least one day prior to mowing. Wet soil is prone to soil compaction. Watering at least one day before mowing will allow time for excess water to drain from the soil. This will minimize any soil compaction that could result from foot traffic and equipment use. In most cases, allowing even a few hours between irrigation and mowing is enough to minimize compaction.

Adjust schedules. Change irrigation schedules as often as necessary to match plant water needs. At minimum, schedules should be adjusted seasonally—more often if the climate changes regularly. In the winter it is common to turn sprinkler systems off in many regions.

Recommend an irrigation schedule to clients. If only the client has access to the irrigation controller, suggest a watering schedule and include updates. Consistent manual watering with hose-end attachments can prove challenging for busy clients. One option is to attach a battery-operated irriga-

tion timer to the outside faucet where the garden hose connects.

Avoid puddling and runoff. Different soil types absorb water at different rates. Applying more water than a soil can readily absorb can lead to puddling and runoff. Sloped turf areas are also prone to runoff. For more information, see "Irrigating Sloped Areas" on page 65.

Promote automatic irrigation systems. In warm climates, newly planted lawns that are not irrigated by an automatic irrigation system inevitably experience moisture stress and compete poorly with weeds and invasive grasses. As a result, these lawns can deteriorate over one or two years, if not sooner. Encourage clients with valuable landscapes to have an automatic irrigation system professionally designed and installed as soon as possible to protect their investment.

Use rain shutoff devices. A rain shutoff device, sometimes called a rain sensor, is a moisture sensor that is mounted outside and wired to the irrigation controller. When it rains, the rain sensor overrides the controller's programmed schedule, saving water. Encourage clients to have a rain sensor installed if they don't have one already.

Consider installing direct-burial soil moisture sensors. Direct-burial soil moisture sensors are buried in the turf and wired to the controller via a separate control unit. They conserve water by preventing the irrigation system from operating when there is enough soil moisture in the root zone. More advanced direct-burial sensors also initiate irrigation when conditions are dry (Nelson Turf 2005).

Direct-burial applications have not been popular among turf professionals, but this could change as the technology continues to advance and the water-saving potential of these devices is realized. Check with your city or county to see if permits are required to install rain sensors and direct burial soil moisture sensors in your area. Utility companies sometimes offer rebates for the installation of these devices.

Estimating Soil Moisture

You can confirm irrigation schedules with a manual soil moisture estimate. To make a rough estimate of the soil moisture, press a screwdriver into the ground in several locations throughout the lawn. If the screwdriver only enters the top inch or two of soil, the soil may be compacted or longer run times may be needed. It could also indicate an irrigation system malfunction or a different soil texture in a particular area.

A more accurate way to estimate soil moisture involves taking a small soil sample from the root zone and forming it into a ball. Coarse soil textures will not form a ball as easily as fine texture soils. The soil should be moist and hold its shape. If the soil drips when it's squeezed, it's too wet; if the soil crumbles or doesn't hold its shape, it's too dry. This method can be used to check the soil moisture for any plant.

General impressions of soil moisture are usually enough to make scheduling adjustments. Soil moisture tables, like tables 3 and 4 on the next page, can also be used. For example, using table 3, you judge a soil to be medium texture and 50 percent moisture deficient. Table 4 shows that the available moisture capacity of a medium-texture soil ranges from 1.4 to 2.4 inches per foot. Calculating the amount of water needed to apply to refill the root zone is as follows: 1.9 inches of available moisture per foot (average) x 50% = 0.95 inch. If you were irrigating 6 inches deep,

you would only need to apply 1/2 inch of water. With practice, manual methods of checking soil moisture can be used with your turf and plant observations to work out accurate irrigation schedules.

Irrigation Factors and Equations

Precise irrigation scheduling is complex because soil, plants, irrigation systems, and microclimates vary from landscape to landscape. And the atmosphere changes seasonally and daily. The general guidelines presented earlier can be used to manage most lawns. This topic introduces a more technical approach to irrigation scheduling. Technical scheduling methods are typically used to increase water savings.

Turfgrass experts have developed equations to determine accurate irrigation schedules for turfgrass. To use these equations, you need to understand irrigation factors, and you must select or determine appropriate values for those factors. For instance, AWHC stands for available water holding capacity. Once you understand what is meant by a soil's available water holding capacity, you can select the appropriate value based on soil type and enter it into the equation. The following equations have been reproduced with permission from *Professional Turf Manager's Guide to Efficient Irrigation Practices and Equipment* (Lit-263), Hunter Industries, 2004.

$$\text{Frequency} = \frac{\text{AWHC x RZ x MAD}}{\text{ET x K}_c}$$

$$\text{Run Time} = \frac{60 \text{ x F x ET x K}_c}{\text{PR x EA}}$$

The following discussion of irrigation factors explains how to choose values for the equations. Equation examples are provided later. Note that when using technical approaches to irrigation scheduling, you must still manually test the soil moisture to determine if scheduling adjustments

Table 3. Soil Moisture Interpretation Chart.

Soil Moisture Deficiency	Moderately Coarse Texture	Medium Texture	Fine and Very Fine Texture
0% (field capacity)	Upon squeezing, no free water appears on soil but wet outline of ball is left on hand.		
0-25%	Forms weak ball, breaks easily when bounced in hand.*	Forms ball, very pliable, slicks readily.*	Easily ribbons out between thumb and forefinger.*
25-50%	Will form ball, but falls apart when bounced in hand.*	Forms ball, slicks under pressure.*	Forms ball, will ribbon out between thumb and forefinger.*
50-75%	Appears dry, will not form ball with pressure.*	Crumbly, holds together from pressure.*	Somewhat pliable, will ball under pressure.*
75-100%	Dry, loose, flows through fingers.	Powdery, crumbles easily.	Hard, difficult to break into powder.
*Squeeze a handful of soil firmly to make ball test.			

Reprinted with permission from Colorado State University Cooperative Extension, 4.700, *Estimating Soil Moisture,* 1998.

Table 4. Usable Soil Moisture Capabilities.

Texture	Available Moisture in./ft.
Moderately coarse (fine sandy loam, sandy loam)	1.0 to 1.6
Medium (silt loam, sandy clay loam, loam, very fine sandy loam)	1.4 to 2.4
Fine and very fine (clay, silty clay, sandy clay, silty clay loam, clay loam)	1.6 to 2.5

Reprinted with permission from Colorado State University Cooperative Extension, 4.700, *Estimating Soil Moisture,* 1998.

are needed. See the previous topic "Estimating Soil Moisture" for more information.

Even if you don't use the scheduling equations, the explanations of irrigation factors shed light on the interaction of water, soil, plants, and the atmosphere. Below is a description of each irrigation factor used in the equations.

AWHC: Available Water Holding Capacity

Available water holding capacity (AWHC) refers to the amount of plant-available water a soil can hold, commonly expressed in inches per foot (in./ft.). The AWHC of a soil influences the frequency of irrigation and the application amount.

Available Water

To understand what is meant by *available water,* you must understand the terms *field capacity* and *permanent wilting point.* A soil saturated with water contains no space for air. If a soil remains saturated for an extended period of time, plants can be damaged or die. Under normal conditions, gravity drains water from a saturated soil until it reaches a condition known as *field capacity.* When a soil is at field capacity, gravity cannot drain any more excess water from the soil, and the soil space contains enough air for plant roots to function. A soil at field capacity can be compared to a wet sponge that does not drip.

The *permanent wilting point* refers to the level of soil moisture at which plants wilt and cannot recover. Soils at the permanent wilting point still contain water, but plants cannot make use of it. *Available water* is the amount of water held by a soil between field capacity and the permanent wilting point. Available water is the water that can be absorbed by plant roots.

Note: The closer the soil moisture level is to the permanent wilting point, the more difficult it is for plants to extract water from the soil. For this reason, irrigation is scheduled well before the permanent wilting point is reached. See the upcoming topic "Management Allowable Depletion" for more information.

Soil Type

Available water holding capacity varies with soil type. Different soil types have different structures and textures. The structure and texture of a soil determine its porousness and influence how much water and air it can hold. In general, fine-texture soils (e.g., clay) are capable of holding the most total water, but medium-texture soils (e.g., loam) are capable of holding the most available water.

- Sandy soil is made up of relatively large soil particles, which give it a coarse texture. It drains quickly and has a relatively small capacity to hold water. For instance, only one-quarter inch of water may be needed to penetrate the turfgrass root zone on sandy soil, whereas one-half inch or more may be needed to penetrate the turfgrass root zone on clay soil. Because sandy soil holds less water, it requires more frequent irrigation than clay or loamy soils. Applying more water than a sandy soil is capable of holding can cause excess water to drain below the root zone, wasting water. Loamy sand and sandy loam are other examples of soil types with a coarse texture.

- Loamy soil has a relatively balanced proportion of large, medium, and tiny soil particles, which gives it a medium texture. Loam holds more water and drains more slowly than sandy soil, enabling it to retain moisture for longer intervals between irrigations. Loam is considered an ideal soil type. Silt loam and silty clay loam are other examples of soil types with a medium texture.

- Clay soil has tiny soil particles, which give this soil a fine texture. Because of its small pore spaces, clay soil drains slowly and plants can have a difficult time extracting water from it. Compaction is a common problem with clay soil, and runoff can occur if too much water is applied at one time. Silty clay is another example of a soil type with a fine texture.

An online search for "determining soil texture" will turn up charts that aid in classifying a soil type based on feel. Soil labs can also determine a soil's textural class. And your county's cooperative extension office will have information on the soil types in your area, including how much available water each can hold. For more information, see "Soil Types" on page 98 and "Web Soil Survey" on page 103.

Table 5 provides estimates of available water holding capacities of common soil types. Keep in mind that data on available water only tell you the amount of available water a soil is capable of holding, not how much is in the soil.

To determine AWHC for the irrigation frequency equation, take a soil sample from beneath the turf, and feel it to determine its texture. Then consult table 5 to find the AWHC for that soil type, and enter it into the frequency equation.

Table 5. Moisture Available (AWHC)

Soil Type	Average in./ft. soil depth
Sand	0.75
Sandy Loam	1.25
Loam	2.00
Silt Loam	2.25
Clay Loam	1.85
Clay	1.25

From *Irrigation Notes: Scheduling Irrigation* (LIT-088), Hunter Industries, 1999. Reproduced with permission.

Example: You sample the soil and judge it to be clay loam. Table 5 gives a value of 1.85 inches of water per foot for clay loam. This is the AWHC value entered into the frequency equation.

$$\text{Frequency} = \frac{\textbf{1.85} \times RZ \times MAD}{ET \times K_c}$$

RZ: Root Zone

Root zone (RZ) refers to the area and volume of soil a plant extracts water from. A plant's root zone depth is one of the factors influencing irrigation scheduling. Compared to shallow rooted plants, deeply rooted plants have access to moisture for longer intervals because they draw water from a larger volume of soil. Note that plant roots can extend much deeper in the soil than is necessary to irrigate. Often, you can keep plants healthy and

attractive by irrigating a limited portion of a plant's root zone, called the *effective root zone*. The goal of irrigation is to replenish the water in the effective root zone.

Bentgrass has a root depth potential of 1 to 8 inches; Kentucky bluegrass, red fescue, ryegrass, and St. Augustine have a root depth potential of 8 to 18 inches; and tall fescue, Zoysia, and Bermuda have a root depth potential of 18 to 60 inches (Wu 1985).

It is commonly said that the effective root zone for turfgrass is 6 to 8 inches. Irrigating deeper than the effective root zone is not necessary for turfgrass health or appearance. Grasses with a greater root depth potential, such as tall fescue or Zoysia, can be watered to a depth of 1 foot, though 6 to 8 inches may still be adequate.

Common values for turfgrass RZ used in the irrigation frequency equation are 0.5 ft. (6-inch root depth) and 1.0 ft. (12-inch root depth) (Hunter Industries 2004).

Example: You are scheduling irrigation for a lawn of St. Augustine grass, which has a rooting potential of 8 to 18 inches. An RZ value of 1.0 or 0.5 could be used.

$$\text{Frequency} = \frac{AWHC \times \textbf{1.0} \times MAD}{ET \times K_c}$$

MAD: Management Allowable Depletion

Plants must be irrigated before all the available water in the root zone has been depleted and the permanent wilting point is reached. Management allowable depletion (MAD) refers to the acceptable level of moisture depletion in a soil. More precisely, MAD is the percentage of the soil's available water that is allowed to deplete before irrigation. Depletion of soil moisture beyond the MAD percentage can lead to plant stress.

A MAD value of 50 percent is a reasonable selection for most soil types; though clay soil is sometimes given a 30 percent MAD value; clay loam, a 40 percent MAD value; silty clay, a 40 percent MAD value; and sand, a 60 percent MAD value. Monitor the site closely at first when using a MAD value greater than 50 percent. For the irrigation frequency equation, the percentage is changed to a decimal (e.g., 50% = 0.50).

Example: You determine the soil to be loam, which has a MAD value of 50 percent.

$$\text{Frequency} = \frac{\text{AWHC x RZ x } \textbf{0.50}}{\text{ET x } K_c}$$

ET_O and K_C: Reference Evapotranspiration and Crop Coefficient

Evapotranspiration (ET) refers to the evaporation of water from the ground plus the transpiration of water from the leaves of a plant. Transpiration primarily keeps plants cool. It can be likened to sweating, though no water appears on the leaves.

ET is most strongly influenced by climate. Sun, wind, temperature, and humidity all influence the rate of evapotranspiration. Heat, low humidity, and wind cause water to evaporate from the ground and transpire from plant leaves more quickly. ET is greatest during the warmest times of day and the warmest times of year. ET also varies according to plant species and the phase of the life cycle a plant is in. For example, a small sunflower plant has a lower ET rate than a large one because it has less leaf area for transpiration.

The ET rate tells how much water is lost from a crop over a given period of time (usually in inches of water per day) and serves as an estimate of how much water to apply through irrigation. If you know how much water a plant uses in a day (its ET rate), you can select irrigation run times that replenish that amount. The result is efficient water use.

Regional facilities record local ET data and make it available to the public. The ET data provided is called reference ET (ET_O). According to L. R. Costello and K.S. Jones of the University of California Cooperative Extension, "Reference evapotranspiration (ET_O) is defined as water loss from a large field of 4-to-7-inch-tall, cool-season grass that is not water stressed. Although ET_O can be measured directly, it is usually calculated from weather data" (Costello, Clark, and Matheny 2000). You can think of reference ET as generic ET data for a region.

To use reference ET, scientists have come up with crop coefficients for many plant species, including turfgrass. The crop coefficient (K_C) is a factor that is multiplied by the reference ET (ET_O) to determine a plant's evapotranspiration rate (ET_C). In other words, multiplying a plant's unique crop coefficient by the reference ET tells you how much water the plant uses. This is all represented in a simple formula, called the ET_C formula:

$$ET_C = K_C \text{ x } ET_O$$

This means that the evapotranspiration rate of a plant (ET_C) is determined by multiplying the crop coefficient (K_C) by the reference evapotranspiration (ET_O).

ET_C = Crop evapotranspiration
K_C = Crop coefficient
ET_O = Reference evapotranspiration

For example, the crop coefficient for cool-season turfgrass is approximately 0.70. If the reference ET is 0.25 inches per day, the ET rate of the grass is calculated as follows:

ET_C = 0.70 x 0.25 = 0.18 inches per day, or 1.26 inches per week. The turfgrass in this example uses about 1.25 inches of water per week.

The irrigation frequency and run time equations make use of the ET_C formula, but include additional factors. Daily or monthly reference ET data can be found online. CIMIS (California), AZMET (Arizona), CoAgMet (Colorado), and FAWN (Florida) are a few online sources of ET data. Your cooperative extension office can provide you with historical ET data for your area. Another alternative is to use a table of potential evapotranspiration rates, as provided in table 7 on the next page. Table 6 includes crop coefficients for turfgrass and a few other landscape plants.

Table 6. Crop Coefficient (K_C)

Vegetation Type	Coefficient
Mature Trees	0.80
Vines & Shrubs (over 4 ft. tall)	0.70
Small Shrubs (under 4 ft. tall)	1.00
Warm-Season Turfgrass	0.50 - 0.70
Cool-Season Turfgrass	0.60 - 0.80
Arid Climate Natives	0.35

From *Irrigation Notes: Scheduling Irrigation* (LIT-088), Hunter Industries, 1999. Reproduced with permission.

Table 7. Potential ET (ET_0) Rates*

Climate Type**	Daily Loss (in inches)
Cool Humid	0.10 - 0.15
Cool Dry	0.15 - 0.20
Warm Humid	0.15 - 0.20
Warm Dry	0.20 - 0.25
Hot Humid	0.20 - 0.30
Hot Dry	0.30 - 0.40

* "These potential evapotranspiration rates are the maximum average ET rates for the climate types. Actual daily ET rates typically are less than these values."

** "'Cool' applies to areas with average high temperatures in midsummer of under 70 F. 'Warm' refers to mid-summer highs between 70 F and 90 F. 'Hot' indicates mid-summer averages over 90 F. Areas in which the average relative humidity is over 50% in mid-summer qualify as 'Humid,' while under 50% is considered 'Dry'."

From *Irrigation Notes: Scheduling Irrigation* (LIT-088), Hunter Industries, 1999. Reproduced with permission.

Example: You will be irrigating tall fescue in an area with warm, dry spring conditions. Table 7 shows a daily water loss of 0.20 to 0.25 inches for warm, dry conditions. This is the value range for ET_0 used in the irrigation frequency equation. Table 6 gives a K_C of 0.60 to 0.80 for cool-season grass. This is the

value range for K_C used in the irrigation frequency equation. If conditions are exceptionally hot and dry, you would use the higher end of the range.

$$\text{Frequency} = \frac{\text{AWHC x RZ x MAD}}{\mathbf{0.25 \text{ x } 0.60}}$$

PR: Precipitation Rate

Precipitation rate (PR) is the depth of water applied by an irrigation system over a given period of time. It is usually expressed in inches per hour. A standard test of a sprinkler system's precipitation rate is called a catchment or catch-can test. The catchment test involves placing empty containers on the lawn, running the sprinklers for a set time, measuring the amount of water in the containers, and using the measurements in a formula, which is provided below.

The containers should be of equal size and shape, and they should have straight sides and flat bottoms. Empty cans or coffee mugs work. Use between 8 and 20 containers. Place one container near each sprinkler in a zone and one in between each sprinkler (see table 8, next page). A zone is an area irrigated by a group of sprinklers that are operated by one valve. (To quickly see where a zone is, manually open a valve, as described on page 152.)

Run the sprinklers for 10 or 15 minutes, measure the depth of water in each container with a ruler or tape measure, and record the measurements. Do this for each zone, and run each zone for the same length of time. The formula is as follows:

$$\text{Avg. PR} = \frac{\text{Total inches}}{\text{Number of cans}} \div \text{Run time x 60}$$

Where: *Total inches* = total inches from all cans. Add up the measurements from all cans to find the total inches.

Number of cans = number of cans per zone x number of zones. For example, if you used 12 cans per zone and measured 3 zones, the number of cans is 36.

Example: After tuning up a sprinkler system, you perform a catchment test for three zones that irrigate the turf. You use 12 cans and a 15 minute run time for each zone. The total depth of water from all cans comes to 14 inches. The number of cans used is 36 (12 cans x 3 zones). The formula is shown below:

$$\text{Avg. PR} = \frac{14}{36} \div 15 \text{ minutes } x \ 60 = 1.55$$

This sprinkler system has a precipitation rate of 1.55 inches per hour. The PR is entered into the run time equation as follows:

$$\text{Run Time} = \frac{60 \ x \ F \ x \ ET \ x \ K_c}{1.5 \ (\text{avg.}) \ x \ EA}$$

Alternative PR Formula

The following alternate PR formula, called the Total Area Method, requires you to know the irrigation system's operating pressure and the gallons per minute of the sprinkler nozzles. It is included for the sake of reference:

$$\text{PR (in./hr.)} = \frac{96.3 \ x \ GPM}{\text{Area}}$$

Where: *PR* = precipitation rate in inches per hour.

96.3 = factor that converts gallons per minute to inches per hour.

GPM = total gallons per minute of the sprinkler nozzles in a zone. Nozzle GPM data is available from sprinkler nozzle manufacturers.

Area = square feet of the area covered by the sprinklers in a zone.

Example: A zone has eight sprinklers. Two deliver 1.5 gpm, four deliver 0.75 gpm, and two deliver 3 gpm. The total gpm for this zone is 12. The area covered is 30' x 20' = 600 square feet. The equation is as follows:

$$\text{PR (in./hr.)} = \frac{96.3 \ x \ 12}{600} = 1.93 \text{ inches per hr.}$$

Can Distribution

Table 8 is a pattern for can distribution. The black dots represent sprinkler heads. The circled numbers represent empty containers. Other patterns are also acceptable.

Table 8. Catchment Placement

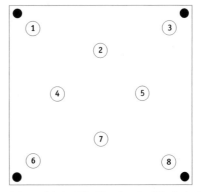

Adapted from *The Handbook of Technical Irrigation Information*, Hunter Industries, 2006. Reproduced with permission.

EA: Application Efficiency

Application efficiency (EA) is a measurement of how much water applied through irrigation is stored in a plant's root zone. EA is expressed as a percentage. No system is 100 percent efficient. Water is lost to runoff, wind drift, overspray, evaporation, and percolation through the soil. Distribution uniformity, explained next, also influences application efficiency. Many causes of water loss can be managed through equipment selection and adjustment, the repair of leaks, and accurate scheduling.

For turf irrigation systems, 80 percent efficiency is excellent, 70 percent is very good, 65 percent is good, and 40 percent is poor. Most systems are 50 to 70 percent efficient. It is reasonable to estimate a system's application efficiency because some of the variables that affect efficiency, such as climate, cannot be fixed (Hunter Industries 1999, 2004).

Example: Assess the sprinkler system's efficiency as excellent, very good, good, average, or poor, and use the corresponding percentage listed above. Convert the EA percentage to a decimal for the irrigation run time equation (e.g., 65% = 0.65).

$$\text{Run Time} = \frac{60 \times F \times ET \times K_c}{PR \times \mathbf{0.65}}$$

Distribution Uniformity. Distribution uniformity (DU) is a measurement of how evenly an irrigation system applies water. To illustrate, a sprinkler system that applies $1/2$ inch of water in one area of turf and $1/8$ inch in another area has low uniformity. If run times are set according to the lower application rate, some turf areas will be over-irrigated. DU is one aspect of a sprinkler system's overall efficiency. A sprinkler system with low DU will have low application efficiency; however, a system with high DU may still have low application efficiency, depending on other factors.

Uneven distribution occurs in all sprinkler systems to varying degrees. Gross unevenness can be caused by poor system design, alterations to the system's original design, and operating pressure differences, among other factors. (For repair suggestions, see "Solving Coverage Problems In Spray-Head Systems" on page 154.)

DU is calculated using the results of a catchment test (see "PR: Precipitation Rate" on page 62). To calculate distribution uniformity, start by arranging the measurements from the individual containers in the order of lowest to highest. Then determine the average of the lowest 25 percent of the results, divide that amount by the average of all results, and multiply by 100 to get a percentage. This is represented in the following formula:

$$DU\% = \frac{\text{Avg. of the lowest 25\% of results}}{\text{Avg. of all results}} \times 100$$

A high DU percentage corresponds to even application. According to Hunter Industries, a DU of 75 to 85 percent is excellent and a DU of 65 to 70 percent is good (2004). If a sprinkler system has poor DU, a low value should be selected for EA (see previous topic). If a sprinkler system has high DU, other factors that influence application efficiency need to be considered before selecting an EA value.

Irrigation Frequency Equation Example

We now have enough information to use the irrigation scheduling equations. The irrigation frequency equation is used to calculate how often the sprinklers should be operated:

$$\text{Frequency} = \frac{AWHC \times RZ \times MAD}{ET \times K_c}$$

Example: You will be irrigating tall fescue, a cool-season grass, growing in clay loam. The location is Sacramento, California, where spring conditions are warm and dry.

AWHC for clay loam = 1.85 inches (From table 5, page 60.)

RZ for Tall Fescue = 1 foot

MAD for clay loam = 40%

ET for warm dry = 0.20-0.25 (From table 7, page 62.)

K_c for tall fescue = 0.60 (From table 6, page 62.)

Based on these values, the equation is as follows:

$$\text{Frequency} = \frac{1.85 \times 1.0 \times 0.40}{0.25 \times 0.60} = \frac{0.74}{0.15} = 5$$

According to the equation, the lawn in this example should be irrigated every fifth day—for example, Monday, Saturday, Thursday, and so on. This type of schedule is known as an interval program. Note that if you base the calculation on an RZ factor of 0.50 instead of 1.0, the interval would be 2.47 days.

Irrigation Run Time Equation Example

The second equation is used to calculate the irrigation run time:

$$\text{Run Time} = \frac{60 \times F \times ET \times K_c}{PR \times EA}$$

Example: You will be irrigating tall fescue growing in clay loam in Sacramento, California during spring. The sprinkler system's average precipitation rate is 1.5 inches per hour, and the application efficiency is estimated to be 65 percent. "F" stands for frequency of irrigation (the watering interval, in days), which is determined using the frequency equation.

F = 5-day interval (Based on the frequency equation example.)

ET for warm dry = 0.20-0.25 (From table 7, page 62.)

K_c for tall fescue = 0.60 (From table 6, page 62.)

PR = 1.5"

EA = 65%

Based on these values, the equation is as follows:

$$\text{Run Time} = \frac{60 \times 5 \times 0.25 \times 0.60}{1.5 \times 0.65} = 45$$

According to the equation, the lawn should be watered for 45 minutes every fifth day. Since the soil in the example is clay loam, the run time may need to be divided into multiple applications to prevent runoff.

The scheduling equations are meant to be used alongside your turf observations. If the schedule results in wilting, stress, or runoff, make adjustments as needed.

Irrigating Sloped Areas

If more water is applied to an area than the soil can readily absorb, puddling or runoff can occur. In technical terms, puddling or runoff occur if the precipitation rate (PR) exceeds the infiltration capacity (IC) of a soil (PR > IC = runoff). The infiltration capacity is the maximum rate at which a soil can absorb water.

Runoff is less common on coarse-texture soils because of their high infiltration capacity. Fine-texture or compacted soils have a lower infiltration capacity and are more prone to runoff. Sloped areas also have a higher incidence of runoff. Measures taken to relieve soil compaction and improve soil texture will increase a soil's infiltration capacity.

The problem of runoff is commonly addressed through multiple cycling: the practice of dividing a turf's water requirement into multiple applications of shorter duration. Only as much water is applied as the soil can absorb without runoff. A short interval between applications allows the water to soak in, and cycling is continued until the turf's water requirement has been met. Table 9 on the next page shows the maximum precipitation rates for sloped areas.

Turfgrass Aeration

Aeration, also called aerification or cultivation, is the practice of punching holes in turfgrass to loosen the soil and help oxygen and nutrients reach the roots. After aeration, grass roots fill in the soil spaces, resulting in a thicker turf that is more disease resistant. Aeration is effective at reducing soil compaction and thatch. A good time to apply fertilizer or soil supplements is after aerating.

Large lawn areas require a power aerator. The preferred power aerator is called a hollow tine or core aerator. This machine punches hollow tines (metal tubes) into the soil and removes soil cores, which are deposited on the soil surface. Cores are usually left on the lawn to break apart over several days to several weeks, gradually becoming undetectable. The fragmenting cores serve as topdressing, which

Table 9. Maximum Precipitation Rates for Sloped Areas

SOIL TEXTURE	Maximum Precipitation Rates (in Inches Per Hour):							
	0 to 5% slope		5 to 8% slope		8 to 12% slope		12% + slope	
	Cover	Bare		Bare	Cover	Bare	Cover	Bare
Coarse sandy soils	2.00	2.00	2.00	1.50	1.50	1.00	1.00	0.50
Coarse sandy soils over compact subsoils	1.75	1.50	1.25	1.00	1.00	0.75	0.75	0.40
Uniform light sandy loams	1.75	1.00	1.25	0.80	1.00	0.60	0.75	0.40
Light sandy loams over compact subsoils	1.25	0.75	1.00	0.50	0.75	0.40	0.50	0.30
Uniform silt loams	1.00	0.50	0.80	0.40	0.60	0.30	0.40	0.20
Silt loams over compact subsoil	0.60	0.30	0.50	0.25	0.40	0.15	0.30	0.10
Heavy clay or clay loam	0.20	0.15	0.15	0.10	0.12	0.08	0.10	0.06

From *Irrigation Notes: Scheduling Irrigation* (LIT-088), Hunter Industries, 1999. Reproduced with permission.

helps to fill in the holes and increases the activity of microorganisms at the soil surface.

Power aerators can be rented from equipment rental centers. Some aerators are large and heavy, making them challenging to transport and operate. If you maintain a number of medium- to high-quality lawns, consider purchasing your own aerator. Alternatively, you can subcontract this work as needed.

Soil Compaction and Aeration

In compacted soil, soil particles are compressed, and the soil contains less room for water and oxygen. Grass roots have less oxygen to draw on and less room to grow; roots become shallow, and lawn health can decline as a result. Soil compaction in turf areas is primarily the result of extensive foot traffic or equipment use. And wet soil compacts more easily than dry soil. Fine-texture soils, such as clay, are the most prone to compaction. By loosening compacted soil, aeration increases soil oxygen levels and allows water and nutrients to penetrate the soil more easily. Aeration, proper

watering, and fertilization can help to relieve soil compaction over time.

It is ideal to apply a thin layer of top-dressing or high-quality, well-aged compost after aeration. Compost serves as a food source for beneficial soil organisms, such as earthworms and microorganisms, which aggregate soil particles and increase soil porosity naturally. The application of topdressing to large turf areas is time and energy intensive and can damage the turf if not done correctly. For these reasons, topdressing is not commonly applied to turf in residential landscapes.

Thatch and Aeration

Thatch is a matted layer of living and dead grass roots and stems that can form on the turfgrass soil surface. Up to 1/2 inch of thatch is beneficial because it cushions the turf and helps retain soil moisture. Thatch in excess of 1/2 inch reduces water infiltration and can prevent nutrients and pesticides from reaching the soil. Thatch can also become home to damaging insects, and it causes grass roots to

Aeration and Preemergent Herbicides

Natural or chemical preemergent herbicides are sometimes applied to turfgrass in spring to control annual weeds (e.g., crabgrass). There are different views on aerating after preemergents have been applied. The effectiveness of preemergents depends on coverage of the soil surface, so the concern is that aeration will breach the chemical barrier, giving weeds a foothold. For this reason, some experts recommend delaying aeration for four to six weeks after applying a preemergent herbicide (Goatley and others 2005). Karl Danneberger, professor of turfgrass science at Ohio State University, says that the preemergent barrier will not be compromised after aeration if the turf is dense. He says that some crabgrass may germinate in thin turf, but aeration is probably needed to help the turf grow denser (Brophy 2004). Ultimately, you must decide which course of action is best. Online forums can be used to get a range of views on more obscure topics like this one. Some popular online forums are listed in appendix A on page 238.

form in the thatch itself, making the grass more susceptible to disease and temperature stress.

Grasses that spread by stolons and rhizomes are more prone to thatch than bunch-forming grasses. The over-application of nitrogen can promote thatch by causing grass stems and roots to accumulate faster than soil microorganisms can decompose them. Low soil pH can promote thatch by hindering the activity of microorganisms. And pesticides that are harmful to earthworms can be a factor in the buildup of thatch. As earthworms tunnel through the soil, they increase soil aeration and bring nutrient-rich castings to the soil surface, where the castings aid in the decomposition of thatch. Note that grass clippings returned to the lawn do not cause thatch if mowing is done properly and regularly.

Aeration punches holes in the thatch, helping water and nutrients reach the roots. And the improved penetration of water and oxygen increases the activity of microorganisms that decompose thatch. Note that aeration alone is not enough to combat a thick layer of thatch, which must be dethatched with a power rake or a vertical mower, depending on the grass type. Dethatching can damage the turf if it is not done properly. Dethatching is not explained here.

When to Aerate

The grass should be actively growing at the time of aeration. For warm-season grasses, a good time to aerate is after the first mowing in spring. It is best not to aerate in summer when the grass is stressed from heat. Some experts suggest that mid-summer aeration of warm-season grasses is acceptable, provided the soil is sufficiently moist (Goatley and others 2005). Note that spring aeration can encourage the germination of annual weeds. For this reason, natural or chemical preemergent herbicides are sometimes applied to the turf after spring aeration.

Early autumn is the preferred time to aerate cool-season turfgrass because the grass is putting energy into root production in preparation for winter (Brophy 2004). And there is generally less weed seed germination in the fall. Spring aeration of cool-season grasses is also sometimes practiced, and is often followed by the application of a preemergent herbicide. Lawns need about a month to recover from aeration. Do not aerate later than one month before the grass goes dormant.

How to Aerate

Irrigate deeply two to three days before aerating so the soil is moist, but not wet or saturated, at the time of aeration. Before aerating, mark the location of sprinkler heads by placing a small landscape flag next to each one. Use caution when aerating turf areas that have shallow irrigation pipes. Pipes laid to code are generally one foot in the ground and should not be harmed by aeration. If you aren't sure how deep the pipes are, carefully dig near a sprinkler head to see where the riser joins the in-ground lateral pipe. For an irrigation system overview, see page 151.

Aeration cores should be approximately $3/4$ inches in diameter, 2 to 4 inches deep, and spaced 2 to 3 inches apart. A 3-inch core spacing may require two or more passes. Make one complete pass over the turf, then another pass at 90 degrees to the first.

Note that bunch-forming grasses, such as tall fescue or perennial ryegrass, generally do not form thatch. If you aerate these grasses to relieve soil compaction, fertilize and overseed afterward to speed recovery time and minimize weed problems (Stier 2000).

How Often to Aerate

Aeration is not necessary if a lawn does not have a soil compaction problem, though most lawns can benefit from aeration every one to five years (Stier 2000). Compacted clay or other fine-texture soils can benefit from aeration twice a year for several consecutive years. Layers of thatch greater than 1 inch should be dethatched, which is the practice of cutting the grass with a vertical mower (dethatcher) or a power rake.

Integrated Pest Management

All of the turfgrass management practices described up to this point are designed to keep turfgrass growing optimally and pest problems to a minimum. However, pests—in the form of weeds, insects, and diseases—will inevitably arise, and it is necessary to have a strategy to deal with them.

Integrated pest management (IPM) is a widely accepted strategy that relies on a combination of pest control methods, with an emphasis on the least toxic. Pesticides are used in IPM, but only as a last resort. The goal in IPM is not to eliminate pests from the landscape, it is to keep their populations at an acceptable level. IPM combines cultural, mechanical, biological, and chemical pest control strategies to minimize aesthetic damage, costs, and environmental impact.

This brief discussion of IPM is meant to serve only as an extended definition. Since IPM is a general pest control strategy, not limited to turfgrass, IPM for landscape plants is also touched upon. Additional training is necessary to learn how to monitor or scout for pests in the landscape and implement control strategies. This is best learned through courses devoted to the subject.

Cultural Practices

Turfgrass pest management begins with site preparation before the turf is seeded or sodded. A fertile, well-prepped soil promotes a disease-resistant soil environment, and a well-designed sprinkler system promotes a dense, deeply rooted turf. The selection of a grass species suited to the environment will also minimize problems. Landscapes that require considerable pest management efforts may need one or more landscape features redesigned.

A dense, healthy turf is the best defense against many turf pests. Proper mowing, fertilizing, irrigating, and aerating are cultural practices that keep turfgrass growing optimally and reduce the incidence of pests. Maintaining the proper height of cut, fertilizing at the correct times of year, watering deeply and infrequently, correcting compaction or thatch problems, and maintaining proper soil pH are all ways to keep turfgrass healthy and competitive.

These practices also support conditions less favorable to pests. For example, overwatering or frequent, light watering and a low cutting height can promote the germination of crabgrass. Selecting the proper cutting height and watering deeply and infrequently will support conditions less favorable to this weed. Other control methods may still be required, but cultural practices form an integral part of an IPM strategy.

Mechanical Controls

Mechanical controls include traps for insects or animals, and straightforward tactics like hand weeding. Some insects, such as aphids, mealy bugs, thrips, and spider mites can be temporarily controlled by hosing off stems and the undersides of leaves with a high pressure stream of water. Some turfgrass weeds, such as dandelion, can be removed at the roots with a forked-tip weeding tool. If this task is tended to before weeds go to seed, minimal time and effort may be required. Mechanical controls may be all the pest control needed in some landscapes. Landscapes requiring more meticulous care or more extensive weed abatement may require additional controls.

Biological Controls

One of the basic concepts in IPM is that beneficial organisms serve as natural controls on pest populations. When chemical pesticides are used, harmful and beneficial organisms are killed. By turning to chemical controls as a last resort, IPM encourages the presence of beneficial organisms and natural pest predators in the landscape.

Insect predators include lady beetles, which limit aphid and mite populations; lacewings, which eat aphids and whiteflies; big eyed bugs, which eat aphids, spider mites, and leaf hoppers; certain beneficial wasps, which attack moth eggs; and praying mantids, which feed on a variety of insect pests. Limiting pesticide use can allow these and other natural predators to be present in sufficient populations to benefit the landscape.

IPM practices also include introducing beneficial organisms into a landscape. Bacillus thuringiensis (Bt) is a naturally occurring soil bacteria used as a biological insecticide in the control of certain damaging insect larvae, such as sod webworm. Bt strains are toxic only to a limited number of insects and are non-toxic to other insects, animals, and humans. Bacillus popilliae is a bacteria sometimes used to control Japanese beetle grubs. And beneficial nematodes are microscopic worms that are sometimes used to control damaging larvae. It cannot be said that all biological controls are as potent or reliable as chemical controls, but some

are effective, and new developments continue to emerge.

Finally, some turfgrass species are enhanced with endophytes, which are fungi that live inside a grass plant without harming it. The presence of endophytes makes the plant undesirable to insect pests, such as sod webworm and chinch bugs, and it improves the stress tolerance of the grass. The higher the percentage of endophyte living in the plant, the greater the plant's resistance to pests that feed above ground.

Chemical Controls

Chemical controls become an option in IPM when pest populations cannot be maintained below a predetermined threshold with other controls or if no other controls are available. For example, if the population of grubs (damaging beetle larvae) beneath the turf exceeds a predetermined threshold (e.g., 10 grubs per square foot), chemical controls are warranted in IPM. Thresholds are selected based on the number of pests likely to cause unacceptable damage or aesthetic harm. Different pest species require different thresholds, pointing to the importance of accurate pest identification.

Considerations for selecting a pesticide include its effectiveness against the target organism, its compatibility with the host plant, its effects on beneficial organisms, the degree of environmental and user safety, and cost (Texas A&M University 2002). IPM favors pesticides that are effective against the targeted pest, have low toxicity, and the least environmental persistence. Maximum benefit is derived by applying pesticides at the most effective time during the pest's life cycle. And environmental toxicity is reduced through the judicious use of pesticides. Spot treatments are used when appropriate (e.g., for localized infestations), and broadcast applications of pesticides are avoided unless warranted.

Chemicals with low toxicity are the first choice. Insecticides made from plants are one line of defence. Neem (Azadirachtin) is an organic insecticide derived from seeds of the Neem tree. Neem is used to repel a variety of pests and is non-toxic to humans.

Pest Control Applicator's Licensing

The commercial application of pesticides requires a pesticide applicator's license, which is granted by the agency in your state that regulates pesticide application. To be granted a license, you must fulfill your state's licensing requirements. To maintain your license, you must complete ongoing recertification and file pesticide application reports. You must also have insurance coverage for the commercial application of pesticides. The responsible and legal use of chemical pest controls requires specialized knowledge and training, which certification helps ensure. If used improperly, pesticides can harm humans, animals, beneficial organisms, and the environment. Note that some states do not allow any unlicensed commercial use of pest controls, even plant-based controls. Homeowners are sometimes exempt from licensing when applying pesticides on their own property.

You can find the contact information for your state agency in charge of pesticide licensing through the website of the National Pesticide Information Center at http://npic.orst.edu/state1. htm, or by calling 1-800-858-7378. The NPIC provides scientifically based information about pesticides and works under a cooperative agreement with the U.S. Environmental Protection Agency. The NPIC can also provide you with pesticide manufacturers' contact information.

Businesses that specialize in the chemical control of insects, weeds, and diseases in the landscape serve accounts on an as-needed or regular basis. If you intend to subcontract this work, be certain your clients understand that they will have to pay a separate service for pesticide application. Pest control businesses can be found under "pest control" or "weed abatement" in the phone book. Your IPM efforts can be defeated if the subcontractor does not practice IPM. Take the time to understand the chemical controls used, even when they are applied by a separate business. Finally, if you have a pesticide- or chemical-related emergency, you can call the toll-free number of the Poison Help Hotline at 1-800-222-1222. The Poison Help Hotline is staffed 24 hours a day, seven days a week.

Pyrethrins are an insecticide derived from the Chrysanthemum plant. Pyrethrins have a relatively low toxicity to humans. They also break down with exposure to sunlight and air and do not persist for a long time in the landscape. Synthetic pyrethrins are more toxic and can persist for longer periods.

Insecticidal soaps are specially formulated soaps used as insecticides. They work on contact and are most effective against small, soft-bodied insects, such as aphids, spider mites, and whiteflies. Insecticidal soaps are less effective against large or hard-bodied insects, and they can kill some beneficial insects. Insecticidal soaps are sometimes combined with horticultural oil to increase their effectiveness.

Turf Repair

Areas of bare soil in turf or dead patches of turf can be caused by pests, compacted soil, foot traffic, a malfunctioning sprinkler system, or other causes. Once the problem has been addressed, areas of bare soil should be repaired to prevent the germination of weed seeds.

Fertilizer is sometimes enough to encourage grasses that spread by runners (rhizomes/stolons) to fill in small areas of bare soil. Bunch-forming grasses will not spread by runners and form new plants, but fertilizer can also help these plants increase in size and fill in smaller gaps.

Seeding is used to repair areas of bare soil in turf. Reseeding is sometimes performed on bunch-forming grasses every few years to keep the turf dense. To ensure uniform lawn color and texture, use the same seed type as the existing turfgrass. If the lawn contains several varieties of grass, use a suitable seed mix. For example, a "shade mix" contains grass varieties that do well in shade. Nurseries can aid in grass identification and selection based on a turf sample.

Small areas of bare soil can be seeded any time during the growing season as long as the soil is warm enough and follow-up irrigation is adequate. The best time to seed cool-season grasses is late summer, and the best time to seed warm-season grasses is late spring or early summer. These are also the best times for establishing new turf. Timing can be critical in some regions, so consult a nursery professional or extension service expert for regional recommendations.

If you will be seeding or sodding a new lawn, have the soil tested first to determine if it is deficient in phosphorus or potassium, or if lime is required. Fertilizer and other amendments should be incorporated into the soil before seeding. Soil testing is explained on page 108.

For large turf areas, follow the recommended seeding rate on the seed label. In general, clump-forming grasses, such as tall fescue and perennial ryegrass, spread slowly, if at all, so they are seeded at a relatively high rate to make a dense stand. Spreading grasses steadily grow outward from the original grass plant at rates that vary by grass type; they are generally seeded at lower rates. An online search for "turfgrass seeding rates" will turn up this information. It is not critical to follow the seeding rate when repairing small turf areas.

Before applying seed, loosen and level the soil in the repair area. Then broadcast the seed over the area with a mechanical spreader or by hand, being careful not to scatter seed into flower beds. Lightly rake the area and gently tamp the soil to ensure the seed make good contact with the soil. The seed should be no more than $1/4$ inch deep. A thin layer of weed-free straw is sometimes used to retain soil moisture and prevent erosion.

At the time of seeding, a starter fertilizer that is low in nitrogen and high in phosphorus should be applied to the soil surface according to the product directions. Starter fertilizer is recommended even if a soil test indicates the soil is high in phosphorus (Christians 2007).

The recommended nitrogen rate for newly seeded turf is $1/2$ pound per 1000 square feet. An additional $1/2$ pound per 1000 square feet can be applied after two weeks (Rosen, Horgan, and Mugaas 2006). Note that the risk of nitrogen leaching and fertilizer runoff is increased in the first year after seeding or sodding because the turfgrass root system is not fully established.

Irrigate lightly and frequently for the first few weeks after seeding to keep the soil in the shallow root zone moist. Multiple light irrigations per day are often necessary to ensure that the soil does not dry out. As the grass starts to become established, irrigation can be progressively deeper and less frequent. The soil should not remain saturated for extended periods.

Mow the grass for the first time when it reaches approximately 1 inch taller than its ideal cutting height. Reduce the lawn's height by no more than $1/3$ to avoid stressing or damaging the grass.

Landscape Plant Management

The majority of landscape plants can be successfully managed by following some general principles of plant care. This chapter is an introduction to selecting, planting, fertilizing, and irrigating landscape plants.

Plant Selection

Plants that are suited to their growing environment have fewer problems and cause fewer problems in the landscape. Local nurseries typically sell plants that are adapted to the region. The conditions of the planting area must also be considered. Before selecting a plant, note the following features of the planting area:

- The height and width of the space allotted to the plant. The space should be suitable to the plant's size at maturity.

- The degree of sun and shade the area receives.

- The amount of wind and heat at the location.

- The level of water use in the zone (low, moderate, high).

- The soil type (described on page 98).

- The soil pH (described on page 105).

Other questions are also helpful: Does the plant need to serve a particular purpose in the landscape, such as block a view or prevent erosion? Is there a plant shape, flower color, or foliage texture that would look good in this spot? Answers to these questions will help you find candidate species.

Plant encyclopedias contain information on plant growth habits and characteristics, and they can be used to gather ideas. A few encyclopedias are the *Sunset Western Garden Book* (alternatively, the *Sunset National Garden Book,* for U.S. regions other than the West), *The American Horticultural Society A to Z Encyclopedia of Garden Plants,* and more focused guides such as *The American Horticultural Society Encyclopedia of Perennials,* and *Rodale's Illustrated Encyclopedia of Perennials.* Online plant databases can also be used to research plants. And nursery professionals are a good source of plant suggestions.

There is a large variety of low-maintenance plants to keep plant selection interesting. In other words, there is no need to reach for a common landscape shrub, such as a Red Tip Photinia, whenever there is a space in the landscape that needs to be filled. In fact, overuse of some species can lead to pest problems. Diversity is an important principle in landscape design.

Rose selection

Hybrid roses (roses in which the cultivar is grafted onto a different rootstock) are classed as one of three grades: Grade 1, Grade 1½, or Grade 2. Grade

1 roses have the best developed canes and roots. Grade 1 1/2 are less well developed, but can reach the quality of Grade 1 roses with care. Grade 2 roses are of lesser quality. To minimize problems, buy only Grade 1 roses. For lower-maintenance roses, consider some of the landscape and shrub roses, floribundas, carpet roses, and other categories bred for disease resistance and abundant bloom.

Tree Selection

Tree selection begins with an evaluation of above- and below-ground site conditions, including planting area size, amount of sunlight, proximity to power lines and buildings, average rainfall in the area, and soil conditions. The degree of maintenance, such as the amount of pruning and irrigation the tree will receive, needs to be considered as well. It is beyond the scope of this book to outline all the factors that must be considered.

Nursery professionals may be able to suggest trees suitable to the planting area. Certified or consulting arborists can provide tree suggestions based on the unique site characteristics. And your city's Parks and Recreation Department may have tree recommendations for the region. Check with your city before planting a tree in a streetside planting strip. Trees in streetside planting strips are the property of the city, and the city will have tree selection guidelines for these areas.

Online tree selection guides and software are available for some regions. A guide for the northeast (U.S. hardiness zones 2-7) can be found at http://lyra.ifas.ufl.edu/NorthernTrees/index.html. A guide for Florida and the southeast (U.S. hardiness zones 8-11) can be found at http://lyra.ifas.ufl.edu/FloridaTrees/index.html. The Urban Forest Ecosystems Institute (http://www.ufei.org) has an online tree selection guide for California called SelecTree.

Once a species has been selected, choose a nursery tree with strong structure. This means selecting a young tree with a single, dominant leader (central stem or trunk) and branches that are well-spaced vertically and radially on the trunk. Trees with branches that are clustered together require more pruning to develop good structure. Branches

should also be less than 1/2 the diameter of the trunk and not contain included bark, which is a sign of a weak branch attachment. Included bark is described on page 123.

Temporary branches are low-placed branches that are allowed to remain on a tree for only a year or two. Temporary branches produce energy, distribute wind stress, and help the tree develop a sturdy trunk. Temporary branches are headed back to keep their growth in check and are removed as the tree matures. For more information, see page 123.

Preference should be given to trees that remain upright without support staking. Test a tree by bending and releasing the top portion to see if it returns to an upright position. Tapered trunks (larger caliper at the base than higher up) are preferable because they distribute wind stress more evenly than trunks without taper.

It is acceptable to purchase a whip, which is a young tree with no branches. Lateral branches will develop after planting. When a fruit tree is purchased as a whip, branching can be promoted by cutting back the leader at the desired branching height. The leader may need to be reestablished after heading, depending on the training method used. Note that smaller trees establish more quickly than larger transplants of the same species. In general, a five gallon tree (#5) or smaller is a good choice.

Plant Names

All plants have a scientific name; many also have a common name. For example, *Mahonia aquifolium* is the scientific name for the plant commonly called Oregon Grape; *Prunus persica* is the scientific name for a nectarine tree. Scientific names are Latin. They serve to categorize a plant within a genus and species based on certain characteristics.

Common names can vary regionally. For example, depending on where you live, *Trachelospermum jasminoides* will either have the common name Star Jasmine or Confederate Jasmine. For this reason, knowing only a plant's common name can occasionally lead to confusion. However, the common name is usually sufficient; for instance, knowing whether a tree is an apricot or a cherry is enough to make important pruning decisions.

Learning the names of common plants in your area enables you to look them up in a plant encyclopedia or online, where you can read about their preferred growing conditions, growth habits, best varieties, and potential problems. This is a good way to increase horticultural knowledge.

Planting

Annuals, shrubs, and trees can be planted any time of year the ground is not frozen, as long as the plants receive adequate post-planting care. Spring and fall are good times to plant because temperatures are mild, and soil conditions are favorable to root growth, provided there is adequate soil moisture.

The correct planting procedure helps plants establish more quickly and reduces the incidence of plant failure. Planting techniques are similar for most trees and shrubs, though container, bare root, and balled-in-burlap plants each have some unique planting guidelines.

Important: Consult with a certified arborist or certified nursery professional before planting, irrigating, or otherwise disturbing the soil beneath the canopy of oak trees.

Planting Container Plants

Container plants should be planted soon after purchase. If planting is delayed, the rootballs should be kept moist and the containers should be shaded—containers exposed to full sun can heat up and cause root loss. The foliage needs conditions similar to where it will grow; for example, if the plant likes partial shade, it should be stored in partial shade.

Annuals are plants that flower only for one season. Nurseries sell annual flowers in six-pack containers and larger flats. To plant annuals, dig a small hole for each plant using a hand trowel. Make each hole just large enough to hold the plant and some loose soil. Hold the plant by the base of the stem, and gently remove the plant from its container. Place the plant in the hole, and fill the remaining space with soil. Firm the soil with your hands to ensure the rootball is in contact with the field soil.

After planting, the base of the stem should sit slightly above the surrounding soil, not below it. Water the area when you are finished. To plant annuals in heavy clay soil, amend the planting area with high-quality compost or another suitable amendment before planting. Most annuals do poorly if planted directly in heavy clay.

Larger container plants come in varying sizes, or classes, such as #1, #5, and #15. At one time these names had a loose affiliation with the gallon size of the container, but this is not the case any more. The planting hole for container plants should be at least 2 to 3 times the diameter of the rootball. An even wider hole is recommended when planting in compacted clay soil or other restrictive soils. Loosening the soil in a wide area makes it easier for plant roots to spread into the surrounding soil.

The hole should be nearly as deep as the plant's rootball. The goal is to have the plant sit slightly above the soil surface after planting. Plants that sit even slightly below grade after planting are more at risk of failing. And keeping the root collar slightly above grade reduces the chance of water collecting around the base of the trunk. Standing water around the trunk's base can promote diseases such as crown rot (Phytophthora).

To help prevent the soil from settling after planting, the soil the rootball sits on should be undisturbed. If the hole is too deep, add soil to the hole and pack it down firmly. When the hole is finished, insert a spade or garden fork into the walls of the hole to help roots penetrate more easily.

Studies have shown there is no benefit to incorporating an organic amendment into the backfill soil. The exception is sandy soil, which can benefit from an organic amendment. Never use sand or gravel as an amendment for clay soil because the soil can become like concrete. Note that adding sand or gravel to the bottom of a planting hole to improve drainage will have just the opposite effect (Harris, Clark, and Matheny 2004). The addition of fertilizer to the planting hole is covered in the upcoming topic "Fertilizing Landscape Plants" on page 80.

Slide the plant from the container. If necessary, cut the sides of the plastic container with a knife. Gently loosen the rootball by hand, and cut off any damaged portions of roots. Note that plants kept in containers for a long time can develop a mass of roots that encircle the plant. A plant in this condition is said to be root bound. It is preferable to avoid purchasing a root-bound plant, which can usually be identified by roots growing above the soil or protruding from the holes in the bottom of the container. If you buy a root-bound plant, cut through some of the finer tangled roots. Do not cut away larger kinked roots. Even with corrective measures, some plants will not recover from being root bound.

Before this lemon tree is planted, the container will be cut away and the rootball will be slightly loosened by hand. The stake will be removed if the tree can stand without it. Otherwise, the stake will be repositioned so it is not pressed against the trunk.

Set the plant in the hole, making sure the top of the rootball remains slightly above grade. Position the plant so that branch placement is suitable to the location. Consider positioning the less developed side of the plant toward the afternoon sun so it will get more light. Position a fruit tree so the crook in the scion (the upper part of the graft union) points away from the afternoon sun. This area can become sunburned if it is directly exposed to the afternoon sun (Harris, Clark, and Matheny 2004). If necessary, the rootball can be slightly tilted in the soil so the trunk of the tree is vertical.

Fill in half of the hole with the backfill soil, and tamp it firmly around the plant. Then water the soil to get rid of air pockets. Fill in the rest of the soil, and firm it by hand or gently by foot. Do not apply backfill soil to the top of the rootball; this can cause water to flow away from the rootball. If the plant does not sit slightly above the rest of the soil, replant it so it does. Create a berm of dirt around the plant to act as a watering basin, then water the plant.

Apply a 2- to 3-inch layer of mulch around the plant. To reduce the risk of disease, keep mulch away from the main stem or trunk. See "Mulching Landscape Plants" on page 79 for more information. If tags are attached to the plant by wire, remove them to prevent the wire from damaging branches.

Do not cut back trees and shrubs after planting except to remove broken or damaged branches or to maintain the dominance of the central leader. For more information see "Pruning at Planting" on page 77. Check the soil moisture daily, and water as needed to ensure the soil in the rootball stays moist, though not saturated, for the first 4 to 6 weeks after planting. Remember that plant roots need oxygen to function. Saturating the soil for extended periods can kill a plant. For more information, see "Irrigating During Establishment Period" on page 86.

Planting Bare Root Trees and Shrubs

Certain plants, such as roses and fruit trees, can be sold in bare root form in winter. A bare root tree or shrub has the soil removed from its roots. Bare root plants are less expensive than container plants, and they can be packaged and shipped. And since bare root plants use only the soil in the landscape, they avoid soil moisture problems that can arise when the rootball has a different soil texture than the planting area.

Bare root trees and shrubs should be planted before bud break. Plant them soon after you get them. If planting is to be delayed, cover the roots with soil or compost and keep them moist. Before planting, prune away any broken portions of roots, and soak the roots in a bucket of water overnight. If overnight soaking is not practical, soak the roots in a bucket of water while you prepare the planting hole.

Follow the same planting procedure as for container plants. The roots should have enough room to spread out, and the soil the roots sit on should be undisturbed to prevent settling. Backfill and firm the soil, and stake the plant if necessary. Note that most bareroot failures are caused by insufficient water as the plant begins to leaf out. Keep the soil in the root zone moist, not saturated, for 4 to 6 weeks after planting. For more information, see "Irrigating During Establishment Period" on page 86.

Planting Balled-in-Burlap Trees and Shrubs

Balled-in-burlap (B-in-B or B&B) trees and shrubs are removed from the ground with their original soil intact. The roots are wrapped in burlap or a similar material. Carry B-in-Bs by the rootball, not the trunk. Follow the planting procedure for container plants. The roots of B-in-Bs do not need pruning.

Burlap and similar materials often do not readily decompose. Cut away any ties that fasten the material to the trunk, and cut away and remove the top and sides of the material that surrounds the rootball. The material on the bottom of the rootball can remain (Watson and Himelick 1997). Remove any wire or plastic baskets that surround the rootball.

Pruning at Planting

ANSI A-300 pruning standards state that pruning at planting should be limited to cleaning (6.2.6, 2008). Cleaning is the removal of dead, diseased, and broken branches.

Structural pruning, or training, of young trees involves cutting back or removing branches that crowd or compete with the central leader. If a healthy tree with good structure has been selected, little or no pruning at planting is required. If structural pruning is needed, it is best to do it one or two years after planting. Leaving as much foliage as possible on a young tree or shrub will help it establish more quickly. Removing branches diminishes the plant's energy reserves and temporarily slows root growth. Training young trees is discussed on page 121.

It has been a common practice to prune the top growth of a recently transplanted bare root or balled-in-bulap tree to compensate for root loss. The idea is that by removing foliage, the tree will transpire less water, and the plant's reduced water needs will be easier to meet by the compromised root system. Though there are different expert opinions, it is now generally agreed that pruning of this type is not necessary for a tree's successful establishment and may only benefit trees that will not receive regular irrigation. When this practice is performed, the focus is on the reduction or removal of a few poorly placed stems. Significant thinning or heading back all growth by one-third or more is not recommended.

Staking Young Trees

Young, unstaked trees that sway moderately in the wind develop a stronger trunk than staked ones. Therefore, young trees capable of developing properly without staking should be allowed to do so. Staking tends to hinder a tree's ability to stand without support. However, windy conditions can shift the roots of young trees, causing root damage and loss of anchorage; the bark of young trees is vulnerable to lawn mowers and string trimmers; and trees in public spaces are at risk for vandalism. For these reasons, young trees are commonly staked.

Garden stores and lumberyards sell support stakes made of treated wood that resists decay, though any narrow, sturdy piece of wood or steel can be used. Stake pounders are designed for the job, though a sledgehammer will work for the occasional planting. Broad, smooth, flexible ties made of cloth, elastic, rubber, or polyethylene garden tape are preferred. Note that rope, wire, garden hose, or strips made from old car tires may damage bark.

Protective Staking

Protective staking is sometimes used on young trees planted in turfgrass to keep foot traffic and power equipment away from bark tissues. Three or more stakes, three feet long each, are spaced evenly around the tree and hammered into the soil outside the rootball, 1 to 2 feet from the trunk. Approximately 2 feet of each stake should remain above ground, and the stakes should be clearly marked so they are visible to pedestrians. Ties are not used in protective staking.

An alternative to installing protective staking is to create mulched areas around young trees growing in turfgrass. For more information, see "Protecting Trees and Shrubs" on page 40 and "Mulching Landscape Plants" on page 79.

Anchor Staking

Anchor staking prevents a tree's rootball from shifting in the ground. Low-placed ties secure the trunk to stakes. The low tie placement is sufficient to keep the rootball from shifting, and it allows the upper portion of the tree to sway freely. This form of staking can be used on trees that are strong enough to remain upright on their own.

Two to three stakes are placed around the perimeter of the tree, roughly 1 foot from the trunk. The ties should loop around the trunk at about 1/3 the height of the tree. The stakes should not extend higher than the ties. Remove the ties after one season. Large transplants may benefit from two seasons of anchor staking.

Support Staking

Young trees that do not remain upright on their own require support staking. Three stakes can be used, though two is enough. If a single stake is used, there is a risk that the stake will rub against the trunk or branches, damaging the bark. Some commercial products safely use a single stake and tie.

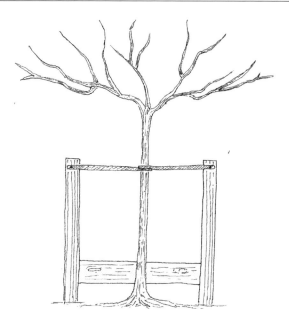

An illustration of support staking. Stakes enter the soil outside the rootball and do not extend higher than the ties. Ties should not be tightly attached to the trunk. In general, ties are removed after one growing season. Note that the low-placed, wood cross tie should not contact the trunk.

The higher the placement of the ties on the trunk, the greater the wind stress on the upper portions of the trunk—wind stress can even break a young trunk if the ties are placed too high. To determine the proper height of the ties, hold the trunk of the tree in one hand and bend the top of the tree with the other hand. Find the lowest support level on the trunk that enables the tree to return to an upright position after the top is deflected, then place the support ties 6 inches above this level. The support level should be a minimum of 3 feet below the top of the leader (Harris, Clark, and Matheny 2004). The absence of a second set of ties lower on the trunk provides the trunk with greater flexibility. Again, the lower the support ties can be placed while keeping the tree upright, the better.

Position the stakes outside the rootball, approximately 1 foot from the trunk, then hammer them into the soil. Once the ties are in place, saw off the stakes a few inches above the ties. Stakes that extend higher than necessary may brush against the trunk or limbs and damage the bark. Connect the stakes together with a low-placed 1" x 3" wood cross tie to keep them properly angled and spaced.

Remove the ties once the tree is able to remain upright on its own. Trees can usually stand on their own after one growing season. Larger trees may benefit from two seasons of support staking. Standards (multi-stemmed plants trained to a single-trunk form), such as crape myrtle trees, may also need several seasons of staking. Rose standards may need permanent staking.

Important: *Ties that remain in place longer than necessary cease to be of benefit and can damage bark or girdle a trunk. Follow up inspection and removal of ties is as important as proper installation.*

Mulching Landscape Plants

Mulch is any material spread on the soil surface to control weeds, reduce evaporation, and moderate soil temperature. Mulched areas can also serve as buffer zones between plants and power equipment. For these reasons and others, it is beneficial to apply mulch around the base of trees and shrubs at planting. Organic mulches are preferred because they contribute organic matter to the soil. Organic mulch can slowly improve soil structure and increase soil nutrient levels.

The majority of nutrient-absorbing tree and shrub roots are near the soil surface. Trees and shrubs growing in turfgrass must compete with the grass for water and nutrients. A ring of mulch around trees and shrubs growing in turfgrass reduces competition from the grass and substantially increases a tree's root and top growth.

For landscape trees up to 3 inches in caliper, a 6- to 9-foot diameter circle of mulch is best (Watson and Himelick 1997). For recent transplants, mulch can be applied one foot wider than the rootball the first year, then gradually expanded over the next several years as the tree develops.

Coarse-texture mulches can be applied up to 4 inches deep, while fine-texture mulches should be limited to a 2-inch depth. Keep mulch several inches away from the base of the trunk. Mulch that

A 4-inch layer of mulch will prevent many weeds from germinating and will smother many existing weeds. These uncomposted wood chips were dontated by a tree trimming business.

contacts the trunk can trap moisture and promote disease and insect damage.

Bark, shredded bark, composted wood chips, pine needles, and rock are common mulch materials. Synthetic products are also available. Uncomposted or raw wood chips are used by many gardeners because these materials suppress weeds and are usually free. At least one expert recommends applying wood chips 4 to 6 inches deep on ornamental sites (Chalker-Scott 2007). Do not use grass clippings as mulch because they can form a mat on the soil surface, restricting air and water penetration.

Add more mulch every few years, or more frequently, depending on how quickly the material decomposes. Fine-texture mulches scatter more easily and decompose more quickly than coarse-texture mulches. Nitrogen fertilizers can be applied directly to the surface of mulch.

Calculating the Amount of Mulch or Soil Amendment

To quickly calculate the amount of mulch or soil amendment needed, see table 10, on the next page. If the depth of mulch you're using isn't listed in table 10, use the following formula:

Cubic feet of mulch = square feet x depth of mulch (as fraction of 1 foot)

First, calculate the square feet of the area to be mulched. For a circular area around the base of a tree, use the formula 3.14 r^2 (3.14 x radius x radius), where radius is half the diameter of the circle. For example, a typical 6-foot diameter mulched area for a tree growing in turfgrass has a radius of 3 feet, so the formula is 3.14 x 3 x 3 = 28 square feet.

Next, convert the depth of mulch, say 4 inches, to a fraction of a foot as follows: 4" ÷ 12" = 0.33. Multiply the result by the square feet of the area to find the cubic feet of material required. This example is worked out as follows: 28 x 0.33 = 9 cubic feet of mulch to fill a 6-foot diameter circle to a depth of 4 inches. Slightly less will be required since the area near the trunk will not be covered. Formulas for some common mulch depths are included in table 10.

Table 10. Calculating Cubic Feet of Mulch*

2-inch mulch depth = sq. ft. of area x 0.167
3-inch mulch depth = sq. ft. of area x 0.25
4-inch mulch depth = sq. ft. of area x 0.33
*Divide the result by 27 to determine cubic yards.

For example, to cover 1000 square feet with 3 inches of bark, the calculation is as follows:

1000 x 0.25 = 250 cubic feet of mulch required.

250 ÷ 27 = 9.25 cubic yards required.

Alternative formula for cubic yards. Here is an alternative formula to determine the cubic yards of mulch to apply to 1000 square feet:

Cubic yards of mulch per 1000 sq. ft. = depth of mulch x 3.086

For example, to cover 1000 square feet with 3 inches of bark, the calculation is as follows: 3 x 3.086 = 9.25

yards. For cubic feet, multiply the cubic yards by 27 (e.g., 9.25 x 27 = 249.75 cubic feet).

Fertilizing Landscape Plants

The Turfgrass Management chapter includes a general introduction to fertilizer and its responsible use in the landscape (see page 44). As with turfgrass fertilization, the emphasis in landscape plant fertilization is on the three primary nutrients: nitrogen, phosphorus, and potassium. Of the three primary nutrients, nitrogen receives the most attention because it is the most important for plant growth and is deficient most frequently.

Experts often provide nitrogen recommendations in terms of "pounds of nitrogen per 1000 square feet". (See page 48 for an explanation of the term "pounds of nitrogen".) To determine how much fertilizer to apply based on these recommendations, some simple calculations are necessary. These are explained in "Calculating the Fertilization Area and Fertilizer Amount" on page 84.

Recommendations in terms of "pounds of nitrogen per 1000 square feet" are useful for fertilizing larger planting areas, but are less useful for fertilizing individual plants. To fertilize individual plants, follow the directions on the fertilizer label (e.g., "apply 1/2 cup along the dripline of each shrub").

Important. Nitrogen rate recommendations are usually the same for trees and shrubs, so you will see recommendations for tree fertilization here. However, tree fertilization is outside the services offered by most landscapers. Many tree problems can cause symptoms similar to nutrient deficiency symptoms. Without properly identifying and understanding the problem, you could apply fertilizer unnecessarily and exacerbate the problem. For this reason, the fertilization of mature trees should be left to a certified arborist.

Nitrogen at Planting

After transplant, a plant may devote more energy to regenerating its root system than to producing new top growth. Once the root system is established in the new location, the plant can resume its normal rate of top growth. Until then, the plant has a diminished capacity to absorb nutrients. For this reason, some experts recommend no nitrogen at planting; other experts make allowances for its use if it is applied at low rates and in slow-release forms. The low-nitrogen phase is said to last typically for a full year after planting (Rosen, Bierman, and Eliason 2008).

If you choose to apply nitrogen at planting, apply a slow-release fertilizer to the soil surface, according to the package instructions (see "Surface Application" on page 84). Quick-release nitrogen at planting may injure plant roots and should be avoided. There is no need to amend the backfill soil with nitrogen. Note that the rootballs of most container plants already contain fertilizer from the nursery.

Phosphorus and Potassium at Planting

Phosphorus is important for a healthy root system, and for this reason phosphorus is often associated with establishing new plantings. Many soils contain enough phosphorus for plant growth. When soil levels are adequate, it is unnecessary to add phosphate fertilizer at planting. A soil test conducted by a soil lab is the best way to determine if phosphorus and potassium are deficient in a soil and, if so, how much of these nutrients to apply. Local experts will also know if the soils in a region have common deficiencies.

If a soil test indicates the need for phosphorus or potassium, the best time to add these nutrients is at planting because fertilizer can be incorporated to the depth of a plant's root zone. Surface applications of phosphorus are less effective because phosphorus does not readily move through the soil as nitrogen does. When a phosphorus fertilizer has been amended into the backfill soil, phosphorus will remain available to a plant for an extended period of time—several years or longer on most soils. Potassium is a nutrient that binds to clay and organic matter particles. As a result, soil levels of this nutrient can also remain adequate for extended periods.

Nitrogen During Increased Growth Phase

As young trees and shrubs begin to become established, they enter an increased growth phase that can last one or more years. If rapid growth is sought during this phase, nitrogen can be applied at higher rates: 2 to 4 pounds of nitrogen per 1000 square feet per year. If rapid growth is not sought, 1 pound of nitrogen per 1000 square feet per year or less (or none) can be used.

Determining the Need to Fertilize Established Plants

Most soils contain enough nitrogen, phosphorus, potassium, and other nutrients to meet the needs of established plants. And many landscape trees and shrubs receive nutrients from turf fertilization. So the first question is whether an established plant requires fertilizer at all. In the absence of symptoms of nutrient deficiency, fertilization is probably not necessary. For instance, if the plant is growing adequately each season, has good leaf color, and has an overall healthy appearance, fertilizer is probably not needed.

If the plant exhibits poor color (light green or yellowish leaves), leaves that are smaller than normal, dead twigs at the end of branches, weak growth, or an unhealthy appearance, nutrient deficiency could be the cause, and fertilization may be helpful. However, these symptoms may be indications of other problems, which should be investigated first.

Soil compaction, root damage, lack of water, disease, or insect or pesticide damage are all possible causes of a plant's slow growth rate or unhealthy appearance. Sometimes nutrients are present in the soil but are not available to the plant. For instance, the availability of some micronutrients is influenced by soil pH. If a soil test indicates that the soil pH is too high or too low, the nutrient deficiency may be corrected once the soil pH has been adjusted. A soil test should be performed to help clarify a nutrient or soil pH problem. Coverage of soil pH and soil testing begins on page 105.

Fertilizing Established Trees and Shrubs

When fertilization is necessary, it should be done with a clear objective in mind, such as to increase growth, improve leaf color, or prevent or correct nutrient deficiencies. If soil or foliar (leaf tissue) analysis reveals nutrient deficiencies, the lab's test results will include fertilizer recommendations.

According to *ANSI A300: Tree, Shrub, and Other Woody Plant Maintenance*—the national fertilization standards used by many landscape and tree professionals:

- If slow-release fertilizers are used, they should be applied at rates between 2 and 4 pounds of nitrogen per 1000 square feet, not to exceed 6 pounds of nitrogen per 1000 square feet within 12 months. The amount of water insoluble nitrogen (WIN) should be considered (ANSI A300-2004, 14.2.3.1-2).

- If quick-release fertilizers are used, they should be applied at rates between 1 and 2 pounds of nitrogen per 1000 square feet per application, and shall not exceed 4 pounds of nitrogen per 1000 square feet every 12 months (ANSI A300-2004, 14.2.4).

The ANSI fertilization standards are broad parameters; they do not tell you how much nitrogen to use. The nitrogen fertilization rate depends on a number of factors, including the fertilization objective, plant species and age, the size of the planting area, plant stress levels, irrigation, and soil type. As a rule of thumb, use the least amount of nitrogen necessary to achieve the desired results.

When to Reduce Nitrogen Rates

Most trees and shrubs can tolerate higher nitrogen rates per application than turfgrass. The amount of nitrogen applied in a single application may need to be reduced in the following circumstances.

- On sites where there is a high potential for groundwater contamination from nitrate leaching, 1 pound of nitrogen, or less, per 1000 square feet per application is advisable. If necessary for plant health, several applications can be made during the growing season (Kujawski and Ryan 2000).

- Nitrogen rates for trees with confined root systems, such as street trees, or trees in planters or parking lot islands, should be based on the accessible root area, not the crown spread. These trees should be fertilized on the low side of recommended rates and the fertilizer should bedivided into split applications, made several times per year. Surface application, foliar spray, or another alternate method can be used (Hensley 2005).

- When fertilizing trees and shrubs growing in turf, do not exceed 1 pound of quick-release nitrogen per 1000 square feet to avoid burning the lawn. See "Fertilizer Application Methods" on page 84 for more information.

Fertilizing Palms

Palms have unique fertilization requirements. Use of the incorrect fertilizer on or near a palm can induce severe to fatal K and Mg deficiencies in palms. According to Broschat, "Research has shown that an analysis of 8–2–12 plus 4% Mg and micronutrients is effective on palms growing in sand and limestone soils throughout the Coastal Plain of the southeastern USA. However, there has been no comparable research for palms growing on other soil types in other parts of the country" (Broschat, pers. comm. 2011). Note that 100% of the N, K, and Mg should be in controlled release form because the sandy soils in this region leach nutrients quickly. The micronutrients should be in sulfate form; the exception is iron, which should be in chelate form (Broschat 2008).

The controlled-release palm fertilizer mentioned above should release nutrients for approximately three months, so it is typically applied at three month intervals. The preferred application method is to broadcast the fertilizer over the fertilization area. For more detailed information, including application rates, see "Fertilization of Field-grown and Landscape Palms in Florida" (Publication #ENH1009) at http://edis.ifas.ufl.edu/ep261. Note that palm maintenance fertilizers can be used to fertilize the entire landscape, including turfgrass; see page 55 for more information.

Timing of Tree and Shrub Fertilization

Apart from nitrogen, it is acceptable to apply macronutrients (phosphorus, potassium, calcium, sulfur, and magnesium) whenever the soil is above 40°F and will receive enough water. Fertilizer should not be applied during dry weather if the plants will not be irrigated, or when the soil is frozen. If applied in granular form, water-soluble micronutrients, such as boron and chelates of iron, manganese, and zinc, should be applied to the soil in summer or fall (Harris, Clark, and Matheny 2004).

Nitrogen fertilization of trees and shrubs should be timed so that nitrogen is most readily available to plants for their spring growth flush. In the text *Arboriculture: Integrated Management of Trees, Shrubs, and Vines* (2004), Harris, Clark, and Matheny say that mid-summer to early fall is usually the most effective time to apply nitrogen to trees and shrubs. Roots readily absorb nutrients at this time. Nutrients absorbed in summer and fall are stored in the plant during dormancy and are available for early spring growth.

Cold-winter regions. In regions with cold winters, nitrogen applied at the wrong time or in the wrong amount can encourage a tree or shrub to produce late-season growth that does not have time to harden off before winter. This tender growth can be damaged by freezing temperatures. Some experts say heavy amounts of nitrogen applied during dormancy or moderate rates during the early growing season may promote this late-season growth (Harris, Clark, and Matheny 2004).

Annuals and perennials. Annuals and perennials can be fertilized approximately once a month during the growing season. Longer intervals can be used with slow-release products.

Fertilizer Type

Established trees and shrubs can be fertilized with slow-release or quick-release nitrogen. Preference should be given to fertilizers with a minimum of 50 percent slow-release nitrogen when plant sensitivity or site conditions warrant, such as with new transplants, sandy soils, or trees and shrubs growing in turfgrass.

The fertilizer analysis will list slow-release nitrogen as coated (usually coated urea), natural organic, or water-insoluble (WIN). A product with 10 percent nitrogen contains 50 percent slow-release nitrogen if the total slow-release content is 5 percent.

Typical formulas of complete fertilizers for landscape plants are in the N-P-K (nitrogen-phosphorus-potassium) ratio of 3-1-1, 3-1-2, or 3-1-3 (Gill, Bosmans, MacLachlan 2001). A product with a fertilizer ratio of 3-1-2 has three times as much nitrogen as phosphorus and twice as much potassium as phosphorus. An example of a complete fertilizer with a 3-1-1 ratio is 12-4-4; an example of a complete fertilizer with a 3-1-2 ratio is 12-4-8.

In the absence of soil or foliar nutrient analysis, avoid fertilizers with a high ratio of P_2O_5 and K_2O (ANSI A300-2004, 14.2.1). Assuming that phosphorus and potassium levels are adequate and that the objective is to promote growth, you can consider using a fertilizer that contains only nitrogen (e.g., 12-0-0). To reduce the risk of injuring plants, tree and shrub fertilizers with a salt index of less than 50 are preferred (ANSI A300-2004, 14.2.5).

In addition to palms, a number of other plants have unique fertilizer requirements. Plant nurseries and garden centers commonly sell special fertilizer formulas for roses, citrus trees, "acid-loving" plants, and other plants. Note that certain acid-loving plants, such as azaleas and rhododendrons, have shallow root systems that can be harmed by high rates of quick-release nitrogen.

Do not fertilize trees and shrubs with "weed-and-feed" products containing 2,4-D or other herbicides. These fertilizer-herbicide products can damage or kill plants other than turfgrass. Follow the product label for specifics. Weed-and-feed is described on page 54. Finally, before starting a fertilization program, investigate if there are common regional nutrient deficiencies.

Calculating the Fertilization Area and Fertilizer Amount

To calculate the amount of fertilizer to apply based on a recommended nitrogen rate (e.g., 1 lb. N/1000 sq. ft.), you first need to calculate the square feet of the fertilization area. For most trees and shrubs, the fertilization area is measured from near the trunk to near or just beyond the dripline (ANSI A300-2004, 14.3.2). The dripline is the area of soil directly beneath the edge of the canopy of a tree, shrub, or group of shrubs. Note that tree roots may extend far beyond the dripline, though the fertilization area is not as large. The area from the trunk to the dripline contains a high concentration of feeder roots.

Do not apply fertilizer to the soil near the trunk of trees or shrubs. This "no-fertilizer" area extends approximately 2 to 3 feet around the trunk of mature trees and approximately 1 foot around the main stem of mature shrubs.

The fertilization area can be calculated with the formula: $3.14\,r^2$ (3.14 x radius x radius), where *3.14* (pi) is a mathematical constant, representing the ratio of a circle's circumference to its diameter, and *radius* is the distance from near the trunk to the dripline. For example, if the radius is 7 feet, the fertilization area is calculated as follows: 3.14 x 7 x 7 = 154 square feet.

Areas covered by sidewalks, driveways, or other paved areas are not included in the area calculation. Trees with restricted root systems, such as trees growing in a parking lot island, are typically either not fertilized or are fertilized at a low rate, using split applications.

Columnar tree forms have narrow canopies that are not representative of the root spread. For these forms, multiply the trunk diameter in inches at 4 1/2 feet above ground by 1 to 1 1/2 to find the fertilization radius, expressed in feet. For example, a columnar tree with an 8-inch trunk at 4 1/2 feet above ground would have a fertilization radius of 8 to 12 feet. Fastigiate tree forms also have narrow canopies, but have multiple smaller trunks; use a fertilization radius equal to the tree's height for these forms.

Fertilizer amount. Once you know the size of fertilization area, you can calculate the amount of fertilizer to apply. First, determine the amount of fertilizer to use per 1000 square feet by dividing the desired nitrogen rate by the percentage of nitrogen in the product. For example, if the desired nitrogen rate is 1 pound per 1000 square feet and the fertilizer grade is 24-6-12, the calculation is as follows: 1 ÷ 0.24 = 4.2 pounds of 24-6-12 per 1000 square feet.

Next, divide the square feet of the fertilization area by 1000 and multiply the result by the pounds of fertilizer per 1000 square feet. For example, if the fertilization area is 225 square feet, the calculation is as follows: 225 ÷ 1000 = 0.225. Finally, multiply this result by the pounds of fertilizer per 1000 square feet. For example: 0.225 x 4.2 = 0.95 pounds. This is the amount of 24-6-12 to apply to the 225 square foot fertilization area. Note that 1 liquid measuring cup holds approximately 8 ounces (roughly 1/2 pound) of granular fertilizer. Table 11 is a summary of how to calculate the fertilizer amount.

Table 11. Calculating the Fertilizer Amount

1. Calculate the fertilization area.

2. Calculate the amount of fertilizer to apply per 1000 square feet. To do this, divide the desired nitrogen rate (e.g., 1 lb. N/1000 sq. ft.) by the percentage of nitrogen in the product (e.g., 24-6-12 = 0.24). To illustrate: 1 ÷ 0.24 = 4.2 pounds of 24-6-12 per 1000 square feet.

3. Divide the area to be fertilized by 1000, and multiply the result by the pounds of fertilizer per 1000 square feet (from step 2). For example: 225 square feet ÷ 1000 = 0.225; 0.225 x 4.2 = 0.95 pounds of 24-6-12.

Fertilizer Application Methods

Surface Application

For nitrogen fertilizers, surface application is the most effective fertilization method because the nitrogen can be evenly distributed, and it will readily move into the root zone with rain or irrigation.

Chelated micronutrients can also be applied to the soil surface.

Avoid surface applications of nitrogen where run-off is likely, such as on slopes or bare, compacted soils. When fertilizing trees and shrubs growing in turfgrass, use no more than 1 pound of nitrogen per 1000 square feet to avoid burning the turf. If you need to apply a higher nitrogen rate, divide the total fertilizer amount into smaller applications, and separate the applications by four weeks. Another approach is to use a subsurface application method to place the nitrogen below the turf's root zone.

In general, phosphorus and potassium are more effective if they are placed within the soil profile: either incorporated into the backfill soil at planting or placed in drill holes around mature plants.

Subsurface Application

Subsurface application involves drilling holes in the soil around plants and placing fertilizer in the holes. Subsurface application does not distribute fertilizer as evenly as surface application, but it is a good choice when fertilizing sloped or compacted areas, or when applying phosphorus or potassium fertilizers.

The majority of tree and shrub feeder roots are shallow in the soil. If the holes are too deep, the nutrients will be beyond the plants' reach. Holes should be 2 to 4 inches in diameter, 4 to 8 inches deep, and spaced 12 to 36 inches apart (ANSI A300-2004). Holes can be placed in a grid pattern or in concentric circles. Avoid a 2- to 3-foot area near the trunk, and be careful not to damage large roots with drilling.

Distribute the fertilizer evenly among the holes. Use a funnel to prevent overspill. Leave the top 2 inches of the holes empty, and backfill them with soil or an organic soil amendment, such as compost. Fertilizer packets or tablets can be used as an alternative to granular fertilizer; use the rate recommended for the product.

Drilling may increase the oxygen level in the soil and it reduces soil compaction. The addition of an organic amendment to the holes can increase the latter benefit and is sometimes practiced without fertilizer. A gas-powered drill can be used. A powerful cordless electric drill may work for limited shrub fertilization.

Subsurface Liquid Injection. Subsurface liquid fertilizer injection also places nutrients in the root zone. Spacing and depth are approximately the same as for drill holes. Don't exceed a 12-inch depth. Nurseries and garden centers sell devices called root feeders that attach to a garden hose and use special fertilizer tablets.

Foliar Sprays

Foliar fertilization is sometimes used to correct micronutrient deficiencies. Spraying plant leaves with a liquid form of the deficient nutrient is a temporary solution until soil problems (e.g., low pH, compaction, or nutrient imbalances) can be corrected. Spray applications can also serve a diagnostic purpose.

Trunk Injection

Trunk injection is an application method used by certified arborists to temporarily alleviate minor nutrient deficiency in large-diameter trees. This technique is sometimes used when other methods are less effective. For instance, an iron-deficient tree with most of its roots covered by pavement may be a candidate for this method. Trunk injection is also sometimes used in the application of systemic insecticides. A drawback of injection is that injection areas can become entry points for insects and disease.

Irrigating Landscape Plants

The irrigation of established woody ornamental trees and shrubs is generally less involved and less critical than the irrigation of turfgrass. Some established landscape plants have extensive root systems and are capable of meeting all their water requirements from rain water alone. Other established plants need more water than rain water typically provides and require regular irrigation at certain times of year. Most landscape plants require irrigation during their establishment period.

Irrigating During Establishment Period

Plants lose roots during transplant. Some plants are grown in the ground and a large percentage of their roots are severed at harvest (e.g., bare root stock). Even briefly exposing a rootball to air during transplant can destroy some of the small root hairs that absorb water and nutrients. Because of this root loss, plants are in a compromised condition for a period of time after transplant.

After planting, a plant must begin to spread roots into the new soil environment. During this time, known as the establishment period, the plant's growth rate is reduced, and the plant is more susceptible to moisture stress. The faster the plant can grow roots into the surrounding soil, the sooner it can resume its normal growth rate, and the sooner it will be able to go without supplemental water. Special attention must be paid to irrigation during the establishment period because optimal root growth depends on adequate soil moisture.

Dry soil hinders root growth and increases the time it takes for a plant to become established. Saturated soil contains low oxygen levels, which also hinder root growth and can kill a plant. Plant roots grow fastest in a moist soil environment. Irrigation should be frequent enough to maintain a fairly constant level of soil moisture, without saturating the soil for extended periods.

Soil Moisture in the Rootball

Until a plant is established, the majority of its roots are located in the rootball. Initial irrigation efforts should focus on keeping the soil in the rootball moist. This often requires frequent irrigation because a plant can quickly deplete the water in the rootball. Even if plant water use is minimal, a fine-texture soil that surrounds the rootball can have a sponge-like effect, pulling moisture out of the rootball—the rootball can dry out while the surrounding soil remains wet.

One strategy to keep the rootball moist without saturating the surrounding soil is to build a small watering basin around the perimeter of the rootball and a larger basin outside the small one. The larger basin can be irrigated at longer intervals.

Scheduling During Establishment Period

Water as needed to ensure that the soil in the rootball and a little of the surrounding soil stays moist, though not saturated or wet, for the first 4 to 6 weeks or longer after planting. Soil moisture can be checked by digging a small hole next to the rootball with a hand trowel and inserting a finger into the side of the rootball toward the base. Increase or decrease the irrigation interval or the amount of water applied, as necessary. See "Estimating Soil Moisture" on page 57 for more information.

Another approach is to water the inner basin every day for several days after planting, then let the plant go without water until it begins to show the first signs of wilting. According to Harris, Clark, and Matheny in the text *Arboriculture: Integrated Management of Trees, Shrubs, and Vines* (2004), "An interval 1 day less than the wilting interval can then be used for irrigation for 2 to 3 weeks. Repeat the wilting experiment to adjust the irrigation schedule later" (p. 201. Reprinted by permission of Pearson Education, Inc., Upper Saddle River, New Jersey). The outer basin may only need water every 2 to 3 weeks.

As roots develop during the first growing season, the watering interval can be increased, and the irrigated area can be expanded. According to Watson and Himelick (1997), even as the root system begins to expand into the backfill soil, the rootball remains the most important place to check the soil moisture for the first two years after planting.

Micro-irrigation (drip irrigation) is well-suited to frequent, low-volume irrigation of the rootball. Bubbler irrigation nozzles are also effective. Hand-watering is also common before establishment. Do not rely on the turfgrass irrigation schedule to water young plants growing in turfgrass; micro-irrigation or hand-watering is still necessary. The turf irrigation schedule will meet the water requirements of most established plants growing in turfgrass.

Length of Establishment Period

A plant is established when it resumes the growth rate it had before transplant. According to Watson and Himelick (1997), "A woody plant may be considered established when the watering cycle can be extended to at least two weeks during warm summer weather without substantial water stress."

How long it takes for a tree or shrub to become established depends on the climate, the plant species, the plant size, the soil type, and post-planting care. Plants in regions with warm soil temperatures for much of the year produce more root growth in a single season than plants in regions with colder winters. And transplants with smaller diameter trunks take less time to become established than those with larger diameter trunks.

Many young trees take one to three years to become established. A rule of thumb is to allow one year per inch of trunk caliper (diameter) for establishment. For example, a young tree with a 2-inch caliper trunk will take approximately two years to become established, with variation according to region and plant species.

Irrigating Established Plants

Many established landscape plants have extensive root systems that draw water from an area of soil that is larger than the plants' branch spread. This allows woody ornamental trees and shrubs to survive without supplemental water. Some ornamental plants need more water than is available from rain water and require supplemental irrigation. Many landscape plants, including many large trees, benefit from irrigation during hot weather.

A plant's foliage can indicate the need for irrigation. A plant experiencing moisture stress will sometimes wilt or exhibit greyish-green leaf color, leaf drop, or leaves smaller in size than usual. Stems may also wither or die back. Other problems, such as a mineral deficiency or a root disease, can cause similar symptoms. Wilting may also be a sign of too much water.

In the absence of symptoms of moisture stress, irrigation is probably not necessary. If a plant shows symptoms of moisture stress, check the soil moisture in the plant's root zone, as explained on page 57. If the soil is more than 40 to 50 percent moisture deficient, irrigation may help. Note that the appearance of the soil surface is not a reliable indicator of the amount of water a soil contains. Even if the surface is dry, the soil may contain enough available water for plants.

Tree roots can extend two to three times the distance of the canopy, sometimes farther. A reasonable irrigation area extends from near the trunk to near or just beyond the dripline (the area of soil beneath the edge of the canopy). Note that the fine roots of most trees and shrubs are relatively shallow in the soil. Specifically, fine roots are concentrated in the top 12 inches of soil, with many in the top 2 inches of soil (Gilman 2009).

Irrigation Guidelines for Established Plants

The following guidelines can be used to irrigate established woody landscape plants.

- Irrigation should replenish the available water in the plant's root zone. (Sometimes only a portion of the root zone is irrigated; see page 94.) Whether this is done through deep, infrequent watering or shallow, frequent watering depends on the maturity of the plant, the irrigation system, and, to some extent, personal preference. Micro-irrigation systems are well-suited to shallow, frequent irrigation and are often designed to be run every few days to maintain an ideal moisture level in the root zone. (Available water is explained on page 59.)

- When irrigating plants growing in coarse-texture soils (e.g., sand), use shorter irrigation run times and irrigate more frequently. Applying too much water to sandy soil will cause water to drain below the rootzone, and nutrients will be leached in the process. Clay soils have slower infiltration capacities. If runoff is a problem on clay soil, use multiple cycling as described on page 65. Micro-irrigation systems typically do not cause runoff. A watering basin around a plant's dripline will also curb runoff. See "Soil Type" on page 59 for more detail.

- Water use restrictions during drought may limit the amount of water available for use in the landscape. Of landscape plants, trees are the highest priority for irrigation because they are the most difficult to replace. Irrigate trees every two to three weeks during drought. (Oaks have unique irrigation guidelines; consult a certified arborist or certified nursery professional for advice.) Apply water near the tree's dripline to a depth of $1 1/2$ feet. During dry winter months, irrigate trees and shrubs at least once a month.

- Two to four inches of mulch reduces evaporation and suppresses weeds. For more information, see "Mulching Landscape Plants" on page 79.

- Soil compaction hinders the movement of water and nutrients to plant roots. Plants in compacted soils can benefit from soil aeration and the application of organic mulch around their bases. Keep mulch away from trunks.

- Early morning irrigation allows water to soak in before the evaporative heat of midday.

- Wetting the trunk or the soil at the base of the trunk of trees and shrubs can increase the risk of crown rot disease (Phytophthora). Use low-angle sprinklers or stream splitters to avoid wetting trunks, and place drip emitters at least one foot away from trunks.

- The high salt content of some irrigation water can injure or mar the appearance of plant foliage. Drip irrigation keeps saline water off leaves. If saline water is applied with sprinklers, longer irrigation run times and longer intervals between irrigations may help to prevent damage to foliage.

- Do not fertilize when a plant shows signs of moisture stress.

- Plants are commonly grouped into high, moderate, or low water use zones. When possible, keep landscape plants with similar water needs in the same irrigation zone (hydrozone).

ET-Based Water Requirements

Scientists continue to develop sophisticated methods of estimating plant water requirements based on evapotranspiration (ET) data. ET-based scheduling methods are somewhat technical, and it is not necessary to use them to successfully maintain plants, though their use can increase water savings.

For an introduction to evapotranspiration, see "ET_0 and K_c: Reference Evapotranspiration and Crop Coefficient" on page 61.

The following is an overview of ET-based irrigation scheduling for landscape plants; it is not intended to be complete or to substitute for the instruction found in the source material. For complete instruction, see *A Guide to Estimating Irrigation Water Needs of Landscape Plantings in California: The Landscape Coefficient Method and WUCOLS III* (Leaflet 21493) by Costello, Matheny, and Clark. WUCOLS III is a list of species factors found in Part II of the guide.

A Guide to Estimating Irrigation Water Needs of Landscape Plantings in California can be downloaded from the website of the California Department of Water Resources at http://www.water.ca.gov/wateruseefficiency/publications. The publication was written for landscape professionals in California, though the information can be used in other areas of the country.

In the turfgrass management chapter (page 61) we looked at the ET_c formula: $ET_c = K_c \times ET_0$, which basically says that to determine how much water a plant uses (the ET_c), you multiply the crop coefficient (K_c) by the reference ET (ET_0).

The same basic formula is used to estimate the ET rate for landscape plants. However, instead of using the crop coefficient (K_c), the landscape coefficient (K_L) is used.

$$ET_L = K_L \times ET_0$$

ET_L = Landscape evapotranspiration
K_L = Landscape coefficient
ET_0 = Reference evapotranspiration

In other words, to determine the evapotranspiration rate of a planting area (ET_L), you multiply the landscape coefficient (K_L) by the reference evapotranspiration (ET_0).

The Landscape Coefficient Formula; Determining K_L

Unlike agricultural crops, landscape planting areas are often comprised of different species of trees and shrubs, planted at varying densities, and affected by unique microclimate conditions. Each of these factors affects the amount of water a planting area requires. The *landscape coefficient formula* attempts to address these factors. The landscape coefficient formula is as follows:

$$K_L = k_s \times k_d \times k_{mc}$$

This means that to determine the landscape coefficient (K_L), you multiply the species factor (k_s) by the density factor (k_d) by the microclimate factor (k_{mc}). These factors reflect the water use of a planting area, as affected by the different plant species, the density of planting, and the microclimate features. Note that some landscape coefficient formulas use additional factors.

The challenge of the landscape coefficient formula is in choosing factors that accurately reflect the species, microclimate, and density of the planting area being watered. Imprecise selection of factors results in diminished usefulness of the landscape coefficient. The guidelines for selecting factors presented here are not intended to be complete. For complete instruction, see *A Guide to Estimating Irrigation Water Needs of Landscape Plantings in California.*

Species factor (k_s)

Species factors for many trees, shrubs, and groundcovers can be found in WUCOLS III. The species factor is selected based on the plant's water requirement. Plants with high water requirements are assigned a higher species factor than plants with low water requirements. When a planting area contains plants with varying water requirements, a factor is selected for the plant with the highest water needs (Costello and others 2000).

In choosing a species factor, experience with the irrigation needs of landscape plant species in a region is helpful. Local experts, such as extension service agents or certified nursery professionals, can also assist with species factor selection. Note that values in between those listed in table 12 may be appropriate for some plants. Species with very low water requirements may be assigned a species factor of 0.1 or less.

Table 12. Species Factor (k_s) for Plant Types

Vegetation [a]	High	Average	Low
Trees [b]	0.9	0.5	0.2
Shrubs	0.7	0.5	0.2
Groundcover [c]	0.9	0.5	0.2
Mixture of trees, shrubs, and ground cover [d]	0.9	0.5	0.2
Turfgrass: [e]			
Cool season	—	0.8	—
Warm season	—	0.6	—

Table and notes from *Landscape Irrigation Scheduling and Water Management*, Irrigation Association 2005; reproduced with permission.

Table 12 notes: "In the table, the 'average' k_s values represent the typical or average species factor, in relation to water use, within a given vegetation category. Similarly, the 'high' values represent the high end of the range of species factors within the category and the 'low' values represent the low end of the range. For instance, the low range for groundcover is 0.2 which is appropriate for a selected group of drought tolerant groundcover species. However, this value may not be appropriate for many typical ornamental groundcovers.

a. The tree, shrub, and groundcover categories listed are for landscapes that are composed solely or predominantly of one of these vegetation types.

b. Species values for trees were based on research from agricultural tree crops.

c. Groundcover estimates were based on preliminary research findings in California.

d. Mixed plantings are composed of two or all three vegetation types (i.e., where a single vegetation type does not predominate).

e. This category was added by the Irrigation Association to distinguish between warm and cool season turfgrasses.

Note: It is important to consult with local sources including land grant universities, extension agencies or water purveyors for the correct species factor (k_s) to apply to the plants in each hydrozone. If warranted, it is entirely appropriate to use values in between those listed in the table, or values not listed in the table."

Density factor (k_d)

The density factor is selected based on the "collective leaf area" of all plants in the irrigation zone. Planting areas with greater leaf area lose more water to evapotranspiration than areas with less leaf area. Areas of shrubs and ground cover that provide less than 90 percent ground shading (canopy cover) are considered "low". Less than 70 percent ground shading for trees is considered "low". Zones with full coverage by only one plant type (e.g., all ground cover) are considered "average". Areas with multiple tiers of plants (e.g., trees over shrubs) can raise the density factor (Costello and others 2000). See the *A Guide to Estimating Irrigation Water Needs of Landscape Plantings in California* guide for more guidance in selecting a density factor.

Table 13. Density Factor (k_d) for Plant Types

Vegetation	High	Average	Low
Trees	1.3	1.0	0.5
Shrubs	1.1	1.0	0.5
Groundcover	1.1	1.0	0.5
Mixture of trees, shrubs, and ground cover	1.3	1.0	0.6
Turfgrass	1.0	1.0	0.6

Table and notes from *Landscape Irrigation Scheduling and Water Management*, Irrigation Association 2005; reproduced with permission.

Table 13 notes: "The table assumes that bare soil surfaces within the landscape planting are not wetted by irrigation. Otherwise, k_d should be increased 10 to 20% due to soil surface evaporation, especially for trees and shrubs.

Note: Worst case, if the k_{mc} and k_d adjustments cannot be determined, then set them to one. In doing so however, K_L becomes k_s, and opportunities for additional water savings may be missed."

Microclimate factor (k_{mc})

Planting areas that have conditions similar to reference evapotranspiration conditions (i.e., the site is not excessively windy, exposed to heat-increasing landscape features, or shady) are considered "average". Areas that experience an increase in plant water use from heat, such as exposed planting areas surrounded by concrete or an area that receives reflective heat from a building, are considered "high". Areas exposed to excessive wind are also considered "high". "Low" is assigned to areas that use less water than average, such as an area shaded by trees or buildings for the majority of the day (Costello and others 2000). See table 14.

Table 14. Microclimate Factor (k_{mc})

Vegetation	High	Average	Low
Trees	1.4	1.0	0.5
Shrubs	1.3	1.0	0.5
Groundcover	1.2	1.0	0.5
Mixture of trees, shrubs, and ground cover	1.4	1.0	0.5
Turfgrass	1.2	1.0	0.8

From *Landscape Irrigation Scheduling and Water Management*, Irrigation Association 2005; reproduced with permission.

Calculating the Landscape Coefficient (K_L)

Once factors have been selected, the landscape coefficient can be calculated. Example: Using tables 12, 13, and 14, the landscape coefficient for a landscape planting with one plant species of low water use planted as a groundcover at 100 percent coverage in a parking lot island is calculated as follows:

$$K_L = k_s \times k_d \times k_{mc}$$

$$K_L = 0.2 \times 1.0 \times 1.2 = 0.24$$

Calculating Landscape Evapotranspiration (ET$_L$)

Once you have the landscape coefficient, you can calculate the landscape water requirement (ET$_L$). For example, if the landscape coefficient is 0.24 and the reference evapotranspiration (ET$_O$) for a location is 10.64 inches for the month of July, the ET$_L$ is calculated as follows:

$$ET_L = K_L \times ET_O$$

$$ET_L = 0.24 \times 10.64 = 2.55 \text{ inches}$$

The planting area requires 2.55 inches of water in the month of July. You can also estimate the daily ET$_L$ by using a daily reference ET. For example, if the daily reference ET is 0.35 inches, the daily ET$_L$ is calculated as follows: 0.24 x 0.35 = 0.084 inches of water per day.

Application Efficiency (EA)

The ET$_L$ is how much water a planting area requires. Since no irrigation system is 100 percent efficient, the amount of water applied should be greater than the ET$_L$. To calculate how much water to apply through irrigation, you need to estimate the efficiency of the irrigation system.

See "EA: Application Efficiency" on page 63 for information on estimating the efficiency of a spray head system. The efficiency of a micro-irrigation system can be estimated to be 85 percent in a dry-warm or hot climate, 90 percent in a moderate climate, and 95 percent in a humid climate (Kourik 1992). Drip systems that don't use pressure-compensating emitters typically have lower efficiency.

Total Water to Apply in Inches

Once you estimate the irrigation system's application efficiency, you can calculate the amount of water to apply using the following formula:

$$TWA = \frac{ET_L}{EA}$$

This means that to calculate the total water applied (TWA), you divide the landscape evapotranspira-

tion (ET$_L$) by the application efficiency (EA). For example, using an ET$_L$ of 2.55 inches and an application efficiency of 70 percent, the total water to apply is calculated as follows:

$$TWA = \frac{2.55}{0.70} = 3.64 \text{ inches}$$

In this example, the planting area requires 2.55 inches of water for the month, but 3.64 inches should be applied, because of the limited efficiency of the irrigation system. For daily TWA, divide the daily ET$_L$ by the application efficiency. For example, 0.084 ÷ 0.70 = 0.12 inches per day.

ET-Based Scheduling

Once the TWA of a planting area has been calculated, you can determine the irrigation run time and frequency. Below are two methods of calculating the irrigation run time. Method 1 is simpler, but you need to determine the irrigation frequency on your own. Method 2 adapts the run time and frequency equations used for turfgrass. The irrigation factors used in the equations (e.g., PR, AWHC, MAD, etc.) are explained on page 57.

Method 1: Run Time

To calculate run time you have to know the irrigation system's precipitation rate (PR). Run time can be calculated using the following formula:

$$\text{Run Time} = \frac{\text{TWA (in inches per day or month)}}{\text{PR (in inches per hour)}} \times 60 \text{ min.}$$

Where: *TWA* refers to the total water applied for a planting area; see the previous topic "Total Water to Apply in Inches".

PR refers to the precipitation rate of the irrigation system. See "PR: Precipitation Rate" on page 62 for a method of estimating the PR of a spray head system. A method of estimating the application rate of one configuration of micro-irrigation system is shown on page 95.

Example: The TWA of a planting area is estimated to be 3.64 inches per month. The precipitation rate of the irrigation system is 1 inch per hour. The formula is as follows:

$$\text{Run Time} = \frac{3.64}{1.0} \times 60 = 218 \text{ min. per month}$$

A daily run time can be calculated using the daily TWA:

$$\text{Run Time} = \frac{0.12}{1.0} \times 60 = 7.2 \text{ min. per day}$$

Divide the monthly run time into multiple applications to avoid runoff or percolation beneath the root zone. Keep in mind that new plantings require frequent irrigation.

Method 2, Part 1: Irrigation Frequency Equation

Method 2 is calculated in two parts: Part 1 is the frequency equation, part 2 is the run time equation. The frequency equation is used to calculate how often to run the irrigation system. This is the same equation used to calculate irrigation frequency for turfgrass except that K_L has been substituted for K_c.

$$\text{Frequency} = \frac{\text{AWHC} \times \text{RZ} \times \text{MAD}}{\text{ET} \times K_L}$$

Example: Using the landscape coefficient formula, you determine the K_L of a planting area to be 0.24. The plants are growing in clay loam. The location is Scottsdale, Arizona, where summer conditions are hot and dry.

  AWHC for clay loam = 1.85 inches (From table 5, page 60.)

  RZ for established plants = 1 foot

  MAD = 40 percent (From page 60.)

  ET for hot dry = 0.30-0.40 (From table 7, page 62.)

  $K_L = 0.24$

Based on these values, the equation is as follows:

$$\text{Frequency} = \frac{1.85 \times 1.0 \times 0.40}{0.35 \times 0.24} = \frac{0.74}{0.084} = 8.8$$

According to the equation, this planting area should be irrigated approximately every 9 days. This estimate is for established plants. Recent transplants would require more frequent irrigation.

Method 2, Part 2: Irrigation Run Time Equation

The run time equation is used to calculate how long to irrigate at each interval. This is the same equation used to calculate a run time for turfgrass except that K_L has been substituted for K_c.

$$\text{Run Time} = \frac{60 \times F \times \text{ET} \times K_L}{\text{PR} \times \text{EA}}$$

Example: Using the landscape coefficient formula, you determine the K_L of a planting area to be 0.24. The plants are growing in clay loam in Scottsdale, Arizona during summer. The sprinkler system's average precipitation rate is 1 inch per hour, and the application efficiency is estimated to be 70 percent. "F" stands for frequency of irrigation (the watering interval, in days), which is determined using the frequency equation.

  F = 9-day interval (Based on frequency example.)

  ET for "hot dry" = 0.30-0.40 (From table 7, page 62.)

  $K_L = 0.24$

  PR = 1

EA = 70%

Based on these values, the equation is as follows:

$$\text{Run Time} = \frac{60 \times 9 \times 0.35 \times 0.24}{1 \times 0.70} = \frac{45.4}{0.70} = 65$$

According to the run time and frequency equations, this planting area should be watered for 65 minutes every 9 days.

The scheduling equations are meant to be used alongside your observations. If the schedule results in wilting, stress, or runoff, make the necessary adjustments.

Micro-irrigation

Micro-irrigation, also called drip or point source irrigation, supplies low volumes of water at low pressure above a plant's root zone. Micro-irrigation avoids the water waste associated with overspray from spray heads. And the slow application of water from micro-irrigation helps to maintain an ideal air/water balance in a plant's root zone.

Micro-irrigation systems attach to irrigation valves or outside faucets. Attached to the valve is the micro-irrigation main assembly, which typically consists of a backflow preventer, a filter, a pressure regulator, and sometimes a fertilizer injector. The backflow preventer prevents water in the irrigation lines from returning to the house's water supply; the filter removes contaminates that could clog emitters; the pressure regulator reduces the water pressure to approximately 25 psi; and the fertilizer injector allows special fertilizer to be delivered to plants through the irrigation system.

Drip hose, or tubing, attaches to the main assembly and conducts water to the planting area. Sometimes PVC pipe serves as a sub-main line, connecting the valve to a remote drip-tube connection. Drip tubing is a flexible polyethylene tubing that is buried or laid on the soil surface in the planting area. Various types of tubing can be used in the planting area. Porous pipe (soaker hose) has tiny holes that leak water onto the soil surface. In-line emitter tubing has built-in drip emitters. Solid drip hose is designed for use with separate emitters. A hole punch is used to make holes in solid tubing, and emitters of various flow rates and watering patterns are inserted.

Different diameters of drip hose can support different volumes of water over varying lengths. Table 15 on the next page shows some common drip tubing sizes and capacities. Different sources may list different capacities. In-line emitter tubing, which is not listed, has different capacities from those of solid drip hose.

Note that there are several sizes of drip tubing labeled as 1/2 inch. (The following sizing descriptions are standardized in many locations, but may not be universal to all manufacturers; check the manufacturer's specifications before purchasing.) The typical hardware-store variety of 1/2-inch tubing is 0.620 outer diameter (OD) and has green rings on fittings. Commercial 1/2-inch tubing is 0.700 OD with black rings on fittings or 0.710 OD with blue rings on fittings. (Commercial 3/4-inch tubing is typically 0.940 OD with grey rings on fittings.)

Note that Rain Bird makes multi-diameter compression fittings, as part of their Easy-Fit Compression Fitting System. Easy-Fit compression fittings work with a range of 1/2-inch polyethylene tubing sizes (0.630" to 0.710", or 16mm–18mm OD).

Bubblers, micro-sprays, and drippers are some of the emitters that can be used with solid drip hose. Each emitter type is available in different flow rates. Table 15 can be used to determine the number of emitters solid drip hose can support. For example, if 240 feet of 1/2-inch drip hose can supply 235 gallons per hour, 235 one-gallon-per-hour drip emitters can be used on that line. You can determine the number of 1/2-gallon-per-hour emitters the drip hose can support as follows: 235 ÷ 0.5 = 470 emitters. Exceeding the hose's gallons-per-hour capacity can reduce the water pressure and diminish the flow rates on the line.

Plants with similar water requirements are often planted in the same area to conserve water and simplify irrigation scheduling. When plants with

Solid drip hose joined by a compression "T". Fitting sizes are color-coded. There are slightly different sizes labeled as ½ inch.

markedly different water requirements are ir-rigated in the same micro-irrigation zone, more emitters are placed near the plants with greater water needs. In this way, one irrigation schedule can meet a range of plant water requirements. Note that all the emitters on a drip tube should be the same flow rate. Mixing emitters of different flow rates on a drip tube can create water waste, as the some of the water released by the larger emitters may percolate below the root zone.

Plant health and appearance can often be main-tained by irrigating a limited volume of soil in a plant's root zone. According to Harris, Clark, and Matheny, emitters should wet 50 to 75 percent of the soil within the dripline or within a diameter equal to the plant's height, whichever is greater (2004). Under certain conditions, it may be appropriate to wet a larger or smaller percentage of soil within the dripline. (The dripline is the area of greatest feeder root concentration.) As the plant matures and

the dripline increases, emitters should be moved farther out, and more emitters may be required.

Drip emitters create different wetting patterns in different soil types. Water moves horizontally and vertically in all soils. In coarse-texture soils, such as sand, the predominant movement of water is downward, and the wetting pattern resembles a thin oval. In medium-texture soils, such as loam, a half-circle wetting pattern is created beneath the soil surface. In fine-texture soils, such as clay, wa-ter penetrates downward slowly and more readily spreads horizontally, resulting in a shallow, broad wetting pattern.

With knowledge of wetting patterns, you can space emitters to create a zone of continuous soil mois-ture, which is useful for dense planting areas. For a zone of continuous moisture, spacing between drip emitters *and* rows of drip tubing is, in general, 12 inches for coarse-texture soils, 18 inches for medium-texture soils, and 24 inches for fine-texture soils (Rain Bird 2000). In-line emitters provide this set spacing. Not all planting areas require a zone of continuous moisture.

Micro-Irrigation Scheduling

A practical way to schedule micro-irrigation sys-tems is to check the plants for signs of moisture stress, sample the soil moisture in the plants' root zones, and make the appropriate scheduling adjustments. If necessary, add or remove emitters

Table 15. Maximum GPH and Maximum Length of Common Drip Tubing

Tubing	Size	PSI	Max. gph	Max. length (flat ground)
Feeder	1/8" 1/4"	20 20	15 30	5' 15'
Solid Drip Hose	3/8" (400) 1/2" (700) 3/4" (900)	25 25 25	110 235 475	120' 240' 300'

Adapted from *Drip Irrigation for Every Landscape and All Climates,* Kourik 1992, p. 87. http://www.robertkourik.com.

to match the water use of individual plants. When adding emitters, the new emitters should have the same flow rate as the existing ones. Run the system long enough to replenish the available water in the effective root zones. Note that a common problem with micro-irrigation scheduling is that systems are not run long enough. For more information on micro-irrigation, see "Micro-Irrigation System Maintenance" on page 176.

Application Rate of In-line Emitter Tubing in a Grid

The flow rate of a micro-irrigation system is measured in gallons per hour or gallons per minute. The following formula enables you to calculate the application rate in inches per hour for micro-irrigation systems that are laid out in a grid pattern. The formula assumes that all emitters have the same flow rate.

Application rate =

$$\frac{231.1 \times \text{emitter flow rate (gph)}}{\text{Dripline spacing (") x Emitter spacing(")}}$$

Where: *Application rate* is the inches of water the system applies per hour.

231.1 converts gallons per hour to cubic inches per hour. For millimeters per hour, multiply instead by 9113.

Emitter flow rate is the flow rate of one emitter in gallons per hour (gph). In-line emitters have the same flow rate.

Dripline spacing refers to the distance, in inches, between the rows of drip tubing. For example, a drip system may have 4 rows of drip tubing, each spaced 24 inches apart.

Emitter spacing is the space, in inches, between emitters in the in-line drip tubing.

Example. A planting area has 3 rows of in-line emitter tubing spaced 18 inches apart. The tubing has emitters spaced 12 inches apart, and each emitter

has a flow rate of 1 gallon per hour. The application rate is calculated as follows:

$$\frac{231.1 \times 1 \text{ gallon per hour}}{18 \text{ inches x } 12 \text{ inches}} = 1.07 \text{ in./hr.}$$

Soil

Plant roots absorb water and nutrients through the soil. Favorable soil conditions support optimal plant growth and health; poor soil conditions hinder plant growth and diminish plant health. With a basic understanding of soil, you can adopt practices that improve less-than-ideal soil conditions and that maintain the benefits of fertile soil. From a practical standpoint, an understanding of soil will inform your decisions regarding planting, irrigating, fertilizing, and even mowing.

This chapter provides a brief introduction to soil structure, soil texture, soil types, organic matter, soil pH, and other topics. The emphasis is on measures you can take to promote fertile soil in the landscape.

Soil

Soil consists of minerals, organic matter, air, water, and living organisms. Optimal soil conditions for plant growth include a porous soil structure that contains adequate levels of oxygen and water; organic matter; soil organisms and microorganisms to conduct beneficial chemical processes; and a sufficient amount of available nutrients. In these ideal soil conditions, plants have what they need to thrive. If the soil lacks nutrients, drains poorly, or has too little space for oxygen, plants will not grow well and will be more susceptible to drought stress and disease.

Soil Structure

Soil contains mineral particles of different sizes. Sand particles are the largest, ranging from 2.00 to 0.05 mm; silt particles are smaller than sand particles and range from 0.05 to 0.002 mm; and clay particles are less than 0.002 mm. Soil particles, along with organic matter, naturally adhere to each other, forming larger structures or aggregates. Soil structure refers to the arrangement of soil particles and the space between them.

Soil structure affects a number of soil properties, including water infiltration and drainage (permeability), root penetration, and the availability of nutrients. Soil structure also affects soil porosity—that is, the amount of pore space that exists between soil particles or aggregates. Pore space affects the volume of water and air the soil can hold. Fine-texture soils, such as clay, have greater porosity than coarse-texture soils, such as sandy soil. As a result, fine-texture soils can hold more water than coarse-texture soils.

Soil structure is influenced by soil texture, organic matter, burrowing insects, and microorganisms such as bacteria and fungi. To illustrate, as earthworms burrow through soil, they loosen and aerate it, improving soil porosity. Microorganisms decompose organic matter until it becomes humus, which is a spongy, porous substance composed of organic compounds. Among other benefits, humus retains nutrients and soil moisture, and improves soil structure.

Soil structure can be negatively affected by various landscaping practices, including tillage and the use of chemicals that are harmful to soil organisms. Foot and machine traffic, particularly in wet soil conditions, can compress the soil and lead to soil compaction. One of the primary ways gardeners attempt to improve soil structure is by incorporating nutrient-rich organic matter into the soil. An organic amendment will improve drainage or water retention, depending on the existing soil type. Organic matter also serves as food for microorganisms, increasing their activity and, in turn, their beneficial effects on soil structure.

Soil Texture

Soil scientists assign a textural classification to a soil based on the ratio of sand, silt, and clay particles it contains. Organic matter is not considered when determining soil texture. In the U.S., there are 12 textural classes. Each textural class has unique physical properties that affect water infiltration and drainage, nutrient availability, and more. We look at some of these physical properties when we discuss soil types.

The major textural classes are sand, silt, and clay. Loam is another textural class; it is comprised of a relatively balanced proportion of sand, silt, and clay particles. Other textural classes are loamy sand, sandy clay, silty clay, sandy loam, clay loam, silty clay loam, sandy clay loam, and silt loam. The names describe the textural composition of the soil. For example, sandy loam is loam with a high percentage of sand, and clay loam is loam with a high percentage of clay.

Ribbon test. Short of a soil texture test conducted by a soil lab, the simplest way to determine a soil's texture is by performing a ribbon test, which is done as follows: Start by shaping a small piece of moistened soil into a ball. Using your thumb and forefinger, try to form the ball into a ribbon. Sandy soil will feel gritty and loose, and it will not form a ribbon. Sandy loam will also feel gritty, as well as slightly sticky owing to the presence of silt and clay; it will shape better than sandy soil, but it will not form a ribbon either. Clay loam will form short ribbons. And clay feels sticky and will form a ribbon. The ribbon test can help you determine what soil type you're working with.

Jar test. You can also determine a soil's textural class using the results of a jar test and a soil texture triangle. To conduct the jar test, place 1 inch of dry soil in a quart jar. Fill the jar 3/4 full with water, and add 1 teaspoon of salt or liquid dish soap. Seal the lid and shake the jar until the soil is thoroughly suspended in the water. Set the jar down and let the mixture settle.

After a minute, the sand layer will settle at the bottom of the jar. Make a mark on the side of the jar at the top of the sand layer. After several hours, the silt layer will settle; mark the jar at the top of the silt layer. After several days, the clay layer will settle to a large degree; mark the top of the clay layer. Determine the percentages of each layer, then use a soil texture triangle to determine the soil's texture.

To use the soil triangle (see next page), find the sand percentage on the bottom of the triangle and draw a line from that point up and to the left (using the lines as guides). Find the silt percentage and draw a line down and to the left. Find the clay percentage and draw a horizontal line at that point. Next, find the point where the three lines intersect: The labels in the soil triangle reveal the soil's texture. For example, if the soil is 50% sand, 10% silt, and 40% clay, the lines you draw on the triangle should intersect in the area marked "sandy clay".

Soil Types

Gardeners commonly group soils into one of six soil types: sandy, loamy, silty, clay, peaty, and chalky. Understanding a soil type's unique physical properties enables landscapers to adopt suitable irrigation and fertilization practices and to take measures to offset a soil's negative attributes.

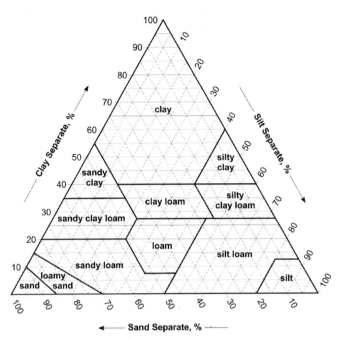

Soil texture triangle. For instructions on using the soil triangle, see "jar test" on the previous page. Reproduced from the United States Department of Agriculture, NRCS.

Sandy Soil

Sandy soil has large soil particles, which give this soil type excellent drainage. Some drawbacks to sandy soil are that it dries out faster than other soil types and requires more frequent irrigation. Sandy soil contains few nutrients, and those present can be leached by rapid water drainage. This leaching of nutrients tends to create low fertility and acidic soil conditions. It is common to attempt to counter the low fertility of sandy soils through lighter, more frequent fertilization. Amendments such as compost and aged manure can improve the structure of sandy soil, increasing its moisture retention and nutrient content. However, the high aeration of sandy soil can cause organic matter to decompose quickly. For information on the water holding capacity of sandy soil, see "AWHC: Available Water Holding Capacity" on page 59.

Clay Soil

Clay soil has tiny soil particles that are packed closely together. This soil feels heavy, lumpy, and sticky when wet, and drainage tends to be poor.

Young plants often struggle when planted directly in clay, and established plants can have difficulty extracting water from clay because it holds water tightly.

Organic amendments can improve drainage and increase space for oxygen in clay soil. It is best to incorporate amendments into a planting bed before planting. Adding organic amendment to a planting hole for a tree or shrub is not beneficial unless you're amending sandy soil. Clay soil is capable of retaining a higher percentage of organic matter than other soil types, giving it potential for good fertility. Don't use sand as an amendment for clay soil because the resulting structure is similar to concrete.

Clay soil is prone to compaction. Avoid unnecessary foot or machine traffic when this soil is wet. Rototilling or excessive digging will also damage the soil structure and promote compaction. Clay soil can be rich in nutrients, making it a good soil for many plants as long as drainage is adequate. For information on the water holding capacity of clay soil, see "AWHC: Available Water Holding Capacity" on page 59.

Loamy Soil

Loam contains a relatively balanced proportion of sand, silt, and clay particles. It is an ideal soil type because it drains well, it contains many nutrients, and it retains nutrients and water better than sandy soil. For information on the water holding capacity of loamy soil, see "AWHC: Available Water Holding Capacity" on page 59.

Silty Soil

Silty soil is composed of fine mineral and organic particles. It has many of the same positive qualities as loam. Some of its distinctions are that it feels floury or smooth, and it is more susceptible to compaction than loam.

Chalky Soil

Chalky soil is alkaline because it contains a high proportion of calcium carbonate, or lime. (Soil pH is described on page 105.) The high soil pH can make certain nutrients unavailable to plants. Chalky soil also contains an abundance of stones, and it tends to dry out quickly. This soil type can benefit from the regular addition of fertilizer and organic amendments; however, the alkalinity is difficult to alter, and most plants will do better in a different soil type. When planting in chalky soil, choose calcicoles, which are species adapted to alkaline soils. (Calcifuges are species adapted to acidic soils.)

Peaty Soil

Peaty soil is darker than most soil—a sign of its high proportion of organic matter. Because of its high organic content, peaty soil can get waterlogged. This soil type is acidic and contains few nutrients, but with the addition of fertilizer it can be a good medium for plant growth. Compost or aged manure are good amendments for this soil type. Sand can improve drainage.

Organic Matter

Organic matter is anything in the soil that came from a living organism. Examples of organic matter are compost, manure, fallen leaves and branches, severed roots, and lawn clippings. Organic matter is an essential component of fertile soil.

While organic matter is found in all soil in varying proportions, soils with a relatively high percentage of organic matter (e.g., 4 to 6%) are often associated with greater microbial activity, porous soil structure, and higher nutrient levels. In particular, organic matter is a significant source of nitrogen and phosphorus, two of the most important plant nutrients.

Organic matter in the soil is either in the process of decomposition (the active fraction) or is fully decomposed (stabilized organic matter, or humus). The fibrous quality of organic matter in the active fraction can improve soil structure. It increases moisture retention in sandy soil and improves drainage in clay soil.

The decomposition of organic matter is facilitated by small animals, earthworms, and microorganisms (bacteria and fungi). Microorganisms feed off the sugars, proteins, carbohydrates, and other nutrients contained in organic matter, and they release nutrients into the soil in forms that plants can use. These beneficial microorganisms also break down many potential pollutants, such as pesticides, and combat microorganisms that cause plant diseases.

Many nutrients, including nitrogen, phosphorus, sulfur, and iron, are made available to plant roots throughout the decomposition process. The quantity of nutrients that become available to plants depends on the percentage of organic matter in the soil, the type of organic matter, and the factors affecting the rate of decomposition, such as soil moisture, soil temperature, and soil pH.

For soils with a pH of 6 to 7, it can generally be assumed that each 1 percent of organic matter in the soil contributes $1/4$ to $1/2$ pound of nitrogen per 1000 square feet per year (Kujawski and Ryan 2000). This explains why many trees and shrubs don't require nitrogen fertilization. While these rates won't meet all the nitrogen needs of turfgrass, it is still a significant contribution.

The benefits of organic matter go beyond its contribution to soil nutrients. The full decomposition of organic matter results in humus. Humus is a dark, porous, crumbly material that no longer looks like organic matter. It is called stabilized organic matter because it is made up of complex organic compounds that cannot be readily decomposed further. Humus improves soil structure (retains air and moisture, and improves drainage) and holds nutrients in forms that are readily available to plants.

Humus, like clay particles, is colloidal. This means it attracts and holds soil nutrients such as calcium, magnesium, and potassium. Soils with a high humus content have a high nutrient holding capacity, scientifically called cation exchange capacity (CEC). This makes humus a valuable soil resource for plants and soil organisms. For these reasons and others, humus-rich soil is valued by gardeners.

Mycorrhizal Symbiosis

This scientific term may sound obscure, but an understanding of the concept will shed more light on the role of organic matter in soil. Mycorrhizal symbiosis is a mutually beneficial relationship between plant roots and certain fungi, called mycorrhizal fungi. In this relationship, the mycorrhizal fungi either contact or penetrate a plant's root cells to exchange nutrients. The plant provides the fungus with carbon compounds (sugars), and the fungus provides the plant with mineral nutrients and water that it gathers through its extensive branching structures in the soil. It's a good deal for plants because the fungi can get nutrients from the soil that plants have a harder time extracting. As a result, plants with a symbiotic relationship with fungi have access to more nutrients over a larger volume of soil. You can think of mycorrhizal fungi as a plant's extended root system. Mycorrhizal fungi also aid in the uptake of phosphorus and help prevent root diseases. The majority of all plant roots are teamed up with mycorrhizal fungi in this way. Other microorganisms also form mutually beneficial relationships with plant roots. The fact that mycorrhizal fungi and other microorganisms depend on organic matter as a food source highlights the importance of organic matter in soil.

Only a small percentage of organic matter added to the soil eventually becomes humus, and it can take years to significantly increase a soil's humus content. Once stabilized humus has formed, it can be broken down and depleted in unfavorable soil conditions. However, under the right conditions, it can last hundreds, even thousands of years. This is one reason it is important to preserve the organic matter already present in a soil.

Microbial activity influences the decomposition rate of organic matter. Conditions that increase microbial activity indirectly cause organic matter to break down faster. Once organic matter in the soil decomposes, more needs to be introduced, or soil organisms will deplete the nutrients and the soil will become less fertile.

Soil labs can test for the percentage of organic matter present in a soil. Four percent or higher is desirable, though not always attainable. If the soil contains less than 2 percent, amendments should be considered. Clay and loam soils can hold greater amounts of organic matter because clay particles bond to organic compounds. Sandy soil contains high levels of oxygen, which speeds up decomposition, so sandy soils usually contain less than 2 percent organic matter.

Influencing Organic Matter Levels

In a natural environment, such as a forest, organic matter is constantly entering the soil. Plants grow, die, decompose, and nutrients are released into the soil again, creating a cycle. Urban landscapes typically have much less organic matter falling onto the soil surface than do natural environments. In some landscapes, leaving plant debris on the ground can create an eyesore or potential for disease. While backyards don't function like a forest ecosystem, organic matter is still important for soil structure and fertility. Here are a few practices used to influence organic matter levels.

Amendments and Mulches

Incorporating organic amendments into the soil, such as adding high-quality, weed-free compost to planting beds, is a simple way to increase a soil's organic content and fertility. Mulching grass clippings and leaves with a mulching mower is a way to return organic matter to turf. Other measures might include top-dressing lawns with a thin ($1/8$- to $1/4$-inch) layer of high-quality, fine-texture compost once or twice a year.

Organic mulches on bare soil will increase soil organic matter levels over time. Leaf matter is often removed from decorative mulches and groundcovers. Leaf matter can also be removed from bare soil surfaces if aesthetics is a concern. However, leaf matter is beneficial organic material; allowing it to remain on the soil surface will contribute organic matter and nutrients to the soil.

Tillage Reduction

Another way to influence a soil's organic matter content is by reducing tillage. Earlier it was said that tilling the soil has a negative effect on soil structure. Another result of tillage is that it introduces more oxygen into the soil. Under the right conditions, this increase in oxygen can accelerate the activity of microorganisms, which will then consume organic matter more quickly. The faster the organic matter is consumed, the more quickly it needs to be replaced. Reducing tillage helps to preserve soil structure and keeps nutrients cycling at a sustainable pace. A slow and steady supply of nutrients is best for plants.

By not disturbing the soil structure, organic matter levels can increase over time, provided other conditions support this. Grass clippings and fallen leaves naturally accumulate, and earthworms tunnel through the soil, increasing soil porosity and producing nutrient-rich castings. And many grass roots sprout and die each year, contributing from $1/2$ to 4 tons of organic matter per acre (Sachs and Luff 2002).

Soil Temperature Moderation

High soil temperatures, along with moisture and oxygen, can increase microbial activity and speed up the decomposition of organic matter. Mulching around trees and plants and cutting turfgrass taller in the summer will help to shade the soil, reducing soil temperature and helping to preserve organic matter.

Lime Only As Needed

Lime is a soil conditioner used to raise soil pH. Most plants do best in a soil that is slightly acidic. The microorganisms involved in the decomposition of organic matter do best in conditions that range from slightly acidic to alkaline (pH 6 to 8). Indiscriminate or excessive applications of lime can increase microbial activity and speed up the decomposition of organic matter. Lime should be applied only when a laboratory soil test indicates the need for it. Soil pH is covered on page 105.

Organic Amendments

The following organic amendments can be used to improve soil structure and increase microbial activity; most will also add nutrients to the soil. When adding an organic amendment to the soil, incorporate it thoroughly so that the soil does not contain pockets or layers of organic material. To calculate the amount of an amendment to purchase, see "Calculating the Amount of Mulch or Soil Amendment" on page 79.

Note that microbes need nitrogen to decompose organic matter. If the organic matter contains too little nitrogen, microbes will take nitrogen from the soil, reducing the amount available to plants. One solution is to add a nitrogen source, such as bloodmeal or another fertilizer, when using low-nitrogen organic amendments.

Aged Manure

The cow and chicken manure available at nurseries is aged and composted. Fresh manure may contain weed seeds and can contaminate vegetable gardens with E. coli, a bacteria that can cause severe illness. Fresh manure or manure that is not fully composted can also contain high salt levels, which can damage plants. Composted manure is a good source of organic matter. It supplies low levels of nitrogen, as well as phosphorus, potassium, and trace elements.

Peat Moss

Peat moss is a soil conditioner comprised of partially or fully decomposed peat. It has a high water holding capacity, making it useful for sandy soils.

Web Soil Survey

The Web Soil Survey is an online application created by the United States Department of Agriculture Natural Resources and Conservation Service (NRCS; http://websoilsurvey.nrcs. usda.gov). It provides regional technical soil information, including data on available water (in centimeters). Whether or not many landscapers use the Web Soil Survey, it is an extensive database that is worth knowing about. Keep in mind that in urban environments, landscapers sometimes import topsoil, and general construction frequently disturbs the soil surface. For these reasons, surveys don't always provide relevant information.

Don't use peat moss in clay soils because it holds too much water and reduces aeration. Peat moss does not contain many nutrients, and it will not be as beneficial to soil organisms as compost or aged manure. Peat moss (sphagnum peat) is acidic and can be a used to lower soil pH. Soil pH is covered on page 105. Note that there is debate among peat producers and conservationists about the sustainability of peat as a resource.

Earthworm Castings

Earthworm castings improve soil aeration and water retention. They contain nitrogen, phosphorus, potassium, and trace elements, as well as humus. Castings are not acidic and can be used as a soil amendment or as potting soil.

Compost

Compost is decomposed organic matter. Compost is a popular organic soil amendment because it can be rich in nutrients and, in general, it does not contain weed seeds. It also increases a soil's aeration and moisture retention. Soil organisms consume the organic matter in compost and release nutrients into the soil. Compost may also play a role in suppressing soil pathogens.

Compost is a good soil amendment, though it should not be used as a stand-alone medium to grow plants. Specialists in organic lawn care sometimes apply a thin ($1/8$- to $1/4$-inch) layer of fine-texture, high-quality compost to lawns once or twice a year. Compost improves soil texture and

provides the lawn with low levels of nutrients. Layers of compost thicker than $1/4$ inch may increase the risk of damaging turf.

The amount of nutrients compost contributes to the soil depends on the feed stock, that is, the materials used to make the compost. Composts made from wood products (i.e., sawdust or wood chips) tend to be low in nitrogen. Composts made from manure tend to be high in phosphorus and potassium. And composts made from yard waste tend to be high in potassium. The nitrogen content of compost derived from yard waste depends on the amount of green matter (e.g., leaves and grass clippings) in the feed stock.

Compost quality can vary greatly, and low quality compost may do more harm than good. For instance, a compost that is not mature (i.e., that has not fully decomposed) can consume nitrogen in the soil and may contain substances that inhibit seed germination or plant growth.

Selecting Compost: Rules of Thumb

The following rules of thumb can be used to select high quality compost:

- Compost should be free from rocks. The presence of some small wood pieces is acceptable, but the compost should contain little or no undecomposed green matter (i.e., grass or leaves).

- Mature compost has an earthy or musty smell; it should not smell like ammonia and it should not smell foul.

- Mature compost is dark brown to black and looks and feels like rich soil, though it is not as heavy as soil.

- The compost pile should not be very hot (120°F). If it is very hot, the compost is not yet mature.

- When you squeeze the compost in your hand, it should not release more than a few drops of water.

Selecting Compost: Technical Guidelines

The following technical characteristics of high quality compost have been adapted from "Compost: A Guide for Evaluating and Using Compost Materials as Soil Amendments" written by William Darlington and produced by Soil and Plant Laboratory, Inc. You can access the complete article from http://www.soilandplantlaboratory.com/pdf/articles/CompostAGuideForUsing.pdf. The following guidelines require you to have access to the compost test results, which commercial compost producers should have on record. For landscape use, compost should have the following characteristics:

- A minimum of 90% of the material by weight should pass a 1/2-inch screen.

- The compost should contain a minimum of 50% organic content based on dry weight (250 lbs. of organic matter per cubic yard of compost).

- The compost should have a maximum carbon to nitrogen ratio of 35:1 if the material is nitrogen stabilized.

- The compost pH should be in the range of 5.5–8.0 (near-neutral [pH 7] is desirable).

- Sodium should account for less than 25% of the total soluble nutrients in the compost. (See Darlington's article for a technical explanation of how to estimate the maximum allowable soluble salt concentration of compost at the desired use rate.)

- The compost's moisture content should be 35-60%.

- The compost should be as free as possible from glass, metal, and plastic. Commercial compost producers are required to test their products for heavy metals and for diseases that may pose a risk to human health. Note that these tests may be particularly important to clients who use compost in vegetable gardens.

Gypsum

Gypsum (calcium sulfate) is a soil conditioner used to reduce sodium in high sodium (sodic) soils. It is a good source of calcium and sulfur, and it has little or no effect on soil pH. Gypsum does not contain organic matter.

Gypsum is sometimes applied in granular or powdered form to compacted clay soil to improve aeration, but in most cases it is of little benefit. Gypsum is most effective at improving soil structure on clay soil that has a high sodium content. It is not likely to improve the structure of any soil type other than clay. And it may not even benefit clay if the soil has a high calcium content. After testing the soil in question, a soil lab can tell you if gypsum will help relieve compaction. Soil testing is covered on page 108.

Earthworms

Earthworms improve soil structure and fertility in several ways. Because of their beneficial effects on the landscape, it is usually a good idea to adopt soil and turf management practices that encourage their presence.

Earthworms can be found in most soils, with the exception of sandy or overly acidic soils. Many species exist, the most common being *Lumbricus terrestris*, also known as the "night crawler" for its nocturnal habit. Earthworms form burrows several feet deep in the soil, and they search for food in the top 12 to 18 inches. They eat soil, leaves, and other decomposing organic matter. Often they remove organic matter from the soil surface and drag it into their burrows to consume it. Digested minerals and organic matter are excreted as castings, which are rich in nutrients. These castings get distributed throughout the soil, and some are deposited on the soil surface.

The two common conceptions that earthworms are good for the soil and are a sign of healthy soil are true. Their burrowing activity serves as a natural method of soil aeration, increasing water infiltration and drainage. This aeration can reduce the potential for runoff, erosion, and pooling—concerns frequently associated with clay soils. Aeration also increases soil oxygen levels and promotes the growth of beneficial microorganisms. By feeding on organic matter on the surface of lawns, earthworms are allies in the battle against thatch, which is a buildup of slowly decomposing grass stems on the soil surface of turfgrass.

Earthworm castings can be raked into the soil surface if they become noticeable. Excessive castings can be problematic, particularly in high-maintenance environments such as golf courses. Even when earthworms are a problem, turf managers recognize their many benefits and only seek to reduce their numbers, not eliminate them. Note that earthworms favor soils with a near-neutral pH (pH 6.5 to 7).

Attracting Earthworms

The following measures will help to increase the earthworm population in a landscape. It can take several years before numbers rise significantly.

- When possible, mow with a mulching mower to return grass clippings and leaves to the soil.

- Amend or top-dress the soil with organic amendments such as compost or aged manure.

- Select pesticides that are known to be less toxic to earthworms.

- When possible, refrain from using pesticides in the spring and fall when earthworms are most active near the soil surface.

- Maintain a soil pH in the range of 6.5 to 7.

- Use chemical fertilizers in moderation to avoid creating acidic soil conditions.

Soil pH

Soil pH is a measurement of soil acidity or alkalinity. It is measured on a pH scale of 1.0 to 14. A pH of 7.0 is neutral, a pH of less than 7.0 is acidic, and a pH of greater than 7.0 is alkaline, or basic. The higher the value over 7.0, the greater the alkalinity; the lower the value under 7.0, the greater the acidity. Soil pH is logarithmic: each one point change on the pH scale represents a tenfold change in pH. For instance, a pH value of 5.0 is ten times more acidic than a pH value of 6.0.

Soil pH is influenced by base nutrients, such as calcium and magnesium. In areas with low rainfall, these nutrients accumulate in the soil, and the soil is more alkaline. In wet regions, high rainfall washes these nutrients from the soil, and the soil is more acidic. Excessive irrigation can have the same effect as high rainfall.

Acidic soil can also be created by other factors. Certain fertilizers, such as those containing ammonium forms of nitrogen, can have an acidifying effect. Areas with high levels of organic matter decomposition will also tend to be acidic. Soil pH can also be affected by regional water quality. For instance, some water supplies contain significant quantities of bicarbonates, which raise soil pH.

Soil pH can affect nutrient availability in a soil. For example, a soil that is too acidic (below 5.5) can reduce the availability of phosphorus. A low pH can also hinder the activity of microorganisms, which convert organic matter into nutrients plants can use. Very low pH (4.0 to 5.0) can create toxic levels of aluminum and manganese in the soil water. In contrast, if the soil is too alkaline (above 7.5), nutrients such as phosphorus and iron can become "locked up", or insoluble, and plants cannot use them. Lack of available iron can cause iron chlorosis, a plant disease that causes slow growth and yellowing of leaves.

Most landscape plants, including turfgrasses, do best in soils with a pH of between 6.0 and 7.0, and

6.5 is considered optimal. This range is also favorable to microorganisms. Bentgrasses typically need a pH that is slightly more acidic (5.5 to 6.5). Blueberries, azaleas, and rhododendrons are examples of acid-loving plants that do best with a soil pH of between 4.5 and 5.2. Evergreens do best with a soil pH of between 5.0 and 6.0. These ranges are for mineral soils—that is, soils that are predominantly composed of minerals as opposed to organic matter. The optimal pH range for most organic soils is roughly 5.4 to 6.2 (University of Minnesota 2004).

While most plants can tolerate a pH modestly outside their optimal range, a pH lower than 6.0 or greater than 7.0 will reduce the availability of nutrients and should be modified, as described later.

Testing Soil pH

Soil pH can be tested quickly with a soil pH probe, a soil pH test kit, or a handheld pH meter. Probes provide a pH reading upon insertion into the soil. Inexpensive probes are readily available, but their reliability is questionable. Nurseries and garden stores also sell soil pH test kits. Using these simple and reasonably accurate tests involves adding soil, distilled water, and a dye to a test container and comparing the color of the solution to a chart. Handheld pH "pens", or meters, are more expensive than test kits, but provide a more accurate analysis.

Soil testing labs provide the most accurate analysis. Labs initially conduct either a water pH test or a salt pH test. These tests indicate whether lime is needed. If lime is needed, most labs will conduct a separate test, called a buffer pH test, to determine how much lime to apply. The buffer test is sometimes called a lime requirement test. The more clay and organic matter the soil contains, the more acid-forming elements (hydrogen and aluminum) the soil can hold, and the greater the quantity of lime required to offset these elements and raise the pH.

It is possible to determine the amount of lime to apply using a store-bought pH test and a chart that provides lime recommendations by soil type. However, charts can vary in their recommendations. It is better to leave lime recommendations to a lab.

It is important to be as accurate as possible when adding lime to avoid raising the pH too much.

One approach is to test the soil with a pH test kit or pH pen and then, if the soil is acidic or alkaline, to send samples to a lab for professional analysis and recommendations. Testing should be done in the spring and fall before fertilization. Not all soils need testing this frequently, though sandy soils can acidify quickly and should be tested regularly.

Tell the lab whether you will be applying lime to the soil surface or incorporating it into the soil. Surface (no-till) applications require less lime and are less effective than incorporated applications. Selecting a lab and collecting soil samples are covered later this chapter.

Raising Soil pH

If a lab test reveals that the soil is too acidic, calcium carbonate ($CaCO_3$) must be added to the soil to raise the pH. Limestone is a source of calcium carbonate widely used in landscapes and agriculture. Note that lime should only be applied when indicated by soil test results; it should not be applied according to a yearly schedule.

Various types of lime can be used to raise soil pH. Calcitic limestone and dolomitic limestone are classed as agricultural lime, and they are the most common. Calcitic limestone is mostly calcium carbonate, while dolomitic limestone contains calcium carbonate and a significant amount of magnesium carbonate. Dolomitic limestone is only used if the soil shows a magnesium deficiency. Sandy soils may benefit from dolomitic limestone.

Burned lime (calcium oxide; also called quicklime) and hydrated lime (calcium hydroxide; also called slaked lime) are more concentrated and raise pH more quickly than ground or dolomitic limestone. However, burned and hydrated lime pose a risk of burning plant roots, and this makes them more hazardous to work with—in general, they are not used on turfgrass.

Landscapers typically use calcitic or dolomitic limestone. Powdered products are a good choice when the lime will be tilled into the soil. The smaller the particle size, the faster the neutralizing effect. Pelletized lime is easier to apply than powdered lime. Water thoroughly after applying pelletized lime to break down the pellets.

Lime products vary in how much calcium carbonate they contain. The calcium carbonate equivalent (CCE) is a measure of the acid-neutralizing capacity of a lime product relative to pure calcium carbonate. The calcium carbonate equivalent will be listed on the lime label as a percentage. If a soil test result provides a recommendation in terms of pounds of pure calcium carbonate ($CaCO_3$) per 1000 square feet, you'll need to make a simple calculation to determine how much of a liming product to use. See table 16.

Table 16. Calculating the Amount of Lime

> Amount of product to apply =
>
> $$\frac{\text{Pounds of pure } CaCO_3 \text{ (from soil test)}}{\text{CCE percentage of product}}$$

For example, if a soil test recommends 70 pounds of $CaCO_3$ per 1000 square feet, and you intend to use a ground limestone product with a CCE of 80 percent, the formula is as follows:

$70 \div 80\% = 87.5$ pounds

Another way to calculate this is:

$(100 \times 70) \div 80 = 87.5$ pounds

In this example, you need to apply 87.5 pounds of product per 1000 square feet to apply 70 pounds of pure $CaCO_3$ per 1000 square feet.

Lime spreads into the soil slowly, and it is most effective on the soil it contacts. For this reason, it is ideal to apply any necessary lime before planting, when the soil can be tilled to a depth of 4 to 6 inches.

Applications of calcitic and dolomitic limestone to established turfgrass should not exceed 50 pounds per 1000 square feet per application. If a lab's

recommendation for surface application is higher, apply half in the spring and half in the fall. If only one application is needed, fall is the preferred time. Do not apply lime during the heat of summer. When applying lime to established turfgrass, water the lawn after application to wash the lime off grass blades. Aerating a lawn before liming will help the lime contact more soil.

Lime applied to the soil surface will penetrate fine-texture soil at about 1/2 inch per year, and only the top 2 to 3 inches of soil will eventually react with the lime. It can take up to six months after liming for the pH to change significantly, and it can take two to three years to see the full effect (Mamo, Wortmann, and Shapiro 2009).

Lowering Soil pH

If a lab test indicates that the soil is too alkaline, the soil pH may need to be lowered. It may also need to be lowered if the soil is being prepared for acid-loving plants such as rhododendrons, azaleas, and blueberries, which need a soil pH of between 4.5 and 5.2.

Nitrogen fertilizers such as ammonium sulfate and sulfur-coated urea have an acidifying effect on soil. These fertilizers can be used to gradually offset soil alkalinity, though only the top few inches of soil may be affected. Sandy soils can quickly become acidic if these fertilizers are used. The pH reduction provided by these fertilizers should be considered a side-effect; apply them according to the plants' nutrient needs. Fertilizers such as ammonium sulfate are sometimes used to maintain a low pH for acid-loving plants.

Peat moss (sphagnum peat) is an acidic organic amendment (pH 3.6 to 4.2) that can be used to lower soil pH. It is most effective when incorporated into the soil before planting. Peat moss decomposes slowly. See "Peat Moss" on page 102 for more information.

Elemental sulfur changes to sulfuric acid in the soil through the activity of soil bacteria. Sulfuric acid lowers soil pH by removing carbonates from the soil. For elemental sulfur to be effective, the soil needs to be at least 60°F, the temperature at which soil bacteria become more active. For this reason, sulfur is usually applied in the spring. It is preferable to incorporate it into the soil well in advance of planting. Follow the product directions closely if you will be applying it to established turfgrass. Elemental sulfur is slow acting, taking up to a year to have full effect. Elemental sulfur is a yellow powder; it is not the same as the sulfate sulfurs found in fertilizers.

Iron sulfate acts faster than elemental sulfur, but greater quantities are required. Iron sulfate may help alleviate iron deficiencies in plants. Note that iron sulfate can burn existing plants, including turfgrass; follow the product label closely. Apply the product evenly and irrigate after application. Iron sulfate can stain concrete if it falls onto paved areas and gets wet, so use it with caution around walkways, driveways, and pools.

Aluminum sulfate is sometimes used to lower soil pH. If it is applied in excess, it can damage plants by creating toxic levels of aluminum in the soil. Closely follow the product directions. Hydrangeas can benefit from aluminum sulfate.

Note that alkaline clay soil tends to be calcareous, meaning high in calcium carbonate (lime). The large quantities of amendments needed to offset the high percentage of naturally occurring lime can make it impractical to lower the pH of these soils. The consensus is that any pH reductions in calcareous soils are short-lived and ultimately not worth the effort. Similarly, in some areas of the country, irrigation water contains significant quantities of bicarbonates. In these areas, the tendency is for soils to become more alkaline over time, making pH reduction more challenging, if not pointless.

Alkaline soils can lack available phosphorus, as well as micronutrients such as copper, iron, manganese, and zinc. It is often more effective to apply nutrients in chelated forms or by foliar spray to correct deficiencies instead of attempting to lower the pH of alkaline soil.

Soil Tests

Soil testing laboratories—sometimes called soil fertility labs—serve farmers, landscape professionals, and homeowners. In addition to testing soil pH, soil labs measure soil nutrients, soluble salts, total nitrogen, organic matter, and the base nutrient holding capacity of the soil (cation exchange capacity, or CEC). Alternative soil testing labs can provide organic fertilizer recommendations. These labs frequently conduct additional tests on compost, soil humus, and microbial levels.

Some experts recommend a soil test for the home landscape every three to four years. Sandy soils should be tested more frequently. Consider getting a soil test for each new account to determine levels of phosphorus and potassium. If levels of these nutrients are adequate, additional testing may not be necessary for many years (Rosen, Horgan, and Mugaas 2006).

Selecting a Soil Lab

Soil labs in your state are more likely to be familiar with the nutrient requirements of the soils in your region. Many universities or university extension services offer soil testing. Soil labs can also be found through the phone book and the internet.

Alternative soil testing laboratories can provide organic fertilizer recommendations for landscape professionals. The website of the National Sustainable Agriculture Information Service (ATTRA; http://attra.ncat.org) has listings for alternative soil testing labs. The following are points to consider when selecting a soil lab:

- Find out if the lab is a North American Proficiency Testing (NAPT) member. The NAPT program works with member labs to increase test accuracy through double blind sample testing.

- Ask if the lab does testing for the home landscape. Results should be in pounds per 1000 square feet as opposed to pounds per acre.

- Ask if the lab offers a buffer pH test, which is needed to determine any necessary lime requirements.

- Find out how long it will take the lab to conduct a basic soil test. Three to five days is common, though labs may be busier at certain times of the year. You will need to fill out a soil information form with your samples. To speed up the process, some labs accept soil information forms over the internet and post results online.

- Ask if the lab offers plant tissue analysis. Plant tissue analysis is sometimes used to diagnose plant problems caused by nutrient excess or deficiency.

- Continue to have your soil testing performed by the same lab if you will be comparing test results over time; test results can vary from lab to lab.

Collecting Soil Samples

Take soil samples several months before planting so there is enough time to apply any necessary lime and let it take effect. For established plants, soil samples can be taken most times of year, though late summer through early fall is ideal because lime is most commonly applied in the fall. Below are some general suggestions for collecting soil samples. Follow the lab's recommended sampling procedures if they differ from those provided here.

Use clean tools to gather soil samples. Steel or nickel-plated tools are preferred. Brass or galvanized tools can affect the copper or zinc readings of tests and should be avoided when testing for micronutrients. For the same reason, place samples in a clean plastic bucket, not a galvanized metal one.

Take a separate soil sample for each area of the yard thought to have unique soil characteristics. Typically, you need a separate sample for the front lawn, the back lawn, areas of trees and shrubs, and any distinct planting areas, such as a vegetable garden or a perennial bed. Also take separate samples for areas with unhealthy plants. For example, if one area of the lawn looks unhealthy, sample that area separately.

Each soil sample should be a composite of several samples in an area. For example, to take a composite sample of a front lawn, you would take a slice or core of soil 1 to 6 inches deep from various parts of the lawn, then mix them together to form one sample. Typically between five and eight cores make up one composite sample. In general, the sample should include at least 1 quart (4 cups) of soil, though some labs only require 1 pint (2 cups).

Samples should be representative of the root zone of plants in that area. According to Soil and Plant Laboratory, Inc., turfgrass, annuals, and groundcovers should be sampled at a depth of 1 to 6 inches; shrubs, roses, and vegetables should be sampled at a depth of 1 to 12 inches; trees should be sampled at a depth of 6 to 18 inches; and trees with deep roots should be sampled at a depth of 24 to 36 inches. Discard the top 1 inch of soil from all samples because it may contain matter not representative of the root zone. When sampling plants watered by drip irrigation, sample near emitters, and do not use the top 2 inches of soil (Soil and Plant Laboratory 2005). Some miscellaneous points:

- Avoid taking soil samples from areas that have been recently fertilized because fertilizer can affect soil pH.

- Take samples when the soil temperature is above 50°F (Voigt, Fermanian, and Wehner 1998).

- Dry soil samples at room temperature before sending them to the lab. This will reduce the activity of microorganisms and help to preserve the field characteristics of the soil. Do not heat the samples to speed drying.

- Wait several months before retesting a limed area.

Fill out the lab's soil information sheet or soil sample submittal form for each sample. Submittal forms can sometimes be downloaded from the lab's website. Make a note on the form of the area of the yard the sample is from and the plants that grow there. Ask the lab to provide you with interpretive information, so you will know what the test results mean. Finally, follow the lab's instructions on how to bag, label, package, and ship the samples.

Pruning

Pruning is the removal of branches to create a desired effect, such as to improve a plant's health, structure, appearance, and fruit or flower production. Shearing a bush with hedge clippers can be considered a form of pruning, though pruning is generally thought of as the selective removal of individual branches.

Not all plants need pruning—though most benefit from it—and not all plants are pruned the same way. Pruning reference books describe in detail how to prune a variety of plants. This chapter covers general pruning principles and techniques. Subsequent chapters examine the common tasks of pruning roses and fruit trees.

It takes study, practice, and, preferably, guidance from an experienced landscaper or certified arborist to develop confidence in pruning. Weekend pruning workshops provide the opportunity to get hands-on experience, which can make pruning principles easier to grasp. You can also become skilled at pruning through study and practice on your own.

Tree Pruning in Landscaping

Residential landscapers typically prune roses, perennials, shrubs, vines, hedges, and small trees such as fruit trees and crape myrtles. The pruning of large trees is beyond the scope of services offered by most landscapers. Professional tree pruning requires licensing, insurance, and specialized training and equipment.

Trees pruned by unqualified individuals are often left unsightly and prone to sunburn, decay, and structural defects—the trees become hazardous and their life spans are reduced. ISA-certified arborists have the necessary training. Arborists write pruning specifications that outline the pruning objectives and methods for each job, and they perform the work in accordance with ANSI A300 pruning standards.

Although the pruning of large trees should be referred to a certified arborist or qualified tree care company, landscapers must still know the right way to prune tree branches. Some basic tree pruning guidelines are included in this chapter. To learn how to become a certified arborist or certified tree worker, contact the International Society of Arboriculture at 1-888-ISA-TREE (1-888-472-8733) or online at http://www.isa-arbor.com. The ISA has local chapters that sometimes offer membership at reduced rates.

Important: *The incorrect pruning of a mature landscape tree can reduce its value, threaten its health, and make it dangerous. Refer tree work to an ISA-certified arborist or qualified tree care company.*

Time of Pruning

The correct time to prune can vary with plant species, plant condition, and the pruning objectives. Other factors, such as prevalent diseases, can also influence the time of pruning. It is a good idea to research a plant's pruning requirements before pruning. Information can be found in pruning manuals or online; certified nursery professionals can also answer questions. Pruning at the wrong time of year can hinder a plant's development or disrupt fruit or flower production. In some cases, pruning at the wrong time of year can harm or kill a plant.

The best time to prune most trees and shrubs is the late dormant season—that is, late winter or early spring, before growth begins (specifically, before bud swell). There is less insect and disease activity at this time, and pruning wounds close quickly with spring growth. It is also easier to see the branches of deciduous trees and shrubs in late winter. Do not prune during a plant's spring growth flush; pruning at this time depletes the plant's energy reserves and weakens its health. And avoid pruning deciduous trees during leaf drop in the fall. Dead, diseased, and broken branches can be removed any time of year.

Pruning in summer, once growth has begun to slow for the season, is also an acceptable time to prune many plants. Summer pruning removes growth the plant uses for energy production and reduces some of the energy reserves stored in woody growth. This may reduce the vigor of the next year's spring growth and have a restricting effect on plant size. For related information, see "Pruning and Growth" on page 137.

Summer pruning results in a weaker growth response than winter pruning. For this reason, and because of the potential for water stress, it is best not to cut trees and shrubs back hard in summer. In general, hard pruning—sometimes called rejuvenation pruning—of temperate zone plants should be done in late winter or early spring.

An advantage of summer pruning is that the presence of leaves makes it easier to judge how much thinning is needed to increase light penetration into the plant or the tree canopy. Dead wood is also easier to identify in summer. Avoid late-summer pruning in regions with cold winters. The growth that develops after pruning may not have time to harden before winter and may be damaged by winter freezes. Vigorous plants may need both dormant and summer pruning.

Time of Pruning for Flowering Trees and Shrubs

The time of pruning for flowering trees and shrubs varies according to when the plant produces flowers. Spring-flowering trees and shrubs produce flowers on growth from the previous season (1-year-old wood). Pruning a spring-bloomer in late winter or early spring will remove flower buds, reducing the flower display for the season. For this reason, spring bloomers are pruned soon after flowering in spring. The growth that develops after the spring flower display contains flower buds for the next year.

Examples of spring bloomers include redbud, crabapple, flowering cherry or plum, lilac, forsythia, azalea, rhododendron, Indian hawthorn (*Raphiolepis*), and Japanese quince. If a spring-bloomer is neglected or overgrown, it is acceptable to prune it hard in late winter or early spring, sacrificing many of the season's flowers to rejuvenate the plant.

Flowering shrubs that bloom in summer produce flower buds on growth that developed the same season (new wood). These plants are pruned in late winter or early spring. Common examples of summer-bloomers are modern bush roses, clematis, butterfly bush (*Buddleia*), and crape myrtle (*Lagerstroemia*).

Other Considerations

- Roses and subtropical plants, such as hibiscus, lantana, and bougainvillea, should not be pruned in winter unless the area is frost-free. In cold-winter areas, prune roses and subtropicals after the danger of frost has passed.

- Some trees exude large amounts of sap from pruning cuts when pruned in late winter or early spring. This "bleeding" does not harm the tree and will eventually stop, though the standard practice is to prune when the tree will exude less sap. Experts recommend pruning in early to mid-winter when the trees are dormant; alternatively, some experts recommend pruning in late spring or early summer, once the trees have fully leafed-out. Examples of trees that exude sap include maple, birch, and walnut.

- Timing of pruning can be critical when diseases that can spread through pruning cuts are a concern, as they are with oak and elm trees. The timing of pruning in these cases varies according to the tree species and the disease. For example, where oak wilt disease is a problem, experts recommend not pruning oaks between April and June because a beetle that can spread the disease is most active at this time. Timing of pruning for fruit trees is also frequently influenced by prevalent diseases. See "Time of Pruning for Fruit Trees" on page 138 for more information.

Pruning and Plant Biology

At the tip of a branch is the terminal bud, sometimes called the apical bud. The terminal bud is the main growth bud on a branch. Along the side of a branch are lateral buds, which in time can become separate branches. The tallest terminal bud on a tree is usually on the central stem, which is called the central leader.

The terminal bud releases a hormone called auxin, which limits the growth of lateral (axillary) buds lower on the stem. Removing the terminal bud through pruning stops the flow of auxin to the lower buds. Once the inhibitory effect of the auxin has ceased, the lower buds will begin to grow or

An example of how pruning influences branch development. This crape myrtle stem was headed back the previous winter. In the spring, the plant directed its growth energy into the two buds beneath the cut. Notice that the branch nearest the cut has grown the most vigorously.

will grow more vigorously; the bud nearest the cut usually grows the most vigorously.

In other words, cutting off the tip of a stem (the terminal bud) causes the stem to develop side shoots (lateral shoots). Horticulturalists use this understanding to control the direction of growth and the overall shape of a plant.

Branches also contain latent buds. Latent buds usually remain dormant until the terminal bud is lost. Latent buds can sometimes be seen in the bark with a close look. Some plants have latent buds along all areas of their bark; other plants do not have latent buds in all areas.

A plant can be permanently disfigured if you cut it back to woody growth that does not contain latent buds. Therefore it is important to research if a plant can tolerate hard cutting back before pruning it. Juniper and most other conifers will not produce new growth from woody branches; a few exceptions are yew (*Taxus*), hemlock (*Tsuga*), and the coast redwood (*Sequoia sempervirens*).

Plants do not regrow branches that have been removed; instead, they seal off pruning wounds and direct growth energy into other buds and branches. With this understanding, you can prune to direct growth. For example, removing all lateral growth from a shoot will increase the amount of growth energy available to the shoot. As a result, the shoot will elongate more than if the laterals remained. Similarly, heading back a vigorous shoot encourages the plant to direct growth energy into the shoot's remaining buds, which will grow vigorously.

Before pruning wounds have sealed off, a plant is more vulnerable to disease and decay organisms. It's preferable to limit pruning cuts to small-diameter branches, because small-diameter branches seal off faster than large-diameter ones. In addition, plants store energy in their branches, trunks, and roots. The removal of large branches or large sections of a plant depletes the plant's energy reserves and temporarily reduces its capacity to produce energy.

Cut Placement

When pruning, always cut branches back to where they originate or to a lateral branch. Branches less than two years old can be headed back to a bud. These techniques are described in "Thinning, Reduction, & Heading back" on page 117.

Do not leave stubs. A stub is a section of branch that remains after a pruning cut. Stubs are susceptible to disease and decay. On trees, stubs can promote the growth of poorly attached branches called watersprouts. Do not leave stubs longer than approximately 1/8 inch on small-diameter branches and 1/4 inch on large-diameter branches. Heading back a shoot to a bud does not leave a stub because new growth will soon form near the cut.

Cut Placement for Tree Branches

The correct cut placement for a tree branch is just outside the branch bark ridge and the branch

The branch bark ridge is the line of rough, raised bark in the branch crotch (arrow). Not all branches have branch bark ridges and not all branch bark ridges are as long as this one. Do not cut into the branch bark ridge or the branch collar when removing a branch.

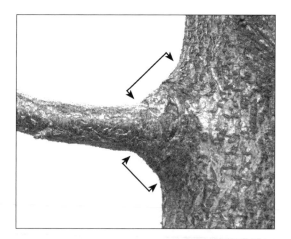

The branch collar is the bulge at the base of the branch. The areas marked by the arrowed brackets indicate the upper and lower portions of the collar. Not all branch collars are as distinct as this one. Never cut into the branch collar when removing a branch. Cut just at the edge of the collar and do not leave a branch stub.

collar, if these features are present. See "Diagram 1" on page 116. The branch bark ridge is the wrinkled, raised bark found in the branch crotch (see photo, previous page). Not all branches have a branch bark ridge. The branch collar is an area of raised or swollen bark at the base of a branch where it intersects with the parent branch or trunk (see photo, previous page). Not all branches have a branch collar.

Branch collars vary in shape and size; some are distinct, while others appear as a subtle flare in the wood. Collars are most visible on branches that are significantly smaller in diameter than the parent branch or trunk. Note that branches with collars are better attached to the trunk than branches without collars. Also, inside the branch collar is an area called the branch protection zone, which acts as a barrier to infection if the branch is removed. Cutting into the branch collar interferes with the branch protection zone and hinders the tree's ability to stop the spread of disease and decay organisms.

If you can't see the branch collar at the bottom of the branch, you will need to estimate the angle of cut; see "Diagram 2" on page 116 for guidelines. Branches with included bark (page 123) have unique pruning guidelines (not explained here). Note that wound dressings and pruning paints do not help seal wounds and may interfere with wound closure.

Cutting Technique

To minimize the risk of damaging the branch collar, prune small-diameter branches with hand pruners and large-diameter branches with a saw. For small-diameter branches, position hand pruners so that the blade, not the hook, is next to the originating branch or trunk, and cut upward or sideways through the branch to avoid damaging the branch collar.

Three-cut Method

When branches over 1 inch in diameter are cut, they can peel the bark down the trunk or parent branch as they fall. To prevent this, use the three-cut method for removing large tree branches. The first cut should be about 1 foot out from the trunk;

This saw cut leaves no stub and correctly avoids cutting into the branch collar. The branch shown is small enough that it can be removed with a single cut. The weight of the branch will be supported by hand as the cut is nearly through.

An example of a large branch tearing midway through a cut. This can be avoided by using the three-cut method. See "Diagram 1" on page 116.

Diagram 1

For large-diameter branches, use the three-cut method. The first cut, which is made on the underside of the branch, prevents the bark from tearing. The second cut is made on top of the branch, farther out from the first cut; the branch falls midway through this cut. The final cut is made in the area indicated by the dotted line. The dotted line shows the correct cut placement when a branch bark ridge and a branch collar are present. The cut is made just outside the branch bark ridge and the branch collar.

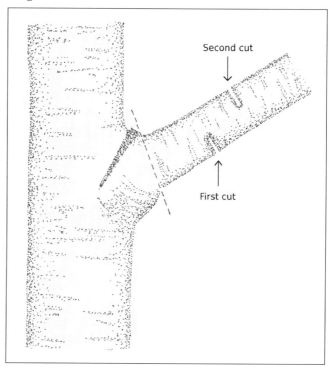

Diagram 2

Diagram 2 shows how to estimate the angle of cut when there is no visible branch collar at the bottom of a branch. Angle A is the angle formed between the branch bark ridge and an imaginary vertical line. Angle B is the estimated angle; it should be equal to or greater than angle A. Cut at the outer edge of angle B. In the diagram, cut placement is marked by the dotted line. Start the cut outside the branch collar on the top of the branch. The cut should not enter the top of the branch bark ridge. Use the three-cut method for large-diameter branches. (Adapted from An Illustrated Guide to Pruning *by Edward Gilman, 2002; p.64.)*

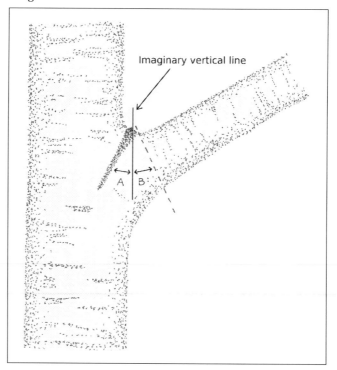

it should begin on the underside of the branch and should enter no more than halfway through the branch. Do not cut so far into the branch that it sags and locks down on the saw. The undercut eliminates the risk of the bark tearing. A few inches farther out from the undercut, cut the branch, starting on top. The branch will drop to the ground midway through this cut. Once the branch falls, return to the stub and make the final cut. See "Diagram 1" on page 116.

Common Pruning Techniques

Cleaning

Cleaning involves removing dead, diseased, and broken branches. Suckers and watersprouts are also commonly removed. Cleaning is a simple way to begin pruning any plant. Removing unhealthy and broken branches is all the pruning many plants need.

Suckers and Watersprouts

Suckers are undesirable branches that originate from the roots or low on the trunk of a tree or shrub. These branches grow upright and have few leaves. Some species are more prone to suckering than others. To remove suckers from a shrub, dig down to where they originate and pull them off the roots by hand. Avoid cutting suckers off at ground level because they will only send up more shoots from dormant buds. A persistent sucker problem may require the application of a chemical product containing naphthaleneacetic acid (NAA). Never use an herbicide to attempt to control a sucker problem.

Many roses and fruit trees are propagated through grafting. The cultivar chosen for its flowers or fruit is grafted onto a variety with a favorable rootstock. Remove suckers that originate from below the bud union (the graft) because these shoots lack the quality characteristics of the cultivar.

Watersprouts (epicormic shoots) are similar to suckers but develop on the trunk or branches, often as a response to excessive pruning or other injury. A tree that has produced a mass of watersprouts is attempting to replace live wood that has been re-

This apple tree was overpruned the previous winter. Vertically growing watersprouts can be seen even from a distance.

moved. Cutting off all watersprouts will only incite the tree to produce more. On an overpruned tree, allow watersprouts to develop for several years to help the tree restore its energy reserves; the watersprouts can then be thinned and cut back selectively. See "Renovating Overpruned Fruit Trees" on page 143 for guidelines. When removing watersprouts, cut them off just above the swollen area near their base.

Thinning, Reduction, & Heading back

Thinning involves removing entire branches by cutting them back to their point of origin (the trunk or parent branch). Thinning relieves overcrowded growth and allows more light and air to reach the center of a plant. Light will activate any latent buds that are present, stimulating the growth of new branches. Shrubs that are congested with woody branches are good candidates for thinning. Remove older, unproductive branches first to encourage new growth.

Reduction, drop-crotching, or cutting back involves pruning a branch back to a lateral shoot that is a minimum of one-third (preferably one-half) the diameter of the branch being removed. Cutting back is a way of directing the vigor of a plant. It is also sometimes used to reduce the height of a tree. Cutting back also helps to stiffen developing branches and encourages a plant to remain more compact. Note that heading back a tree branch to a bud or to a branch that is less than one-third the diameter of the branch removed is unprofessional; see "Topping, Tipping, & Lions-tailing: Techniques to Avoid" on page 119.

Heading back involves removing the growth tip of a branch by pruning to a bud or to a random point on the branch. Heading back stimulates the growth of new shoots below the cut; it also stiffens existing growth. Only make heading cuts on branches less than two years old. And do not head back to a random point on a branch unless you know the plant has latent buds in that area. Latent buds can sometimes be seen in the bark with a close look. Shearing a hedge is a form of heading back. Heading back is also commonly performed in rose pruning, where it is used to encourage outward-facing buds to grow.

Renovation

Renovation is the practice of cutting back a shrub drastically—sometimes to the ground. It is a technique commonly used in late winter or early spring on shrubs that are overgrown or that contain a lot of woody, unproductive growth. After renovation, latent buds begin to grow and will form productive new shoots. A more gradual way to rejuvenate a plant is to remove 1/3 of older stems each year for three years. Some flowering stems may need to be sacrificed on plants that bloom on year-old wood.

Most conifers (e.g., juniper) do not respond well to renovation. When renovating grafted plants, do not head back below the bud union; also remove any suckers arising from the rootstock. Not all plants respond well to thinning, cutting back, or renovation, and some may be damaged or killed. When in doubt, research the plant in question.

Renovation pruning on storm-damaged trees should be left to a certified arborist. Neglected fruit trees can be renovated by a professional landscaper, provided the heavy pruning is spread out over several years. See "Renovating Neglected Fruit Trees" on page 142 for guidelines.

Espalier and Topiary

Espaliers are trees or plants trained to grow into a decorative shape, flat against a wall, or along a fence or wire. A topiary is a plant shaped into a decorative form such as a geometric shape or the form of an animal. Espaliers and topiary take time to create and maintain. Any general book on pruning will describe how to create these forms.

An example of renovation. This six-foot-tall Mexican Bush Sage (Salvia leucantha) has purple flowers much of the year. The right photo shows three sages cut down to two feet in winter. These plants will regrow again in the spring. Renovation of this plant keeps the canes young and the flowers vibrant. Not all plants respond well to hard heading back or renovation.

Tree Pruning Ordinances

▪ Cities have tree protection ordinances that require arborists to get a permit before pruning a city-owned tree. City-owned trees grow on city property, which includes streetside planting strips. Do not remove branches from streetside trees without getting the necessary permits. In some cases, permits are also required to prune protected species. Call your city to learn the tree protection ordinances for your area.

▪ If a client asks you to cut back the branches of a neighbor's tree that overhangs onto her property, have the client get permission from the neighbor first. In these circumstances, failure to prune the tree to industry standards could result in a liability. It is not acceptable to simply prune the tree's branches or roots back to the property line (Gilman 2002).

Topping, Tipping, & Lions-tailing: Techniques to Avoid

Topping refers to the indiscriminate heading back of large branches in the crown or canopy of a tree to reduce its height. No effort is made to cut back to suitable laterals, and stubs remain. Topping is an unprofessional pruning technique that should not be used unless there are no alternatives to improve or correct a structural defect. Limbs that have been severely headed back are subject to decay and can be entry points for disease. Cracks may form in the trunk below the cuts. Extreme pruning can also cause the tree to produce numerous watersprouts the following season (see page 117). And removing large portions of the canopy puts the tree at risk for sunburn, which cracks and dries the bark, and potentially reduces the tree's life span.

Tipping involves heading back branch tips to buds or weak laterals in an attempt to reduce the width of a tree. Tipping is another unprofessional practice that should be avoided. Tipped limbs are subject to decay and often produce a mass of poorly attached growth at the point of the cuts.

Lions-tailing is the excessive thinning of interior tree branches or the removal of the majority of branches on the lower $2/3$ of a branch. Branches are left bare except for the branch tips. Lions-tailing shifts weight to the end of branches, weakens branches, increases the risk of sunburned bark,

and promotes watersprouts. It is an unprofessional practice that should not be used.

Shrubs and Hedges

Pruning shrubs involves removing weak, crowded, crossing, and diseased growth, and heading back branches that grow out of bounds. A common technique is the selective removal of older growth to promote new growth, which produces better flowers and foliage. Beyond these generalities, pruning requirements can vary considerably between species, so it is important to consult a pruning reference before pruning. Many (though not all) broad-leafed shrubs respond well to renovation if they become too large or woody. Plants can be renovated in a single season; more often, it is better to renovate over two to three years.

Shrubs and hedges are pruned in an informal (natural) or formal (sheared) manner, depending on the plant species and sometimes personal preference. Formal treatment involves shearing plants to a consistent size and shape. A formal style tends to look best on plants with a tighter branch structure and smaller leaves. Boxwood and yew are examples of shrubs commonly treated in a formal manner.

Informal pruning techniques allow plants to develop their natural form, apart from light, general shaping. Plants maintained in an informal manner

Hedges need shearing in the spring and summer. Cut to the underlying shape, leaving some new growth, and avoid cutting into woody growth. Selective thinning cuts can be made once or twice a year to help prevent the hedge from developing a thin shell of foliage.

often have a looser branch structure and larger foliage that is marred by uniform cutting with hedge clippers. Branches are thinned or headed back selectively, not sheared. In general, large-leafed evergreens look poor when sheared. Flowering hedges are usually treated in an informal manner. Camellia is a common example of a broad-leafed, flowering plant pruned in an informal or semiformal manner.

It is a common error for untrained maintenance workers to shape all shrubs and hedges with hedge clippers. Regardless of one's personal preference, some plants should not be sheared. Ornamental plants such as fortnight lily (*Dietes vegeta*), heavenly bamboo (*Nandina domestica*), and ornamental grasses that have been marred through shearing should be allowed to grow out to regain their natural form, then pruned in an informal style. Extensive plant knowledge is not needed to identify these plants. If the general impression is that the plant does not look right sheared, it probably should not be.

Shearing Formal Hedges

Many landscape shrubs and hedges have been shaped into round or rectangular forms; some are used as topiary—plants shaped into decorative forms. To maintain the form of previously shaped shrubs and hedges, shear new growth back to the underlying shape, leaving some new growth (1/3 to 1 inch). This will cause the hedge to increase in size over time, but it maintains new foliage.

Shearing may be necessary once or several times throughout the spring and summer. The final shearing of the season should be the most precise; consider using stakes and twine to serve as guides. Note that a properly trained hedge is narrower at the top than at the base; see "Training Formal Hedges", next.

The branches of woody ornamental plants are green and tender at the tip and become more brown and woody closer to the main stem. As a general rule, cuts made in the tender green growth will result in new growth. Most shearing and shaping cuts are in this tender growth. Deep shearing cuts made in the woody growth can permanently disfigure some plants. For instance, deep shearing cuts into conifers, such as juniper, will leave the area bare and unsightly. Restrict shearing cuts to tender green growth, or research to learn if the plant can tolerate harder heading back.

Note that consistent shearing with hedge clippers can create a thin shell of foliage, which can weaken the health of the plant. Intermittent thinning of broad-leafed shrubs and hedges can improve light penetration into the shrub and help to maintain dense foliage. If thinning is done in early spring, new growth will quickly fill in any gaps.

Most vigorous broad-leafed shrubs and hedges can be headed back hard (by 50 percent) in late winter or early spring if they become too large or woody. Most slow-growing shrubs and coniferous shrubs should not be cut back hard. Pruning reference books or online research will reveal if the shrub can tolerate renovation (described on page 118).

Finally, some hedge plants, such as Xylosma, grow rapidly in the spring. Some landscapers use plant growth inhibitors to reduce the trimming required to manage these plants. Plant growth inhibitors are chemicals that are sprayed on the leaves of a plant to slow plant growth. The commercial use of growth inhibitors requires a pest control applicator's license.

Training Formal Hedges

Hedges are used to partition areas of a landscape, screen views, and reduce wind. To establish a hedge, select hedge plants that suit the growing conditions and the allotted space. Regardless of the species used, small, wide plants are preferred because they establish more quickly and need less corrective pruning to promote branching low to the ground.

Plant spacing varies with the plant species. The plants' branches must overlap to form the hedge, so plants are spaced closer than is recommended for freestanding plants. Space the plants 1 to 2 feet apart; dwarf species can be spaced 4 to 6 inches apart (Brickell and Joyce 1996). Three-foot spacing or greater may be acceptable for large-growing deciduous plants.

If hedge plants are not trained, they will develop a loose branch structure, which does not make for an effective screen or an attractive formal hedge. Training of hedge plants involves regularly heading them back to promote a dense branch structure that begins low to the ground. Pruning at planting varies with the plant species. Vigorous plants with an upright growth habit, such as privet, are headed back hard at planting, to within 6 to 12 inches of the ground.

Subsequent training involves heading back new growth by approximately 1/2 whenever it reaches 6 to 12 inches in length. This should be done for the first few years after planting, until the hedge reaches the desired size. Most evergreens need minimal pruning at planting. Conifers are not pruned hard at planting, and the central stem or leader should be left intact during training.

A well-trained hedge has dense foliage from its top to the ground. For this to come about, light must reach the base of the hedge. Branches on the lower portions of the hedge are at a disadvantage because they receive less sunlight. Compensate for this by training hedges to be wider at the base and narrower on top—this gives the properly trained hedge a slight wedge-like shape when viewed from the side.

Training Young Trees

Many young trees need training, also called structural pruning, to develop a strong and attractive branch structure. Training involves correcting structural problems and selecting suitable branches to form the tree's main branch structure. Without proper training, landscape trees are more at risk for storm damage as they mature. Proper training results in a safer tree with greater longevity and reduces the pruning required over the tree's life span.

Training is a significant part of pruning for the first 25 years of a shade tree's life. Because of the size of maturing landscape trees and the specialized knowledge required to manage them, training should be performed by a certified arborist. However, in the first few years after planting, a landscaper can promote good branch development with some selective pruning. This early training is discussed here. For a discussion of pruning at planting, see page 77. For information on training fruit trees, see "Training Fruit Trees" on page 133.

Most trees have either an excurrent or decurrent form. Excurrent trees maintain a central leader to the top of the tree and have a cone-shaped or pyramidal structure. Most conifers (e.g., pine, spruce, fir, sequoia) are naturally excurrent; they develop strong central leaders and typically do not need training. If a young conifer develops more than one leader, known as multiple leaders or codominant leaders, keep the more vigorous of the two and remove the other. In the event of a dead or damaged leader, train a new leader by tying the most upright stem to a vertical stake or splint.

Decurrent trees form lateral branches that compete with the leader, giving these trees a rounded crown. A single trunk should dominate for the majority of a decurrent tree's height. The following five steps have been adapted from the video *Training Young Trees for Structure and Form,* produced by UC Television (http://www.uctv.tv/search-details.aspx?showID=5598). See the video for complete instruction. These guidelines apply to most decurrent trees.

1. Remove Broken, Diseased, or Dead Branches

Start by removing broken, injured, diseased, dying, and dead branches. If a young tree has good structure, no other pruning may be needed in the first few years.

2. Select a Leader and Remove or Cut Back Competing Leaders

A tree's central stem, called the central leader, will continue to grow vertically unless it is cut back or damaged. Keeping the leader intact promotes a strong branch structure. Remove or shorten branches that compete with the central leader. If there are multiple leaders, remove or shorten some of the competing stems so that the strongest, most vertical stem dominates. This shortening of competing growth is called subordination. Note that some shrubs trained as trees, such as crape myrtle, naturally produce many low stems, and it is acceptable to trains these trees in a multistemmed form.

3. Select and Establish the Lowest Permanent Branch

City ordinances dictate the minimum height of the lowest permanent branch on a tree that is near sidewalks and streets. Generally, the lowest permanent branch above a sidewalk should be a minimum of 8 feet high; the lowest branch along a street should be a minimum of 14 feet high. Where there is no foot or vehicle traffic, the height of the lowest permanent branch may be lower. Keep in mind that branch height does not change as a tree matures.

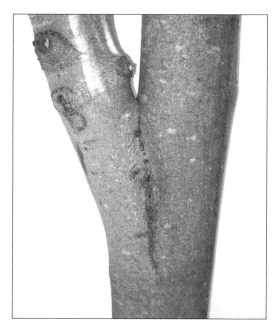

Stems with nearly the same diameter are known as codominant stems. Codominant stems are structurally weak. When selecting scaffold branches, choose branches that are one-half the diameter of the trunk or less, and that do not contain included bark.

Included bark is bark that becomes pinched or enclosed in the branch union. Unlike a branch bark ridge, which is rough and raised, included bark often looks like a crease (arrow). Included bark is a sign of a weak branch attachment. Avoid branches containing included bark when selecting scaffold branches.

The tree may need to increase in height before the lowest permanent branch can be selected.

To help ensure that the lowest permanent branch has a strong attachment to the trunk, select a branch that is $1/2$ the diameter of the trunk or less at the point of attachment and that does not contain included bark. Included bark is bark that has become pinched in a branch crotch. Unlike the branch bark ridge, which is wrinkled and raised, included bark often appears sunken or creased; it is a sign of a weak branch attachment (see photo, previous page). In general, branches with a "V"-shaped crotch may contain included bark, and branches with a "U"-shaped crotch indicate a strong branch attachment. Remove any branches that crowd the lowest permanent branch.

4. Select Scaffold Branches and Remove or Cut Back Competing Branches

Scaffold branches, also called primary scaffold limbs, are permanent branches that form the main branch structure of the tree. The lowest permanent branch is the first scaffold branch. Several other scaffold branches should be selected above the lowest permanent branch.

Scaffold branches should be $1/2$ the diameter of the trunk or less at the point of attachment. This size difference promotes the development of the branch collar. The branch collar is an area of trunk tissue that surrounds the base of a branch (see "Cut Placement for Tree Branches" on page 114). Branches with collars are better attached to the tree than branches without collars. A branch with a diameter larger than $1/2$ the diameter of the trunk should be cut back to slow its growth. Branches with included bark have weak attachments and should not be selected as scaffold branches.

To form a balanced crown, scaffold branches should be well-spaced radially around the trunk and vertically on the trunk. Vertical spacing between scaffold branches should be 18 inches for trees that will have a 12-inch-diameter trunk at maturity; a 12-inch vertical spacing is recommended for smaller trees. Remove branches that crowd the framework branches and cut back others. Remove

This tree's scaffold limbs have inadequate vertical spacing, which increases the risk of limb breakage. Training young trees involves maintaining a single dominant leader and selecting scaffold limbs with adequate vertical spacing.

or shorten branches that have included bark, and leave small branches between scaffolds to serve as temporary branches.

5. Select Temporary Branches Below the Lowest Permanent Branch

Branches growing below the lowest permanent branch are called temporary branches. Temporary branches produce energy and help the trunk increase in diameter near the base. This results in a tapered trunk, which helps the tree withstand wind stress. Temporary branches also help to protect the trunk from sunburn and physical injury, such as bark damage from power equipment.

Head back temporary branches to 2 to 3 buds to slow their increase in diameter. Temporary branches of low vigor are preferred and may not need to be headed back. Remove temporary branches that are larger than $1/2$ the diameter of the trunk. Temporary branches can usually be removed once the trunk is 3 to 4 inches in diameter.

Felling Small Trees

Cutting horizontally through the trunk of a small tree will cause the trunk to pinch down on the saw. A horizontal cut also provides little control over the direction the tree will fall. To fell a small tree correctly, start by choosing the direction you want the tree to fall. On that side, cut a wedge shape out of the trunk. The top of the wedge should be at approximately a 60 degree angle; the bottom of the wedge should be horizontal. The wedge should enter approximately 1/3 of the way into the trunk. This is the notching cut.

On the side of the trunk opposite the notching cut, saw through the trunk horizontally, approximately 1 inch above the bottom of the notching cut. This is the felling cut. Do not cut all the way through the tree on the felling cut. Leave some wood to act as a hinge and gently coax the tree to fall. Leave some trunk to use as leverage if you intend to dig up the roots; if not, make a final cut close to the ground. See diagram 3. To reduce the risk of personal injury or property damage, limit the use of this technique to trees that are in open areas and that have a trunk diameter of 5 inches or less.

Diagram 3

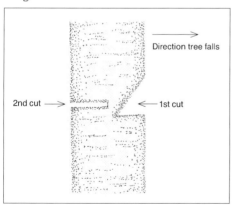

This diagram shows the technique for felling a small tree. The first cut is the notching cut. The notching cut should enter no more than one-third of the way into the trunk. The second cut is the felling cut. The felling cut is made opposite the notching cut, approximately one inch above the base of the notching cut. Do not cut all the way through the trunk during the felling cut; leave some wood to act as a hinge and gently push the tree until it falls.

Stopping Stump Sprouts

Many tree stumps send up unwanted new growth called stump sprouts. To prevent stump sprouts, apply a stump killing product to the freshly cut stump. Note that the commercial use of chemical garden products requires a pest control applicator's license. See page 70 for information.

To speed up decomposition, make several deep line cuts in the stump with a chainsaw and cover the stump with soil. If the client wants the stump removed immediately, refer him to a stump grinding service.

Pruning Roses

Roses are grouped into different classes, and each class of rose is pruned differently. This chapter focuses on the pruning of modern bush roses, since they are the most common roses in residential landscapes. The pruning of standards, ramblers, climbing roses, and shrub roses is also covered.

Modern Bush Roses

Modern bush roses are a combination of two different roses: the rose chosen for its flowers and the rose chosen for its rootstock. The two are grafted together at the base, called the bud union. Hybrid teas, grandifloras, floribundas, and miniatures are all examples of modern bush roses.

In the simplest terms, the goals of pruning modern bush roses are to thin them out and head them back. More specifically, the goals are to remove unproductive and poorly placed stems and to promote the growth of strong new flowering stems. Annual pruning in late winter, after the risk of frost has passed, encourages strong new growth each spring. This new growth produces the best flowers. Below are six guidelines for pruning modern bush roses. The recommended pruning cuts can be made in any order.

Six Guidelines for Pruning Modern Bush Roses

1. Make Proper Pruning Cuts

Use sharp hand pruners when pruning roses. Dull pruners can leave stems with rough edges, which may make the rose more susceptible to disease. Always head back to a bud or remove an entire branch. When heading back to a bud, make the cut 1/4 inch above the bud at a 45 degree angle that slopes away from the bud. An angled cut allows water to run off, helping to prevent disease.

Cuts made even 1/2 inch above a bud will leave a section of branch—a stub—that can die back. This "die-back" can creep down the entire branch. A dead stub is a probable indication that the cane is diseased. Diseased canes can be identified by their brown centers; the center of a healthy rose cane is white. Areas of die-back must be removed below the point of infection. This often requires hard corrective pruning, which depletes the plant's energy reserves and weakens its health over time. Proper pruning cuts help the rose recover disease-free. See photos, next page.

Left: This rose stem has been cut too far away from the nearest bud, leaving a stub. The correct cut placement is 1/4 inch above a bud at an angle that slopes away from the bud.

Right: Stubs often lead to die-back. Die-back will progress into the healthy cane if left untreated. Infected canes are brown in the center. Cut infected canes back below the point of infection.

2. Remove Dead, Weak, or Crossing Growth

The removal of dead, weak, or crossing growth is a good way to begin rose pruning. Cut dead or diseased branches back to a healthy juncture. And cut off any growth less than the thickness of a pencil. This weak growth does not produce many flowers and it is prone to disease. Remove one of any two stems rubbing against each other. Rubbing can tear the outer layer of a stem, making the plant susceptible to disease.

Note: For roses growing in cold-winter regions, limit fall pruning to these sanitary measures, and leave the more extensive pruning, described in the next steps, until spring. See "Winterizing Roses" on page 131 for more information.

3. Remove Stems That Grow Toward the Center

Remove stems that grow toward the center of the plant. This helps to prevent crossing growth and improves air circulation in the center of the plant, reducing the risk of disease. Because of the absence of branches in the center, a well-pruned rose is sometimes said to have a vase-like shape.

4. Remove Older, Unproductive Canes

The base of a modern bush rose is called the bud union. The bud union is where the cultivar (the desirable rose variety) was grafted to the rootstock. Stems that originate at the bud union are called canes. As canes age, they become woody and produce less vigorous growth and poorer quality flowers. The removal of old canes is perhaps the most neglected aspect of pruning modern bush roses. Many people are reluctant to remove what seems like an essential branch. However, when an old cane is removed, a rose often sends up a productive new cane from the bud union or from a bud low on an existing cane.

Stems branching from a cane should be vigorous and produce good-sized flowers. If the majority of growth arising from a cane is weak (less than a pencil's thickness), remove the entire cane. Most brown, woody canes are less vigorous than green or partially green canes. Remove old canes at their base using a pruning saw. If a new cane has sprouted from the base of an old cane, cut back to the new cane.

If all the rose canes are unproductive, you can remove them all. This extreme measure is an example of renovation. With proper irrigation and fertilization, the rose should produce new canes in the spring. A more gradual method of renovating a rose involves removing one or two old canes per year until the entire plant has productive new growth. This gradual approach helps the plant maintain its energy reserves, and it is less likely to raise concerns among clients.

Some rose experts recommend cleaning the bud union gently with a wire brush to stimulate basal breaks (new canes). At least one rosarian recommends removing canes greater than 3/4 inch in thickness during the growing season, rather than during dormancy, to facilitate callusing (Kuze 2003).

5. Remove Suckers By Hand

The rootstock of a modern bush rose can produce suckers that divert energy from the cultivar. A rose sucker is easy to identify because it sprouts from the soil or below the bud union, indicating it has sprouted from the rootstock. Rose suckers typically have seven leaflets and are often a different shade

This modern bush rose is crowded with unproductive growth. Branches near the top are spindly and produce small flowers. This happens when old, woody canes are not removed.

When older, unproductive canes are removed near the bud union, a rose typically sends up new canes that will produce more vigorous growth and more attractive flowers. Renovation is best done by removing only a few old canes each year.

Woody, old cane

Young cane

of green than the cultivar. Dig away the soil to find where the sucker begins, then pull off the sucker at its source. Suckers cut off at the soil surface will only send up more shoots.

6. Head Back Remaining Canes

Head back the remaining canes to outward-facing buds. Heading back to an outward-facing bud helps to keep the center open and encourages a desirable, vase-like shape. Modern bush roses vary in how far they should be headed back. See the following categories of modern bush roses for guidelines.

Note that heading height is partly a matter of preference. Harder heading back tends to produce fewer but larger flowers. However, several consecutive seasons of hard heading back can weaken the plant's health. In general, vigorous roses should be allowed to remain larger.

In cold winter areas, the canes of modern bush roses should be headed back to 2 to 3 feet in the fall to reduce the risk of damage by winter winds. More extensive pruning is postponed until spring. See "Winterizing Roses" on page 131 for more information. Below are some categories of modern bush roses and their unique pruning requirements.

Hybrid Teas

Hybrid teas are the most common modern bush rose and the most popular rose overall. Most hybrid teas are 3 to 6 feet tall. Each stem produces one or several roses, and the plant blooms repeatedly throughout the growing season, as do all modern bush roses. Follow the six guidelines for rose pruning, and leave 3 to 6 canes when finished. Finally, remove the top 1/3 to 1/2 of each cane, heading back to outward-facing buds. Harder heading back is not necessary unless you live in a cold winter area where it is sometimes necessary to remove frost damage.

You can also decide how far to head back based on a cane's thickness. For instance, if a cane is 1/2 inch thick at 3 feet, this indicates that the hybrid tea is vigorous—the cane won't need to be cut back far for it to produce strong growth that season. Ideally, vigorous roses are allowed to increase in size and are not pruned to a predetermined height. Larger roses are more resilient and produce more flowers. With that said, it is acceptable to prune hybrid teas back harder if you want the rose to produce fewer but larger flowers.

Before-and-after photos of a hybrid tea or grandiflora. Branches growing toward the center have been removed, giving the plant a vase-like shape. In temperate climates, many modern bush roses do not drop all of their leaves in winter. Remove leaves when signs of disease are present. Leaves should also be cleared from the ground around the base of the rose.

Grandifloras

Grandifloras are a category of modern bush rose that look like large hybrid teas. Many grandifloras are over 5 feet tall. Grandifloras are sometimes mistaken for hybrid teas, and vice versa; however, pruning is nearly the same for both. Leave 4 to 6 canes, and reduce the height of the canes by 1/3.

Floribundas

Floribundas are distinct in that they produce bunches of flowers per stem. The flowers are smaller than those of hybrid teas, but not as small as the flowers of polyanthas. Floribundas are usually 3 to 4 feet tall and are bushier than either hybrid teas or grandifloras. For this reason, they are often grown as shrubs or hedges. Leave all productive canes (usually 6 to 8), and reduce the height of the canes by 1/4.

Polyanthas

Polyanthas produce many small flowers. They are smaller plants than floribundas, and they are not common in residential landscapes. Leave all productive canes, and reduce the height of the canes by 1/2.

Miniatures

Miniatures are usually less than 1 1/2 feet tall and produce tiny flowers. Remove dead stems, and reduce the plant's height by 1/2 or more. Thin congested growth as necessary.

Other Roses

Standards

A standard, also known as a tree rose, is a bush rose grafted onto a tall, bare rose cane from another variety: the result is a rose that looks like a 4- to 5-foot-tall tree. The head is usually a modern bush rose, such as a hybrid tea or floribunda, and pruning is mostly the same as for these roses. Remove suckers that grow from the trunk, and support the trunk with staking. Deadhead during spring and summer. See "Deadheading", next page.

Standards tend to be top heavy and have to balance on a bud union that is off the ground, so prune them

A standard rose in summer. Standards have to balance on a bud union that is off the ground, so they are kept more compact than other modern bush roses. Notice the permanent stake supports.

a little harder than you would normally prune a hybrid tea or floribunda. It is also important to maintain symmetry in the top growth. An imbalance of growth can be countered by pruning slightly harder on the side with *weak* growth. Harder pruning on the side with weak growth encourages the plant to produce new growth on that side, helping it to balance out.

A weeping standard is a standard with the head of a weeping rose. Weeping standards produce long, arching shoots that bend to the ground. Do not cut weeping roses back like modern bush roses. Allow the rose to develop its weeping habit for the first few years after planting, then thin out older shoots at the bud union as the head becomes crowded.

Ramblers

Rambling groundcover roses produce long canes that root when they touch ground. These roses spread and fill in the space available to them, so they are frequently used as groundcovers. Ramblers can be identified by their seven leaflets; climbing roses have five leaflets. Ramblers usually bloom once a year on growth from the previous season. Prune them after flowering to preserve the current season's blooms. Remove dead and diseased branches, and cut back stems that grow out of bounds. Ramblers respond well to renovation if they become too large or tangled.

Climbing Roses

Climbing roses are commonly grown along wires or a trellis. Some bloom repeatedly throughout the spring and summer, others bloom only once, in the spring. To train young climbers, spread out several canes in a fan-like fashion, then tie them loosely to their support with garden tape. Allow the plant to develop for two to three years, and tie the main branches in vertically.

The main branches will produce lateral growth that should be tied in horizontally. The horizontal position activates flower buds and discourages growth buds along stems. Even bending a bare, vertical stem to a horizontal position encourages it to produce flowers. As an alternate, more informal training method, allow canes to develop, then tie them to a support in a broad, back-and-forth manner. Crossing branches are unavoidable in this type of training.

Annual pruning is different for repeat bloomers than for spring-only bloomers. In the winter, cut the flowered stems of repeat bloomers back to 2 or 3 upward- or outward-facing buds; some gardeners leave more buds. These buds will produce flowers in the spring. Tie in vigorous new canes in a back-and-forth manner. Deadhead during the spring and summer. Remove old canes on repeat bloomers as you would for hybrid teas or grandifloras.

Prune spring-only bloomers in spring, just after the blooms are spent. The horizontal canes will produce new growth that will flower the following spring. If you prune spring-only bloomers in winter, you risk cutting away the growth that the next year's flowers will form on. Cut thinner stems back to 2 to 3 buds. Leave the horizontal framework. Remove unproductive canes at their base.

Shrub Roses

Many shrub roses, such as species and old garden roses, are closer to how roses are in the wild. They vary greatly in height and have either an upright or spreading habit. Many of these roses flower on older wood and, therefore, should not be cut back each year as modern bush roses are. It can be difficult for the amateur to identify species or old garden roses; when in doubt, ask a nursery professional. Older properties will be more likely to have shrub roses than newer developments. These roses are frequently used as hedges.

Once established, shrub roses don't need much pruning. Remove dead, diseased, crossing, or weak growth, and remove old canes that are no longer productive. Don't cut these roses back except for purposes of light, general shaping. Prune repeat bloomers in the winter, and prune spring-only bloomers after the blooms are spent in spring. The homeowner is likely to know if the rose blooms only one time per season. Shrub roses can be renovated. Deadheading is acceptable for repeat bloomers. Stop deadheading in mid-summer to encourage the formation of hips (see photo, opposite page). More detailed pruning instructions for shrub roses can be found in pruning reference texts.

Deadheading

Deadheading is the practice of cutting off faded flowers on repeat-flowering roses. Deadheading prevents the rose from directing its energy into seed production and encourages the continued production of flowers throughout the growing season. Deadheading is not often the highest maintenance priority, though it does keep roses looking their best. It is also an easy part of rose pruning that some clients enjoy doing themselves. Modern bush roses respond well to deadheading. Deadheading is not necessary for groundcover roses and some shrub roses.

To deadhead, cut the spent flower back to a bud just below the flower. Some rose experts recommend cutting back to the first stem with five leaves—a strong bud can be found here in the leaf axil. When deadheading cluster-flowering roses such as floribundas and polyanthas, wait until all the roses in the bunch fade, then remove the flowered stem. In cold winter areas, stop deadheading in late summer and allow the rose to form hips. This will help the plant harden off for winter.

Rose Pruning Tools

Most rose pruning is done with hand pruners, also called secateurs. Bypass pruners provide a cleaner cut on green growth than anvil-type pruners. A pruning saw can be used to remove old, woody canes at the bud union; loppers can also be used, though they can be more difficult to position, and the hook may damage canes. Avoid cheap pruners and loppers because their stamped metal blades flex and cause cutting problems. When the job is finished, dirty blades should be cleaned with steel wool, sharpened with a suitable sharpening stone, and lightly coated with metal lubricant.

To help prevent the spread of disease between stems, some experts recommend cleaning blades and saws with a household disinfectant cleaner or ethyl-alcohol-based hand sanitizer after cutting through diseased wood. Other experts think this is unnecessary, stating that disease infection is less related to mechanical transmission than it is to varietal susceptibility and environment.

Sanitation and Dormant Spray

In mild-winter areas, modern bush roses sometimes retain leaves through the winter. Leaves containing signs of insect damage or fungal disease should be stripped from the plant after pruning. All leaves and stems should be removed from around the base of roses. Diseases can overwinter on fallen leaves and reinfect the plant in the spring.

Roses can be sprayed with a dormant spray to reduce overwintering insects and disease. Dormant sprays commonly consist of a sulfur or copper product to control disease, coupled with horticultural oil to smother overwintering insects. Copper-based products protect against a broader range of diseases than sulfur-based products. The same dormant spray that is used for fruit trees and berries can be used for roses. For more information, see "Dormant Spraying of Fruit Trees" on page 146.

In the winter, many shrub roses form attractive seed pods, called hips. The hips shown here have shades of red, orange, and yellow. Do not deadhead repeat-bloomers after mid-summer if you want to encourage the formation of hips.

Winterizing Roses

Modern bush roses growing in areas that experience winter temperatures below 28 degrees F for extended periods require winter protection. Roses that are not protected can be damaged by the freezing/thawing cycles of winter and may not recover in spring. Winterization practices aim to prepare roses for dormancy and insulate them so they remain dormant through the winter. Roses that grow on their own root systems, such as species roses and miniatures, are better suited to endure freezing winter conditions and may not require winterization.

Hardy roses, by definition, are those which are better able to withstand harsh winters. Measures taken to keep roses disease-free during the growing season will benefit roses during dormancy. Cease nitrogen applications in late summer to avoid promoting tender growth that is susceptible to freeze damage. After the first frost, strip away all leaves and clear fallen leaves from around the base of the rose. Apply a dormant spray if necessary.

Limit fall pruning to removing dead, diseased, and damaged growth. Long canes can be cut back to 2 to 3 feet to prevent them from being damaged by winter winds. More extensive pruning should be delayed until spring. Stop deadheading in late summer and leave spent flowers on the plant so hips can form. This will help the plant harden off for winter.

Dormancy can begin after the first frost, and this is the time to insulate roses, not sooner. Insulation protects roses from winter temperature fluctuations and helps to keep them dormant. A heavy snow cover that remains through the winter can help to moderate temperatures, though insulation should still be considered. Water the rose once before applying insulation.

Hilling is a common insulation technique that involves mounding 10 to 12 inches of soil around the canes and bud union. Digging near roses can expose roots to winter damage, so the soil should be dug up from a different part of the yard. Sandy soil is preferred. Alternatively, manure, compost, or another organic material can be used. Mulch is sometimes added on top of the soil. Before mounding the soil, tie the canes together with synthetic twine or other material that won't damage the canes. Roses can also be insulated with commercial products, such as rose cones.

The canes of modern climbers can be removed from their support and pinned flat to the soil, or laid in a shallow trench and then covered with soil. If this is not practical, burlap or other forms of insulation can be wrapped around the canes, though this provides less protection. Standards can be dug up, laid in a trench, covered with mulch, and buried for the winter. Some experts recommend digging up standards that are growing in the ground and moving them to a cold, sheltered location for the winter. Either of these techniques can also be used for potted roses. Roses stored in a sheltered location require some water during the winter to keep them from drying out.

Wait until freezing temperatures have passed before removing insulation in the spring. Cut away any winter-damaged growth and prune as appropriate for that rose. Nursery professionals may be able to suggest additional winterization products and practices.

Pruning Fruit Trees

When left unpruned, many full-scale fruit trees produce hundreds of pounds of small fruit, mostly on the tallest branches. Fruit growers learned long ago that pruning could be used to produce larger fruit that was easier to pick, while maintaining good yields each year. Even with the arrival of semi-dwarfing rootstocks, the goals of pruning fruit trees today are the same: size control and fruit management.

More specifically, the goals of pruning fruit trees are to reduce the amount of fruit (which increases the size of the remaining fruit), to renew fruiting wood, to increase light penetration into the canopy (which stimulates new growth and improves the red color of fruit), to maintain the framework of the tree, and to control tree size. Often a single pruning cut will accomplish several of these goals.

Training Fruit Trees

In general, the goal of fruit tree training in the residential landscape is to create a tree with a strong branch structure that produces most of its fruit at a relatively low picking height. The most common fruit tree training systems are the central leader, modified central leader, and open center systems.

In the central leader system, the tree's central leader is left intact to provide extra support for the framework branches. Some orchardists train apple trees using the central leader system because these trees bear heavy loads of fruit. The central leader system is also well suited to the natural growth habit of apples. Pears are also sometimes trained using the central leader method for similar reasons. The open center system can be used to train all fruit trees in the residential setting, and it is the system described here.

Training a fruit tree usually takes three to five years and involves both dormant and summer pruning. Dormant pruning is done in late winter after the risk of extreme cold, but before bud break. During the first two to three years, fruit production should be minimized so the tree can devote its energy to the development of a sound branch structure. Thin the crop as needed to ensure that fruit does not bend young scaffold limbs to undesireable positions. The following guidelines can be applied to all sizes of fruit trees except genetic dwarfs.

Open Center System

In the open center system, the central leader of a young tree is headed back, and three to four branches are selected to form the main branch framework. Removing the central leader allows more sunlight to penetrate through the center of the tree to lower branches. Sunlight activates flower buds, resulting in more fruit on lower limbs.

At Planting: The training of a fruit tree to the open center system can begin at planting. The central leader should be headed back to 1 1/2 to 3 feet above the soil. Heading the leader will promote branching near the cut. Branching can be promoted higher than 3 feet, though this will increase the height of fruit picking.

If a young tree already has several well-placed branches 1 1/2 to 3 feet above the soil, they can be used as scaffold limbs, provided they are well-spaced radially and vertically. Cut the leader back to the existing branches. If these young branches are of low vigor, head them to 2 to 3 buds to encour-

age them to grow vigorously. Cut all other shoots back to approximately 6 inches—these will serve as temporary branches, shading the tree and producing energy. Finally, paint the trunk and any exposed branches with a 50/50 mixture of white latex paint and water to prevent sunburn.

First Growing Season: Lateral shoots will form at the height of the cut leader and below. Choose 3 to 4 laterals to be the primary scaffold limbs, that is, the tree's main framework branches. Primary scaffolds should have angles of attachment of 45 to 60 degrees and be well-spaced around the tree, with at least several inches of vertical spacing between them. Well-placed shoots with narrow angles of attachment can be spread to wider angles using toothpicks or clothes pins. Some trees, such as pears, naturally tend toward upright growth and benefit from manual spreading.

Head back or remove any branches that compete with the young framework limbs, and head back any branches below the framework limbs. Leave

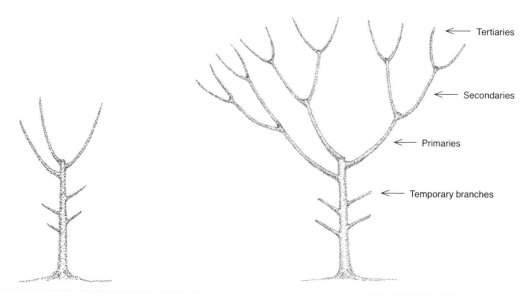

Diagram 4. In the central leader training system, the central leader of a young fruit tree is headed back to three or four well-spaced branches, which will become the tree's primary scaffold limbs. The leader is headed back even if no suitable scaffold branches exist; shoots will develop at the height of the cut and below. Temporary branches on the trunk are headed back to two or three buds.

Tertiaries

Secondaries

Primaries

Temporary branches

Diagram 5. This diagram illustrates the main branch framework of an open center tree. Though it is not shown in this diagram or in diagram 4, smaller shoots should be kept on all of the framework limbs to provide shade and produce energy. Temporaries are headed back to slow their growth; they are removed before they reach two inches in diameter.

enough small branches to provide shade in the center of the tree. These shading branches can be headed back.

First Summer: Once the primary scaffold limbs increase in length, head them back to 2 to 2 1/2 feet to promote branching. The branches that develop here are called secondary scaffold limbs. When heading the primary limbs to promote the secondaries, examine the branch to find the growth buds in the bark. Head each primary scaffold back to outward- and upward-facing buds pointed in directions that will eventually fill out the crown evenly. If branches have already formed on the primary scaffolds, secondaries can be selected from these.

First Winter After Planting: If the primary scaffolds didn't grow much during the first growing season, cut them back to 2 to 3 buds to promote their vigorous growth the next season (Ingels and Dong 2000).

If the secondary scaffolds were not selected during summer pruning, select and cut back to secondaries during dormancy (late winter). If the secondaries have grown enough, cut them back to 2 to 2 1/2 feet.

The framework branches that develop from the secondary scaffolds are called the tertiary scaffold limbs. Again, if suitable tertiary shoots exist, cut back to these. If not, head back the secondaries to buds aiming in suitable directions. The aim is to fill out the tree's crown in a vase-like fashion.

Throughout the training process, remove any suckers that develop from the rootstock, maintain enough shoots to provide shading and energy, and head back or remove branches that compete with the scaffold limbs. Training can be considered complete once the tertiary limbs have developed. The result is a strong, open framework of branches that will support many smaller, fruit-bearing branches. Prune as a mature fruit tree from this point on.

If a fruit tree is not trained in the first few years, corrective pruning may be needed to create well-spaced framework branches. Removing large portions of misplaced wood and further delaying fruit production may be warranted.

A plum tree trained to the open center system. Branching has been promoted close to the ground for ease of fruit picking. The dark band at the base of the tree is a sticky insect barrier; see "Aphids" on page 147 for more information.

Fruit Tree Physiology

Understanding the following aspects of fruit tree physiology will help you make pruning decisions.

Flower Buds

Flowers develop from flower buds that form in the shoots and branches of fruit trees. (Technically, flowers develop from flower buds or mixed buds, depending on the species.) Flower buds look similar to growth buds but tend to be larger and rounder. Their relative plumpness is the easiest way to identify them; this is true for most fruit trees. Flowers produce fruit when pollinated.

Fruit trees differ in how they produce flower buds and fruit. Apples, pears, cherries, almonds, plums, and apricots produce most of their fruit on spurs, which are short lateral shoots containing one or several flower buds. Most spurs develop on wood that is at least two years old. Each spur produces fruit for several years before becoming unproductive. Spur life refers to the number of years a spur remains productive.

Spur life varies with tree type. For example, the spurs on most pear trees remain productive for a little over five years, whereas the spurs on certain apple varieties can produce fruit for up to twenty years. The spur life of common fruit tree varieties is provided in "Pruning Guidelines for Common Fruit Trees" on page 140. On average, spurs remain productive for three to five years. Some varieties of the above-mentioned trees, most notably apples, can be tip-bearing instead of spur-forming. Tip-bearing describes varieties that produce fruit at the tips of branches.

Peach and nectarine trees do not produce spurs but instead produce flowers on year-old wood, sometimes called second-year wood. This means that in one season a peach tree grows a branch containing flower buds, and in the next season those buds blossom and produce fruit. Many peach and nectarine buds come in clusters of three: usually the outer two are flower buds, and the center bud is a growth bud (see photo). Still other trees, such as figs, fruit on growth that developed the same season. Figs also produce fruit on year-old wood. Note that cherries, apricots, and plums produce most of their fruit on spurs, though they also produce some fruit on year-old wood.

Sunlight stimulates the development of flower buds. Without pruning, fruit trees tend to become congested with branches. This prevents light from reaching the center and lower portions of the tree, which hinders fruit production in these areas. The majority of fruit will naturally develop higher in the canopy, but this can be countered to a degree. Thinning increases light penetration through the canopy, stimulating the development of flower buds on lower branches.

A horizontal branch produces more flower buds than a vertical one. Even bending an upright shoot to a more horizontal position will cause it to develop more flower buds. Growers use this knowledge to increase fruit yields. When choosing between two closely spaced branches, the more horizontal one is usually the one to keep.

Rootstocks

Growers propagate fruit trees through grafting. The scion—that is, the species chosen for its fruit—is grafted onto the rootstock of another variety. This can be done to reduce a tree's height, increase its resistance to disease, and/or increase its tolerance of different soil conditions. Semi-dwarf and dwarf rootstocks reduce a tree's height by restricting its natural vigor.

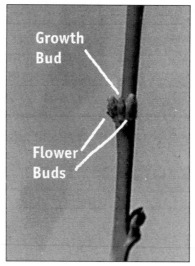

Left: Flower buds on the short spurs of a cherry tree. Most spur systems are larger and longer than those found on cherries.

Right: Typical bud configuration on peaches and nectarines. A narrow growth bud sits between two fatter flower buds. This branch grew the previous spring and will fruit the next.

Trees grown on standard rootstocks are the largest, with heights ranging from 15 to 40 feet. Standard rootstocks do not provide size-reduction and are the most hardy. Semi-dwarfing rootstocks produce a mid-size tree, with heights ranging from 12 to 20 feet. Dwarfing rootstocks produce trees with heights ranging from 6 to 12 feet. Dwarfing can also be produced by genetic breeding. The reduced size of genetic dwarfs is not the result of restricting rootstocks.

Rootstocks also vary in their disease resistance and tolerance of different soil conditions. For example, peaches and nectarines don't naturally grow well in poorly draining soil, but with the right rootstock they can be grown in these conditions. Catalog growers in your state can help with scion/rootstock selection. Fruit trees purchased from a local nursery should be well-suited to regional growing conditions.

Chill Factor

During the winter, fruit trees go dormant and temporarily cease growing. To overcome this dormancy, fruit trees must have a certain number of chill hours each winter. A chill hour refers to one hour below 45 degrees F (7°C). Temperatures below 32 degrees F or above 60 degrees F will not provide the necessary chilling effect. To illustrate, figs may require as little as 100 hours of winter chill, while some apples may require 1000 hours. If the required hours of winter chill are not met, the tree may experience delayed leaf production in the spring, prolonged blossoming, bud deterioration or drop, and few, if any, flowers; all resulting in little or no fruit production (Pittenger 2002).

Note that chill hours do not have to be consecutive. However, mid-winter heat spells (temperatures over 65°F) can have a "negative chilling" effect, and hours spent at these temperatures are subtracted from the accumulated chill hours. Growers include chill requirement information (sometimes called minimum chill requirement, or MCR) for the trees they sell and can suggest trees well-suited to a region. Note that different microclimates on a property may produce different chilling effects, so planting location can be important.

This photo shows one gardener's attempt to counteract the vertical growth habit of a pear tree. By forcing the branch to a more horizontal position, it will produce more flower buds and fruit.

Alternate Bearing

Alternate bearing, also called biennial bearing, describes a fruit tree that produces a heavy crop one year and little or no fruit the next. Common examples of trees prone to alternate bearing are pecans, apricots, and some apples, though all fruit tree types can be affected. Regular pruning helps prevent this problem. One corrective measure for alternate bearing involves pruning heavily following a year with a light crop, and pruning lightly following a year with a heavy crop. Hand-thinning young fruit in heavy bearing years is another remedy.

Pruning and Growth

To prune fruit trees correctly, you must consider the immediate effect of pruning cuts as well as your prediction of the tree's growth response. As described in "Pruning and Plant Biology" on page 113, a shoot's terminal bud produces a hormone called auxin, which suppresses the growth of lateral (axillary) buds below it. When the terminal bud is pruned away, the lateral buds are freed from the effects of the auxin and begin to grow.

The harder a young shoot is cut back, the more vigorously the lateral buds will grow. For example, if a 3-foot shoot is cut back several inches, it may produce only a small amount of lateral bud growth in the spring and summer; if the shoot is cut back moderately, lateral bud growth will be more pronounced; if the shoot is cut back hard, lateral bud growth will be vigorous and often several new branches will develop near the point of the cut. In general, the more vigorous the original shoot, the stronger the resulting bud growth will be in response to pruning.

This understanding might be used to encourage a well-placed shoot to fill in a gap in the crown or to correct an imbalance of growth on a tree. Note that the harder a shoot is cut back, the fewer flower buds that shoot will produce.

After pruning, the tree produces new vegetative growth to compensate for the growth that was removed. Skilled fruit tree pruning makes use of this understanding. By removing a percentage of older fruit wood each year, a tree is encouraged to grow new shoots that will produce fruit in future seasons. Note that hard pruning will not cause a tree to increase in overall size. Pruning stimulates a growth response, but has an overall dwarfing effect.

Overpruning

As a general rule, no more than 10 to 15 percent of a tree's live foliage should be removed in a single season. Overpruning, or cutting off too much growth in one season, can cause a fruit tree to produce vigorous, upright growth called watersprouts (described on page 117). Watersprouts are unsightly, poorly attached, and produce less fruit. In addition, the tree withdraws energy from fruit production until it produces new growth. Overpruning also exposes limbs to sunlight, which puts them at risk for sunburn. Topping is the most common cause of overpruning. Significant thinning of congested growth may need to be carried out over several seasons to avoid stimulating watersprouts. See "Renovating Neglected Fruit Trees" on page 142 for more information.

Time of Pruning for Fruit Trees

Fruit tree pruning is generally done in late winter before bud break, because there is less risk of winter damage at this time. It is also easier to see branches in the absence of leaves, and the labor demands of other tasks are lower at this time of year. Trees that are susceptible to fire blight, such as apples and pears, are usually pruned in late winter to reduce the risk of infection.

Summer pruning is commonly used to keep growth in check on trained form trees. Summer pruning is thought to have a dwarfing effect because pruning slows root growth and removes vegetative growth that would otherwise be used to produce energy. The dwarfing effect is strongest when trees are pruned just after they complete their branch extension growth in early summer. In some areas, stone fruits, such as plums, apricots, and cherries, are more susceptible to disease when dormant pruned, and summer pruning is recommended. In cold-winter areas, pruning should be done no later than midsummer to prevent late-season growth that may be damaged by freezing temperatures.

Three Steps To Pruning Fruit Trees

Fruit tree pruning can be divided into three steps: cleaning, thinning, and size control. These guidelines apply to most fruit trees. The specific pruning requirements of common fruit trees are included in the next topic. As with all pruning, make proper pruning cuts, and use the three-cut method as necessary (see "Cut Placement" on page 114).

1. Cleaning

Cleaning is the removal of dead, diseased, and broken branches. Rubbing branches, suckers, and watersprouts are also frequently removed. Suckers and watersprouts are vigorous, upright branches with relatively few leaves. Suckers should be cut or torn off where they originate below the soil. Cutting them off at the soil surface results in continued growth. Watersprouts can be removed where they originate on a branch; it is best to rub them off when they are less than 1 inch long.

A tree that has been overpruned in a previous season may have numerous watersprouts. In this situation, it is best not to remove all the watersprouts in a single season; refer to the topic "Renovating

Overpruned Fruit Trees" on page 143. If a tree has recently been topped or otherwise overpruned, allow watersprouts to develop for several years before beginning thinning. This will help the tree rebuild its energy reserves. For related information, see "Suckers and Watersprouts" on page 117.

Remove mummies, which are old, shriveled fruit from the previous season that remain on a tree. Mummies can harbor diseases that can infect the new crop. Rake up fallen fruit and leaves around the base of the tree for similar reasons. Cleaning is all the pruning some trees require.

2. Thinning

Thinning cuts remove branches where they originate. Thinning serves multiple purposes: It relieves congestion so that light can penetrate into the canopy, stimulating growth on lower branches; it reduces the crop on trees that produce excessive fruit, which increases the size and quality of the remaining fruit; and it encourages the growth of new fruit wood that will produce crops in future years.

The tree type determines the amount of thinning required. To illustrate, apricot spurs produce fruit for three years before becoming unproductive. To ensure a supply of new fruit wood on apricot trees, 1/3 of older spur-bearing branches should be removed each year. Sweet cherries have spurs that can produce fruit for as long as 10 years and, therefore, need much less annual pruning.

Unpruned fruit trees often appear as a congested mass of branches. To orient yourself, it's helpful to identify the tree's framework branches. Visually trace your way along the primary scaffold limbs to the secondaries and tertiaries (see diagram 5 on page 134). Initial thinning can focus on congested growth in the tree's center and around the framework branches. Note that trees don't neatly conform to the diagram of an open center tree. A branch can be considered a part of the framework if it helps to fill in space in the crown.

Additional thinning may be necessary depending on the tree's spur life and the degree of shade in the canopy. Thin no more wood than is recommended for the tree type. For specifics, see "Pruning Guide-

lines for Common Fruit Trees", next. In general, congested, weak, or unproductive growth, and upright and downward shoots are candidates for thinning. Long shoots that extend through the tree's center can be thinned or headed back, though some foliage should be preserved in the tree's center.

It is preferable to limit pruning to poorly placed smaller growth. It can be acceptable to remove larger misplaced wood, provided that too much growth is not removed in one season. As a general rule, remove no more than 10 to 15 percent of growth from a fruit tree per year. In some cases, it may be acceptable to remove up to 25 percent of growth in a single year.

Neglected fruit trees tend to have numerous large branches that crowd each other. To minimize the risk of excessive watersprouts and sunburn, prune neglected trees over several seasons. See "Renovating Neglected Fruit Trees" on page 142.

3. Size Control, If Necessary

The semi-dwarf rootstock is the most common fruit tree rootstock in the residential setting. It produces trees 15 to 20 feet in height on average. Even at these heights, semi-dwarf trees can produce too much fruit, too high in the canopy. They can also pose maintenance challenges and take up too much space in small backyards. For these reasons, some backyard orchardists choose to maintain semi-dwarf fruit trees at low picking heights. This involves more frequent cutting back of wayward growth, but because the trees are smaller, maintenance is reduced overall.

Fruit tree height is largely a matter of personal preference. Picking height, quantity of fruit, maintenance level, planting-area constraints, and the tree's purpose in the landscape (e.g., aesthetics as well as fruit) are all points to consider. When training a young tree, there is nothing wrong with selecting a tree height based on ease of maintenance and fruit picking. Of course, the rootstock's natural vigor cannot be ignored. A semi-dwarf fruit tree can be maintained below 10 feet with regular pruning, but this is not suitable for trees growing on standard rootstocks. (Continued, next page.)

The ultimate size of a fruit tree should be decided at planting. The tree can be grown to the desired height and not allowed to grow taller. For established trees, the client will have already chosen a height, and pruning involves maintaining the tree at that height.

In general, a tall fruit tree should not be topped in an attempt to reduce the picking height. Topping promotes watersprouts, increases the risk of sunburn, and can cause cracks to form in the cut limbs and the trunk. If the tree has enough low branches, thinning will increase light penetration into the canopy and stimulate the development of flower buds lower in the tree.

If the client requests height reduction of a mature fruit tree, reduce the tree's height over several years to avoid causing a vigorous growth response. Reduce the height by no more than $1/4$ in a single season. When shortening a branch, cut it back to an outward-facing branch that is a minimum of $1/3$ (preferably $1/2$) the diameter of the branch being cut. Paint any limbs exposed to direct sunlight with a 50/50 mixture of white latex paint and water to protect them from sunburn.

An extreme form of height reduction involves removing all major limbs except one. This technique should only be used at the client's request. Bark exposed to direct sunlight should be painted with a 50/50 mixture of white latex paint and water to protect it from sunburn. New growth can be trained at a lower picking height. If the tree recovers, it will take several years for it to produce fruit. Note that trees renovated this way lose much of their natural beauty and are at greater risk of structural problems and decay. Consider simply removing the tree and planting a new one.

Fruit trees maintained at low picking heights require regular summer pruning. Pruning for size control is generally done once in early summer and once in late summer. Early summer pruning involves hard heading back of excessively long shoots that form in spring. The second pruning in late summer involves heading back any additional wayward growth to 2 to 3 buds. Vigorous trees may require pruning three times during the summer.

Pruning Guidelines for Common Fruit Trees

The three steps to pruning fruit trees provide general guidelines that apply to most fruit trees. Each fruit tree type also has specific pruning requirements, which are described here.

Apples and Pears

Apples and pears need only modest pruning. Most apple trees have spurs that last five to eight years, though some varieties have spurs that can bear much longer. Pear spurs last a little over five years. Spurs develop on two-year-old wood for both apple and pear trees. To prune, follow the three pruning steps and thin only enough to allow some sunlight through the canopy when leaves are present. This will encourage new spur development. Avoid over-pruning, and reduce height as necessary.

Apple branches tend to bend downward with the weight of fruit, so pruning should promote some vertical replacement growth. Allow a well-placed shoot with a favorable angle of attachment to develop, and cut back to this branch in a future season when neighboring branches begin to droop. Pear branches can also bend downward, though their general tendency is to grow upright. Pears should be pruned to develop a more open form. Thin congestion in the center of the tree, and cut upright growth back to suitable outward-facing laterals.

Apple and pear spurs develop naturally on two-year-old and older wood. Limit pruning to cleaning and thinning, and allow the tree to produce spur systems on its own. Pruning techniques can be used to encourage spur development, though these methods are not a necessary part of yearly pruning.

Apple and pear spurs can become congested with growth, reducing the space fruit has to develop in. To relieve congestion, thin some of the short shoots on the spurs themselves. It is often possible to see sections of spurs that lack flower buds, and these should be removed first. Entire spurs can be removed in areas of high congestion.

Some varieties of apples and, rarely, pears are tip-bearing. Renewal pruning for tip-bearing trees involves heading back fruited shoots to 1 or 2 buds or removing them entirely. This will result in replacement growth that will bear fruit in a future season. To ensure a crop for the current season, head back or thin only a percentage of fruited shoots each year.

Apricots

Apricot spurs produce for roughly three years before becoming unproductive. To ensure a steady crop, remove approximately one-third of spur-bearing branches each year, focusing on those that have older spurs. Thin enough to allow some light to penetrate the canopy when leaves are present. Head-back long shoots to promote branching. These thinning and heading cuts also help to thin the crop. Reduce height if necessary, cutting back to suitable lateral branches.

Hand-thinning fruit in spring will result in larger fruit and can help prevent diseased fruit. In some areas, dormant pruning may increase the risk of certain diseases, such as Eutypa canker, which is carried by rainwater and enters through pruning cuts. For this reason, summer pruning of apricots is sometimes recommended. When summer pruning is performed, it is in late summer with six weeks of rain-free weather following pruning (Ingels, Geisel, and Unruh 2002).

Cherries

The spurs on sweet cherry trees produce fruit for many years; therefore, these trees need minimal pruning to remain fruitful. Thin the canopy enough to allow some light to reach lower limbs when leaves are present. Remove crossing branches, weak growth, and branches growing through the center. Encourage a more open form by cutting back to outward-facing branches when possible. These trees are naturally tall. Height reduction is acceptable. Sour cherry trees fruit on one-year-old wood. Annual thinning of a portion of the wood that has already fruited will stimulate new fruiting shoots. Otherwise, pruning is mostly the same as for sweet cherries.

Cherry trees have thin bark, and overpruning puts them at risk for sunburn. Paint exposed trunks and limbs with a 50/50 mixture of interior white latex paint and water. Commercial tree wraps will also protect from sunburn. In some areas, dormant pruning may increase the risk of disease. For this reason, cherries are sometimes pruned in late summer. Follow the recommended time of pruning for apricots.

Peaches and Nectarines

Peaches and nectarines are pruned the same way. These trees bear fruit on year-old branches—in one season the shoots form, and a year later they bear fruit. These branches are reddish in color and are generally 12 to 24 inches long. Moderate annual pruning of peaches and nectarines trees helps to reduce the crop and encourages replacement growth for a future crop. Because they need relatively heavy pruning, these trees account for the bulk of fruit tree pruning each year.

Start by removing dead, diseased, and damaged growth, and remove any vertical watersprouts. Next, thin growth that crowds the framework branches, and remove any branches that grow through the center; fruiting shoots that grow toward the center don't need to be removed, but can be shortened. The aim is to maintain the framework, lighten the crop, and increase light penetration into the center of the tree. Reduce height if necessary by cutting back to outward-facing branches. Branches that are becoming too long and beginning to droop can be cut back to more vertical growth.

Finally, thin a portion of the year-old shoots. Start by removing any upright or downward-angled shoots and short or weak growth. (Clingstone peaches naturally produce downward-angled branches that are acceptable.) Thin the remaining year-old shoots so they are spaced at approximately 4 to 6 inches. Year-old shoots longer than 24 inches can be shortened by one-third.

Persimmons

Persimmons produce fruit on the tips of the current season's growth. Thin deadwood and areas of congested growth. Remove some young shoots to encourage growth for a future crop, and head back overly long growth. Do not overprune. Height reduction is acceptable but not necessary. More detailed methods of renewing persimmon fruit wood can be found online.

Figs

Figs produce a first crop on growth from the previous year and one or two late summer crops on new growth. They are terminal-bearing, meaning fruit forms near the ends of branches. Figs don't need pruning to remain productive. Remove crossing branches and shoots that form from the base. To control tree size, cut back as necessary. Figs can be maintained as either small or large trees.

Citrus

Citrus trees include lemons, oranges, limes, and tangerines, among others. In frost-free regions, citrus trees can be pruned any time. Otherwise, prune citrus trees in spring, after the risk of frost has passed. Prune to maintain the tree's shape. Remove twiggy growth and overly vigorous upright shoots. Upright growth that fills in space in the crown does not need to be removed, but can be headed back. University of California pest management guidelines recommend pruning the lowest branches to 2 feet above the ground to help prevent brown rot. The brown rot fungus arises from the soil and can splash onto fruit during rain.

Old citrus trees can be renovated, with the client's consent, by cutting back branches several feet to encourage new growth. An extreme form of renovation involves cutting back large limbs to 1-foot stubs. (Some experts recommend pruning only one large limb per year.) It will take some time for the tree to fruit again and should only be done if the tree is vigorous. After renovating a citrus tree, paint exposed limbs with a 50/50 mixture of interior white latex paint and water to protect them from sunburn. Commercial tree wraps will also protect limbs from sunburn. In cold winter areas, prune these trees in spring or later.

Citrus trees are heavy feeders. They often show micronutrient deficiencies and can benefit from special fertilizer formulations sold as "citrus food".

Citrus fertilizer is similar to rose fertilizer and can often be used interchangeably. Begin fertilizing in spring, when new growth is forming on the tree. Some gardeners recommend fertilizing every other month during the growing season. Do not fertilize between October and February. Follow the product directions.

Renovating Neglected Fruit Trees

Neglected fruit trees can become congested with growth, preventing light from reaching the center and lower portions of the tree. This results in smaller, lower quality fruit that is higher in the canopy. Significant thinning is often required to improve light penetration. Height reduction will also help to accomplish this. This heavy pruning should be spread out over two to three years to prevent the tree from responding with excessive upright growth. As a rule of thumb, remove no more than $1/4$ of the crown each year (Brickell and Joyce 1996).

Always cut branches back to outward-facing laterals that are a minimum of $1/3$ (preferably $1/2$) the diameter of the branch being cut. Upright growth may develop near the site of previous cuts, and this can be removed during the summer or the following dormant season. Prune according to the following guidelines:

- Remove low-hanging branches that limit access around the tree.

- Pull off or cut suckers where they originate. Suckers cut off at ground level will continue to grow.

- Limit the amount of wood removed in one season to avoid vigorous upright growth. Avoid removing large-diameter branches if possible.

- Reduce the width of the tree as necessary, cutting back to suitable laterals. Trees trained to the central leader method should have narrower branches higher up to allow light to enter the canopy from the sides.

- Remove dead, diseased, or damaged growth. And remove vertical growth, downward growth, and one of any two crossing branches. Remove watersprouts by cutting them just above the swollen area near their base.

- Continue thinning over several years until some sunlight enters the canopy when the tree is in full leaf.

- Avoid fertilizing during renovation so as not to encourage watersprouts.

Renovating Overpruned Fruit Trees

Fruit trees can be overpruned through topping or excessive thinning. Overpruned fruit trees produce less fruit, and they respond to the extreme pruning with watersprouts (described on page 117). Renovation involves gradually thinning this upright growth over two to three years, while training some of the upright shoots to become framework branches. The process is similar to training a young tree except that framework branches are selected from the upright shoots.

Remove 50 percent of the upright shoots in the first year, then 50 percent of the remaining upright shoots in the second year. The remaining shoots should be evenly spaced. Each year, tip-prune the upright shoots to promote branching, and remove any new upright growth that develops around previous pruning cuts. Select suitable framework branches from the remaining growth. The tree should fruit again by the third year. Prune as a mature tree from that point forward.

Pruning Trained Forms

Fruit trees are sometimes trained into specialized forms such as a cordon, double cordon, spindle bush, fan, palmette, or espalier. Forms serve a decorative purpose, but they also maximize fruit production in minimal space by allowing sunlight to reach more of the tree. In some cases, the use of specialized forms allows more trees to be planted in an allotted space. In addition to following the

This photo shows the results of overpruning. Too many large branches were removed from this limb the previous winter. To compensate, the tree has produced a thicket of unfruitful and poorly attached vertical branches (watersprouts). The pruning goal is to thin out this vertical growth over several seasons, while training a few of the upright branches to become part of the framework.

These peach trees have been trained to a double cordon form. With this form, more trees can be grown in an alotted space and maneuvering a ladder for pruning and picking is easier. The two branches on each tree are joined by a rope for support. Notice that the trees are grown on an area of raised soil to reduce the risk of disease associated with standing water around the base of the trunk.

specific pruning requirements for the tree type, the form must also be maintained.

To maintain a trained form tree, head back new growth that strays from the desired shape. This is best done during summer to reduce the tree's vigor. Head back wayward shoots in the early summer, then head back subsequent growth to 2 to 3 buds toward the end of summer. Heading back young shoots also encourages fruit spur development on spur-bearing trees.

Pruning Grapes

Grapes are a vine, but the goals of grape pruning are similar to fruit tree pruning: to keep growth in check and to reduce the amount of fruit, thus improving the quality of the remaining fruit. Grapes live for many years. Old, woody growth supports the structure of the plant, and new growth produces fruit. Grapes are pruned in late winter before bud swell. Grapes are also thinned in summer to improve light penetration and air circulation. The latter is helpful in preventing disease.

Grape pruning systems remove or head back growth to make room for the next season's canes. The two pruning systems are spur pruning and cane pruning. The system used depends on the variety of grape. On spur-pruned varieties, such as Flame Seedless, the canes are thinned so they are spaced at roughly 4 to 6 inches and then headed back to 2 to 3 buds. When selecting canes to keep and spur prune, choose canes growing high on the plant.

Cane-pruned varieties, such as Thompson Seedless, bear fruit from buds farther out on the canes. If cane-pruned varieties are spur pruned, they won't fruit that year, or will only fruit a small amount. Cane pruning involves removing all growth except 2 to 4 one-year-old canes and a few spurs near the head (the top of the main woody structure). This means removing the "arms" of the plant, that is, the thicker, two-year-old growth that grows horizontally along wires. The remaining one-year-old canes will be tied in horizontally to replace these arms. These canes are headed back to roughly 10 to 20 buds.

A spur-pruned grape.

A grape trained to the curtain method. One shoot is trained up a support and two are trained horizontally across wires or other supports. In spur-pruned varieties, the horizontal canes, or arms, remain for the life of the plant. In cane-pruned varieties, the arms are removed each year and new one-year-old canes are tied in horizontally to replace them.

When selecting canes to keep, choose canes that are long, medium thickness, growing high on the plant, and growing close to the head. In addition to the main canes, keep a few canes near the head and spur prune them; the canes that develop from these spurs can be used as replacement canes the following season.

If you don't know the grape variety, you must decide whether to spur prune it or cane prune it. If the arms—the main branches extending from the top of the trunk—are nearly as thick and woody as the trunk, the grape is probably spur pruned. One strategy is to spur prune 50 percent of the canes and head back the other 50 percent to 8 to 10 buds.

If the spur-pruned canes don't produce fruit, cane prune the entire plant the following winter.

Pruning overgrown grapes involves removing wayward growth and cane pruning or spur pruning the remaining canes. For a grape grown over an arbor, keep enough canes to cover the area, and head back the remaining canes to 2 buds—8 or more buds if it's a cane-pruned variety. Note that grapes are at risk for powdery mildew, a powdery-looking fungus that thrives on dry, warm days and cool nights. Control is an involved process. University extension websites, such as UC IPM Online (http://www.ipm.ucdavis.edu) provide detailed control guidelines.

Training Grapes

Young grapes need to be trained. Many methods are available. The curtain method is a common and simple method used for grapes. Allow the plant to grow for one season, then choose one vigorous stem to train up a support. Remove the other branches, and head back the stem to promote branching at approximately 3 to 4 feet high. Choose two laterals that develop in the spring and train them horizontally along a wire so that the grape resembles the letter "T". From then on, begin spur pruning or cane pruning, depending on the variety.

Pruning Berries

Blackberry and raspberry plants send up new canes from the ground each year and bear fruit on canes that are one year old. Annual winter pruning involves removing canes that have already fruited and leaving new canes. Autumn-fruiting raspberries are an exception; these produce fruit on canes that develop the same year. Cut autumn-fruiting raspberries down to several inches each winter. Note that berry canes can be trained up and over wires several feet off the ground for improved air circulation and higher quality fruit. Unpruned berries can be renovated by removing all but several new canes.

Pruning Tools

Fruit trees can be pruned from the ground with a pole pruner and a pole saw, or from a ladder with

Orchard ladders are stable on soil. The single support leg fits in tight spaces, allowing close access to trees and shrubs.

hand pruners and a pruning saw. Pole pruners can cut branches up to approximately 1 1/2-inch diameter. Note that a long-reach pruner is not the same as a pole pruner. A long-reach pruner looks like a hand pruner on the end of an extendable pole. It's used to prune small shoots (up to 1/2-inch diameter) that are high in a canopy.

Pruning from the ground with a pole pruner saves time repositioning and climbing a ladder, and it provides perspective on how the crown is shaping up. A few of the drawbacks of pruning from the ground are that it can be awkward to prune large branches and small shoots, and it can be more difficult to make proper pruning cuts. Looking upwards for extended periods can also be uncomfortable.

Pruning from an orchard (tripod) ladder with hand tools provides good control. Fruit wood can be examined up close, and saw cuts can be made quickly. Proper pruning cuts are not a problem. On the downside, there is less perspective up close, so you need to regularly climb down the ladder to see how the tree is shaping up.

In general, it's fastest to prune small trees by ladder. Medium to large trees can be pruned with a combination of tools. Eight-foot orchard ladders are versatile. Ten- or twelve-foot models put more in reach, but they can be cumbersome to position, haul, and store. Large orchard ladders are needed to prune trees growing on standard rootstocks, though standards are not common in residential landscapes. Note that climbing a fruit tree may scuff the bark and create an entry point for disease.

Disinfect hand tools after cutting through diseased growth. Hand sanitizer based on ethyl alcohol or a household disinfectant cleaner can be used. A bleach solution may harm tools. Tools can be cleaned with steel wool after pruning, and a thin coating of a light metal lubricant will help to keep them in good condition.

Dormant Spraying of Fruit Trees

Fruit trees are sometimes sprayed during the dormant season to help control diseases and harmful insects. Dormant spray is not applied routinely each year, but is warranted if the tree had a pest problem the previous season. Because peach leaf curl is common, peach and nectarine trees are typically sprayed each year.

Copper sulfate, also called fixed copper, is used as a dormant spray in the control of a variety of diseases. It comes in a powder that is mixed with water. Copper sulfate can be used as a dormant spray on all fruit trees. Lime sulfur is a foul-smelling liquid made by boiling lime and sulfur together. It is also used as a dormant spray to control a variety of diseases and insects, though *lime sulfur should never be used on apricot trees.*

Horticultural oil is applied as a dormant spray to smother insect pests and their eggs that overwinter on a tree. Certain caterpillars, aphids, and mites are some of the insects controlled. The dormant oil can be mixed in the same tank with copper sulfate or lime sulfur when spraying during dormancy. The oil helps the spray stick to the tree.

If rain is predicted, an appropriate amount of spreader-sticker should be substituted for the horticultural oil. Sticker improves coverage and helps the product stick to the tree during rain. If there is no rain in the forecast, horticultural oil is preferred because it has more protective benefits. If it rains within 24 hours after application and sticker was not used, the product should be reapplied. Do not mix both sticker and horticultural oil into a tank of copper sulfate.

One to one-and-one-half gallons of mixture will cover most trees. Start at the top of the tree and work your way down. Shake the sprayer occasionally to keep the solution mixed. An extension wand will eliminate the need to climb a ladder with the sprayer. After spraying, the tree will have a blue-green cast from the copper.

An alternative to mixing a tank of spray is to apply a copper or lime sulfur product with a hose-end attachment. Since copper in wettable powder form will plug hose-end sprayers, liquid copper must be used. Note that liquid copper products will be of benefit, but they are less effective than wettable powders for dormant use (Shor 2008).

Dormant oil is low toxicity, though copper sulfate and lime sulfur can irritate the skin and eyes. The appropriate personal protective equipment (PPE) should be used, including goggles and chemical-resistant gloves. A long-sleeve shirt should also be worn and you may need to wear a respirator. Follow the product directions for specifics. Spray on a day with little or no breeze to minimize drift. Note that dormant spray may stain certain landscape features such as wood patios, brickwork, concrete, aluminum siding, and roofs. Cover these areas with a suitable material, as necessary.

A rule of thumb is to spray three times during dormancy: late November, late December, and early to mid-February before bud swell (Thanksgiving, Christmas, and Valentines). If there is time for only two sprayings, late November and mid-February are preferred. If there will only be one application,

The Commercial Use of Dormant Sprays

Copper sulfate, lime sulfur, and horticultural oil are the most common products used for dormant spraying in landscapes. As dormant sprays, all three are currently approved on the national level for use in organic crop production (with a few limitations). States may have different regulations. The National Organic Program's "National List of Allowed and Prohibited Substances" can be found on the United States Department of Agriculture website at http://www.ams.usda.gov/AMSv1.0/nop.

Regardless of the status of these products, you may need a pest control applicator's license to apply them commercially in some states. Questions regarding the need for certification can be directed to the state agency that handles licensing. You can find the contact information for your state agency through the website of the National Pesticide Information Center at http://npic.orst.edu/state1.htm or by calling 1-800-858-7378.

make it in late winter. Exact spray times depend on the product being used, the pest being controlled, and the weather. Follow the product directions.

The same mixture of dormant spray can be applied to roses, grapes, berries, and ornamental fruit trees such as ornamental pears and flowering plums. Excess copper sulfate or lime sulfur that has been mixed in a spray tank should be used up. To clean the empty sprayer, refill the tank with fresh water, pressurize the tank, and spray it until it is empty.

Common Fruit Tree Pests

A few fruit tree pests are so common as to warrant an introduction. Dormant spraying is used as a control for a number of these pests. Books and websites devoted to integrated pest management (IPM) will provide more detailed methods of control than those presented here. One website is UC IPM Online at http://www.ipm.ucdavis.edu. A nursery professional or county farm advisor will be familiar with the prevalent pests in a region and can also suggest controls. See "Integrated Pest Management" on page 68 for additional information.

Aphids

Aphids are tiny, soft-bodied insects that gather on leaves and shoots and feed on plant fluids. Small populations of aphids are not usually a cause for concern. Large populations of aphids can disfigure leaves and branches and stunt growth, making them particularly problematic for young, developing trees. These insects secrete a sticky residue called honeydew. Honeydew is unsightly, and it can promote the growth of a dark-colored fungus called sooty mold.

High-pressure water is effective at temporarily removing aphids from leaves and stems. Applying a dormant horticultural oil can help reduce overwintering aphids. Ants can exacerbate an aphid problem, as they harvest aphids to feed on the honeydew. Clearing weeds from around the base of the tree and applying a sticky insect barrier, such as Tanglefoot, to a small section of the trunk blocks the ants and can help control the problem.

Before applying a sticky barrier around the trunk of a tree, wrap a wide band of masking tape or fabric tree wrap around the trunk, then apply the product to the tape. Duct tape does not stretch and should not be used. The tape makes it possible to remove the sticky barrier, which should be done before winter. The band of Tanglefoot should be 6 to 8 inches wide. Applying the sticky barrier higher on the trunk can prolong its usefulness because it will accumulate less dirt. Tanglefoot is also used to control various harmful worms, caterpillars, weevils, and other pests.

Bark Borers and Sunburn

Bark borers are insects that dig into vulnerable or damaged tree bark. Borers can weaken or kill a tree. Control is complex, but simple measures can aid in prevention. Drought-stressed trees are more susceptible to borers, so irrigation during the summer can help. Trees that have experienced sunburn are even more at risk. Sunburn is caused by prolonged exposure of a tree's trunk or limbs to direct sunlight in the growing season. This exposure is usually caused by overpruning. Bark damage from sunburn is not usually detectable until long after the damaging sun exposure, so preventive measures are the best defense.

For aesthetic reasons, commercial tree wraps are the best choice of sunlight protection for most landscape trees. For some clients, appearance may be less of a concern for backyard fruit trees. With the client's consent, trunks and limbs that will be exposed to direct sunlight for extended periods can be painted with a 50/50 solution of interior white latex paint and water, which will help prevent sunburn.

In some regions, tree injury called sunscald can also damage tree bark. Sunscald occurs in winter when sunlight warms an area of bark to the point where some cells temporarily come out of dormancy. Temperatures soon drop, causing the cells to freeze, and this results in cracked bark or split trunks or limbs. Young trees with thin bark are particularly at risk. When tree wraps are used to prevent sunscald, they are applied in early winter and removed in spring.

Codling Moth

Codling moth worms bore into apples, pears, walnuts, prunes, and some plums. Infected fruit shows the small entry point of the larvae. A number of controls exist, and pesticides are sometimes necessary. Remove infected and fallen fruit to lessen

Though it is not evident from this photo, this peach tree has been overpruned. The home gardener has applied a 50/50 mixture of white latex paint and water to the limbs to protect them from sunburn.

the number of damaging larvae. Pheromone traps can be used to good effect in landscapes where only one or two infected trees exist. Pheromone traps lure male moths with a synthetic female sex pheromone and trap them on a sticky surface. The traps are placed in the upper third of a tree's crown.

Use one to two traps for a small tree and two to four for a large tree. Install the traps between March and April, and change the pheromone and sticky lining according to the directions for the product. UC IPM Online (http://www.ipm.ucdavis.edu) suggests attaching traps to a simple pulley using a loop of twine hung over a branch high in the canopy. This allows the traps to be raised or lowered from the ground. Remove the traps at harvest. Treatment of the problem should be effective by the second year; traps are less effective in the first year.

Brown Rot

Brown rot is a fungus that causes fruit to rot on the tree. It affects apricots, plums, cherries, nectarines, and other stone fruits. The recommended treatment is to spray the tree with a copper sulfate mixture when the flower buds begin to swell and again at early bloom; that is, when the first few blossoms open. If only one application is possible, it should be applied just before full bloom. No applications should be made once the tree is in bloom. (Citrus is an exception; see below.)

Additional preventive measures include fruit thinning and the removal of fallen fruit and diseased fruit (mummies). Infected shoots can be identified by dead leaves. Prune away infected growth in early summer, when it is easy to identify.

Brown rot on citrus can be significantly reduced by pruning branches at least 2 feet above the ground, as the fungus arises from the soil and gets splashed onto the tree during rain. A copper fungicide can also be applied to the lower portion of the tree (up to 4 feet from the ground) and to the ground beneath the tree. Apply the copper in the fall, shortly before or after the first rain. If it rains excessively in the period after spraying, you may need to reapply the copper in January or February (UC IPM Online 2008).

Fire Blight

Fire blight is a bacterial disease that quickly attacks a shoot and turns it black, making it appear scorched by fire. The bacteria enter through flower buds, but can also enter through pruning cuts. Rain and warm temperatures during bloom increase the risk for fire blight, making this disease prevalent in spring. Apple and pear trees are most commonly affected. One preventative measure is to spray fire-blight-prone trees with copper sulfate at bud break; that is, when green color can first be seen in the buds. If fire blight is detected, cut out small infected shoots 12 inches below the die-back area, preferably at a branch collar; cut out larger branches 24 inches below the die-back area. Disinfect pruning tools with a household disinfectant cleaner or hand sanitizer based on ethyl alcohol before continuing to prune healthy wood. Monitoring and early detection will help to limit fire blight damage.

Peach Leaf Curl

Peaches and nectarines are subject to peach leaf curl, a fungus that puckers and curls the leaves, hindering the tree's growth and fruit production. The fungus can also distort shoot growth, negatively affecting the development of young trees. If infected leaves are stripped away, the tree will usually grow healthy new ones; however, this does not control the disease. Stripping leaves increases the risk of bark sunburn, and it forces the tree to use energy reserves to produce new leaves, potentially weakening the tree's health over time. Treatment for a tree that was recently infected with peach leaf curl is to spray it with a copper sulfate or lime-sulfur mixture once between mid-November and mid-December, and again in early spring before the buds begin to swell. In some cases, one application is enough.

Irrigation System Repair

Irrigation systems require regular inspection and maintenance to continue to perform as designed. Adjustments and minor repairs are common. Troubleshooting malfunctioning irrigation systems is also part of the landscape manager's job, though this work can be contracted out if necessary. This chapter covers sprinkler and pipe repairs and provides instruction on troubleshooting and repairing irrigation valves, controllers, and field wire. We start with a basic introduction to irrigation system components.

Irrigation System Overview

Sprinkler heads connect to lateral irrigation lines (PVC pipes or polyethylene tubes) that are buried in the ground. These lateral lines connect to the house's water supply at a juncture called an irrigation valve, also called a station valve. Station valves serve as gates that control the flow of water to a section, or zone, of lateral irrigation lines. For example, one station valve might control six sprinklers in the front lawn, another might control five sprinklers in the side yard. Four to six valves is typical in residential landscapes, though more or less may be installed. See diagram, next page.

Station valves can be manual or automatic. Automatic valves connect by low-voltage wiring to the controller, sometimes called a "timer". The control-

ler stores an irrigation program, or schedule. At the scheduled time, the controller sends an electric signal to the station valves, causing them to open. When a station valve is open, pressurized water flows from the house's plumbing to the lateral lines, out to the sprinklers. Most controllers operate only one valve at a time to maintain adequate water pressure at each zone. Occasionally a system is designed so that two to three valves operate at a time.

Controllers are either closed control loop or open control loop. With a closed-loop controller, the user defines some general parameters, and the controller then makes "decisions" about irrigation run times and frequency based on feedback provided by sensors mounted in the landscape, such as a direct-burial soil moisture sensor or an evapotranspiration (ET) sensor. Special ET controllers are designed to receive ET data remotely. These controllers require the user to pay for a service that provides daily ET updates.

Open-loop systems are the most common in the residential setting. With an open-loop controller, the user enters the irrigation run times and frequency into the controller's memory. Open-loop systems use either electromechanical or electronic controllers. Electromechanical controllers use gears and an electric clock to signal the valves. These controllers have fewer features than electronic

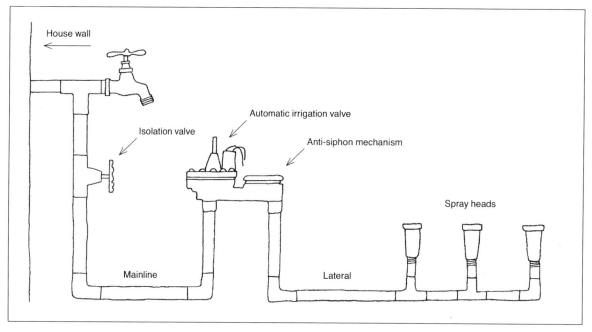

The layout of a typical residential irrigation system, not drawn to scale. The wires on the automatic irrigation valve are solenoid wires. They attach to field wire that runs to the controller. The field wire is usually taped to the underside of the mainline. The anti-siphon mecanism, also called a backflow preventer, prevents potentially contaminated water in the lateral lines from returning to the house lines or the water supply.

controllers, but they are reliable—mechanical programming maintains schedules despite power outages or surges.

With their extensive programming capabilities and ease of use, electronic controllers are the standard today. Electronic controllers have the advantage of allowing multiple irrigation programs, which can be used to water flower beds separately from turf or to make multiple shorter applications to sloped areas to avoid runoff. Many electronic controllers are also capable of supporting sensors, such as a rain sensor, that increase water savings.

Programming most residential electronic controllers involves little more than turning a dial to the appropriate setting (e.g., "Set Watering Times") and entering the schedule information, such as the run-time minutes for each station. Directions are sometimes posted on the inside cover of the controller. Missing manuals can be downloaded from the manufacturer's website or mailed from the manufacturer upon request.

Manually Operating Automatic Valves

Sprinkler adjustments are made with the water on. Automatic valves are usually located near an outside water faucet or in a green irrigation box in the landscape. Occasionally valves are buried in the soil, and special electronic equipment is needed to locate them.

Manual valves are opened and closed by rotating the valve stem. Automatic valves can be operated from the controller or from the valves. They are opened manually by rotating the bleed port screw or the solenoid. The bleed port screw is a small, raised screw on the top of the main valve housing. The screw is usually black and plastic. Sometimes the bleed port screw is located at the top of the flow control stem—the raised stem in the center of some automatic valves (see photo, next page).

To manually operate the sprinklers, turn the bleed screw slightly to the left with your fingers. Do not remove the screw. Water will trickle from beneath the screw and in a few moments the sprinklers will come on. On some models, water does not trickle beneath the screw, but instead empties directly into the pipes. To shut the sprinklers off, turn the bleed screw all the way to the right using gentle pressure only. In a few moments, the valve will close and the water will shut off. The valve may make a popping noise as it closes. Turn on only one valve at a time to maintain adequate water pressure.

Rotating the solenoid, also known as the coil, is another way to manually operate some automatic valves. The solenoid is a black, cylindrical or hexagonal device with two wires coming out of the top. Some solenoids are roughly the size of a camera film container. Other solenoids are smaller and may be enclosed in a metal bracket. The solenoid's job is to open the valve when it receives the electric signal from the controller. Rotate the solenoid to the left until you hear the valve open. Do not rotate the solenoid so far that it comes off. To close the valve, gently hand-tighten the solenoid. The water will shut off in a moment. Some valves have a lever at the base of the solenoid that is used to raise the solenoid and open the valve.

Repairing Sprinklers

The three most common sprinklers in residential landscapes are spray heads, impact-drive sprinklers, and gear-driven sprinklers (rotors). Spray heads come with quarter-circle, half-circle, full-circle, or adjustable spray nozzles. Some are brass, and some are plastic with two-inch or four-inch pop-up extensions. Mowing and general turf use frequently cause spray heads to rotate out of position. To adjust the sprinklers, turn them on and rotate them back into position by hand. Though it's less precise, sprinklers can also be adjusted with the water off; marks on the nozzles show the direction of spray. To rotate a pop-up spray head, raise the stem and turn it. It will make a clicking noise as it turns.

Plastic pop-up spray heads contain a screen (filter) that occasionally clogs with debris, reducing water flow. On some models, the filter is located at the base of the pop-up section. To access it, unscrew

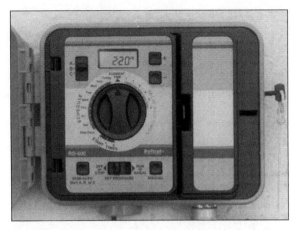

Controller instructions are usually posted inside the front cover. Irritrol is the manufacturer of the controller shown here.

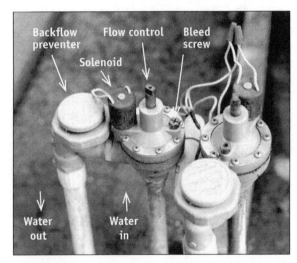

The external components of a typical solenoid valve. Automatic valves can be opened manually by rotating the bleed screw or, on some models, the solenoid.

the top of the sprinkler (not the nozzle), and remove the pop-up section from the body. The sprinkler housing can remain attached to the riser.

Many models place the screen beneath the nozzle, which is the screw-on spray tip in center of the head. With the water turned off, raise the stem and grip it firmly, or hold it up using a pair of vice grips with the teeth wrapped in duct tape. Unscrew the nozzle by hand. (Do not turn the metal screw in the center of the nozzle. This screw is for adjusting the distance of throw.) Next, remove the screen and clean it by rinsing it with water and going over it with a toothbrush. Reinsert the screen and screw the nozzle back on. If the stem slips down during the repair, screw the nozzle back on and pull it up again.

Brass spray heads frequently malfunction but are durable and easy to repair. Rocks and debris can lodge between the stem and housing, preventing the stem from rising and lowering freely. With the sprinklers on, step on the raised nozzle so it is partially lowered. Water will flow past the stem, clearing small debris. (This quick-fix can also be tried on plastic pop-up heads that leak water around the stem.) If this does not work, unscrew the spray head from the riser, and force the stem up by pressing the lower part of the stem onto concrete, then shake out the rocks.

Since brass pop ups don't have filters, the nozzles tend to clog with dead bugs, rocks, and other debris. To clear the nozzle, unscrew the hex nut spray tip and turn the water on. This will force debris out of the stem. Another method is to unscrew the entire spray head, and tap the hollow stem onto a piece of wood to force out debris. A toothbrush can be used to brush rocks out of the nozzle. Note that all the spray heads mentioned so far have variants that are attached to an above-ground riser that does not pop up.

Replacing Spray Heads

To replace a broken spray head, unscrew it counterclockwise from the riser and screw on a new sprinkler. The riser is a short section of pipe that is connected to a tee fitting in the lateral PVC pipe buried in the soil. The most common riser is made of polyethylene and is called a poly cut-off riser or a flexible cut-off riser. It is a 6-inch plastic pipe with male-threaded sections that can be cut to size. The soft plastic of the poly riser helps to take the brunt of any impact to sprinkler heads, reducing the incidence of damage to sprinklers and PVC pipe.

PTFE tape, more commonly known as Teflon tape, is a thin, white, non-adhesive tape applied to threaded sprinkler parts to seal the connection. According to landscape architect Jess Stryker, Teflon tape is not needed when connecting spray heads to poly

cut-off risers because the plastic is soft enough to seal itself (2006). Teflon tape should be used with threaded metal risers or rigid PVC risers. To apply Teflon tape, wrap it clockwise around the male threads several times, then screw the parts together.

Risers are removed with a tool called a stub remover or riser extractor. The stub remover fits into the hole in the riser and digs in with metal teeth, allowing the riser to be unscrewed without damaging the pipe threads. If the existing cut-off riser is too tall, cut it down to size and reuse it. If the riser is too short, replace it with a new poly cut-off riser, and cut it to fit using a PVC cutter (vinyl pipe cutter). If dirt enters the sprinkler line, turn on the water to flush the line before installing the new sprinkler.

Select a new pop-up spray head that is the same size as the one being replaced. The nozzle should have the same pattern, or arc (half circle, quarter circle, etc.) and distance of throw, or radius (8 feet, 12 feet, 15 feet, etc.) as the old one. Select the same brand of spray head or nozzle for every sprinkler in a zone. Nozzles from the same manufacturer and of the same model will have matched precipitation rates, meaning they will apply the same amount of water over a given area. A nozzle or spray head by a different manufacturer may result in more or less water being applied by that sprinkler. Check the sprinkler manufacturer's performance charts when in doubt.

The sprinkler casing should sit flush with the soil; the pop-up section (the stem) provides the necessary clearance. Marks on the nozzle show the direction of spray. Adjust the direction of spray by turning the stem left or right. It will make a clicking noise as it turns.

Solving Coverage Problems In Spray-Head Systems

Improving coverage in a neglected sprinkler system may be as simple as cleaning the screens of pop-up spray heads, cleaning out rocks and bugs from brass heads, replacing worn nozzles, or adjusting the flow controls at the valves. Sometimes a damaged sprinkler head or a cracked PVC pipe is the cause of low water pressure and poor coverage.

Coverage issues can also occur if the system has been altered from its original design, or if the system was not designed correctly to begin with. These problems can be more complex to solve because they require an understanding of irrigation system design. With an improperly designed system, there may be too many spray heads per valve or the heads may be spaced too far apart. Until more recently, the only way to solve these problems was to have a contractor install an additional valve or redesign the system.

One alternative solution is to replace the traditional spray nozzles with rotating stream nozzles, such as the MP Rotator made by Hunter Industries (http://www.hunterindustries.com) or the Rotary Nozzle made by Rain Bird (http://www.rainbird.com). Rotating stream nozzles provide increased coverage with the same or less water pressure. These nozzles have an adjustable arc while maintaining matched precipitation rates. If you use this solution, all the spray heads on the valve must use rotating stream nozzles; do not mix rotating stream nozzles with standard nozzles.

Improper system design or changes to the system can also cause inadequate coverage of the turf area close to the spray head. In some cases, the installation of undercut nozzles can solve this problem. Undercut nozzles have a second spray tip, beneath the main one, that directs more water to the area near the head. These nozzles use more water, so this solution may not work if there is insufficient water pressure available on the line.

Some coverage issues can be corrected by replacing screens with pressure-compensating screens. According to Rain Bird, pressure-compensating screens can be used to compensate for pressure fluctuations and to eliminate misting (fogging) associated with high water pressure. Pressure-compensating screens can also create short throw, reduced-radius patterns when matched with the appropriate nozzles (2007). Some spray heads come pre-assembled with pressure-compensating screens. Irrigation store sales staff can help in

An impact-drive sprinkler. Arc and radius adjustments can be made when the sprinkler is in operation. An impact-drive sprinkler wrench is needed to access the filter or change the internal drive. The sprinkler shown has been installed too high. The casing should sit flush with the soil surface.

proper selection and may be able to suggest other technological solutions for coverage problems. Note that a valve's flow control can be turned down to reduce misting. See "Flow Control Adjustment" on page 165 for more information.

Impact-Drive Sprinklers

Impact-drive sprinklers, sometimes called pop-up impulse sprinklers, rotate as water hits a lever on the pop-up section of the sprinkler. Impact-drive sprinklers are larger than spray heads and can cover larger areas. Like spray heads, they screw onto risers that attach to the underlying PVC pipe or polyethylene tubing. Occasionally a contractor will attach these sprinklers using an inlet on the side of the sprinkler's casing. When repairs are needed, the internal sprinkler mechanism can be replaced without removing the sprinkler casing from the ground.

Adjustments can be made to the coverage arc (distance traveled left and right) and radius (distance of throw). The arc is controlled by two metal adjustment clips called arc adjusters or the trip collar. The arc adjusters are mounted on the pop-up section below the nozzle. Turn on the valve using the bleed screw, then watch the sprinkler go through a few rotations to see how the arc adjusters work. Slide the arc adjusters left or right to get the coverage needed. For 360-degree coverage, raise the trip pin so that it does not contact the trip collar.

A small screw near the nozzle, called the diffuser screw, controls the radius. Tightening the screw causes it to progressively enter the stream of water, reducing the radius and increasing misting. Strike a balance between distance of throw and coverage of turf near the sprinkler. Some models also have a distance control flap or dial that is also used to adjust the radius.

Impact-drive sprinkler filters do not usually need to be cleaned. If you need to access the filter or remove the internal drive for replacement, use the appropriate impact-drive wrench. A few different wrenches exist, and they are available at most irrigation supply stores. To clean the filter, pry open the top of the sprinkler with the thin end of the wrench then pull up on the lid. Insert the wrench into the bottom of the sprinkler housing and unscrew the internal drive. The filter is on the bottom of the drive. Clean and reinstall the filter then reinstall the internal drive.

Failure of an impact-drive sprinkler to rotate can be caused by low or high water pressure, debris in the nozzle, worn or damaged parts, or other causes. Some common problems with old impact-drive sprinklers are bearing wear and reduced arm spring tension. On some models the spring can be tightened or replaced. Bearings can be replaced on some brass models. Otherwise, just replace the internal drive. If replacement drives aren't available, it may be easier or cheaper to replace the entire sprinkler. Note: Impact-drive sprinklers are water lubricated. Do not apply other lubricants.

Gear-Driven Sprinklers

Gear-driven sprinklers, also called rotors, rotate at a steady speed while delivering a solid stream of water. Rotors are common in larger turf areas, owing to their radius range of roughly 20 to 50 feet. More compact models have a radius range of roughly 15 to 35 feet. Rotors have the advantage of being compact, silent, adjustable, and durable. As with other sprinklers, rotors require adequate water pressure to function properly.

There are numerous makes and models of rotors, and many have unique operating specifications and adjustment procedures. The adjustment instructions included here do not apply to all rotors. If the following instructions do not readily lead to the desired adjustments, note the make and model of the rotor, and get the adjustment instructions from manufacturer's website or from a sales person at an irrigation supply store. Note that you may need an inexpensive, specialized tool to make adjustments. A small screwdriver can be used on some models.

Adjusting the Arc. Arc adjustments are made with the water on. The nozzle can be manually rotated left and right as the sprinkler is in operation, providing a fast way to check the existing arc. Always start by turning the nozzle in the direction it is rotating.

Rotors rotate back and forth between a fixed stopping point and an adjustable stopping point. Depending on the rotor, the fixed stop may be at the end of the left rotation (left reversing point) or the right rotation (right reversing point). On some models, the placement of the fixed stop is determined by the position of the sprinkler housing, or "can", on its connection point with the lateral pipe in the ground. To adjust the fixed stop, turn the entire sprinkler on its connection point.

On some models, another way to adjust the fixed stop is to turn off the water, unscrew the top of the rotor, lift out the internal drive, and replace the drive so that the fixed stop aligns with the irrigation boundary. On other models, the stem can be rotated by hand while the rotor is in operation. These models make a ratcheting noise when turned.

To determine if the fixed stop is on the left or right, insert the appropriate tool into the arc adjustment slot, and turn the tool one rotation in either direction to change the arc. The arc side that does not change is the fixed stop. The arc adjustment slot can be identified by the "+" and "-" signs on top of the rotor.

After setting the fixed stop, set the side with the adjustable stop. Insert the appropriate tool into the arc adjustment slot, as described above. Turn the tool in the direction of the "+" sign to increase the arc. Turn the tool in the direction of the "-" sign to decrease the arc. The stem may need to be held stationary at the fixed stop position during this adjustment.

Adjusting the Radius. A rotor's radius can be adjusted by turning the radius adjustment screw or by changing the nozzle. To adjust the radius using the radius adjustment screw, locate the arrow icon on top of the rotor. The radius adjustment screw is located beneath the slot indicated by the arrow icon. Insert the appropriate tool into the radius adjustment slot. A 1/16 inch Allen wrench is required on some models. Turn the screw clockwise to reduce the radius; turn the screw counterclockwise to increase the radius. Rotating the radius adjustment screw too much in either direction will cause the screw to fall out. If the screw comes out, the nozzle will come loose because the radius adjustment screw also holds the nozzle in place.

Note that using the radius adjustment screw will not change the flow rate. In other words, if the radius is reduced with the radius adjustment screw, the same amount of water will be applied over a smaller area, which can result in uneven coverage. For this reason, irrigation professionals recommend making significant radius adjustments by changing the nozzle. Smaller nozzles reduce the radius while simultaneously reducing the flow rate, thereby maintaining even coverage. Assuming the system was designed correctly to begin with, minor radius adjustments can be made using the radius adjustment screw.

Adjusting the Flow Rate. A rotor's flow rate is measured in gallons per minute and is determined by the operating pressure (PSI) and the nozzle. Rotor nozzles are replaceable and come in a range of sizes. Replacing an existing nozzle with a larger nozzle is a way to increase the precipitation rate. Larger nozzles also provide a larger radius, and smaller nozzles provide a smaller radius. Low-angle nozzles also reduce the radius and are sometimes used to clear low branches or reduce wind drift, among other uses. Only use nozzles made by the rotor's manufacturer.

Keep in mind that rotors rotate at a set speed. This means that a rotor passes over a quarter-circle area twice as frequently as a half-circle area. If nozzles with the same gallons per minute (GPM) are used for both quarter-circle and half-circle areas, the quarter-circle area will receive twice as much water as the half-circle area, assuming the radius and run time are the same for both. To match rotor precipitation rates, a nozzle for a quarter-circle area should have 1/2 the flow rate as a nozzle for a half-circle area. Similarly, the nozzle for a half-circle area should have 1/2 the flow rate as a nozzle for a full-circle area.

Replace rotor nozzles with the water off. The rotor's stem must be raised to access to the nozzle. To raise the stem, a simple, specialized tool made

Gear-driven sprinklers, also called rotors, rise on a stem and rotate back and forth. They deliver a larger volume of water than spray heads.

Pipe Threads

National Pipe Thread (NPT) is a tapered pipe thread common in the U.S.. Threaded PVC fittings are NPT. NPT is still sometimes referred to as iron pipe thread (IPT). The abbreviations "mipt" and "fipt" stand for "male iron pipe thread" and "female iron pipe thread". Hoses use a different thread called hose thread or garden hose thread (GHT). "Mht" and "fht" stand for "male hose thread" and "female hose thread". PTFE (Teflon) tape is used for sealing NPT fittings. Hose threads seal with a washer. Threaded fittings are never cemented.

by the rotor manufacturer is required. Insert the tool into the lifting socket, turn the tool 90 degrees, and lift. Hold it in the raised position. Some models can be held in the raised position with a different specialized tool.

With your free hand, insert the appropriate tool into the radius adjustment slot, and turn the radius adjustment screw counterclockwise until it is no longer holding the nozzle in place. Remove the existing nozzle per the manufacturer's directions. On most models, the nozzle will come out when the radius adjustment screw is removed. On other models, it is also necessary to insert a screwdriver into a tab on the nozzle and pry it out. Insert the new nozzle, and turn the radius adjustment screw clockwise until the new nozzle is held in place. Release the stem, turn on the water, and adjust the radius.

PVC Pipe Repairs

PVC (polyvinyl chloride) pipe is a white plastic pipe commonly used in sprinkler systems. PVC pipe is buried roughly one foot in the ground and is laid out according to the landscape architect's or contractor's design.

PVC pipe is available in different diameters and different thicknesses or pressure ratings. *Schedule pipe* is rated by the thickness of the pipe walls, with Schedule 80 being thicker than Schedule 40. Schedule 80 and 40 are required in valve installations. Schedule 80 is UV resistant and so it is sometimes used for above-ground applications. *Class pipe* has an operating-pressure rating. Class 200 and Class 125 are common in residential landscapes; class 125 has the lower pressure rating of the two. Some contractors don't like class pipe and use only Schedule 40 for laterals and main lines. The most common size of PVC pipe used in residential sprinkler systems is three-quarter inch. One inch and one-half inch are also common.

PVC pipe is cut to size and cemented together using slip fittings. Slip fittings are smooth on the inside and require cement, unlike threaded fittings. Couplers, elbows, and tees are common slip fittings. Couplers join two pieces of pipe in a straight line, elbows join two pieces of pipe at a 90 degree angle, and tees join three pieces of pipe—two in a straight line and one at a 90 degree angle. Some PVC fittings convert a slip connection to a threaded connection; a common example is a riser tee fitting that has two slip connections and one threaded connection (to hold a threaded sprinkler riser). Most residential PVC fittings are schedule 40 and can be used with schedule or class pipe.

PVC Cements

PVC cement is used with slip fittings to join sections of PVC pipe. PVC cement is never used with threaded fittings. PVC cement is a solvent cement—it softens the outer layer of the PVC pipe and bonds to it. Different types of PVC cement are used under different conditions and for different ratings of pipe. Use the cements and primers required by your local building codes. Some choices of PVC cement for residential repairs are the all-weather type, which can be used at low temperatures, or the wet-or-dry type.

PVC primer can be used to soften and clean the PVC before cementing. Primer creates a longer lasting seal. Use a primer as required by local codes or when repairing main line PVC pipe (as opposed to laterals). PVC cements and primers come with warning labels and directions, which should be read thoroughly. These products are flammable, and their vapors can be harmful to breathe.

Repairing PVC Pipe

The following instructions explain how to repair broken PVC pipe by cementing in a new section of pipe. Compression couplers and telescoping couplers are described later. To begin a repair, clear the soil around the pipe a few feet beyond the break on both sides. Water may leak from the pipe when it is cut, so clear enough soil under the pipe to prevent water from interfering with the repair.

Next, determine the diameter of the existing pipe and the parts needed for the repair. Most residential PVC pipe is three-quarter inch, though it could be one-half inch, one inch, or larger. If in doubt, take a piece of the broken section to the store. It is better to have the repair parts on hand before cutting the pipe, but not essential. The replacement pipe should be the same diameter as the existing pipe and have a rating that is equal to or higher than the existing pipe. Short sections of pipe can usually be found in a remainders box at irrigation or garden supply stores.

Start by cutting out the cracked section of pipe. This can be done with a small hacksaw or a wire saw, though the ideal tool is a PVC cutter because it fits in tight spaces and makes a clean cut. Sawing can leave the pipe with burrs, or rough edges, which must be filed smooth or cut clean with a knife before cementing. When the broken section is removed, water may trickle from the pipe. Clean both pipe ends with a rag, and file away any burrs on the ends of the PVC pipe in the ground. Dry the pipe if the PVC cement being used requires a dry surface.

Check the fit of the parts. Once cement is applied, there is not much time to adjust the connection. Insert the tip of the pipe into the coupler, then remove it. Do not press the pipe deeply into the fitting because it will be difficult to remove. The last step before applying cement is to make sure the in-ground pipe is flexible enough that the repair pipe can be inserted; if not, dig away more soil. Over-flexing PVC pipe can break it.

If primer will be used, apply it according to the product directions before applying the cement. It is strongly recommended that you use primer when repairing pipe that has been buried because the primer removes dirt and cleans the pipe.

Finish the repair with PVC cement. Cement both couplers to the ends of the in-ground pipe in the following manner: First, apply a liberal coat of PVC cement to one end of the in-ground pipe. Next, apply a thin coat of cement to the inside of the coupler. Don't puddle the cement inside the coupler because this can create a weaker bond. Apply cement to the repair pipe one more time, then fit the parts together, giving the coupler a quarter-turn as you insert it.

The cement must be fluid. If the cement dries, both parts will need to be recoated before being fit together. Hold the parts together for one minute. Cement the other coupler to the other end of the in-ground pipe in the same manner. Cement only one fitting at a time because PVC cement dries quickly.

Once the couplers have been cemented onto the in-ground pipe ends, cut the repair pipe to size, and file away any burrs on the repair pipe. Use the same method of cement application: cement only one side at a time; apply a liberal coat of cement to the clean, burr-free repair pipe; apply a thin coat of cement inside the coupler; insert the pipe deeply into the coupler with a quarter-turn as it is inserted; and hold for one minute.

Cementing the last pipe-to-slip connection involves applying the cement as described above, flexing the in-ground pipe, and fitting the parts together. The pipe should enter as far into the coupler as possible. An alternative and simpler method is to use a slip coupler for one end of the repair and a compression coupler for the other end. With this approach, the pipe does not need to be flexed for the final fitting.

Let the PVC cement set per the product directions. In general, cement takes longer to set in colder weather. After a few minutes, the bond should be set enough to check the seal. The cement will fully harden later. Turn on the water. If there are no leaks, bury the pipe and replace any turfgrass.

Compression Couplers

Compression couplers can be used to quickly repair broken PVC pipe. A compression coupler joins two pieces of PVC pipe by means of hand-tightened caps that squeeze a rubber washer around the pipe—no cement is required. To use a compression coupler, the pipes to be joined cannot be more than a few inches apart. A compression tee can be used for repairs near sprinkler risers or other multiple-pipe connections. Compression couplers are available for one-half inch, three-quarter inch, one inch, and larger diameter pipe.

To use a compression coupler, clear the soil approximately one foot on each side of the break, and prepare the pipe as previously explained. No flexing of the pipe is required. Unscrew the end caps from the compression coupler, and slide one over each pipe end. Next, slip one rubber washer over each pipe end. Fit the body of the compression coupler in place over the pipe ends, and hand-tighten the end caps so the washers form a seal between the coupler body and the pipes. Use a wrench to turn the caps an additional one-quarter turn, and test the seal by turning on the water.

Note that if a compression coupler is used within a few feet of an ell (90° angle) fitting, the ell must be braced in place or the pipe will shift and blow out of the coupling. To prevent shifting, drive a stake behind the ell.

Telescoping Couplers

Telescoping couplers are another quick fix for PVC pipe repairs. They have a built-in slip coupler on one end and a short length of PVC pipe that telescopes out on the other end. An additional slip coupler is needed for the repair. As with a compres-sion coupler, the pipes do not need to be flexed, so less soil needs to be removed.

Poly Pipe Repairs

Polyethylene pipe is a black plastic pipe that is used in irrigation systems in many parts of the country. Drip systems use poly pipe, and repairs are typically performed using compression couplers; see "Micro-irrigation" on page 93 for information. Pressure-rated poly pipe that is used for spray head systems is often repaired using barbed insert couplers. Repair with insert couplers is explained here.

Dig down and clear the dirt several inches on all sides of the broken section of pipe. Less dirt needs to be removed from around poly pipe than PVC pipe because poly is flexible and requires less cleaning prior to repair. Note that it's important not to kink poly pipe because this can compromise its strength.

Shut off the water and cut out the broken section of pipe. The pipe ends should be cut square, that is, at a 90 degree angle. Take the pipe with you to the irrigation or plumbing supply store, and purchase a piece of replacement pipe that has the same diameter and pressure rating as the broken pipe. You will also need two barbed poly insert couplers that are the correct size for the pipe. Barbed insert couplers can be brass, stainless steel, or PVC. And you will need four hose clamps. Stainless steel hose clamps are a good choice.

Cut a piece of repair pipe the same length as the section removed from the in-ground pipe. Be sure the cut ends are square. Slide two hose clamps onto the section of repair pipe, then insert one barbed coupler into each end of the repair pipe.

Note that some professionals heat the pipe ends to make it easier to insert the couplers. Heating must be even and uniform to avoid creating thin wall areas that can rupture. Heat guns and blow driers increase the risk of heating the pipe unevenly. An acceptable heating method is to dip the pipe ends in hot water. Avoid heating poly pipe if possible.

Be sure the couplers are inserted all the way—the hose should contact the coupler rings. Slide the clamps over the ends where the couplers are, then tighten the clamps.

Next, slide one hose clamp over each end of the in-ground pipe. Insert the repair pipe couplers into the in-ground pipe. Once the couplers are in all the way, slide the hose clamps over the section where the couplers are, then tighten the clamps. If possible, let the repair sit overnight. The next day, retighten the clamps, check the seal, and bury the pipe.

Troubleshooting Irrigation Systems

Mechanical and electrical irrigation system components are generally durable and trouble-free. When components malfunction, troubleshooting and repair should be performed promptly to avoid causing drought stress to plants, particularly during the summer months. This work can be contracted out, but there is no guarantee that repairs will be done in a timely manner.

Irrigation system malfunctions can have a variety of causes. Identifying and locating the problem(s) are the bulk of the work. Understanding how an irrigation system functions is the key to thinking logically about the potential causes of a malfunction.

Automatic Irrigation System Overview

Solenoid valves are the most common automatic valve in residential landscapes. They consist of a mechanical section (the valve) and an electrical component (the solenoid, or coil). Pressurized water enters the valve from the water supply through an opening in the valve called the inlet cavity. In an open valve, water flows unobstructed through the valve to the outlet cavity and out to the sprinklers. In a closed valve, a circular, rubber component, called the diaphragm, seals off the flow of water between the inlet and outlet cavities. Valve design makes use of hydraulic force—the force of water—to raise and lower the diaphragm.

The solenoid is the electrical device that triggers the hydraulic change in the valve. The solenoid

connects to the controller by low-voltage wires that extend across the landscape below ground. At the scheduled run times, the controller sends an electric signal to the solenoid, causing the valve to open. When the controller stops sending the electric signal, the valve closes.

Basic Valve Hydraulics

To troubleshoot mechanical problems in an automatic valve, you need a basic understanding of valve hydraulics. (The components described here are labeled in the diagram on the following page.) In a closed valve, pressurized water in the inlet cavity exerts upward force on the diaphragm. The diaphragm does not lift because water in a chamber above the diaphragm exerts a greater downward force on the diaphragm, keeping it closed. This chamber above the diaphragm is called the bonnet cavity. The water pressure is the same in both the inlet cavity and the bonnet cavity, but the bonnet cavity has a larger surface area, which accounts for the greater hydraulic force.

When the water pressure in the bonnet cavity drops—due to either an activated solenoid or an opened bleed port—the pressurized water in the inlet cavity forces the diaphragm to lift, and water flows through the valve to the sprinklers.

A small tube, called the inlet port, channels water from the inlet cavity to the bonnet cavity above the diaphragm. This is how the bonnet cavity fills with water. Water exits the bonnet cavity through a slightly larger tube called the outlet port. The solenoid controls the flow of water through the outlet port by means of a small plunger. When the controller sends an electric signal to the solenoid, the solenoid plunger lifts off the outlet port, unblocking it—the bonnet cavity pressure drops, the diaphragm lifts, and water flows through the valve.

When the controller stops the electric signal, a spring in the solenoid forces the solenoid plunger over the outlet port, blocking it. As a result, water pressure increases in the bonnet cavity. The increased bonnet cavity pressure—with the help of the diaphragm spring—forces the diaphragm

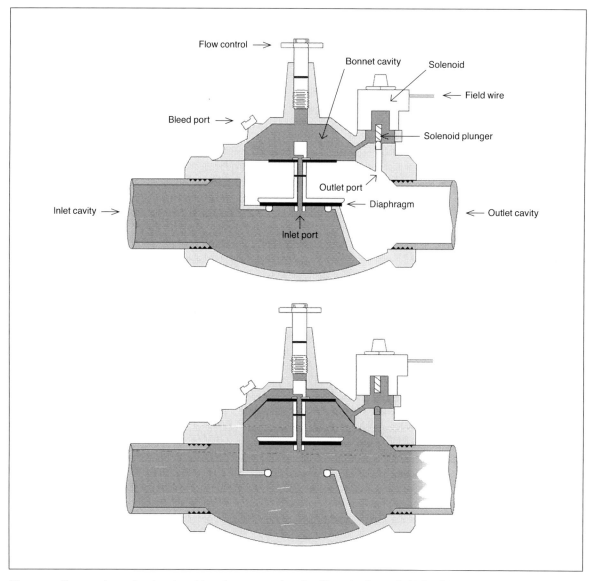

The upper diagram shows the closed position of an automatic valve (Superior Controls Globe Valve, Model 950). The solenoid plunger blocks the outlet port and the diaphragm remains lowered. In the second diagram, the solenoid is activated, causing the solenoid plunger to unblock the outlet port; this triggers the water pressure change that causes the valve to open. Diagrams adapted with permission from Storm Manufacturing Group, Inc.

down over the inlet and outlet cavities, stopping the flow of water.

Rotating the bleed screw or the solenoid are ways to manually release the water pressure in the bonnet cavity. Again, the drop in bonnet cavity pressure causes the diaphragm to lift and the valve to open. Photos of valve components are shown on page 164.

Troubleshooting Low Water Pressure

A properly designed sprinkler system will have sufficient operating pressure and flow (in gallons per minute) to achieve head-to-head water coverage. This means that the coverage radius of one sprinkler extends to the base of the next sprinkler. Sprinkler systems that fall short of head-to-head coverage are at risk for uneven watering, brown spots, and donut patterns. If the sprinkler system was not designed correctly to begin with, the system should be redesigned by a landscape architect or contractor. For other solutions, see "Solving Coverage Problems In Spray-Head Systems" on page 154. The following troubleshooting guidelines are for water pressure problems caused by a malfunction or a recent change to the system.

Low Water Pressure, All Zones

Check for a closed gate or ball valve. If all zones have reduced water pressure, begin troubleshooting by checking for a partially closed gate valve or ball valve. Gate valves and ball valves are installed in the irrigation mainline before the valves. They are sometimes referred to as isolation valves or shutoff valves, and they are used to temporarily shut off water to the valves. Additional shutoff valves can be found on some backflow prevention devices, such as a pressure vacuum breaker or reduced pressure backflow preventer; not all properties have these devices. See "Sprinklers Fail To Shut Off" on page 165 for more information.

On an open ball valve, the handle points in the direction of the pipe. Open and close ball valves slowly to reduce the risk of water hammer, which is a fast water-pressure change that can damage irrigation pipes. Use care when cranking old shutoff valves to avoid breaking off the handle.

Check main water supply. If the isolation valve was already fully open, there could be a problem with the property's water supply. This is likely if the water pressure inside the house is also low. Contact the municipal water supplier to see if there is a problem in the area. Note that water pressure is typically lower in the early morning hours; if this is the case, scheduling systems to run at a later time may avoid the problem. Otherwise, the property's main water shut off valve may be partially closed or the pressure regulator may be malfunctioning or in need of adjustment.

Warning: *Pressure regulators reduce water pressure and prevent water pressure fluctuation. These devices protect a plumbing system from water pressure surges. The incorrect adjustment of a pressure regulator can cause significant plumbing damage. Leave the adjustment of pressure regulators to a contractor or plumber.*

If a single pressure regulator serves both the house lines and the landscape, have a plumber or landscape contractor check and adjust the pressure regulator. If the irrigation system has a designated pressure regulator, you may, at your own risk, attempt to adjust it, though you'll need to get the appropriate instruction; testing water pressure is not explained here.

For reference, rotating the bolt on the pressure regulator clockwise increases water pressure; rotating the bolt counterclockwise decreases water pressure. This is the opposite of adjustments for a flow control on an automatic irrigation valve. According to landscape architect Jess Stryker, "As a general rule most regulators will work well if you set the pressure at least 1,4 bars (15 PSI) lower than the inlet pressure. If the pressure drop is less than required, the regulator tends to not work as accurately, and may allow the pressure to vary up and down considerably." (IrrigationTutorials.com 2011).

Some automatic valves have a built-in pressure regulator, though these valves are more expensive and less common in residential landscapes. Another potential cause of reduced pressure at all valves is a single leaking valve. See "Low Head Drainage and Valve Seeping" on page 168 for information.

Low Water Pressure, One Zone

Check the flow control adjustment. The position of the flow control determines how high the diaphragm rises. The flow control is sometimes used to reduce the water pressure in a zone; it can also be used to shut off the water during an emergency. A partially closed flow control could be the cause of the low water pressure. The flow control is either a short stem (usually black) or a plastic, inset screw on top of the valve casing; see photos on page 153 and page 164. (Unlike the bleed screw, the flow con-

A) This anti-siphon valve's internal components are accessed by unscrewing the large plastic ring on the main valve housing. Some valves use screws to secure the bonnet to the valve body. On this valve, the flow control is the white screw to the left of the solenoid.

B) The same valve with the top removed. In this photo, the right side of the valve body is the anti-siphon mechanism, which prevents water in the irrigation pipes from returning to the house lines.

C) The bonnet, diaphragm, and diaphragm spring. The spring helps lower the diaphragm when the bonnet is repressurizing.

D) An enlarged view of the bonnet and diaphragm. When the outlet port is closed, pressurized water in the bonnet cavity keeps the valve closed. The valve shown is manufactured by Lawn Genie.

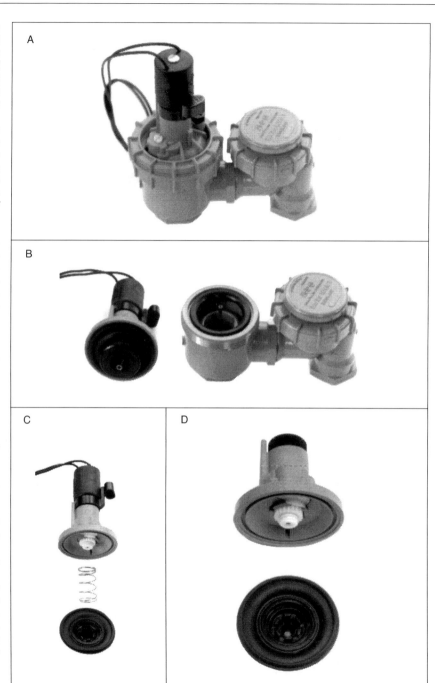

Flow Control Adjustment

The flow control is used to control the flow of water through the valve. It can also be used to close the valve in an emergency. On some models, the flow control is a plastic screw; on others, it is a black stem in the center of the valve. A properly adjusted flow control provides the amount of water needed in a given system. For small systems, the flow control needs to be turned down more than for larger ones. For the correct adjustment, turn the flow control all the way down, then turn the valve on, and start adjusting the flow control up. Stop when the sprinklers provide the desired coverage. If the flow control is fully raised, back it down by rotating it clockwise 2 to 3 full turns. On systems that have a designated pressure regulator, system-wide water pressure adjustments should be made with the pressure regulator.

trol screw requires a screwdriver.) Rotate the flow control counterclockwise all the way. If this was the problem, the water pressure will return to normal. If the flow control will not turn counterclockwise, don't force it; it is already fully open and not the problem. To properly adjust the flow control, rotate it clockwise two to three full turns from the fully open position.

Check for broken pipes or recent system changes. Broken pipes or sprinklers can reduce the flow of water to the rest of the sprinklers in the zone. Puddling and holes in the turf are possible indications of a break. If no pipe breaks or broken sprinklers are detected, find out if there have been any recent changes or repairs to the sprinkler system. If new sprinklers or nozzles have been installed that emit more gallons per minute than the previous ones, all sprinklers in the zone will receive less pressure. For example, if a client replaces a spray head with a rotor, this could cause the pressure drop. A new section of sprinklers added to an existing section can have the same effect.

Sprinklers Fail To Shut Off

If a zone continues to operate after the scheduled run time, the problem could be mechanical or electrical. Begin mechanical troubleshooting by checking to see if the valve's bleed port is closed and the solenoid is hand tightened. If either is loose, water will exit the bonnet cavity and the sprinklers will continue to run.

Check for an activated solenoid. If the controller is sending voltage to the solenoid, the valve will continue to operate. To quickly see if the solenoid is continuing to receive power, feel the solenoid for a slight vibration, or place a small screwdriver across the top to feel for a magnetic pull. If there is no vibration or magnetic pull, the solenoid is not activated. If the solenoid is activated, the problem is electrical. Switch the controller to the "off" or "rain" position, and continue with electrical troubleshooting as described on page 168. Specifically, you should suspect a malfunctioning controller microprocessor. If the solenoid is not receiving power, continue below.

Check the flow control adjustment. In low water-pressure conditions, a fully raised flow control may prevent the diaphragm from lowering. The water does not need to be turned off for this adjustment. Using a wrench, or a screwdriver on some models, turn the flow control counterclockwise all the way. If the flow control won't turn counterclockwise, don't force it. This indicates that the flow control is fully raised and may be the cause of the problem. To adjust the flow control, rotate it approximately three full turns clockwise from the fully open position. Sometimes more turns are necessary. If the valve does not shut off, continue below.

Troubleshoot for bonnet cavity pressure problems. If the bonnet cavity is unable to repressurize, the valve will not close. Anything that prevents

If there is no gate valve for the specific valve or manifold being worked on, shut off the house's main water. Always get prior permission from the homeowner or tenants. The water main is usually located near the street.

water from filling the bonnet cavity or causes water to flow out of the bonnet cavity could be the problem. Potential causes include an open bleed port, a loose solenoid, debris in the inlet port, a torn diaphragm, debris lodged where the diaphragm seals off (seat assembly/valve seat), a misshapen or poorly functioning solenoid plunger, or a loose seal between the bonnet and the valve body. If the valve was recently repaired, it is also possible that the diaphragm spring was accidentally left out.

As a preliminary step, try flushing debris from the valve by opening and closing the bleed port several times. If this does not fix the problem, continue below.

1. Shut off the water. To troubleshoot problems related to valve components, start by turning off the water at the shutoff valve. If there is no shutoff valve in-line before the valves, you may need to shut off the house's main water. In many cities, the main water shutoff valve is located in a landscape box near the street, but it may be elsewhere. The box or shutoff valve should be marked "Water". Be certain it is the right utility box or call a plumber or contractor. Always get the homeowner's or resident's permission before shutting off the house's water supply.

If the property has a pressure vacuum breaker (PVB) or reduced pressure backflow preventer (RP), the water can also be turned off here. These

devices are backflow preventers: they prevent contaminated water in the irrigation system from returning to the water supply. A city may require specific types of backflow preventers. Many properties don't use PVBs or RPs. Reduced pressure backflow preventers are more expensive devices and are typically used in commercial applications. They can often be seen near the street in front of commercial properties.

Pressure vacuum breakers and reduced pressure backflow preventers have two shutoff valves (ball or gate valves), one at each end of the assembly. Either shutoff valve can be used to turn off the water, though it is safer to use the one closer to the water supply to minimize the risk of damaging the backflow preventer's internal components (Charlot 2007).

2. Inspect the solenoid. With the water to the valves off, remove the solenoid by unscrewing it counterclockwise by hand. Some models secure the solenoid with a metal bracket, and removal requires a screwdriver. Inspect the solenoid by depressing the plunger tip. The plunger is a small piston in the solenoid body that raises when the solenoid is energized. The plunger should lift and return to its original position. If it will not lift or will not return, there could be corrosion or debris in the plunger area, or the solenoid plunger spring could be missing. Pry off the rubber plunger tip, and check for either of these problems. The plunger cannot be removed on some models.

If the plunger lifts and returns to position, inspect the rubber plunger tip to see if it is uniform and positioned properly. An improperly seated or misshapen solenoid plunger tip will fail to seal off the outlet port. If the plunger tip is misshapen, replace it, or install a new solenoid.

Finally, check for an improperly seated or damaged solenoid seal, or O-ring. The solenoid O-ring is located in the valve body beneath the solenoid. If the solenoid and its components look all right, reinstall the solenoid. Turn on the water at the shutoff valve to see if the valve closes. If it does not, turn off the water again, and continue with the following procedures.

Backflow Preventers

Backflow preventers are irrigation components that prevent contaminated water in the irrigation system from returning to the water supply. Fertilizers, pesticides, and animal waste, among other contaminants, can reenter the public water supply through irrigation systems if the correct backflow prevention device is not installed or is not functioning properly. For this reason, many cities require the installation of specific types of backflow preventers and require that these devices be tested regularly to ensure their proper functioning. Often, these testing procedures can be performed only by certified testers of backflow prevention devices and assemblies. Contact the Building and Planning department of your city government offices or your local water supplier to learn about the regulations for backflow prevention (sometimes called cross-connection control) in your area.

3. Inspect the internal valve components. The next step is to open the valve casing and inspect the internal components. Unscrew the metal screws or the large plastic ring that secures the top of the valve to the main valve housing. Lift off the top of the valve. This is the bonnet housing. Underneath is the circular, rubber diaphragm. Between the diaphragm and the bonnet housing is the diaphragm spring. The diaphragm may need to be separated from the bonnet housing to see the spring. If the spring is missing, this is the likely cause of the problem. Check for it at the bottom of the landscape box or on the ground. Otherwise, get a replacement spring.

Lift off the diaphragm and inspect it for any breaks. Inspect the circular disk attached to the bottom of the diaphragm (called the seat assembly) for any nicks. And inspect the smooth circular ring in the valve body where the diaphragm seals off (valve seat). Some seat assemblies can be removed, others are built-in to the valve. Look for any nicks or oddities. Remove any debris found inside the valve. Wipe the diaphragm and valve seat clean. Sometimes cleaning is enough to solve the problem. Otherwise, write down the valve's make and model, and replace any nicked or damaged parts.

Sprinklers Fail To Come On

When a valve fails to open at the scheduled time, the problem is usually electrical. Either the control-ler is malfunctioning, the solenoid is not working, or there is a break in the wire connecting the two. Before proceeding to electrical troubleshooting, eliminate the possibility of mechanical failure. Open and close the valve using the bleed port. If the sprinklers come on and shut off, the valve's mechanical components are functioning properly.

If opening the bleed port does not turn on the sprinklers, the shutoff valve may be closed. Occasionally someone will confuse a gate valve handle with a garden hose faucet handle. If the shutoff valve is open, check to see if the flow control on the irrigation valve is fully turned down. If it is, the valve will not open. Turn the flow control counterclockwise all the way, then back it down two to three full turns.

If the valve opens with the bleed screw, eliminate another possible mechanical cause by rotating the solenoid to the left until the valve opens. If the unit has one, use the lever or solenoid handle at the base or top of the solenoid. This raises the solenoid plunger off the outlet port, unblocking it. If the sprinklers don't come on by rotating the solenoid, it is possible that the outlet port is blocked. Turn off the water, remove the solenoid, and attempt to clear debris from the outlet port with a paper clip. If the sprinklers turn on and off with these manual tests, the problem is electrical. Continue with "Electrical Troubleshooting", next.

Low Head Drainage and Valve Seeping

After the sprinklers shut off, water in the pipes may drain out of the lowest head in the zone and eventually stop. This is called low head drainage, and it does not indicate a problem with the sprinkler system. However, low head drainage can cause puddles, runoff, and water waste. The installation of a device called a check valve will eliminate low head drainage. Some check valves screw onto the riser beneath the sprinkler head. Sprinklers with built-in check valves are also available. If a sprinkler head continually leaks water, this indicates that water is leaking through the valve. The solenoid plunger tip may not be seating properly or there may be damage or debris on the valve seat. Follow the troubleshooting guidelines in "Sprinklers Fail To Shut Off" on page 165.

Electrical Troubleshooting

Once the problem has been narrowed down to electrical causes, the next step is to figure out where in the electrical system the problem lies. The problem could be with the controller, the solenoid, or the field wire connecting the two. Troubleshooting electrical malfunctions requires an electronic testing device known as a volt/ohm meter (VOM). An alternative is to use a specialized irrigation testing

An analog volt/ohm meter. The meter shown here is manufactured by GB Instruments.

device that performs a similar function and may include additional features.

Volt/Ohm Meter

A volt/ohm meter, also called a multimeter, is an electronic device used to test for volts (AC and DC voltage), amperes (current), and ohms (resistance) in electric components. Alternating current voltage (ACV) is the current found in a house's electrical outlets. Batteries provide direct current voltage (DCV). Ohms are the units used to describe resistance.

Voltage is electrical pressure. It can be compared to the pressure of water in a pipe. Put differently, voltage is a measure of the force that causes electricity to flow through a conductor. Resistance can be compared to water friction; it is a measure of how easily electricity can flow through a conductor. No resistance is called continuity. We measure AC voltage when testing a controller's power source, and we measure resistance when testing field wires and solenoids.

The volt/ohm meter has a dial on it that can be turned to different settings. To read ACV, turn the dial to one of the ACV settings. Always select a setting that is larger than the power source being tested. For example, to test a wall outlet in the U.S., you might set the volt/ohm meter to 250 ACV. When the volt/ohm meter is set to 250 ACV, the power source being tested should be 250 volts AC or less. The standard voltage in household outlets in the U.S. is approximately 120 volts AC. In comparison, the standard voltage in household electrical outlets in Europe is 220 to 240 volts. Some countries have multiple standards.

You would not use a volt/ohm setting of 50 ACV to test a 250 volt power source, because this would likely blow the fuse in the volt/ohm meter. Similarly, you would not use a DCV setting or an ohms setting, except when specifically testing for DC voltage or ohms, respectively. When testing DC voltage (e.g., when testing a battery), the red lead should touch the positive terminal, and the black lead should touch the negative terminal.

Analog or digital volt/ohm meters are available. Digital volt/ohm meters are more commonly called digital multimeters (DMM). If you purchase an analog volt/ohm meter, select one that has an R x 1 or R x 10 ohms setting. This means that the reading is multiplied by one or ten, respectively. The R x 1K (1000) setting is not suitable for most continuity tests.

Important: *Working with electricity is inherently dangerous. Follow the directions that come with your volt/ohm meter to avoid breaking the instrument or injuring yourself. If you do not have a product manual, contact the product's manufacturer for a replacement.*

Controller Tests

If the sprinklers don't come on at the scheduled time, or don't come on at all, and mechanical causes have been eliminated, the problem could be a malfunctioning controller. The following controller troubleshooting tests will help to isolate the problem. The guidelines presented here do not need to be followed in order, though the order presented is a logical way to investigate a problem.

The troubleshooting instructions provided here will not be as specific as those found in the controller manual. If the controller manual is not posted near the controller, the client may have it. Many controller manuals are also available through manufacturers' websites. The following troubleshooting tests are for solid state controllers; electromechanical controllers are not covered.

The following instructions for testing for power at the controller pertain only to 24-volt irrigation controllers. *Warning:* Some commercial controllers have junction boxes containing wires that may run 120 volts AC or 230 volts AC. And the electrical outlets that supply residential controllers can be 120 volts or greater (220-240 for appliances; 230 volts is standard in the U.K.).

Warning: *Use the following instructions for testing AC voltage at your own risk. Problems associated with electrical outlets, as well as problems associated with controller power wires that have a reading significantly higher than 28 volts AC, should be addressed by a licensed electrician. As an additional precaution, you can wear approved electrical insulating rubber gloves (low voltage; class 0) when testing any household power source.*

Does the controller have power? Begin troubleshooting by checking to see if the controller is on. If the switch or dial is set to the "off" or "rain" position, the controller will not operate. If the controller is on, the next step is to see if the controller is receiving power. The controller receives electricity from a transformer that reduces the house's standard 120 volts AC (or 110 volts AC) down to 24 volts AC. The transformer either plugs into a wall outlet or is wired directly to the house's electricity.

Note that the LCD screen of the controller may appear functional even if the controller is not receiving power. One way to determine if the controller is receiving power is to disconnect its battery. If the LCD screen goes blank, there is a problem with the transformer or the transformer is not receiving power. You may need to reprogram the irrigation schedule after testing for power this way.

Another way to determine if the controller is receiving electricity is to use the volt/ohm meter to test for power at the terminal strip (see photo, next page). Inside the controller, sometimes under a plastic panel, is a row of screws with colored wires attached. This is called the terminal strip or wire terminal. Each color-coded wire—apart from the white common wire and the power input wires—is known as a station control wire. Each station control wire connects to a different valve in the landscape.

Begin volt/ohm meter power tests with an AC setting that is higher than the standard voltage reading for electrical outlets in the area. Set the volt/ohm meter to a setting larger than 120 volts AC (230 volts AC in the U.K.). Next, locate the power input wires on the terminal strip. They will be labeled "VAC", "AC", or "24VAC". Touch one volt/ohm lead to one power input wire, and touch the other volt/ohm lead to the other power input wire. The lead can touch the copper of the wire or the post it connects

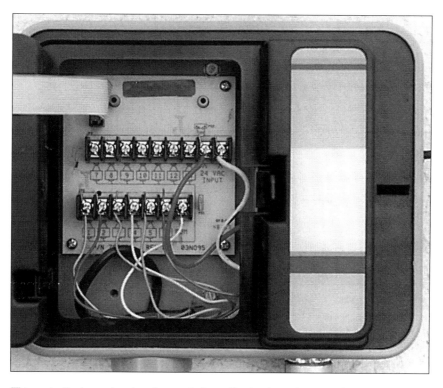

This controller is running six valves, as indicated by the six station control wires on the lower part of the terminal strip. The white wire is the common wire and attaches to a post labeled "COM". There are seven unused stations. The "24 VAC" posts are the power inputs, which have been stepped down to 24 volts by a transformer.

to. Do not let the volt/ohm leads touch each other during this test.

A reading of approximately 24 volts (up to 28 volts) reveals that the transformer is doing its job stepping down the power and delivering it to the controller. If this is the case, there is no need to test the outlet: proceed to "Does the Controller Activate Each Station?" If there is no reading with this test, either the transformer is bad or the electrical outlet is not providing electricity. Proceed to test the electrical outlet as described below.

Does the outlet have power? If the controller is wired directly to the house's electricity, check the circuit breaker. If the circuit breaker is all right, have an electrician troubleshoot the power problem. If the controller's transformer plugs in to a wall outlet, troubleshoot as follows:

If the electrical outlet has a ground fault circuit interrupter (GFCI), press the black "test" button on the outlet. This will cut off power to the outlet and cause the red "reset" button to raise. If the GFCI has already been tripped, the red reset button will be raised. Press the reset button to restore power to the outlet. If the controller still does not have power, check the circuit breaker that governs that electrical outlet. Reset the breaker if necessary.

If the circuit breaker is all right, the next step is to test the power supply at outlet using the volt/ohm meter. Unplug the transformer from the outlet, and follow the instructions that came with your volt/ohm meter for testing electrical outlets. The instructions included here are only for testing a household 110-120 volt power plug.

In the U.S., set the volt/ohm meter to a setting above 120 volts AC. As a standard safety precaution, begin the test by putting the meter on the highest ACV setting. Next, insert the black lead into one vertical slot in the outlet and the red lead into the other vertical slot in the outlet. You may need to move the leads around to get them to contact the electricity.

The meter should read approximately 120 volts on the AC scale. Some variance is normal: usually 110-125 volts. You can contact your power supply company to find out what the acceptable voltage range is for the area. If the meter shows no reading, or the reading is outside the range quoted by the power company, there may be something wrong with the outlet, and an electrician should be called to repair the problem. If the outlet has power but the controller does not, the transformer is bad and should be replaced with a comparable (usually 24-volt) transformer.

Is the rain sensor activated? A rain sensor is an optional device that overrides the controller's programming during rain. The sensor can be adjusted to interrupt the controller at different rainfall levels; it can also be adjusted to dry at different rates. Once the rain sensor dries out, the sprinklers will come on at the scheduled time. The rain sensor connects to designated sensor posts on the controller. Alternatively, the sensor may have one wire attached to the common (COM) post on the terminal strip and another wire attached to the white common wire that connects to the valves. Some rain sensors are wireless. Many systems don't have a rain sensor.

The irrigation system will not operate, automatically or manually, if the rain sensor is activated. If the rain sensor is activated, it must be bypassed for the sprinklers to operate. Some controllers have a built-in bypass switch; if the controller does not have one, the best solution is to install a jumper wire to bypass the switch. Some rain sensor models can be bypassed by removing the cap on the sensor. This will close the circuit and allow the sprinklers to operate.

Is the fuse blown? A blown fuse could also cause the sprinklers to fail to come on at the scheduled time. Some controllers have a circuit breaker instead of a fuse. A blown fuse is usually caused by a short or a bad splice in the field wire. Test and

repair the field wires before replacing the fuse. Proceed to "Continuity Testing: Introduction" on page 172 for instructions. Replace the fuse with an identical fuse. Do not use a fuse with a larger amperage. If the fuse or circuit breaker are all right, continue below.

Does the controller activate each station? When the controller is receiving power, it delivers electricity to each station at the programmed times. Each station on the controller corresponds to a valve in the landscape. It is rare for a controller to fail to deliver electricity to a station, but this can also be checked. First, activate a station using the manual feature of the controller. Put the volt/ohm meter on an AC setting greater than 120 volts. Next, hold the black volt/ohm lead to the common (COM) post and the red lead to the post of the activated station. There should be a reading of approximately 24 volts, up to 28 volts. This can be done for each station. Remember, each station will show that it is receiving power only if it is activated.

- If all stations have power when activated, check the station run times. If the run times are not what was programmed, the microprocessor may be malfunctioning. Troubleshoot for a malfunctioning microprocessor, as described in "Is the microprocessor malfunctioning?", below.

- If all stations have power except one, that station is malfunctioning. Reset the controller microprocessor, as described in "Is the microprocessor malfunctioning?" If this does not restore power to the station, one solution is to move the wire to an unused station on the controller. Otherwise, the controller should be serviced if it is expensive or replaced if it is inexpensive.

Is the microprocessor malfunctioning? Power surges can damage a controller's microprocessor or cause it to malfunction. Controllers with built-in surge protection are less prone to these problems. Weak batteries can also cause microprocessor malfunctions, including oddities such as scrambled LCD digits and alterations to the program run times. These malfunctions can usually be corrected by resetting the microprocessor memory and installing a new battery.

If the controller has non-volatile memory (i.e., preserves data in the event of power outage), you must follow the instructions in the controller manual to reset the microprocessor memory. To reset the microprocessor memory on controllers that don't have non-volatile memory, turn the controller off, disconnect the battery, and unplug the transformer. The battery may be located behind a panel inside the controller. If there is not a plug-in transformer, disconnect the power wires from their posts. The power wire posts will be labeled "24V", "VAC", or similar. Wait several minutes, then reconnect the battery and the transformer or power wires. If the problem persists, try disconnecting the power for a longer interval.

Sometimes a battery will test as "good" but doesn't have enough strength to power the controller; therefore, it is usually best to install a new battery. If this solves the problem, reprogram the time, date, and station run times. If this does not solve the problem, the controller is malfunctioning and should be serviced if it is expensive, or replaced if it is inexpensive.

If, after conducting the previous tests, the valves still fail to operate from the controller, the common wire to the valves may be disconnected or broken. Proceed to "Continuity Testing: Introduction" on the next column for instructions.

Field Wire

Field wire is a polyethylene (PE) or polyvinyl chloride (PVC) insulated, low-voltage, direct-burial cable used for irrigation. Field wire that will be buried must be Underwriters Laboratories (UL) approved underground feeder wire (UF). Field wire is either single strand or multi-strand. Multi-strand (multi-conductor) field wire houses several color-coded copper wires. All the wires in a cable are the same gauge; the colors simply aid in identification.

Irrigation field wire runs from the controller to a group of valves, which is called a manifold. The wire may run underground or along the outside of a building. Contractors typically lay the wire in the trench with the mainline PVC pipe to protect it and make it easier to locate. Sometimes the wire is taped to the underside of the pipe.

Each automatic valve has a solenoid with two wires coming out of it. One wire from each solenoid connects to the common wire in the field wire strand. The common wire is usually the white wire. This common wire attaches to the common post (COM) on the controller. The other solenoid wire attaches to its own colored wire (station control wire) in the field wire. Each station control wire connects to its own numbered post on the controller terminal strip. Either solenoid wire can be attached to the common wire.

For example, a landscape with four valves requires four colored station control wires and one common wire. Occasionally the field wire contains more wires than are used. Note that some systems have multiple common wires attached to the common post on the controller. Each common wire is from a different manifold.

Resistance. When electrical energy travels through a copper wire, some of the energy is lost to resistance. The energy loss associated with resistance can be compared to the pressure loss of water from friction. To illustrate, the farther water travels through a pipe, the greater the water pressure loss; similarly, the longer the length of field wire, the more energy is lost to resistance.

American wire gauge (AWG) is a measurement standard for the diameter of electrical wire. The thicker the wire, the lower the gauge number and the farther the wire can carry electricity without problematic energy loss. Owing to the relatively short wire runs in most residential landscapes, problems associated with incorrect wire gauge are rare. The most common diameters of field wire in residential landscapes are 18 gauge and 14 gauge.

Continuity Testing: Introduction

A broken, shorted, or poorly connected field wire or solenoid can prevent the controller's electrical signal from activating the valve. A volt/ohm meter can be used to test for wire breaks, bad splices, or short circuits from the terminal strip on the controller. This is done by performing a continuity test. A continuity test is a test of resistance in the field wire and the solenoid.

Note that some controllers are equipped with a short-circuit protection feature that skips a faulty station, allowing the remaining zones to run at the scheduled times. Error symbols on the LCD screen reveal which station is malfunctioning. These newer controllers speed up troubleshooting, though continuity testing is still needed to locate the source of the problem in the faulty circuit.

A continuity test is performed with the ohm setting on the volt/ohm meter. When set to read ohms, the volt/ohm meter sends a small current through the circuit to test resistance. In a properly functioning circuit, the current will travel through one field wire to the solenoid and back through the other wire. Resistance levels outside the acceptable ranges indicate a problem with the wiring or the solenoid. The problem can then be narrowed down further.

Calibrate an analog volt/ohm meter before conducting a continuity test; see your meter's manual for instructions. Briefly, to calibrate the meter, set

the meter to read ohms, then touch the red and black leads together. Adjust the dial on the side, or an adjustment screw, until the needle points to zero. This should be done before each use. Digital multimeters do not need to be calibrated.

Continuity Test

Before beginning a continuity test, turn the controller's dial or switch to the off position. This is important to do because the volt/ohm meter can be damaged if volts run through the meter while it is set to read ohms. As an added precaution, unplug the transformer, or disconnect the power wires (24VAC) on the terminal strip.

Next, disconnect the common wire from the post marked "COM" on the terminal strip. The common wire is usually white, but may be a different color. Set the volt/ohm meter to read ohms (resistance or Ω) at the R x 1 or R x 10 setting. Touch the meter's black lead to the white common wire, and touch the red lead to one of the station control wires. Each station control wire is connected to a numbered valve post. Make note of the resistance reading on

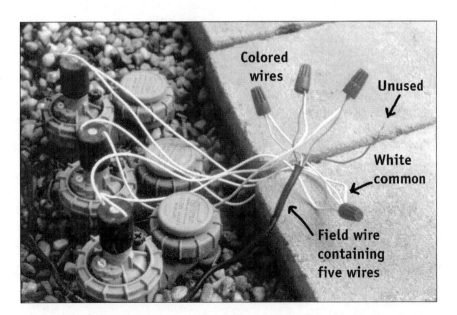

This manifold has three valves. Each solenoid has two wires coming out of it. One solenoid wire connects to the white common wire, the other wire connects to its own colored wire in the field wire. The wires are joined using waterproof connectors. Breaks, shorts, and bad splices can be detected with electrical tests performed at the controller. Note that these valves have been installed incorrectly: they sit too low in the ground.

the meter. Do this for each station on the terminal strip. The readings can be interpreted as follows:

20 to 60 ohms = Acceptable. A range of 20 to 60 ohms is acceptable (Rain Bird 2006). Some experts suggest that a good wire run can safely range between 10 and 60 ohms (Urban Farmer Store 2003). Various factors determine the resistance level, including the make and model of the solenoid and its age. If one circuit has a markedly different ohm reading from the others, this could indicate a problem.

Below 20 ohms = Short Circuit. A reading below 20 ohms indicates a short circuit (Rain Bird 2006). Some sources suggest that a reading below 10 ohms indicates a short circuit. Again, when testing several circuits, any reading that stands out could indicate a problem.

A short circuit occurs when two wires make contact at a point that was not originally intended. This contact allows the electrical current to complete the circuit without traveling the full length of the intended circuit. Short circuits generate less resistance and increase voltage. This can cause the controller's fuse to blow or circuit breaker to trip.

A short circuit can occur in the field wire or the solenoid. To determine which is the cause of the short, locate the valve connected to the problematic station. To locate the valve, use a controller chart (explained on page 175) if available. Otherwise, note the color of the station control wire at the faulty station, and locate the valve with that colored station control wire. If the valves are buried, wire tracing equipment is required to locate them.

Once you locate the valve, disconnect the two solenoid wires from the field wire, and test the resistance of the solenoid. With the volt/ohm meter still set to read ohms at the R x 1 or R x 10 setting, touch one volt/ohm lead to one solenoid wire and the other lead to the other solenoid wire. A properly functioning solenoid will have a resistance reading of 20 to 60 ohms.

If the resistance of the solenoid is below 20 ohms, the solenoid has a short and should be replaced

(Rain Bird 2006). Some sources suggest that a reading of 10 ohms or less indicates a shorted solenoid. Again, comparing the resistance of the solenoid to that of several other solenoids in the system may be useful. If the solenoid's resistance is low, but several other solenoids in the system have the same resistance, the solenoid may be functioning properly and the short may be in the field wire.

To replace a bad solenoid, shut off the water to the valve using the shutoff valve to the manifold. It may be necessary to shut off the house's water main (see page 166). Disconnect or cut the two solenoid wires, unscrew the solenoid counterclockwise, and remove it. Screw on the new solenoid, and splice the wires to the field wire. One wire connects to the white common wire, which is shared by the other valves in that manifold; the other wire connects to the color-coded station control wire. See the sidebar for guidelines on making a good wire splice.

If the solenoid's resistance is within the acceptable range, simply re-splicing the solenoid wires to the field wire may fix the problem. Otherwise, the short circuit is in the field wire and wire tracing equipment may be needed to find it. See "Locating Buried Valves and Field Wire", next, for more information.

Above 60 ohms = Open Circuit, Break, or Bad Splice. A reading of infinity indicates an open circuit. No current can complete the circuit because of a disconnected or broken wire. A reading of 70 to 150 ohms indicates a bad splice (Ewing Irrigation 1999). If the reading is above 60 ohms, suspect a bad splice or nicked wire. These problems increase resistance and reduce the electrical energy available to the solenoid.

If a station shows a reading above 60 ohms, locate the valve on the problematic circuit as described previously. Remove the wire connectors and disconnect the solenoid wires from the field wire, or cut out the old splices. Test the solenoid for a resistance reading above 60 ohms, and replace the solenoid if necessary. If the solenoid tests in the acceptable range (approximately 20 to 60 ohms), proceed to test the resistance of the field wire.

How to Make a Good Wire Splice

Faulty wire splices are responsible for many irrigation electrical problems. To make a good wire splice, strip one-half inch of insulation from each wire, being careful not to scrape into the copper wire. Next, twist the wires together using lineman's pliers (combination pliers). Don't make the connection too loose or too tight. Complete each splice with waterproof wire connectors. Waterproof wire nuts contain silicon or lithium-based grease and are generally required for outdoor splices. Regular wire nuts or electrical tape should not be used for outdoor splices. Failure to waterproof the wire splices at the valves is a common cause of valve solenoid failure (Stryker 2001). Field wire that is buried should be repaired with a direct-burial splice kit.

The following method of troubleshooting field wire is based on a recommendation in Rain Bird's *Irrigation Troubleshooting Guide*. With the wires disconnected from the solenoid, temporarily connect the white common wire to the station control wire, and return to the controller to re-test the resistance of the circuit. The reading at the controller will only reflect the condition of the field wire because the solenoid is not attached. Field wire resistance is low, and so the reading should be only a few ohms.

A resistance reading higher than a few ohms indicates a nick or bad splice in the field wire somewhere between the valve and the controller. If the resistance reading is no higher than a few ohms, the problem was a bad splice between the solenoid wires and field wire. Return to the valve and make new splices. Re-test at the controller to confirm this solved the problem.

Locating Buried Valves and Field Wire

Locating shorts or "opens" in buried field wire between the valve and the controller requires special electronic equipment. Buried field wire and valves can be located with wire and valve locating equipment. Alternatively, the city permit department may have the property's irrigation blueprint on file. Pulsers are electronic testing devices that can be used to locate breaks and nicks in the wire. These devices are relatively expensive, and their use requires training and practice. Irrigation technicians who troubleshoot on a regular basis can

justify purchasing these tools. Many tool rental companies have this equipment.

If you know the problem is isolated to the field wire, and bad splices are not the cause, you can rent and learn how to use a wire locator and pulser, though it may be simpler to have a landscape contractor or irrigation technician find the break. Fortunately, hard-to-locate wire breaks and shorts are relatively rare.

Controller Chart

Continuity tests are conducted at the controller. Once a problematic circuit is located, further troubleshooting is conducted at the valve. Valves can be identified by the color of their station control wire, though this approach can take some time. A controller chart is a diagram of the landscape that shows which irrigation zone is activated by each controller station. Some controllers charts use written descriptions to explain the irrigation layout. Controller charts speed up troubleshooting, and they are necessary for irrigation scheduling.

To make a simple controller chart, set the controller to run each station for one minute using the manual function on the controller. Run all the valves in sequence. Next, stand by the valves with a pencil, paper, and screwdriver ready. The first zone to operate is station #1, the second zone is station #2, and so on.

When the sprinklers come on, identify which valve is operating. Sometimes water will trickle from the backflow preventer of an operating anti-siphon valve. Alternatively, an open valve will produce a subtle vibration. Another method is to lay a screwdriver or other steel object across the top of the solenoid; an activated solenoid will have a magnetic pull.

Take notes briefly describing the area of the yard served by each valve; for example, "Station #1: South valve at front of house. Serves lawn west of driveway." Set the controller to automatic mode when you are finished. Post the controller chart near the controller for future reference.

Micro-Irrigation System Maintenance

Drip systems should be monitored monthly to ensure proper functioning. Systems at new accounts can be monitored more frequently to ensure that debris accumulation and emitter clogging are minimal. For an introduction to micro-irrigation systems, see "Micro-irrigation" on page 93.

Begin micro-irrigation system maintenance by turning on the system and walking the irrigated areas to inspect for obstructed emitters. Drip emitters can clog with sediment, microbial growth, and mineral deposits. Some malfunctioning emitters can be taken apart and cleaned; others must be replaced. Occasionally a clogged emitter can be cleared by holding a finger over the opening for a moment, then releasing. Replace faulty emitters with emitters of the same flow rate. If the original emitter is pressure compensating, the replacement emitter should be as well. Pressure compensating emitters maintain a consistent flow rate despite changes in water pressure or elevation.

As a plant increases in size, emitters should be added to the drip tube in order to wet the entire area within the plant's dripline. The dripline is the area of soil aligned with the edge of a plant's foliage. The majority of feeder roots are located in this area of soil. Note that the maximum GPH of the drip tubing needs to be taken into consideration

The filter (the black cylinder pointing downward) and pressure regulator of a drip system. Filters need occasional flushing and cleaning.

when adding emitters or sections of tubing (see page 93).

Micro-irrigation systems are equipped with a filter that prevents debris from clogging drip emitters. Filters require occasional flushing to clear accumulated debris. Flushing frequency depends on the rate at which debris accumulates. Generally, micro-irrigation systems connected to a municipal water supply require minimal flushing. To flush the filter, turn on the water to the drip system, and unscrew the cap at the base of the filter casing. The pressurized water will flush out debris. From time to time, remove the filter casing and inspect the filter for damage and mineral build-up (the system should be shut off for this inspection). Mineral build-up on the filter can be treated by soaking it in white vinegar or a chemical mineral remover, and scrubbing it with a toothbrush.

Once a month, flush sediment from the tubing by opening the end of one of the lateral lines and turning on the water. Open only one line end at a time. If there is no noticeable sediment after several months, the interval between flushings can be increased. Soaker hoses (porous pipe) should also be flushed from time to time. Leaks in solid tubing can be repaired with "goof plugs" or main line couplings. Flush the lines after repairs.

Treatment for algae growth is the same as for sediment. Flush main lines from time to time and replace clogged emitters as necessary. Chlorine dioxide can be injected into the lines to prevent algae buildup, though this is not typically performed in residential drip systems. Attempting to treat microbial growth that has been building up in a drip system for years may result in dead microbial growth clogging emitters.

Winterization of a micro-irrigation system is necessary in areas with winter freezes or hard frosts. When water freezes, it expands, and this can damage pipes and components. Winterization of a drip system involves draining the water from components and tubing and bringing the main assembly indoors. Most main assemblies consist of a backflow preventer, a filter, and a pressure regulator. Other winterization practices may be necessary. See the following topic for more information. In the spring, reinstall the main assembly, and flush the lines before operating the system.

Winterizing Irrigation Systems

Irrigation systems require winterization in areas of the country that experience freezes or hard frosts. Winterization procedures protect irrigation pipes and components from damage resulting from the expansion of water as it freezes. Considerable damage can be done to an irrigation system if winterization procedures are not performed correctly. Get the proper training, or leave the winterization of irrigation systems to experienced contractors.

Spring start-up of an irrigation system that has been winterized also requires special procedures to avoid causing damage. Fully opening a shut-off valve in the spring can cause water hammer—a pressure surge that can break pipes and fittings. Spring start-up procedures describe how to recharge the system with water without damaging components.

Included below are the web addresses of several articles that provide information on irrigation winterization and spring start-up procedures. Note that some of the procedures are high risk (e.g., using pressurized air to blow out an irrigation system) and can cause personal injury and property damage. Educate yourself thoroughly before attempting winterization, and call the help lines of major irrigation manufacturers if you have questions. If you attempt to winterize an irrigation system on your own, keep landscape architect Jess Stryker's

words of wisdom in mind: "The goal is to blow OUT the sprinklers not blow UP the sprinklers!"

- Stryker's *Winterizing Your Irrigation System* can be found at http://www.irrigationtutorials.com/winter.htm. This article also includes winterization practices for temperate climates.

- Rainbird's *Homeowner's Guide to Winterization* can be downloaded from http://www.rainbird.com/documents/diy/WinterizationGuide.pdf. Alternatively, search for the article using a search engine.

- *Winterizing Your Irrigation System* by Hunter Industries can be downloaded from http://www.hunterindustries.com/winterizing-your-irrigation-system.

Part III

Business Management

Part III

Part III covers selected business topics, including calculating an hourly rate, maintenance contracts, employer requirements, bookkeeping, and taxes.

Calculating an Accurate Hourly Rate

We begin the business section with possibly the most important and neglected topic for landscape management business owners: the calculation of an accurate and profitable hourly rate. No other area of small business management has as much bearing on the financial status of your business. Excellent customer service, meticulous bookkeeping, sound horticultural understanding—all of these are essential to the success of your business, but none of these will ensure that you turn a consistent profit. Only by taking the time to calculate what it costs you to do business and the amount you need to profit in order to sustain and grow your business can you hope to keep your enterprise thriving for the long haul.

Guesstimation

New landscapers tend to think that pricing is a secret that established landscapers keep to themselves. Unfortunately, even many established professionals know less about job pricing than they need to. This leads many in the profession to wing it when it comes to bidding. This casual approach to price calculation is sometimes referred to as "guesstimation".

Without business training, new business owners have little choice but to take their best guess when pricing jobs; or, if possible, to learn what other landscape management businesses charge and bid with those prices in mind. This can help new business owners bid competitively. However, since guesstimation is so common, there is a chance that even established local businesses are not bidding objectively, and that their rates do not reflect accurate pricing.

Guesstimation is frowned upon by experienced landscape management contractors because it lets the market determine the price of labor and fails to factor in the cost of doing business. Every business that bids according to what "the other person" charges will inevitably feel the downward pull of price under-cutters, or "low ballers", on the market. Even many knowledgeable landscape managers can wind up bidding jobs at prices that fail to provide fair compensation, because they didn't take the time to determine what it costs them to run their businesses.

Without an understanding of job costs, there is no way to know if the business is remaining profitable. In fact, the business could be generating minimal profit while the business owner thinks the business is highly profitable. In this sense, guesstimation and poor business management often go hand in hand. Businesses run this way tend to suffer from "undiagnosed" low profit, and many eventually go out of business.

The good news is that for most residential maintenance there is nothing wrong with estimating job *time* based on your experience maintaining properties of similar size and layout. Many residential bids can remain fast and accurate, as long as you calculate an hourly rate that covers all job costs and provides an adequate profit.

Job Costs

Unless an effort is made to quantify all the costs involved in a job, you can wind up cutting into your profit to keep your business afloat. This is a fast route to business failure. However, as long as you accurately determine job costs and pass these costs onto the client, you have a foundation to be consistently profitable.

Some job costs are easy to identify, others are more hidden. Plants, fertilizer, labor, tool usage, and so on, can all be directly tied to a particular job. Other costs are more loosely tied to a job: drive time, load/unload time, and dump fees are examples. Then there are the general costs associated with running the business: advertising, office supplies, insurance, bank charges, and rent for example.

The more accurate and detailed you can be about determining your costs for a particular job, the better your chance of recuperating all your costs in addition to a profit. This is where an estimating system can be of use: it helps you determine your total costs for a job. Bidding, in the technical sense, is the process of adding markups and margins to that cost to reap a profit. We use both of these practices when we calculate an accurate hourly rate.

Estimating Systems

There are many systems for estimating job costs. Some are detailed and methodical, others are homespun procedures created by sole proprietors for their own businesses; some provide accurate, useful information, others are based on conventions that, in the end, may or may not produce accurate bids. The varying methods and explanations and the technical nature of the subject tend to make estimating a source of confusion for many landscape management business owners.

To provide reliable information, *How to Price Landscape & Irrigation Projects,* by James R. Huston, MBA, CPE (J. R. Huston Enterprises, Inc. 2003) has been used as the main reference for this topic. This 600-page book is an authoritative text on job pricing for the green industry. It provides a wealth of instruction for a broad range of bidding situations, including residential maintenance.

Overview of the Lawn Maintenance Package

Huston recognizes that bidding residential lawn maintenance does not need to be as complex or time consuming as bidding commercial maintenance or installation jobs. He presents a method for determining an hourly, daily, and per-minute price based on the costs associated with a generic day of lawn maintenance. This allows the business owner to easily bid lawn maintenance accounts based on an estimate of labor time, and it simplifies the process of determining if a job is remaining profitable. He calls this method the "lawn maintenance package" approach.

Note that Huston's description of the lawn maintenance package approach can serve as an introduction to estimating and bidding in general. Even if you don't calculate your own maintenance package rates, this estimating system reveals many job and overhead costs that small business owners often fail to consider.

A large part of this chapter is devoted to explaining how to calculate lawn maintenance package rates, so it will be helpful to have an overview of what follows: The maintenance package approach aims to systematically account for all costs involved in a generic day of residential lawn maintenance. Once costs are known, markups and margins are added to find the total price for one generic day of maintenance. The daily price is then divided by the number of work (production) hours in the day to get an hourly rate that can be used to accurately bid residential lawn maintenance.

Huston divides the system of calculating maintenance package rates into three phases. *Phase I: Production Costs*, examines costs that are directly connected to the work of landscape maintenance, such as mowing and power tool use. *Phase II: General Conditions*, examines costs that are tied to Phase I costs, such as drive time and load/unload time. *Phase III: Markups and Margins*, covers sales tax, labor burden, overhead, and profit.

Note that these three phases are the foundation for many bidding situations, not just the lawn maintenance package. Huston's book details over 15 special bidding situations, including irrigation service work, large maintenance jobs, lawn fertilization, shrub fertilization and insect control, snow plowing, general tree work, tree fertilization, and others.

The Lawn Maintenance Package

We will follow the outline of the lawn maintenance package as Huston presents it and include explanations of some of the different categories and terms. So it is clear to the reader, the vast majority of the definitions and information about the maintenance package presented here have Huston's book as their source. However, the present text is not intended to represent his work. The selected topics and explanations included here have been taken out of their larger context. For comprehensive instruction, you are encouraged to consult Huston's text.

Note that information has been added to make some topics more applicable to the home-based landscape management business. For instance, if Huston's text examines the costs associated with an office space, our text focuses on the costs associated with a home office. Topics more suitable to larger businesses have not been included here. For a worksheet, see appendix B on page 240.

Phase I: Production Costs

Production costs are the costs associated with the production of the product or service. Mow time, power equipment use, sprinkler parts, and fertilizer are a few examples. In contrast, general condition costs, which are discussed in Phase II, are those costs tied to the product or service, but not directly required to produce it. Drive time, load/unload time, dump fees, and vehicle costs are examples.

Production costs are divided into four categories: materials, labor, equipment, and subcontractor costs. The maintenance package focuses on labor and equipment because these are the most significant costs associated with lawn maintenance. For information on materials, see page 197.

Production Labor Costs Per Day

Calculations for the maintenance package begin with the estimation of production labor costs. (Production labor is also called field labor or direct labor.) For this, you need to determine your *production labor hours* and your *production labor costs per hour* for a generic day of lawn maintenance in your business. You can then calculate your production labor costs for the day.

Production Labor Hours

Production labor time refers to the hours spent performing labor at the job site. Huston gives the example of a 10-hour work day. If 2 of those hours are spent loading/unloading and driving, you are left with 8 hours of production labor. With an employee, it would be 20 hours (2 people x 10 hours) minus 4 hours for load/unload and drive time, leaving 16 production hours.

Keep track of your drive time, load/unload time, and production labor time on your maintenance route over several weeks, and possibly at different times of the year. This will help you establish production labor times that accurately reflect a generic day of lawn maintenance in your business.

After determining your production labor hours for a generic day of lawn maintenance in your business, the next step is to calculate your production labor costs per hour. This involves calculating the crew average wage, overtime factor, and risk factor, as described below.

Crew Average Wage

The crew average wage (CAW) is the total of all hourly wages paid, divided by the number of crew members. Huston gives the example of a crew comprised of a crew leader/driver and a laborer. The crew leader is paid $12 per hour, the laborer is paid $8 per hour. Their combined hourly wage is $20 per hour. In this example, $20 per hour divided by 2 results in a crew average wage of $10 per hour.

As an owner-operator, you will need to decide on a fair hourly labor wage for yourself at this point. (Later, you will give yourself a salary to account for non-labor tasks, such as business management.) You might experiment on paper with different hourly wages for yourself ($20, $30, or $40 per hour, for example) to see how they add up in the total maintenance package rate. Keep in mind that the hourly wage you choose must allow you to bid competitively. If you won't be a member of the crew performing maintenance, don't include your hourly wage in the crew average wage.

Overtime Factor

If you have employees who are paid overtime, you need to add an overtime factor (OTF) to the crew average wage to account for the extra cost of overtime pay.

To determine the overtime factor, divide the number of overtime hours paid by the number of straight-time hours paid (per week). Huston gives the example of a 50-hour work week (where overtime begins after 40 hours) that results in 5 overtime hours paid. The calculation is as follows: 5 overtime hours paid ÷ 50 straight-time hours paid = 0.10 = 10 percent overtime factor.

Multiply the crew average wage by the overtime factor, and add the result to the crew average wage. For example: CAW = $10 per hour x 10% = $1; $10 + $1 = $11 per hour.

Note: Don't confuse "overtime hours paid" with overtime hours. There are 10 overtime hours in a 50-hour work week. However, at the standard overtime rate of time-and-a-half, 10 overtime hours results in 5 overtime hours paid (i.e., 5 additional straight-time hours paid). In other words, in a 50 hour work week, an employee receives the pay equivalent of 55 hours at the straight-time hourly rate.

Risk Factor

A risk factor (RF) is a markup applied to the crew average wage to account for possible discrepancies between the amount of labor you think a job will require and the amount actually needed. It is common to apply a risk factor of 10 percent even if you are confident about the estimated labor time. If you are less confident, you can use a risk factor of 20 percent or more.

To determine the risk factor amount, multiply the crew average wage/overtime factor total by the risk factor. Next, add the risk factor amount to the CAW/OTF amount. To illustrate: multiply the CAW/OTF amount of $11 by a risk factor of 10 percent to get a risk factor of $1.10. Add $1.10 to the $11 CAW/OTF to get $12.10. Round this number down to $12. Huston calls the crew average wage that includes an overtime factor and a risk factor the "loaded crew average wage" (loaded CAW). The loaded crew average wage is the production labor cost per hour.

Once you know the loaded crew average wage, multiply it by the number of production labor hours in the work day to get a production labor subtotal for the generic day of lawn maintenance in your business. Following the previous example: $12 loaded CAW x 16 production labor hours = $192. This is the production labor total. We will return to this example when Phase I production costs are summarized later.

Equipment Costs Per Day

You spend money to purchase, operate, repair, and replace your equipment. Businesses that fail to pass equipment costs on to their clients wind up paying for those costs out of their profit. When calculating a maintenance package rate, your goal is to determine your direct equipment costs for a generic day of maintenance. Again, direct equipment costs are equipment costs that can be "directly attributed" to the service itself.

In landscape management, direct equipment costs are associated with tools such as lawn mowers, edgers, grass-trimmers, leaf-blowers, and so on. This category is only used to cover costs associated with motorized tools. Hand tools and other non-motorized tools are accounted for under general and administrative overhead in Phase III.

The first step is to determine the cost per hour (CPH) for each power tool used for maintenance. Once you know the cost per hour for each tool, you can cost out equipment use for a generic day. If your equipment use changes, so should your equipment costs for the maintenance package. Table 17 on the next page provides some hourly equipment costs for purposes of comparison.

Hourly Equipment Costs

The first goal is to determine the cost per hour (CPH) of each piece of equipment that will be used on the job. To do this, you will need the following information:

The purchase price of the piece of equipment. This is the price you paid, including sales tax and interest, if any. Even if you are costing out used equipment, you should still use the price of a new model.

The "life expectancy" of the tool in hours. An equipment dealer may have this information. If not, you might estimate the useful life of each small engine tool based on two to three hours a day of use for two seasons. (2 hrs./day x 5 days/wk. x 40 weeks x 2 seasons = 800 hours, roughly.) Huston gives a life expectancy for cars and light trucks (under one ton) of 8,320 hours for their useful life (based on four years). For other equipment, such as larger mowers, you might use his approach of approximating 100 hours of useful life for every horsepower the piece of equipment has. Equipment with 50 to 100 horsepower is capped at 5,000 hours. Equipment with over 100 horsepower is capped at 7,500 hours.

The lifetime maintenance costs. If you have been in business long enough, you can use your actual costs to estimate the lifetime maintenance costs of a tool. If not, an equipment dealer may have information you can use. For small engine tools with a useful life of about two years, it is reasonable to estimate maintenance costs at 50 percent of the purchase price for cost-per-hour calculations. Vehicle maintenance costs should be broken down in detail, including insurance, licenses, brakes, clutches, oil changes, tune ups, and so on. Estimate these costs for four years.

The amount of gas the tool uses. Huston provides several methods of determining fuel usage for equipment. Fuel usage for small equipment can be based on the length of time the tool can run on one gallon of gas. See "Fuel cost per hour", next page, for more information. Fuel usage calculations for large equipment can be based on the fuel tank size and the number of fill-ups per month; this is not explained here.

The salvage value, if any. The salvage value is the amount of money you can get for a tool if you sell it at the end of its life expectancy. Most small engine tools, such as hedge clippers or edgers, will have no salvage value.

Once you have gathered the necessary information, determine the hourly cost of a piece of equipment as follows: calculate the acquisition cost per hour, maintenance cost per hour, and fuel cost per hour, and add them together. This is illustrated below.

Acquisition cost per hour: Subtract any salvage value from the tool's purchase price, then divide that price by the lifetime hours. For example, the acquisition cost of a $1200 mower is calculated as follows: $1200 ÷ 800 (lifetime hours) = $1.50 per hour.

Maintenance cost per hour: Divide the tool's lifetime maintenance costs by the lifetime hours. For example, $600 ÷ 800 hours = $0.75 per hour.

Fuel cost per hour: For small equipment, divide the average price of a gallon of gas by the length of time the tool can run on one gallon. For example, $3.50

÷ 3.5 hours = $1.00 per hour. Note that two-cycle gas/oil mix is considered an overhead expense and is accounted for under "Small Tools and Supplies" in Phase III (page 192).

Total CPH: Add all three subtotals together to get the tool's total cost per hour. Following our previous example: 1.50 + 0.75 + 1.00 = $3.25 per hour. Round to the nearest dollar.

Once you know a tool's CPH, you can incorporate that cost into your bids based on the amount of time that tool will be used for a specific job, or into the maintenance package rates as we're doing here.

Common Hourly Equipment Costs

Table 17 provides some hourly equipment costs for purposes of comparison. If you don't intend to calculate your own hourly equipment costs, you might use the hourly costs in table 17; just note that your actual costs could vary because of different equipment purchase prices and fluctuating fuel prices.

Daily Equipment Costs

To calculate the daily equipment cost for each piece of equipment, determine the average number of hours the tool will be used on the job in a typical day, then multiply this time by the tool's cost per hour. If you run the business by yourself, you might base your calculations on a hedge clipper, grass trimmer, edger, blower, and 21" mower. Note that truck costs are accounted for under Phase: II, not here.

To understand how to calculate the daily equipment cost for a lawn mower, consider the example of an owner-operator who averages 25 minutes of mowing per account and eight accounts per day. Daily lawn mower use is calculated as follows: 25 x 8 = 200 minutes or 3.5 hours per day. The cost per day is calculated as follows: 3.5 hours x $3 per hour (based on table 17) = $10.50. This number can be rounded up to $11 per day.

Continuing the example, the owner-operator averages 10 minutes of use at each account for each of the following tools: a hedge clipper, grass trimmer, edger, and leaf blower. Daily use of these tools is

Table 17. Equipment Costs Per Hour

Mini-pickup	$ 4
1/2-ton pickup	$ 6
3/4-ton pickup	$ 7
1-ton pickup	$ 8
Trailer, 1 axle	$ 1
Trailer, 2 axle	$ 2 ($12/day)
21" Rotary Mower	$ 3
36" Rotary Mower	$ 4
48" Rotary Mower	$ 5
51" Rotary Mower	$ 6
60" Rotary Mower	$ 7
72" Rotary Mower	$ 8
Chainsaw	$ 5
Aerator	$ 8
Rototiller, small	$ 6
Hedge trimmer	$ 3
Grass trimmer	$ 3
Edger	$ 3

Adapted from *How to Price Landscape & Irrigation Projects*, J. R. Huston Enterprises 2003.

calculated as follows: 10 minutes x 4 tools x 8 accounts = 320 minutes or 5.3 hours total for all small-engine tools. The cost per day for all of these tools is calculated as follows: 5.3 hours x $3 per hour = $15.90 per day. This number can be rounded to $16. Total daily equipment costs in this example are calculated as follows: Mower $11 per day + Small engine tools $16 per day = $27 per day.

In another example, a two-person crew averages five hours per day on a 36" mower (5 hours x $4 per hour = $20). The crew averages three hours per day on a 21" mower (3 hours x $3 per hour = $9). The crew averages four combined hours for hedge clipper, grass trimmer, edger, and blower use (4 hours x $3 per hour = $12). The total daily equipment cost in this example is $41 per day.

For purposes of comparison, Huston gives an approximate daily (8-hour) equipment cost of $48 for a two-person maintenance crew and $64 for a three-person maintenance crew.

Phase I Summary

Before moving on to Phase II, here is a summary of the two-person-crew example we've been following:

Production labor hours: 16
Crew average wage: $10
Overtime factor: 10% x $10 = $1
Risk factor: 10% x $11 = $1.10
Loaded CAW: $12
Production labor total: 16 x $12 = $192

36" mower: $4 x 5 hours = $20
21" mower: $3 x 3 hours = $9
Clipper, edger, etc.: $3 x 4 hours = $12
Production equipment total: $41

Rework your maintenance package rates if production costs change. Again, Phase I labor and equipment costs are directly attributed to production—that is, to landscape maintenance. There are other labor and equipment costs, as well as costs associated with running the business; these get worked out in Phases II and III.

Phase II: General Conditions

General conditions costs are those costs tied to the end product or service, but not directly required to produce it. A good example of a general conditions cost is drive time. Driving between job sites is labor that is tied to landscape maintenance, but it is not a part of the actual service. General conditions costs tend to be overlooked by many landscape management business owners.

Like production costs, general conditions costs fall into one of four categories: materials, labor, equipment, and subcontractor costs. Again, the emphasis here is on labor and equipment. Huston lists 29 common general condition costs, some of which are most applicable to landscape construction.

Below are some general conditions costs common in landscape management.

Load/Unload Time

Load/unload time is the time spent loading and unloading equipment from the truck at the start and end of the workday and throughout the day.

When calculating a maintenance package rate, your goal is to calculate the load/unload-time labor cost for a generic day of maintenance. This is done by estimating your (or your crew's) load/unload time for a generic day of maintenance and multiplying this time by the loaded crew average wage. Since this is a labor estimate, the average daily load/unload time must be multiplied by the number of people on the crew.

For example, an owner-operator without employees averages 15 minutes load time at the start of each day, 10 minutes load/unload time at each of eight accounts, and 15 minutes unload time at the end of each day. The average daily load/unload time for this example is calculated as follows: 15 + (10 x 8) + 15 = 110 minutes. This time is multiplied by the loaded crew average wage (described in Phase I) to calculate the load/unload labor cost.

Here is another example: A two-person crew averages 10 minutes to load the truck at the start of each day, 5 minutes to load/unload at each of eight accounts, and 10 minutes at the end of each day. The average load/unload time for this example is calculated as follows: (2 x 10) + (2 x 5 x 8) + (2 x 10) = 120 minutes, or two hours a day. This time is multiplied by the loaded crew average wage to calculate the load/unload labor cost. To illustrate: 2 hours x $12 loaded CAW (from previous example) = $24 load/unload labor cost for this crew's generic maintenance day.

Note that Huston gives a separate category called "Clean Up Time" to account for putting tools away and cleaning the worksite at the end of the day. Here, that time has been accounted for in the load/unload category.

Drive Time

Drive time is the time spent driving to and from the job site and between job sites. To determine your maintenance package rate, you need to estimate your drive time labor cost for a generic maintenance day. This is done by estimating your (or your crew's) drive time for a generic day of maintenance and multiplying this time by the loaded crew average wage. Since this is a labor estimate, the average daily drive time must be multiplied by the number of people on the crew.

For example, a two-person crew's average drive time is 10 minutes to the first site, 10 minutes between eight additional sites, and 10 minutes home. The drive time calculation is as follows: 10 + (10 x 8) + 10 = 100 minutes. The drive time needs to be doubled because it is a two-person crew: 2 x 100 minutes = 200 minutes or approximately 3.5 hours. The cost calculation is as follows: 3.5 hours x $12 loaded CAW = $42 drive time labor.

Break Time

If you have employees and provide them with paid breaks, account for this time under general conditions. For example, if you provide two employees with a paid 15-minute break each work day, you must account for the costs associated with this 30 minutes of "labor". To calculate the break time labor, multiply the crew's combined break time by the loaded crew average wage to get the break time labor total. For example: 30 minutes = 0.5 hours; 0.5 hours x $12 loaded CAW = $6 break time labor.

Haul Debris (Labor)

If you haul debris to a municipal composting facility or transfer station on a daily basis, you can factor these costs into your maintenance package rates. Calculate the round trip time to the transfer station, multiply this time by the number of employees, then multiply the total time by the loaded crew average wage. For example: 1 hour round trip x 2 people = 2 hours, 2 hours x $12 loaded CAW = $24 haul debris labor.

Haul Debris (Equipment)

The haul debris (equipment) category is used to account for equipment (primarily vehicle) costs arising from a daily trip to a transfer station. For example, if you spend one hour each work day driving round trip to the transfer station, you would account for one hour's worth of truck use. If truck costs are $7 per hour (see table 17, page 186), then the haul debris (equipment) cost for a generic day is $7. If you have a trailer hitched up when you make the trip, add the hourly cost of trailer use (e.g., $7 for truck + $1 for single-axel trailer = $8 haul debris equipment cost).

Truck

Truck use is determined by the length of the workday, regardless of actual running time. For the maintenance package, multiply the cost per hour for your truck by the number of hours in a typical day of maintenance (see table 17). For example: $7 per hour x 8 hours = $56 in truck costs for a generic day.

Trailer

If you use a trailer, calculate trailer time in the same manner as truck time. For example: $1 (from table 17) x 8 hours = $8.

Materials

Transfer station fees and soil tests are a few examples of materials that are accounted for under general conditions. Soil test costs are not applicable to the maintenance package. However, if you incur a set, daily transfer station fee, include that cost. Or estimate an average daily transfer station fee.

Phase II Summary

Once you have calculated general conditions labor and equipment costs, add them up to get a total for Phase II. Following our two-person example:

Load/Unload: 2 hrs. x $12 (loaded CAW) = $24
Drive Time: 3.5 hours x $12 = $42
Break Time: 0.5 hours x $12 = $6
Haul Debris (Labor): 2 hours x $12 = $24
General Conditions Labor Total: $96

Haul Debris (Equipment): 1 hour x (Truck $7 +
      Trailer $1) = $8
Truck: 8 hours x $7 = $56
Trailer: 8 hours x $1 = $8
General Conditions Equipment Total: $72

Phase III: Markups and Margins

In Phase III, markups and margins are added to the cost information gathered in Phases I and II. All the costs calculated up to this point have been direct costs, meaning costs that arise from doing a specific job. The only other direct costs that need to be calculated are sales tax and labor burden, which are calculated here in Phase III. Once sales tax and labor burden are added, the estimating process is complete and the bidding process begins.

The bidding process starts with the addition of general and administrative overhead. G&A overhead is an indirect cost, meaning that it is a general business cost, not associated with a specific job. Finally, a profit margin and contingency factor are added to get the final price for a generic day of lawn maintenance. It is then possible to calculate an accurate hourly rate.

Sales Tax

In Phase III, sales tax is added to the taxable items in the bid. In most states, materials are the only items subject to sales tax. If you were working out a bid for a job that involved materials, this is where you would account for the sales tax. In calculating a maintenance package rate, we are assuming there are no materials, and, therefore, no sales tax. (For general information on sales tax, see page 219.)

Labor Burden

If you have employees, you have additional costs that are tied to your payroll, such as social security and unemployment taxes (FICA, FUTA, SUTA), workers' compensation insurance, workers' medical insurance (if applicable), general liability insurance, and more. These costs are called labor burden. Huston devotes a chapter to explaining how to calculate labor burden; however, for the maintenance package, he suggests that labor burden be calculated at 30 percent of the total labor cost for a job (production labor and general conditions labor combined). In our two-person example, we determined that production labor was $192 and that general conditions labor was $96. The calculation is as follows: $192 + $96 = $288 total labor cost; $288 x 30% = $86.40 labor burden, rounded to $87.

Total Direct Costs (TDC)

Now we can add up the labor, equipment, and labor burden totals, as well as any sales tax, to get the total direct costs (TDC) for the generic day of lawn maintenance: Labor (Phases I and II) + equipment (Phases I and II) + labor burden (Phase III) + sales tax, if any = TDC. If you had a daily dump fee, you would add that as well. Following our example:

Labor subtotal: $192 from Phase I + $96 from
      Phase II = $288
Equipment subtotal: $41 from Phase I + $72 from
      Phase II = $113
Sales Tax: none
Labor burden: $87 (from Phase III)
Total direct costs: $488

General & Administrative Overhead

Different estimating systems may include different costs under the category of overhead. For instance, some estimating systems may account for some direct costs, such as general conditions, under the category of overhead. Huston uses the term *overhead* to refer only to general and administrative overhead (G&A overhead). General and administrative overhead costs are indirect costs: they are not associated with a specific job. These are the behind-the-scenes costs of running a business. They include things like computers, advertising, insurance, rent, office supplies, utilities, and small tools.

There are different methods of calculating overhead. Most start by totalling the overhead costs for one year. Once overhead is totalled, a portion of those costs is allocated to each job, so that overhead costs are slowly recovered throughout the year. Just as methods for calculating overhead differ, so do the methods of allocating overhead costs to a job. Huston devotes a chapter in his book to showing that, while there is no right way to allocate overhead to a job, there are "mathematically inaccurate" ways.

For this reason, Huston advocates using the overhead per hour (OPH) method. In the overhead per hour method, the total overhead for the year is divided by the projected yearly billable field-labor hours to arrive at an overhead per hour amount. Once the overhead per hour is known, calculating the amount of overhead to apply to a job is simply a matter of multiplying the OPH by the billable field-labor hours in the job (in our case, the generic maintenance day). We will define these terms and explain the OPH method later.

The first step is to determine your total overhead for the next 12 months, regardless of what month you are in now. Overhead estimates are not necessarily linked to the fiscal year. If you have records of overhead costs from the past, you can use that information as a starting point to work out your current overhead. If you are a new business owner, you can make the same educated guesses about overhead costs as established business owners, only without records of past costs.

Huston presents 28 categories of overhead costs. His explanations are detailed, and it is beyond our scope or needs to cover all that he does. Here we provide simplified explanations, suitable to a small residential landscape management business. Consult Huston's text for comprehensive information.

Overhead estimates are based on fair market value, not necessarily actual costs. Fair market value refers to what you could expect to pay for something if you had to buy it today. This means that some overhead estimates may be higher or lower than actual overhead costs. Items that should be judged at fair market value will be pointed out in the category explanations below.

While your total overhead projection may not be 100 percent accurate, it should be within 10 percent accuracy. Note that it is more important to account for all overhead costs than to categorize everything precisely. The categories are useful in helping you

systematically account for all costs. Wherever you categorize an expense, put it in the same category each year.

G&A Overhead Categories

Use the following categories to determine overhead costs for the next 12 months. For complete category descriptions, consult *How to Price Landscape & Irrigation Projects* by James R. Huston.

1. Advertising: Classified ads, phone book ads, brochures, direct mail pieces, truck signs, and website development and maintenance are examples of costs that fit in this category.

2. Bad Debts: If clients owe you money and you can't collect, you can include the amount as an overhead cost. Limit the bad debt amount to one-half of 1 percent (0.5%) of your gross annual sales.

3. Computers, Software, External Drives, etc.: If you use a computer for bookkeeping, letter writing, construction of business forms, online research, and so on, include the cost of a computer and business-related software here. Generally, the useful life of computers and software is three years. Divide the total cost of each item by three to determine the yearly overhead amount.

If you also use your computer for non-business activities, base the overhead cost on the percentage of time you use the computer for business. For example, if you have a $2000 computer that is used for business only 30 percent of the time, your computer overhead is $2000 x 30% = $600. Spread this out (depreciate) over three years. $600 ÷ 3 years = $200 per year. For accounting or estimating software, include the cost of upgrades, and spread the cost over three years.

4. Donations: If your business donates materials or labor as a charitable gesture, include those costs here. Cap this amount at between $500 and $1000.

5. Downtime Labor: Downtime labor refers to the time field employees are paid when they are not working in the field. Potential causes of downtime labor include bad weather, meetings, busywork, and unforeseeable circumstances (e.g., a vehicle break down). Note that downtime labor does not include time spent on equipment repair or driving to jobs. Average downtime labor is one to one-and-one-half hours per week for each full-time field employee.

For example, if your work year is 50 weeks long and you have two full-time employees, you pay for 100 downtime hours (50 weeks x 1 hour per week x 2 employees). If you perform the work, include yourself. To calculate the yearly downtime-labor overhead cost, multiply the total yearly downtime-labor hours by the loaded crew average wage. For example, 100 hours x $12 per hour = $1200. (The loaded crew average wage is explained on page 184.)

6. Downtime Labor Burden: Earlier we calculated labor burden at 30 percent of labor costs. Do the same for the downtime labor total. For example, $1200 x 30% = $360.

7. Dues and Subscriptions: Dues and subscriptions are fees and membership charges for state and national associations/organizations, professional magazines, the chamber of commerce, and so on. Account for the yearly cost of these items here.

8. Insurance: Use this category to account for insurance for office contents, as well as medical and dental insurance for owners, receptionists, accountants, field supervisors, and any other person on the payroll whose work cannot be linked to a specific bid. Unless you are incorporated, no other insurance coverage is included here.

9. Interest and Bank Charges: Examples of interest and bank charges include interest on business credit cards, credit card processing fees, bank fees (including penalties/service charges), and interest accrued on debts to suppliers. Interest on equipment loans and building mortgages are not included. Huston provides an alternate way of accounting for interest overhead that can be used if your business does not use credit.

10. Licenses and Surety Bonds: In this category, include the cost of a city business license, if required. This category does not include licenses for specific jobs, (e.g., sprinkler valve installation).

State contractors can include their license and surety bond fees here.

11. Office Equipment: Use this category to account for the purchase price and repair costs of office equipment—not including computers, phones, pagers, or field equipment. Examples include file cabinets, office furniture, copy machines, calculators, plants, artwork, and so on. Even if you don't have a designated office, consider including the fair market value of a desk and office chair, and possibly a file cabinet.

Spread this cost out over the number of years the equipment is expected to last. For example, if a desk and chair cost $400, spread the cost out over 10 years. This comes to $40 per year. Note that while you must meet certain IRS requirements to claim home office deductions for tax purposes, you are not subject to those restrictions when calculating overhead costs.

12. Office Supplies: Paper, pens, ink cartridges, printing costs for letterhead and business cards, envelopes, and postage are examples of overhead items that can be included here.

13. Professional Fees: Fees paid to a certified public accountant, bookkeeper, or lawyer are examples of overhead costs that can be included here.

14. Cell Phones, Pagers, Two-Way Radios: Costs associated with cell phones, pagers, and two-way radios used for business are considered overhead. Spread the cost of a cell phone over two years; spread the cost of two-way radios over 10 years. Include all monthly charges and any maintenance costs.

15. Rent (Office and Yard): If you rent an office space and/or storage facility, determine the rental costs for the next 12 months. If you operate your business from home, you can still include the fair market value of your home office and storage space. For example, if you store tools in the corner of your garage, you can account for what it would cost you to rent a storage space of equal size. If you handle business phone calls and bookkeeping at a desk in the corner of a bedroom in your home, you can account for the fair market value of an office space of equal size. Be reasonable in your estimations. In other words, don't include the cost of a $500 per month office if you use 30 square feet in the corner of a bedroom. Again, you don't need to meet the IRS's requirements for a home office to account for these overhead costs.

16. Salaries for Office Personnel: If you have an office, this category is used to account for the yearly salaries of any employees that work in the office. If an employee, such as a field supervisor, spends some of the time in the office and some of the time in the field, account only for salary related to time spent in the office; time spent in the field should be bid into jobs whenever possible.

17. Salaries for Owners and Partners: This category includes any salary that you or you and a partner draw from the business. If you don't have a defined salary, you should still include the fair market value of a salary suitable to the amount of work you do running the business.

This salary is for the work you do that cannot be tied to a specific job; for example, office work, bookkeeping, taking client calls, designing fliers, estimating, billing, picking up office supplies, interviewing employees, paying bills, and so on. Don't include work that can be accounted for under downtime labor. Note that time spent on equipment repair is covered under production costs in Phase I, not here.

To determine your yearly salary, estimate the time you will spend in the upcoming year on general business tasks, and multiply that time by a reasonable hourly rate. This hourly rate does not need to be the same as your hourly labor rate. Note that determining the fair market value of your work as the owner does not guarantee that enough funds will be available to pay that salary! You need to bill enough jobs to cover this and all your yearly overhead costs. Huston writes that the combined salary for the owner and all partners should not exceed 12 percent of gross annual sales.

18. Salary Labor Burden: Calculate the labor burden for owner and office employee salaries by

multiplying the total salaries by 30 percent. This is the predetermined percentage we're using for the maintenance package .

19. Small Tools and Supplies: The cost of hand tools is considered an overhead expense. This category can also be used to account for the cost of miscellaneous supplies, such as PVC cement, garden tape, canvas tarps, tie downs, gas cans, two-cycle gas/oil mix, and trimmer line. Safety equipment such as gloves and face masks are included under category 24, below.

20: Taxes (Asset or Mill Tax): An asset tax is a tax on office equipment and furniture that is levied by some cities or counties. Some counties levy a mill tax based on sales. Don't include federal and state taxes; these are not overhead costs.

21. Telephones: This category refers to landlines as opposed to cellular phones. Include the purchase price of phones, answering machines, and fax machines. Include monthly and long-distance charges, the cost of repairs, and internet connection fees.

22. Training and Education: Use this category to account for educational materials or courses for yourself or employees. Include the cost of books, training videos, continuing-education classes, one-day seminars, and so on.

23. Travel and Entertainment: If you have business-related travel or entertainment expenses, account for these overhead costs here. Include transportation costs to and from workshops and classes, and any gifts purchased for clients or employees such a holiday cards.

24. Uniforms and Safety Equipment: Include the cost of any uniform clothing (tee shirts, hats, etc.) for yourself and employees, as well as any associated cleaning costs. Include the cost of seasonal clothing such as rain gear here. Safety equipment such as gloves, dust masks, face mask and cartridges, hearing protectors, goggles, and protective glasses are also included in this category.

25. Utilities: Assuming you don't rent a separate facility for your business, you will need to base your utilities costs on your natural gas and electrical usage in your storage area and/or home office. For example, if your home electric bill averages $150 per month, determine how much of that can be attributed to time spent working at your desk, on the computer, or in the garage. If you estimate 10 percent, that works out to $15 a month or $180 a year for business electricity use. The amount should be reasonable. Don't include the entirety of your home electric bill as an overhead cost. Overinflated overhead estimates can make your bids too high.

26. Vehicles, G&A Overhead: Use this category to account for the cost of business vehicle use by office employees. Crew pickup trucks are not included here. If employees engage in business activity using their own vehicles, and you reimburse them based on mileage, include that cost here.

27. Yard Expense: This category is for costs—primarily material costs—associated with maintaining or improving the yard where crews meet and equipment is stored. For example, the costs associated with installing a fence or irrigation system would be accounted for here. Account for any associated labor performed by employees under downtime labor.

This category is also used for costs associated with leasehold improvements to an office space; for example, painting or the installation of new carpet. If you work from home and operate on a small scale, you can still include the cost of yard expenses and leasehold improvements for your business. For example, if you install a tool shed in the backyard, you could include that cost here. Yard expense costs should be spread out over the number of years the improvement is expected to last. For example, if you install a cyclone fence in the yard for large power equipment, you would spread that cost out over 10 to 15 years.

28. Miscellaneous: Huston recommends using this category as little as possible and that even large businesses keep costs listed here under $500 or $1000.

Overhead Per Hour (OPH)

Add up the amounts in all the G&A overhead categories to arrive at the overhead amount you need to recover over the next 12 months. Once you know your projected overhead costs for the upcoming year, the next step is to calculate the overhead per hour (OPH) amount. Overhead can then be applied to a job (in this case, the maintenance package) based on the number of billable field-labor hours in the job.

To calculate your OPH amount, you need to estimate your projected billable field-labor hours (FLH) for the upcoming year. According to Huston, "Billable field-labor hours are those hours included in a bid and for which a client is billed." Billable field-labor hours do not include downtime hours, equipment repair hours, or other time that the client is not billed for. General conditions labor time is included in the billable field-labor hours as long as the general conditions costs get passed on to the client (e.g., if you factor drive time into your bids, include drive time in the projected billable field-labor hours for the year).

To calculate your yearly billable field-labor hours, multiply the hours per week by the number of weeks in a work year. For example, if you and an employee are on a maintenance route 10 hours a day, 5 days a week, 10 months a year, the calculation for yearly billable field-labor hours is as follows: 20 hours/day x 5 days/week x 43 weeks = 4300 yearly billable field-labor hours. (The calculation is based on the average of 4.33 weeks per month.)

Next, divide the yearly overhead amount by the projected yearly billable field-labor hours to get the overhead-per-hour (OPH) amount. For example, if you estimated your total overhead cost for the next 12 months to be $20,000, you would divide 20,000 by 4300 to get an overhead-per-hour amount of $4.65. Consider another example: If you estimated your yearly overhead cost to be $15,000, and you are on your maintenance route by yourself part time a total of 1200 hours per year, your overhead per hour is calculated as follows: 15,000 ÷ 1200 = $12.50 OPH.

Break Even Point (BEP)

It took some time to come up with the overhead per hour amount. Once the OPH amount is determined, you can add overhead costs to any bid based on the number of billable field-labor hours in the bid.

Our goal is to determine how much overhead to include in the generic lawn maintenance day. To calculate this, multiply the overhead-per-hour amount by the billable field-labor hours in the generic day. Using the example of a two-person crew averaging 10 hours a day, the calculation is as follows: $4.65 overhead per hour x 20 field-labor hours = $93. In this example, the overhead for the generic day of maintenance is $93.

Next, add this daily overhead amount to the total direct costs to get the break even point (BEP). Again, total direct costs include the totals for labor, equipment, labor burden, and sales tax. The break even point is the total for all costs in a job; in our case, the generic day of maintenance. Here is a summary of our two-person-crew example:

Break Even Point Example

Phase I: Production Costs
Labor: $192
Equipment: $41

Phase II: General Conditions
Labor: $96
Equipment: $72

Phase III: Markups and Margins
Sales Tax: none
Labor Burden: $87
Subtotal: $488 (Total direct cost, or TDC)

G&A Overhead: $93
Subtotal: $581 (Break even point, or BEP)

Net Profit Margin (NPM)

The next step in Phase III is to add a net profit margin (NPM) to the break even point. The net-profit-margin amount is all profit (before interest and taxes); it includes no costs. (Gross profit margin, on the other hand, includes the net profit amount, plus overhead and the contingency fac-

tor, if any. Gross profit margin is not explained here.)

The net profit margin for residential and commercial maintenance commonly ranges from 10 to 15 percent. The NPM for residential installation and irrigation service commonly ranges from 15 to 25 percent. Huston makes it clear that the net profit added to a job should vary according to circumstance. He suggests determining an appropriate net profit margin for each of five categories pertaining to a job, then totalling them and dividing by five to get the average.

The five categories are need, size, risk, market, and negotiating ability. To illustrate, if you strongly need the job, you might use a NPM toward the lower end of the range in the need category, say, 10 percent (need). Huston recommends using a higher NPM for small jobs than larger ones (size). Jobs with low risk, such as most maintenance jobs, might be assigned a slightly lower NPM in the risk category (risk). If the market is highly competitive, a lower net profit margin in the market category might be appropriate (market). Negotiating ability is more applicable to landscape contractors. Add up the percentages assigned to the five categories, and divide by five. For example:

Need: 10%
Size: 12%
Risk: 14%
Market: 12%
Negotiating Ability: 15%
Total = 63% ÷ 5 = 12.6% NPM

Huston uses a 10 percent net profit margin in his maintenance package example. Depending on the market, you might experiment with net profit margins higher than 10 to 15 percent.

Correctly Applying the Net Profit Margin

Multiplying the break even point by the net-profit-margin percent will not produce an accurate net-profit-margin amount. You must use the following formula: To apply the net profit margin to a job, divide the break even point amount by 1.0 minus the net profit margin. The net-profit-margin percent must be changed to a decimal for this calculation (e.g., 10% = 0.1). Again, the formula to correctly apply the net profit margin is as follows:

$$\frac{\text{Break even point}}{1.0 - \text{net profit margin (as decimal)}}$$

To illustrate: The break even point for the two-person-crew example is $581. To correctly apply a net profit margin of 10 percent to this amount, divide $581 by 0.9 (1.0 - 0.1 = 0.9) to get $646. Here is another example: To apply a net profit margin of 12.6 percent to the break even point of $581, divide $581 by 0.874 (1.0 - 0.126 = 0.874) to get $665. Note that Huston also recommends a different method of adding profit to a bid based on the number of field-labor hours in the bid. This profit-per-hour approach (PPH) is not discussed here.

Contingency Factor

A contingency factor is a subjective amount of net profit that is sometimes added to a bid to offset risk. Contractors sometimes use a contingency factor in situations where there are unknown variables. A contingency factor is also sometimes applied if a contractor will have to put up with personality differences or deal with difficult work conditions. It is a way of using extra profit as an incentive to tolerate less than ideal conditions. You don't need to apply a contingency factor to your bids, though it is an option. We are not using a contingency factor for the maintenance package.

Final Price

Add the G&A overhead and net profit to the total direct cost to get final price for the job. In this case, we have the total price for a generic day of lawn maintenance. Following our two-person-crew example:

Maintenance Package Day Rate

Phase I: Production Costs
Labor: $192
Equipment: $41

Phase II: General Conditions
Labor: $96
Equipment: $72

Phase III: Markups and Margins
Sales Tax: none
Labor Burden: $87
Subtotal: $488 (Total direct cost, or TDC)

G&A Overhead: $93
Subtotal: $581 (Break even point, or BEP)

Net Profit Margin at 10%: $581 ÷ (1.0 - 0.1) = 581 ÷ 0.9 = $646
Contingency Factor: none

Total Price: $646

The Curb-Time Rate

This is what we have been working toward. Knowing the price for a generic lawn maintenance day allows us to calculate the *curb-time rate*. The curb-time rate is the hourly rate used to bid residential maintenance. *Curb-time* refers to time spent at the job site—it starts as soon as you stop your truck at the curb in front of a residence.

Calculate the curb-time rate by dividing the total price for the generic day of maintenance by the number of production hours in that day. In Phase I, we calculated 16 production hours for our two-person-crew example. Using the daily price of $646, the curb-time rate for this example is calculated as follows: $646 ÷ 16 = $40.38 per hour. Round this to $40. Huston calls this the *curb-time man-hour rate*. The *crew curb-time rate* is the curb-time rate multiplied by the number of crew members. In our two-person-crew example, the crew curb-time rate is calculated as follows: $40 x 2 = $80 per hour.

Calculating the Monthly Rate for Maintenance Accounts

Calculating a monthly labor rate for a maintenance account can be done in one of two ways using the curb-time rate.

Method 1. Determine the per-visit price by multiplying the estimated time per visit by the crew curb-time rate. Next, multiply the per-visit price by the number of visits in a month to arrive at the monthly labor rate. (There are an average of 4.33 weeks per month.) See the formula on the next page:

Time per visit (converted to a decimal) x curb-time rate = price per visit

Price per visit x 4.33 weeks = monthly labor rate

For example: You estimate that a two-person crew perform 45 minutes of maintenance per visit at a particular property. To calculate the per-visit rate, convert 45 minutes to a decimal (0.75), and multiply this by the crew curb-time rate of $80 (from previous example): 0.75 x $80 = $60 per visit. Multiply the per-visit rate of $60 by 4.33 weeks to arrive at a monthly rate of $260.

Method 2. Another way to calculate a monthly rate for a maintenance account is to multiply the per-visit price by the number of weeks in the contract year, then divide the result by the number of months in the contract. Again:

Time per visit (converted to a decimal) x curb-time rate = price per visit

Price per visit x weeks in contract year = price per contract year

Price per contract year ÷ months in contract year = monthly labor rate

For example: Working by yourself, you estimate it will take you 45 minutes per visit to perform maintenance at a particular property. To calculate the per-visit rate, convert 45 minutes to a decimal (0.75), and multiply this by a curb-time rate of $40 (from previous example): 0.75 x $40 = $30 per visit.

Next, assume it is a year-round contract with 52 weeks: 52 weeks x $30 = $1560 per contract year. There are 12 months in the contract, so $1560 ÷ 12 = $130 per month. This is the monthly labor rate. Note that when you use the maintenance package rate, the cost of materials can be added on a time-and-materials basis. Keep in mind that the examples are provided only to demonstrate how to calculate rates.

Variables That Affect Curb Rates

Changes in crew size, equipment, or drive time make it necessary to recalculate the curb time rate. Adjusting for crew size or equipment changes is straightforward; adjusting for drive-time changes requires a brief explanation.

If drive time decreases, curb time increases, assuming you are still working the same total hours for the day. Put differently, if you (or a crew) spend less time driving, you spend more time on the job—enabling you to achieve your daily billable goal with a lower curb time rate. The daily billable goal is explained in the next topic.

For example, if drive time decreased by one hour in our two-person-crew example, each crew member would spend one additional hour on production labor. So instead of dividing the day rate of $646 by 16 production hours, you would divide it by 18 production hours: $646 ÷ 18 = $35.88; rounded to $36 per hour—or a $72 crew curb time rate (as opposed to $78 when there were 16 production hours).

If drive time increases, curb time decreases, assuming you are still working the same total hours for the day. In this situation, the curb time rate will need to increase because you have less curb time to achieve the daily billable goal. For example, if drive time increases by one hour in our two-person-crew example, each crew member spends one hour less on production labor. So instead of dividing the day rate of $646 by 16 production hours, you would divide it by 14 production hours: $646 ÷ 14 = $46.14; rounded to $46 per hour—or a $92 crew curb rate.

Staying Profitable

Track the time you or your crews spend on production labor, equipment use, load/unload time, and drive time to check the accuracy of your maintenance package rate. These simple measures will help to ensure that your maintenance package rate is covering costs and providing adequate profit without being over-inflated.

This information can be recorded onto customized forms or entered into a spreadsheet program with a laptop computer. Keep in mind that a maintenance package rate on paper does not ensure that you are remaining profitable; you must also complete enough jobs each day to cover your day rate.

The Day Rate

If you recall, the day rate is the total price for a generic maintenance day. To stay profitable, your daily billable amount must meet or surpass your day rate.

To calculate the daily billable amount, determine the per-visit rate for each account serviced on a given day, and add all the per-visit rates together. To determine an account's per-visit rate, divide the monthly rate by the number of visits per month (e.g., for weekly maintenance, divide by 4.33). For example, if you bill a client $180 once a month, the per-visit rate is calculated as follows: 180 ÷ 4.33 = $41.57. Again, to get the daily billable amount, total the per-visit rates for all accounts serviced on a given day.

This simple method of assessing profitability points to the importance of setting daily billable goals, or targets, for yourself or your crews. A daily billable goal is the total billable amount that you strive to generate on a given day. Reaching a daily billable goal ensures profitability.

The Minute Rate

The minute rate can also be used to quickly gauge profitability. The minute rate is the day rate divided by the curb-time minutes per day. (To calculate the curb-time minutes per day, multiply the number of curb-time hours by 60. For example: 8 hours x 60 minutes = 480 curb-time minutes per day.) For example: $646 (day rate) ÷ 480 daily curb-time minutes = $1.35 minute rate. You can quickly check the per-visit billing for an account by multiplying the job time by the minute rate.

For example, if a crew averages 30 minutes per visit at an account, the per-visit billing for that account can be calculated as follows: 30 minutes x 1.35 minute rate = $40.50. If the actual billing is lower than this amount, you can reevaluate the account, and adjust the pricing accordingly. Huston writes

that variances in curb rates are fine as long as you continue to reach your daily billable goal.

Materials

Huston recommends marking up materials a minimum of 25 percent and as much as 40 to 50 percent above the wholesale price. (Technically, the price that contractors pay is called the "rewholesale" price, because nursery and other retailers have already purchased wholesale from growers and manufacturers, and marked up before reselling to contractors.) The 40 to 50 percent markup to the wholesale price brings the price close to the retail price that clients would pay if they purchased the materials themselves. Obviously, if you pay retail prices for materials, these percentages are not suitable, and you might just charge the client what you paid. Huston also points out that it is normal to mark up subcontractor costs 10 to 25 percent. Note that including materials or subcontractor costs in the maintenance package calculations is not recommended; calculate these costs separately.

Final Thoughts On The Maintenance Package. The three phases involved in determining maintenance package rates make up a system that can be used to bid any job. In this sense, the maintenance package approach can simultaneously serve as an introduction to estimating/bidding in general. There is a great deal more to learn about job pricing and business management. However, once estimating and bidding are understood, these practices can be used as the foundation for successfully managing your business as it grows.

Sample Maintenance Contract

Legally binding contracts are formed when an agreement is reached between parties regarding services or goods to be provided and payment for those services. Contracts can be verbal or written. Legally, a written contract is not required for normal business contracts one year in length or less.

A written contract defines the terms of service in a landscape management agreement between your business and the client. Contracts protect the property owner and the landscape management business owner by detailing the services to be provided, optional services, licenses and liabilities, and "terms, conditions, and charges".

Some residential landscape managers use written contracts, some do not, and others use them selectively. The size of the property, the complexity of the management required, and the monthly billing rate can all influence whether or not to use a written contract. In general, residential accounts that are predominantly lawn maintenance can be handled with a verbal contract; however, a written contract can still help you avoid misunderstandings and may provide you with greater protection. Written contracts are standard in commercial maintenance.

Sample Contract

The University of Florida IFAS Extension has produced an article entitled *Considerations for Developing a Lawn and Landscape Maintenance Contract*, published online at http://edis.ifas.ufl. edu/pdffiles/lh/lh03100.pdf. Part of the article is reproduced here, with permission, to provide an example of a detailed contract that is appropriate for both commercial and residential maintenance. While the sample contract is specific to Florida, it has broader applicability. The first paragraph of the article is an introduction and the contract follows. Note that some of the landscaping guidelines presented in the sample contract may have changed since the article was produced in 2001.

Considerations for Developing a Lawn and Landscape Maintenance Contract[1]

Sydney Park Brown and Michael J. Holsinger[2]

The following sample contract includes landscape maintenance practices which are in accordance with University of Florida recommendations. These recommendations are based on research and objective-based information specific to Florida and reflect the philosophy of Environmental Landscape Management (ELM). The ELM concept integrates environmental concerns into landscape maintenance. Water and energy conservation, fertilizer and pesticide management, and the reduction and reuse of plant clippings are important components of ELM. The sample contract suggests additional topics which you should consider when creating a contract or reviewing one. This sample was developed as an educational resource for lawn and landscape professionals and users of their services. However, final decisions on what to incorporate in a lawn and landscape contract must be made by individual professionals and their clients. This publication is distributed with the understanding that the authors are not engaged in rendering legal advice or opinion, and that the information contained herein is not to be regarded or relied upon as a substitute for professional legal service. If you require legal advice or opinion seek the services of an attorney.

Sample Lawn and Landscape Maintenance Contract

Part I: Lawn Maintenance Considerations

A. Mowing, Edging, and Trimming: Contractor will mow turf areas as needed according to seasonal growth. No more than 1/3 of the leaf blades should be removed per mowing. Mowing shall be with a (reel/rotary/or mulching) mower. Mower blades will be sharp at all times to provide a quality cut. Mowing height will be according to grass type and variety. Contractor will leave clippings on the lawn as long as no readily visible clumps remain on the grass surface 36 hours after mowing. Otherwise, contractor will distribute large clumps of clippings by mechanical blowing or by collecting and removing them. In the case of fungal disease outbreaks, contractor will collect clippings until the disease is undetectable.

Contractor will edge tree rings and plant beds and all buildings, sidewalks, fences, driveways, parking lots, and other surfaced areas bordered by grass will be edged every other mowing during the growing season. Turf around sprinkler heads will be trimmed or treated with a non-selective herbicide so as to not interfere with or intercept water output. Isolated trees and shrubs growing

in lawn areas will require mulched areas around them (minimum 2-foot diameter) to avoid bark injury from mowers and filament line trimmers and to reduce root competition from grass. Establishment and maintenance of such mulched areas will be charged to the customer. Contractor will clean all clippings from sidewalks, curbs, and roadways immediately after mowing and/or edging. Contractor will not sweep, blow or otherwise dispose of clippings in sewer drains.

B. Fertilization: Contractor will fertilize turf areas as per the maintenance specifications attached (not included here). Complete fertilizers shall be granular in composition and contain 30% to 50% or more of the nitrogen in a slow- or controlled-release form. The ratio of nitrogen to potash will approximate 1:1 or 2:1 for complete fertilizer formulations (Examples: 15-5-15, 16-4-8, 15-0-15, 12-2-14, 14-3-14). While nitrogen fertilization is based on the desired growth rate and type of turfgrass being grown, the phosphorus fertilization rate should be based on the analysis of a lawn soil sample and the recommendations obtained from it. The fertilizer shall also contain magnesium and micro-nutrients (i.e., manganese, iron, zinc, copper, etc.). Iron shall be in the sulfate, sucrate, or chelated form. Fertilizer will be swept off of walks and drives onto lawns or beds. After fertilization, a minimum of 1/4 inch of water will be applied by the client.

C. Pest Control: The contractor will inspect lawn areas each visit for indications of pest problems and advise the client or representative of such problems. Upon confirmation of a specific problem requiring treatment, the contractor will apply pesticides as needed and only in affected spots, whenever possible using the least toxic, effective pesticide. All applications of pesticides and fertilizations will be performed when temperatures are below 90°F and wind drift is negligible. No pesticide will be applied to turf areas without the express approval of the client. This includes weed and feed formulations. The contractor will keep records on pests identified and treatment(s) rendered for control. All pest control service is in addition to the basic contract charges. The contractor will charge the client per job, based on materials cost plus labor. The cost will be agreed on by client and contractor before such service is rendered. Pesticide applications will be made in accordance with the rules and regulations governing use of pesticides in Florida. The contractor will post alerts and notify pesticide-sensitive persons (if applicable) of the pesticide application. The pest control applicator will be operating under License # _____. Expiration Date _____.

D. Thatch Control: (See Part III—Optional Services)

Part II: Landscape Plant Maintenance Considerations: Trees, Palms, Shrubs, Groundcovers

A. Fertilization: Ornamental shrubs, trees and groundcovers planted less than three (3) years shall be fertilized 4 to 6 weeks after planting and then two to three times per year for the following 3 years. Two of the annual applications are normally scheduled around February and October for south Florida, March and September for north Florida. A third application can be made during the summer. Rate will be 1 pound of nitrogen per 1,000 square feet per application. [Brown and Holsinger include palm fertilization guidelines here. For current palm fertilization guidelines, see "Fertilizing Palms" on page 82.] Established shrubs and trees in lawn areas exposed to lawn fertilizations will not be fertilized supplementally. Fertilizer applied to shrubs and trees planted in beds shall be broadcasted over the entire plant bed. Fertilizer may be punched shallowly into the soil on berms and slopes where runoff is likely. Nutrient deficiencies shall be treated with supplemental applications of the specific lacking nutrient according to University of Florida Cooperative Extension recommendations.

B. Pest Control: Contractor shall practice Integrated Pest Management (IPM) to control insects, diseases and weeds on and around perennials, groundcovers, shrubs, vines and trees. This will include frequent monitoring and spot treatment as necessary using the least toxic methods. All applications will be performed when temperatures are below 90°F and when wind drift is negligible. First choice will be insecticidal soaps, horticultural oils and biological controls such as Bacillus thuringiensis (Bt) formulations. Weeds in beds or mulched areas will usually be removed mechanically or by hand. Upon client approval, herbicides may be employed for heavy weed infestations.

C. Pruning: Shrubs will be pruned with hand shears as needed to provide an informal shape, fullness and blooms. Palm pruning will be done one (1) time per year to remove brown fronds and seed heads. No green palm fronds shall be removed. No pruning will be done during or immediately following growth flushes, branches will be pruned just outside the branch collar, and pruning paint will not be applied. Sucker growth will be removed by hand from the base of trees. No herbicides will be used for this purpose. The contractor will remove all litter. It is recommended that an ISA Certified Arborist be consulted and/or utilized for tree work.

D. Mulching: All mulched areas will be replenished once a year during the winter months (Nov-Feb). "Alternative" mulches (pine bark, pine needles, melaleuca, eucalyptus, recycled, etc.) should be considered. Mulch should be maintained at a depth of 3 inches. All curb, roadway and bed edges will be trenched to help contain the applied mulch. Additional mulch will be billed at $____/yard. Mulch will not be placed against the trunks of plants.

Part III: Considerations for Optional Services

A. Annual Flowers: Replacement of existing annuals will be done _____ times per year. Major renovation of annual beds shall be accomplished once per year in _____. Replacement of dead or injured plants due to pests or contractor negligence will be done without cost to client. Replacement of stolen, vandalized or damaged flowers will be charged to the client at a rate of _____/plant. Annuals and perennial bedding plants shall be fertilized monthly, at a rate of $1/2$ pound of nitrogen per 1,000 square feet of area every 3-4 weeks. An optional fertilizer schedule would use a slow-release fertilizer such as Osmocote or Nutricote incorporated in the bed at planting, and applied thereafter according to label directions. The contractor will be responsible for weed control. Pest control will follow IPM principles.

B. Irrigation Systems: The contractor shall inspect and test rain shut-off devices and other components and zones in the irrigation system monthly and shall reset zone times according to seasonal evapotranspiration changes. Minor adjustments and repairs such as head/emitter cleaning or replacement, filter cleaning, small leaks, and minor timer adjustments shall be made by the contractor, with the client paying for parts. Once a year, the contractor will recalibrate each zone to allow for the application of $1/2$ inch–$3/4$ inch of water per irrigation. During weekly maintenance, the contractor will note and report to client any symptoms of inadequate or excessive irrigation, drainage problems, etc. If the contractor is responsible for irrigation scheduling, timers will be shut off during the summer rainy season and the system will be turned on manually as needed. Repairs or system service beyond the above scope will be charged to the client at an hourly rate per worker plus parts. The contractor will notify the client or client's agent, of the nature of the problem before repairs are made.

C. Thatch Removal/Scalping: Removal of thatch (a spongy, build-up of dead and living grass shoots, stems and roots) should be considered when thatch thickness exceeds one inch. The best time for thatch removal is March through August when the turfgrass is rapidly growing. Thatch removal is not included in the basic contract charges. Verticutting, using a vertical mower, is the recommended method of mechanically removing thatch from Bermuda, St. Augustine, Zoysiagrass, and Centipede lawns. Blade spacing shall be 3" for St. Augustine, 2-3" Centipedegrass, and 1-2" for Bermuda grass and Zoysiagrass. Bahiagrass lawns can be power-raked rather than verticut. Contractor will remove resulting debris. Remaining turf will be mowed and irrigated with at least $1/2$ inch of water. One week after dethatching, apply $1/2$ to 1 lb of soluble nitrogen (e.g. 1-3 lbs ammonium nitrate, or 2.5-5 lbs ammonium sulfate per 1000 square feet to encourage recovery). Fertilizers must be watered in immediately following application to avoid plant burn. Scalping (close mowing) is not a substitute for vertical mowing and is not recommended for this purpose.

D. Other Services Available: (Priced per job by contractor)

- Installation of a rain shut-off device for irrigation systems.

- Landscape additions/renovations/transplanting.

- Transplanting of existing trees will be accomplished during January/February for dormant species, and April–August for palms.

- Plant or turf replacement (not attributed to contractor negligence).

- Maintenance of aquatic sites.

- General hauling.

- Major irrigation system modifications. Interior plant maintenance.

Part IV: Considerations for Insurance, Licenses, Permits and Liability

The contractor will carry liability amounts and workers' compensation coverage required by law on his/her operators and employees and require same of any sub-contractors and provide proof of same to the client. The contractor is also responsible for obtaining any licenses and/or permits required by law for activities on client's property.

Situations which the Contractor may deem are his/her responsibility: 1. Any damage due to operation of his equipment in performing the contract. 2. Failure to comply with all laws pertaining to protected plant species, such as the mangrove. 3. Damage to plant material due to improper horticultural practices. 4. Improper replacement or retrofitting of irrigation system components. 5. Injury to nontarget organisms due to application of pesticides.

Situations which the Contractor may deem are not his/her responsibility: 1. Death or decline of plant materials due to improper selection, placement, planting or maintenance done before the time of this contract. 2. Damage due to improper irrigation components existing at the time of contract execution. 3. Exposed cables/wires or sprinkler components/lines normally found below the lawn's surface. 4. Flooding, storm, wind, fire or cold damages. 5. Disease or damage to lawns or landscape plants caused by excessive irrigation or lack of water due to inoperative irrigation components provided he/she reported these to client, or irrigation restrictions imposed by the Water Management District or civil authorities. 6. Damage caused by or to any item hidden in the landscape and not clearly guarded or marked. 7. Damage due to vandalism.

Part V: Property Description, Services Provided, Terms, Conditions and Charges (for possible inclusion).

1. Contracts are normally for maintenance of property at an identified location and specifically described.

2. The term of the contract. A contract can be for a single year or multiple years with a beginning and ending date. A cancellation provision should be included.

3. The charge for monthly services should be specified. A deadline date should be included and late payment charges should also be considered. Any additional or unscheduled services agreed upon by client and contractor could be billed separately.

4. Contract renewal provisions may also be included. The contract is signed and dated by both parties, and can be witnessed or notarized.

The remainder of this article can be found online at http://edis.ifas.ufl.edu/pdffiles/lh/lh03100.pdf. Footnotes and copyright information for this article can be found in appendix E on page 246.

Additional Contract Considerations

You may want to follow the outline of the IFAS sample contract when writing up your own contracts. You'll need to select maintenance procedures appropriate for your region and decide which services to include in the monthly rate. Below are some additional considerations.

Cancellation. The contract should include cancellation terms. A typical cancellation policy states that either party has the right to end the contract with 30 days notice in writing. Without cancellation terms, the client may terminate the contract at any time. Note that some residential clients are reluctant to enter into a written contract and feel more comfortable knowing they can cancel service at any time for any reason.

Winter pruning. A year-round contract might state that limited pruning or general clean-up will be substituted for lawn maintenance during the winter months. This gives clients an incentive to continue service year-round, rather than discontinue during the winter. It is reasonable for the time spent per visit on winter pruning to equal the average time spent on other maintenance. Extensive pruning that cannot be accomplished over several visits should either be factored into the original bid or bid separately on a time-and-materials basis.

Subcontractors. If subcontractors will be performing some of the service (e.g., lawn aeration or herbicide application), include this information in your contract. If you aren't licensed to apply herbicides, inform the client both verbally and in writing that a separate weed abatement service may need to be called from time to time.

Rates for extra work and common materials. If you charge a higher hourly rate for some services, such as general clean-up, lawn aeration, or irrigation system repair, include your hourly rate for these services in the contract. If you are licensed to apply herbicides, include your rates for herbicide application.

Some landscape managers include limited irrigation part replacement in the monthly rate. If you charge for miscellaneous sprinkler parts, include your rates for spray heads or other low-cost parts. Include prices for lawn and shrub fertilization if you intend to bill extra for it. Notify the client in writing of any changes to your prices for extra work or common materials. Some clients will want to be notified before any extra work is done, others will let you use your discretion.

Policy Information

Your contract should include your business policies. Some policy examples are included here.

Service day. If you will not be performing maintenance on a set day, mention this to the client. A flexible-day policy is convenient for you and slightly less convenient for clients, who tend to prefer that maintenance be performed on a set day of the week.

Rain. The contract should include your rain policy. For example, "In the event of rain, maintenance will be performed on the first available non-raining weekday."

Pets and toys. Take measures to keep your clients' pets out of harm's way. Notify clients before applying chemicals, and securely close gates each time you enter or exit a backyard. If a dog will remain in the yard while you work, meet the dog with the owner present. Be sure the dog is not aggressive, even when power equipment is in use. Clients should agree to keep lawn areas cleared of toys and pet waste on maintenance days. Inform clients that the monthly rate does not change if you must avoid an area of the landscape that contains pet waste.

Time off. If you provide year-round service and you intend to take two weeks off per year, include this in the contract. Some gardeners choose to take two weeks off during winter, when work has slowed. The rate is the same during the month time off is taken.

Go over important contract and policy points with clients. Advise them to read the contract at their leisure and contact you if they have questions. Some clients object to the use of herbicides/pesticides in their yard. Discuss the use of these substances with clients before applying them in the landscape. Organic alternatives exist for granular fertilizers, preemergent herbicides, and pesticides, with varying degrees of effectiveness.

Customer Service Guidelines

Relating to clients in a professional manner is a necessary skill and one that will have tangible value for your business. Excellent customer service frequently results in customer loyalty and word-of-mouth referrals. Some homeowners are searching for a landscape management service simply because they are dissatisfied with the customer service of their existing company.

Fundamentally, customer service involves maintaining a respectful and attentive attitude toward clients. This is demonstrated in some of the following ways:

Client Communication and Email

Clear communication with clients will help you avoid many problems and reconcile others. If you are uncertain what your clients' think of your service, talk to them. Encourage clients to make requests and state their preferences as the work progresses. Once clients know they can speak with you, they will be less likely to discontinue service over minor problems. A written survey is an another way to get feedback and is more appropriate for some accounts.

Email can be a convenient way to communicate with clients. Email can be used to keep clients updated on the status of a large job, to get approval for additional work or materials, to provide a job summary for one time jobs, and to reschedule when necessary. Some clients even prefer to receive invoices via email. A group email can be used to notify clients of fertilization or aeration dates or to tell them about additional training or coursework you've completed. The key is moderation—excessive emailing can annoy clients. Note that emailing unsolicited promotions can be considered spamming and should be avoided. If you intend to send promotions through email, get the client's prior consent.

- Answer the phone, when possible, instead of letting it route to voicemail. New clients are more likely to do business with a service that answers the phone. Existing clients will appreciate being able to reach you with questions and requests.

- Return calls as soon as possible. Sometimes this will be the end of the work day; other times calls can be returned on the job. Waiting even 24 hours to return a call will often lose a new client. Existing clients are more understanding of short delays in getting back to them.

- Return all calls even if you are unable to take on more work. Tell the potential client when your schedule will open up, or refer the person to another reputable service.

- Show up to bids on time. Arriving late to a bid makes a poor first impression. Call and reschedule if you are unable to make the original meeting time.

- Respect privacy and property. Don't look in windows, garbage cans, or garages, and don't ask personal questions. Don't slam or damage gates.

See that pets are out of harm's way, and notify the client if there is any reason a pet should be out of the yard on a particular day. Many clients want their pets out of the yard before and immediately after the application of fertilizers or chemicals.

- Show attention to detail. You can do a fine job on the landscape, but if, for example, you leave weeds growing through a crack in the driveway or debris gathered around the edge of the doormat, this will undermine client satisfaction.

- Use mistakes as opportunities to provide outstanding customer service. For example, if the client points out damage to a sprinkler, replace it immediately. Or notice and repair the damage before the client does. What could have been a reason for the client to search for a different service becomes an opportunity to increase customer satisfaction.

- Don't sell your services for less than they are worth or give away your time for free. These gestures may increase customer satisfaction, but they undermine your efforts to stay in business.

Late Payments

Most clients pay their landscape management bill on time. Some tend to be late with their payments, but always come through in the end. It's helpful to set a payment period of Net 10 to encourage timely payment. Net 10 means that payment is due in 10 days from the receipt of a bill. If payment is not received within the payment period, leave the client a note as a reminder.

Client Doesn't Pay

Once in a great while, a client may fail to pay. Tact and persistence will usually result in payment from even an evasive client. An initial strategy is to take steps to elicit payment while maintaining a working relationship with the client. Quickly resorting to letters that demand payment or threats of legal action may rule out any chance of doing business with the person again. This approach may also provoke a stubborn response from a disgruntled client, and getting paid may become more difficult than it needs to be. A diplomatic approach is usually the most effective.

It is possible that the client has specific complaints about the work. Discussing the matter with the client in person or by phone can help you determine if the complaints are justified and what steps you can take to resolve the matter. If the complaints are not justified, and the client still refuses to pay, you can proceed with legal action.

The next step is to send the client a demand letter that includes the amount due, a demand for payment, the date payment is expected by, and a notification that you will be taking the matter to court if payment is not received by the stated date. It is important to restate the facts of the dispute to later demonstrate in court your attempt to collect (Steingold 2005). Send the letter via certified mail. If the client still does not pay after receiving the demand letter, it is time to take the matter to small claims court.

Small-Claims Court

Small-claims court, sometimes called county court, hears civil disputes between private parties over issues concerning small sums of money. Each state sets its own upper limits on the amounts that can be sued for in small claims court. In most cases, lawyers are not involved, and the parties represent themselves.

Call the phone number for the small-claims court or the superior court clerk in charge of civil disputes. You can find the number in the county government pages in the phone book. You will likely receive a handbook from the court that describes the legal process and requirements involved as the plaintiff or defendant. The following describes the general process, though procedures in your area may differ. Consult the printed material provided by your county.

First, the plaintiff files a claim with the court and pays an inexpensive fee. Next, the plaintiff must arrange to serve the defendant with a form that notifies the defendant that he is being sued and when and where he must appear in court. Counties specify how the defendant should be served with the form. For instance, some counties will send the form by certified mail for the plaintiff; other counties recommend that an independent third party hand the form to the defendant and tell him he is being sued.

On the designated court date, a judge will decide the case. In some courts, the case may be decided in favor of the plaintiff if the defendant fails to show up. Bring documents and pertinent photographs with you to prove your case. If you have a witness, have the person come with you on the court day. Depending on the amount of your claim, it may be helpful to consult a book devoted to the topic of small claims court, such as *Everybody's Guide to Small Claims Court* by Ralph Werner (Nolo).

CHAPTER 13

Employer Requirements

In This Chapter

- Federal requirements
- Payroll services and temp workers
- Independent contractors

This chapter provides an overview of common legal requirements for employers—it is intended to serve as an aid for those who are considering hiring employees. Coverage of the selected topics is partial. You will need to consult additional sources to ensure that you comply with all federal and state laws. *The Employer's Legal Handbook* by Attorney Fred S. Steingold (Nolo) is one specialized book on the subject. It is available at many public libraries.

The website of the Small Business Administration (SBA) also includes information on complying with labor laws; search for "Employment and Labor Law" from the SBA website, or go to http://www.sba.gov/content/employment-labor-law. Most of the requirements presented in this chapter are federal. States have additional requirements, which you can learn about from state labor offices.

Employer Identification Number

Employers need an employer identification number (EIN) from the IRS. The EIN is a Taxpayer Identification Number for your business; it is used for legal identification purposes. If your business is structured as a sole proprietorship and you do not hire employees, you may not be required to get an EIN, though it may be a good idea to do so anyway. For instance, if you disclose your business's Taxpayer Identification Number, as is sometimes necessary, you afford yourself greater protection from identity theft when you use an EIN as opposed to your Social Security number. Note that if you change the legal structure of your business, you will need a new EIN. For example, if the business begins as a sole

proprietorship and later becomes a partnership, the business will need a new EIN. See the instructions for *Form SS-4* for details.

To file for an EIN, you will need IRS *Form SS-4* and the *Instructions for Form SS-4*. IRS forms, instructions, and other publications can be downloaded from the IRS website, or ordered over the phone by calling 1-800-TAX-FORM (1-800-829-3676). The SS-4 can be submitted to the IRS over the internet, among other methods. Instructions are also available in Spanish. Note that states issue EINs (State Tax Ids) that are separate from federal EINs.

Workers' Compensation Insurance

In general, employers are required to purchase workers' compensation insurance. Workers' compensation insurance pays for medical expenses and lost wages to employees who are injured on the job. In some cases, it also provides employees with benefits if they are impaired from earning a living in the future. Even if workers' comp is not required in your area, it is prudent to get it to protect your business.

You can buy workers' compensation insurance from a private insurance company or a state fund. A few states require businesses to purchase workers' comp from a state fund. In general, workers' comp does not cover you, the business owner, though it may be possible to add this coverage. Ask your insurance agent if you also need employers' liability coverage, or coverage B.

Contact your state workers' compensation office to learn about your state's workers' compensation requirements. A directory of state workers' comp offices is available on the Small Business Administration website. To locate the directory, go to http://www.sba.gov and enter "workers comp" into the search bar.

Disability Insurance

If your employees work in California, Hawaii, New Jersey, New York, Puerto Rico, or Rhode Island, your are required to purchase disability insurance for employees. Contact the state agency in charge of this program for more information.

Employment Laws

The U.S. Department of Labor (DOL) administers and enforces federal employment laws, including laws of the Fair Labor Standards Act (FLSA), which sets standards for minimum wage, overtime pay, child labor, and employer record keeping. See the *elaws* section of the DOL website for guidance in complying with federal labor laws (http://www.dol.gov/elaws/index.htm).

The elaws *FirstStep* Employment Law Advisor is a primer on employment laws and recordkeeping, reporting, and notice requirements, including necessary workplace posters. Through an interactive questionnaire, *FirstStep* helps you determine which DOL requirements apply to your business. The DOL's *FirstStep* webpage is located at http://www.dol.gov/elaws/firststep.

Note that *FirstStep* does not explain all the employment laws administered by the DOL, only the major ones. If you don't know which laws apply to your business, the DOL recommends that you start with *FirstStep*. The DOL also produces the Employment Law Guide, which is said to provide more "hands-on" information; it can be found at http://www.dol.gov/elaws/elg. If you need help navigating DOL laws and regulations, see DOL compliance assistance at http://www.dol.gov/compliance. The DOL can be reached by phone at 1-866-4-USA-DOL (1-866-487-2365). Remember that state labor agencies have additional laws employers must abide by.

OSHA Requirements

The Occupational Safety and Health Administration (OSHA) is a division of the U.S. Department of Labor that regulates workplace safety. Employers must follow the workplace safety standards set forth in the Occupational Safety and Health Act of 1970 and meet OSHA's requirements, both on the state and federal level. State standards can sometimes be stricter than federal standards.

To learn about OSHA compliance, call the OSHA Compliance Guidance Group at 1-301-515-6796 or visit the OSHA website at http://www.osha.gov. The simplest way to navigate OSHA's site is with the A-Z index in the search bar at the top of the home page. Search the A-Z index for "small business" and follow the link. The direct address for the small business page is http://www.osha.gov/dcsp/smallbusiness/index.html. The small business page includes information on OSHA's On-site Consultation Program, as well as the Compliance Assistance Quick Start feature. OSHA's *Small Business Handbook* is also accessible from this page.

OSHA's Landscape and Horticultural Services page contains important compliance and safety information; see "Safety and OSHA" on page 29. OSHA's *Job Safety and Health: It's the Law* poster is required for all employers. Search for "posters" in the A-Z index. Ordering information for OSHA publications is available through the OSHA Publications Office at 1-202-693-1888. A general OSHA phone number is 1-800-321-OSHA. Note that your state may have its own OSHA website.

Important: Within 8 hours of the death of any employee from a work-related incident or the in-patient hospitalization of three or more employees as a result of a work-related incident, you must report the incident by telephone or in person to the OSHA Area Office that is nearest the site of the incident. You may also notify OSHA via their central phone number, 1-800-321-OSHA (1-800-321-6742).

Posting Requirements

The Department of Labor website provides a list of required posters for the workplace. Not all posters are required for all businesses. To learn which federal posters you are required to show in your workplace, call the DOL, or use the *FirstStep* Poster Advisor on the DOL's website at http://www.dol.gov/elaws/posters.htm. Most posters are also available in Spanish. Required federal posters include, but are not limited to:

- Employee Polygraph Protection Act

- FLSA/Federal Minimum Wage

- Equal Employment Opportunity Is The Law

- Job Safety and Health: It's the Law

State labor agencies have additional posting and notice requirements. For example, you may be required to give employees pamphlets on worker's compensation rights and sexual harassment, among other topics. And when you fire or lay off an employee, you may be required to give the person pamphlets on state unemployment and disability insurance programs. You can find out all of your state's employer requirements through your state's labor office. The U.S. Small Business Administration website (http://www.sba.gov) is a useful resource for determining employer requirements and locating state labor agencies. A search on the SBA website for "managing employees" and "posters" will turn up articles.

Employee File

Employers are required by law to keep a file of records for each employee. See the previous topic "Federal Labor Laws" and answer the Department of Labor's *FirstStep* questionnaires to learn what recordkeeping is required by the Fair Labor Standards Act (FLSA) and DOL laws. The employee file should also include the employee's job description, job application, Social Security number, IRS Form W-4, USCIS Form I-9, and performance and attendance records, among other job-related information. Employee files should be kept confidential and stored in a locked, secure place. For details on setting up and maintaining an employee file, consult a specialized book such as *The Employer's Legal Handbook* by Fred S. Steingold (Nolo).

Eligibility for Employment

Employers are required to verify that employees can legally work in the United States. Verification is performed by completing the U.S. Citizenship and Immigration Services (USCIS) Form I-9, *Employment Eligibility Verification* for each new employee. An I-9 must be completed within three days of hiring. The form must be kept on file for three years or one year after an employee's termination, whichever is later. I-9s can be downloaded from the U.S. Citizenship and Immigration Services website at http://www.uscis.gov. Search for "employment eligibility verification" from the website. The instructions for Form I-9 are included in Form M-274 *Handbook for Employers*, which is also available for download. The USCIS can be reached at 1-888-464-4218.

Employers can also instantly verify an employee's eligibility to work in the U.S. using E-Verify. According to USCIS, "E-Verify is an Internet-based system that compares information from an employee's Form I-9...to data from U.S. Department of Homeland Security and Social Security Administration records to confirm employment eligibility." Visit the USCIS website to enroll in E-Verify. Some state's (e.g., Arizona and Mississippi) require employers to use E-Verify.

New Hire Reporting

Employers are required to report the hiring of new employees, including re-hired employees, to a state directory within 20 days of hiring. In some states, new hire reporting may also apply to the hiring of independent contractors. To find the name and contact information of the state agency in charge of this program, see the New Hire Reporting Requirements web page at Small Business Administration's website: http://www.sba.gov/content/new-hire-reporting-your-state.

Tax Forms and Withholdings

IRS Publication 15 (Circular E), *Employer's Tax Guide* details the federal taxes employers must pay. IRS Publication 15-A *Employer's Supplemental Tax Guide* also includes employer tax information. These publications are available through http://www.irs.gov or 1-800-TAX-FORM (1-800-829-3676). Table 18 is a summary of employers' basic federal

Table 18. Employer's Federal Tax Responsibilities From 2018 IRS Publication 15, *Employer's Tax Guide.*

New Employees:
- Verify work eligibility of new employees.
- Record employees' names and SSNs from social security cards.
- Ask employees for Form W-4.

Each Payday:
- Withhold federal income tax based on each employee's Form W-4.
- Withhold employee's share of social security and Medicare taxes.
- Deposit:
  - ↝ Withheld income tax.
  - ↝ Withheld and employer social security taxes.
  - ↝ Withheld and employer Medicare taxes.

  Note: Due date of deposit generally depends on your deposit schedule (monthly or semi-weekly).

Quarterly (By April 30, July 31, October 31, and January 31):
- Deposit FUTA tax if undeposited amount is over $500.
- File Form 941 (pay tax with return if not required to deposit).

Annually (By January 31):
- File Form 944 if required (pay tax with return if not required to deposit).

Annually (See Calendar for due dates [included in IRS Publication 15]):
- Remind employees to submit a new Form W-4 if they need to change their withholding.
- Ask for a new Form W-4 from employees claiming exemption from income tax withholding.
- Reconcile Forms 941 (or Form 944) with Forms W-2 and W-3.
- Furnish each employee a Form W-2.
- File Copy A of Forms W-2 and the transmittal Form W-3 with the SSA.
- Furnish each other payee a Form 1099 (for example, Form 1099-MISC).
- File Forms 1099 and the transmittal Form 1096.
- File Form 940.
- File Form 945 for any nonpayroll income tax withholding.

Table 18 is a brief summary of employers' basic tax responsibilities. Since employer circumstances can vary, responsibilities for withholding, depositing, and reporting employment taxes can differ. See the current IRS Publication 15 for detailed instruction.

tax responsibilities. See Publication 15 for complete explanations of each task listed in table 18.

Workshops that provide instruction on completing employer tax requirements are available, but can take some effort to locate; the IRS website is worth searching, and so are the websites of the Small Business Administration (http://www.sba.gov) and SCORE (http://www.score.org). Call the IRS at 1-800-829-1040 for assistance. IRS Publication 910, *Guide to Free Tax Services* also lists educational sources. Keep records of employment taxes for at least four years. Some tax professionals recommend getting a separate checking account for employee tax withholdings.

You may be required to pay state unemployment insurance tax for employees or other state taxes. Contact your state tax agencies to learn more. Links to state tax agencies can be found on the Small Business Administration website at http://www.sba.gov/content/learn-about-your-state-and-local-tax-obligations.

Advertising, Interviewing, Hiring, Terminating

Once you have an EIN and unemployment insurance, met OSHA requirements, and know how to complete employee-related tax requirements, you still need to interview and hire employees, as well as train, manage, pay, and sometimes fire them. Many laws regulate the hiring and firing process, as well as employer-employee relations. While you are free to hire whomever you wish, it is illegal to discriminate based on race, color, religion, national origin, sex, age, disability, or genetic information. Additional anti-discrimination rules exist. You cannot do extensive background searches without the applicant's written consent. You must also be sensitive to the types of questions you ask during an interview. It is important to understand these and the many other laws governing employer-employee relations before hiring people. *The Employer's Legal Handbook* by Fred S. Steingold (Nolo) is one book that explains the legalities of employer-employee relations.

Payroll Services

A simpler alternative to making tax deductions and writing paychecks is to hire a payroll service to make the appropriate state and federal deductions and generate employee paychecks or calculate paycheck amounts. Many payroll services will also deposit employee withholdings to the IRS on a regular schedule and report the hiring of new employees to the pertinent state agencies, if required. For an extra fee, some payroll services will obtain workers' compensation insurance and file W-2 forms and 1099-MISC on your behalf. You can find payroll services in the phone book. Request a quote, and be sure you understand what services the quote does and does not include. Software and Web-based services are also available.

Temp Workers

One way to avoid the hiring process, workers' compensation insurance, and paycheck deductions is to obtain help through a temporary employment agency. A "temp" agency will handle the legalities of hiring and paying employees, for a fee. The temp agency makes money by charging the business an hourly rate that is higher than what the employee is paid. It is less expensive to hire employees yourself, but if you want to avoid the extra bookwork or if you only need help for a few months, a temp agency is worth considering. Note that when you hire a temp worker, you must still abide by the laws governing employer-employee relations.

Independent Contractors

An independent contractor performs work for another business but is not an employee of that business. Since independent contractors are considered self-employed, you do not need to deduct payroll taxes or to obtain workers' compensation insurance on their behalf. And, in most circumstances, your business is not held responsible for the negligent actions of an independent contractor.

When you hire an independent contractor, you are obligated to fill out and send Form 1099-MISC to both the IRS and the independent contractor at the end of the year if you paid the independent contractor $600 or more for services and materials during the year. See the IRS publication *Instructions for 1099-MISC* for current figures and complete details. It is important for business owners to file Form 1099-MISC because it provides them with presumptive evidence that the individuals listed on the 1099s are actually independent contractors (Fujie 2009).

There may be additional state reporting requirements associated with hiring independent contractors. For example, in California, business owners must file Form DE 542 with the Employment Development Department (EDD) within 20 days of paying or entering into a contract to pay an independent contractor $600 or more in any calendar year. Form 542 helps state and county agencies locate parents who are delinquent in their child support obligations (Form DE 542 2005).

Independent Contractor or Employee?

Because of the minimal bookwork and legal obligations associated with hiring independent contractors, you may be tempted to classify someone as an independent contractor when they are better classified as an employee. However, the IRS aggressively penalizes businesses that incorrectly classify employees as independent contractors. If you claim workers are independent contractors, and they are not, the IRS can force you to pay the back employment taxes those workers would have owed as employees, as well as penalties and interest. Note that this is an area of tax law that the IRS and some state agencies actively investigate.

The IRS provides guidelines to help business owners make the distinction between an independent contractor and an employee. A general rule is that you can classify someone as an independent contractor if you control or direct only the result of the work, not how the work will be done. This "degree of control" is what needs to be considered in each situation. Generally, if the person advertises his services to the public, works for different people, owns his own equipment, sets his own hours, has his own workplace or office, determines how the work gets done, and is not reimbursed for expenses,

the person can be considered an independent contractor (Pakroo 2004).

For example, a professional window washer acts as an independent contractor when she cleans windows for local small businesses. She decides how to clean the windows and how much she is willing to make. Additionally, she has her own business license, owns her own tools, and meets the legal requirements for her trade. If the window washer accidentally causes property damage at a restaurant where she is working as an independent contractor, she is financially responsible for that damage. If the window washer were a regular employee of the restaurant, she would not be financially responsible.

Consider another example: You may wish to hire a friend to maintain some lawns for you because he has his own truck. You loan him your equipment, tell him the addresses of the accounts you need serviced, describe how you want the work done, and state how much you will pay. You would be safer hiring your friend as an employee rather than as an independent contractor because he does not operate his own business, and he will be performing the work in the ways you dictate. If you classify him as an independent contractor, and the IRS later rules against this classification, you can be held responsible for taxes that employee should have paid as well as financial penalties.

In contrast, if you have a friend who advertises his own landscaping services, owns his own equipment, and has his own maintenance accounts, and you hire him to provide basic maintenance at several accounts for a week while you are out of town, he can probably be classified as an independent contractor. For more detailed information on determining whether a person should be classified as an independent contractor or an employee, see IRS Publication 15-A, *Employer's Supplemental Tax Guide,* or a specialized book such as *Hiring Independent Contractors,* by Stephen Fishman (Nolo). If you have any doubt about the proper classification of a worker, have a professional tax advisor decide, or file IRS Form SS-8 and the IRS will make the correct classification for you.

Bookkeeping

The IRS requires business owners to keep records of business income and expenses to verify the accuracy of income tax reporting. This practice of recording business financial transactions is known as bookkeeping. From a practical standpoint, bookkeeping helps you stay organized in preparation for tax time, when you must report your income and deductions to the IRS. If you have employees, bookkeeping is also necessary to document payroll deductions. Another function of bookkeeping is to provide accountants or accounting software with accurate financial information that can be used to generate reports on a business's financial status. Note that accounting encompasses bookkeeping, but is not limited to it.

The IRS has certain bookkeeping guidelines you should follow. This chapter looks at some of these guidelines, as well as some fundamental bookkeeping concepts. It also shows you how to set up and use a manual, single-entry bookkeeping method. Even if you end up using accounting software, the simplicity of a hand-entry system can make learning the basics easier.

It can be helpful to consult with a small-business accountant or certified public accountant (CPA) before choosing an accounting method. These professionals can provide you with guidance in setting up your books and answer some of the obscure bookkeeping and tax-related questions that inevitably arise. Many CPAs also specialize in tax preparation for small businesses. Note that a knowledgeable accountant or CPA is a valuable business associate; every small business owner should consider hiring one. For more information, see "Tax Professionals" on page 231.

This introduction to bookkeeping is intended to serve as a practical overview; it is not meant to be complete. You are encouraged to seek out the appropriate sources of information to comply with all requirements for your business. It is also helpful to take a course in small business bookkeeping as soon as you are able. Additional information on bookkeeping can be found in the following IRS publications:

- Publication 583 *Starting a Business and Keeping Records*

- Publication 334 *Tax Guide for Small Business*

- Publication 538 *Accounting Periods and Methods*

- Publication 535 *Business Expenses*

- Publication 463 *Travel, Entertainment, Gift, and Car Expenses*

- Publication 587 *Business Use of Your Home*

- Publication 946 *How to Depreciate Property*

You can request IRS forms and publications by calling the IRS at 1-800-TAX-FORM (1-800-829-3676), or you can download publications from the IRS website at http://www.irs.gov. Note that IRS publications can, at times, be challenging to read. Books on accounting, bookkeeping, and taxes for small business can make the subjects easier to grasp. Several books are listed in appendix A.

Income and Expenses

Money generated by your business—in the form of cash, check, or credit card—is income. According to the IRS, property and services can also qualify as income. For example, if you receive a rent reduction for managing the landscape where you live, the fair market value of the bartered service is considered income. The IRS lists some less common forms of income in Publication 334, *Tax Guide for Small Business*.

Business expenses are costs associated with running your business. For example, advertising, business cards, equipment, and gardening supplies all qualify as business expenses. Business expenses are deductible. This means that you do not have to pay income tax on the amount of the expense. For example, if you purchase a power hedge clipper for $250, you can claim it as a business expense; this will reduce your taxable income by $250. If you need a new piece of equipment, buy it and take the tax write-off. In general, you should avoid purchasing things only to reduce your taxes.

You have some discretion in deciding what qualifies as a business expense, but ultimately the IRS has to agree with you. As a guideline, the expense must be "ordinary and necessary". According to the IRS, "An ordinary expense is one that is common and accepted in your trade or business. A necessary expense is one that is helpful and appropriate for your trade or business. An expense does not have to be indispensable to be considered necessary."

Business expenses are broadly divided into two categories: current expenses and capital expenses. Current expenses are expenses associated with running a business; these items are generally used up within one year (e.g., supplies, equipment repairs, and advertising). Capital expenses are expense items with a useful life longer than one year (e.g., equipment and vehicles).

Note that inventory is not labeled a business expense; it is a business asset that gets "expensed" as it is sold (Daily 2005). Consequently, inventory purchases made at the end of the year will not reduce your taxable income for the year. For instance, purchasing $400 in irrigation parts would not reduce your taxable income by $400 at tax time because these are inventory items.

We will explore some of these topics more later. For now, you only need a general understanding of what the terms *income* and *expense* refer to. We now look at three essential components of a bookkeeping system: bank account, records, and ledgers.

Bank Account

Keep your personal finances separate from your business finances by opening a separate checking account for your business. In some states, it is illegal to cash a business check without depositing it in a business bank account (Kamoroff 2005). While you may not be legally required to open a separate business bank account, it is a logical first step in organizing your business finances.

Bank statements can provide another form of income and expense documentation for your business. If you deposit all income into your business bank account and pay all expenses from that account, the bank statements can be used to verify the accuracy of your bookkeeping. Depositing personal income into your business account or paying business bills from a personal checking account creates disorganization, and extra efforts must be made to keep track of transactions.

It is a good business habit to deposit all income into your business checking account. This applies to all forms of payment, including cash, checks, money orders, and credit card transactions. Obviously, it is illegal to hide income, and doing so can result in legal consequences, including the payment of past taxes, fines, and penalties. The IRS is good at finding holes in financial records. They have the authority to inspect any documents related to your business and personal finances, including (but not limited to) ledgers, receipts, invoices, bank statements, and credit card bills.

After withdrawing money from your business account for personal use, record the transaction in your expense ledger and business checkbook as "Owner's Draw". Finally, balance your business checkbook every month to keep your records accurate and up to date.

Records

Save all records of business income and expenses to support the income and expense claims on your tax return. In the event of an audit (explained on page 232), the IRS may ask to see your business records to verify that your income and expense claims are legitimate. Without receipts or other supporting documentation, you may not be entitled to all the expense deductions claimed on your tax return. You should also keep documentation of business loans or your personal financial contributions to the business.

Below are some guidelines on maintaining income and expense records. For more information on what constitutes an adequate income or expense record, see IRS Publication 583, *Starting a Business and Keeping Records* and IRS Publication 463, *Travel, Entertainment, Gift, and Car Expenses.*

Income Records

Keep copies of all income receipts and invoices. Invoices should include a description of the items or services sold (e.g., "Maintenance for July"), the total amount of the bill, and the date. Items that are subject to sales tax should be clearly marked, and the sales tax total should be included. Sales tax is described on page 219.

If you photocopy invoices that you designed yourself, fill out a separate copy for yourself each time you write an invoice. Carbonless or NCR invoice pads produce a copy when the original invoice is filled out. If you make an error while filling out a carbonless invoice and cannot use it, write "void" on it and hang onto it—gaps in the numbered sequence of invoices can raise a question for the IRS.

Expense Records

You need records or supporting documents for all business expenses claimed on your tax return. Receipts or cancelled checks serve as records of transactions. Paid bills can be used as supporting documents for certain business expenses, such as utilities. Note that some receipts include a cash register print out and a credit card slip: staple them together to avoid mistaking them for separate transactions.

After getting an expense receipt, you will enter the expense into your expenditure ledger (explained later) and file the receipt away. Expenses get recorded in separate categories in the expenditure ledger. Keep receipts of the same expense category (e.g., "office supplies") in a single envelope or folder to make them easier to find. Once all expense receipts for the year have been sorted and your taxes are done, write the tax year on each envelope, and store the envelopes in a file cabinet with your income tax returns and other business records. For information on how long to keep business records, see "Length of Time to Keep Records" on page 232.

Ledgers

A ledger is a book with rows and columns used to record, or "post" in bookkeeping jargon, business income and expenditures. Paper ledgers are available at stationery or office supply stores. Accounting software has built-in ledgers.

The two primary ledgers used by small businesses are the income (revenue) ledger and the expenditure ledger. Depending on the size and nature of the business, additional ledgers may be used. A business may have separate ledgers for payroll deductions, inventory, fixed assets, petty cash, accounts receivable, accounts payable, travel expenses, and vehicle expenses, among others. These designated ledgers provide more detailed records of the financial information that is summarized in the income and expenditure ledgers. The needs of your business determine which ledgers to use. For instance, if a business has few travel expenses, a separate ledger for these expenses is not necessary.

The next few topics present some of the choices available to you when setting up a bookkeeping method. This is followed by an explanation of how to set up and use income and expenditure ledgers.

Calendar vs. Fiscal Year

Income tax returns are filed for a 12-consecutive-month accounting period called a tax year. There are two types of tax years. The tax year most businesses and individuals use is the same as the calendar year: it begins on January 1st and ends on December 31st. Some corporations have the option of reporting income and expenses in a fiscal year, which is a different time period from the calendar year. If you have a legitimate reason, you can request to use a fiscal year for your business by filing IRS Form 8716 *Election To Have a Tax Year Other Than a Required Tax Year*. For more information, consult IRS Publication 538, *Accounting Periods and Methods*.

Single- vs. Double-Entry Systems

Businesses can choose between a single-entry or double-entry bookkeeping system. In a single-entry bookkeeping system, each transaction is recorded in a ledger only once, either as income or as an expense. Single-entry systems are similar to a checkbook register, making them simple to use. One of the drawbacks of a single-entry system is that there is not a built-in method of checking for input errors, as there is with a double-entry system.

In double-entry bookkeeping, each transaction is recorded twice—as a debit in one account and as a credit in another account. For example, if you purchase a box of 20 sprinklers, and you are using the double-entry system, the transaction would be recorded as a debit (increase) in the inventory account and a credit (decrease) in the cash account.

Because of the complexity of double-entry accounting, you need to take a course on the subject to understand how to do it properly. One advantage of a double-entry system is that it forces you to check for math errors, as the debit and credit amounts must balance.

Most large businesses and many small businesses use the double-entry accounting system. Some small businesses can be run with a manual, single-entry system. A business with few or no employees and low revenue is sometimes referred to as a "microbusiness". A single-entry system may be adequate for a microbusiness. Some residential landscape management businesses fit the description of a microbusiness, others do not.

Starting out, it is reasonable to adopt a system that is easy to learn. In time, you can get additional training and change the system if you need to. (Prior IRS approval may be required; see "Changing Your Accounting Method", next page.) Most introductory books on bookkeeping emphasize manual, single-entry systems for simple small businesses. Some accounting software, such as Quicken, uses a single-entry system; Quickbooks has both single- and double-entry features. Data entry for accounting software is relatively simple because the double-entry process is automated and happens behind the scenes.

Cash vs. Accrual Method

Businesses must also choose between the *cash* and *accrual* methods of accounting. These methods have to do with the date you record transactions in your ledgers. With the cash method, you record income when you receive a payment (i.e., when funds become available to you), and you record an expense when you make a payment. For example, if you buy a piece of equipment on store credit, you would not record the expense in your ledger until the day you paid the bill.

With the accrual method, you record income when you bill the client, even if you have not been paid yet; and you record an expense when you acquire an item, even if you have not paid for it yet. For example, with the accrual method, if you buy a

Changing Your Accounting Method

If you decide to change your accounting method after you have filed the first tax return for the business, you will need to get approval from the IRS. Approval is obtained with IRS Form 3115. See the instructions for Form 3115 and IRS Publication 538, *Accounting Periods and Methods* for more information. This is another example of a bookkeeping-related task that an accountant can help with.

piece of equipment on February 20th, but don't pay the bill until March 10th, you would still record the expense on February 20th.

Each method has the potential to affect your taxable income for the year. For example, if you are using the accrual method and you bill a client $400 near the end of 2019, but don't receive payment from the client until 2020, you must pay taxes on the $400 in 2019. If you were using the cash method, you would not pay taxes on the $400 until 2020.

The cash method is the simpler one to use. However, the IRS provides rules regarding who is and is not allowed to use the cash method. The rules are complex, so it is advisable to consult with an accountant before deciding. See IRS Publication 538, *Accounting Periods and Methods* for more details. According to Bernard Kamoroff, CPA and author of *Small Time Operator,* if the gross annual sales for your business are $1 million or less, you can use either method (2005). Some accounting software is based on the accrual method.

Setting Up and Using an Income Ledger

All income (revenue) generated by your business must be recorded in an income ledger. Income records are used to complete tax returns and generate financial reports. For the income ledger, purchase ledger paper with approximately seven columns. Depending on your business, you may need more or fewer columns. To demonstrate how to label columns and make entries, we will follow the format of the sample income ledger shown on the next page.

The first column in the sample ledger, *Date*, is used to record daily sales. Note that the rows in the sample are numbered according to the day of the month. However, a blank column is more convenient because it allows you to post daily sales in more than one row. For example, you may choose to have three rows designated to March 3, each row listing a different client's payment.

The next column, *Sales Period,* is used to post income acquired over a certain time period (e.g., March 27–31). If you use the sales period column, you don't need to use the date column. Postings for a sales period are comprised of more than one individual sale. This is generally most useful for businesses that do numerous transactions a day, such as a retail store or a large maintenance contracting business. Small landscape management businesses tend to have much fewer income transactions, so it is often possible, and more useful, to list individual payments in the income ledger. For example, instead of posting the sales total of $240, generated in the sales period "March 2–3" (see the sample ledger), you might list each sale separately. For example, "March 2, Watson Clean-up, $100," "March 3, Smith Maintenance for April, $140."

Remember, if you are using the cash method, the transaction date is the date payment funds become available to you. If you are using the accrual method, the transaction date is the date you leave the client an invoice, regardless of when you receive payment.

The *Taxable Sales* column is used to isolate the income that is subject to sales tax. Use this column to enter the total for all taxable items in a job. For

| | | | | Nontaxable Sales | | | |
Date	Sales Period	Sales Tax	Whole-sale	Nontaxable Services	Other	Total Sales
1		$59.95	$5.25		$115.00		$180.20
2							
3	March 2 - 3				$240.00		$240.00
4							
5							
6					$177.50		$177.50
...31	March 27 - 31				$595.00		$595.00
Totals		$59.95	$5.25		$1127.50		$1192.70

Sample Income Ledger / March

example, if you charged sales tax on $40.00 in materials, you would enter $40.00 in the taxable sales column. The *Sales Tax* column is used to record the amount of sales tax collected for the taxable items. For example, if the total of all taxable items is $40 and the sales tax rate is 8.25 percent, the sales tax collected for the job is $3.50—this amount would be entered in the sales tax column. Assuming you mark the taxable items and sales tax total on invoices, these totals can be transferred from invoices. If the ledger entry is for a sales period, these columns would include the totals of all taxable sales and sales tax in that period.

Note: The taxable sales and sales tax columns are used only for taxable items you have marked up and resold. If you paid sales tax when you purchased the item and have not marked up the cost of the item before reselling it, you would not enter the amount of these items in the taxable sales or sales tax columns. Instead, the totals for these items might be included in the category marked "other" under non-taxable sales.

Next to the sales tax column is *Non-Taxable Sales*. Non-taxable sales are those items on an invoice

or sales receipt that are not subject to sales tax. Generally, labor and services are not subject to sales tax. However, some states or municipalities do impose sales tax on services. For more information, see "Sales Tax" on the next page.

In the sample ledger, the non-taxable sales are divided into three columns: *Wholesale, Non-Taxable Services*, and *Other*. You can add categories to suit your needs. For example, you might create three columns under the non-taxable services column labeled *Maintenance, Clean-ups*, and *Irrigation Repair*. These subcategories will be of no interest to the IRS, but they can help you analyze your business. If these services are taxable in your area, you could include these categories under *Taxable Sales*.

Ultimately, the income ledger should meet the needs of your business. If a category does not pertain to your business, you don't need to include it; if additional categories are useful to you, include them. For instance, you might include a column labeled *Payment Type* to record check numbers or to note which payments were in cash. Most payments are by check, but the IRS likes to see that you claim cash payments and may be suspicious if it does not

Sales Tax

As the owner of a small business, you are required to collect sales tax from clients for any applicable goods or services you sell and send that sales tax to the appropriate authority in your state. Sales tax law can vary from state to state and within a state. In general, only materials are subject to sales tax, though some states and municipalities also levy sales tax on services. A few states do not have a sales tax (though cities and municipalities within these states may have a sales tax). Contact your state's sales tax agency or your city government offices to find out the sales tax and related accounting requirements for your business. Small-business accountants will also have this information.

find any. You might also include bank and checking account information for each check, to make it easy to follow up if a client's check fails to clear.

Once you've posted all income for the month, write the totals for each column at the bottom of the ledger sheet. Begin a new income ledger page each month. At the end of the year, add up the monthly totals on a new income ledger page to get your income totals for the year.

Note that your income totals may include reimbursement from clients for materials you purchased, but in the end, you will not pay income tax on the amount you paid for these purchases. These materials costs are considered business expenses ("supplies") and, as such, they get deducted on the Schedule C tax form, which is covered in the next chapter. Also note that income from loans or your personal financial contribution to the business is not recorded in the income ledger.

Setting Up and Using an Expenditure Ledger

The expenditure ledger is similar to a checkbook register in that it contains a record of payments made by your business. Unlike a checkbook register, the expenditure ledger shows all business payments, not just those paid by check. The other unique feature of this ledger is that expenditures are grouped into categories. Categorizing expenditures enables you to analyze where you are spending money in the business and helps you prepare

for tax time, when you must categorize expenses for the IRS.

When setting up your expenditure ledger, choose categories for common expenditures in your business. For example, if you have many transfer station fees, you could create a "Transfer Station" category. While many of the expenditure ledger categories will be business expenses, other categories can also be included, such as inventory and fixed assets. This is what makes the expenditure ledger a complete record of the funds paid out in your business.

Sole proprietors must complete a Schedule C tax form at the end of each year. You can save time on tax preparation by setting up your expenditure ledger to include some of the Schedule C expense categories. A reduced-scale copy of Schedule C is included on page 228. Another idea is to base some expenditure ledger categories on your G&A overhead categories (described on page 190). This can help you speed up the calculation of overhead costs.

If you are using the cash method, the date you record will be the date you paid for the expenditure. If you are using the accrual method, the date you record will be the date the transaction occurred, regardless of when you pay the bill. Under the *Payment Method* column, include the payment type, and the check number if you paid by check. Include a *Payee* column to show who the payment

Sample Expenditure Ledger / March									
Date	Payment Method	Payee	Total	Inventory	Payroll	Adver-tising	Supplies	Misc.	Non-Deduct.
3-1	Visa	ACE Hard.	$42.50				$31.25		$11.25
3-1	Visa	CT Irrigation	$34.50					$34.50	
3-5	Ck.# 472	RB Nursery	$18.70				$18.70		
3-12	Ck.# 473	Daily Star	$28.40			$28.40			
March Totals			$124.10			$28.40	$49.95	$34.50	$11.25

was to. It is also useful to include a column labeled *Transactions* to describe what the payment was for.

Each transaction amount is recorded in at least two columns: the *Total* column and the column of the expenditure category that the payment went toward. For example, on the sample expenditure ledger, the transaction on 3-12 for $28.40 is recorded in the *Total* column and the *Advertising* column. If the payment went toward multiple expenditures, you would write the amount in the *Total* column and split the total between the appropriate categories. Note that your expenditure ledger is likely to have more categories than are shown in the sample.

The expense categories for Schedule C are described in the IRS publication *Instructions for Schedule C*, which is downloaded separately from the Schedule C tax form. You can also find category descriptions in "Expense Categories" on page 225. These descriptions can help you decide where to categorize expenses. Otherwise, use your judgment about where to list each expenditure. Accountants can provide guidance when you are uncertain. Miscategorizing an expenditure is not usually a big deal. However, you should be consistent from year to year about where you categorize an expenditure.

At the end of each month, add up the amounts in each column, and write the totals on the next empty line. Draw a line beneath the monthly totals, and continue recording expenditures for the next month on the same ledger sheet; you don't need to begin a new ledger page each month. At the end of the year, add up the totals from each month on a separate ledger page.

Other Ledgers

Depending on the complexity of your business, you may need additional ledgers to keep track of other aspects of your business. Designated ledgers for inventory, employee payroll, petty cash, fixed assets, vehicle expenses, accounts receivable, and accounts payable are common. Books that contain detailed coverage of small business bookkeeping explain how these ledgers work.

Two popular books are *Small Time Operator* by Bernard Kamoroff and *Keeping The Books* by Linda Pinson. Both are available at many public libraries, and both contain various blank ledgers that can be photocopied. These and similar books can also show you how to generate financial statements, such as a balance sheet, profit and loss statement, and cash flow statement. Note that accounting software can generate various reports automatically.

Accounts Receivable Ledger

An accounts receivable ledger contains a record of payments owed to you by clients. Typically, invoices are left for maintenance clients at the end of the month, and payment is due within a designated time period. Net 10, for instance, means that pay-

Accounting Software

Accounting software has advantages and disadvantages. One of the drawbacks of accounting software is that—because complex functions are performed automatically—some users may occasionally find it difficult to understand where a figure came from or what it means. This is more likely to be the case for those who lack a basic understanding of accounting. Another drawback of accounting software is that it is subject to the general pitfalls of computer use, such as hard-drive crashes, viruses, theft, and other maladies. If these observations speak to you, remember that hand-entry bookkeeping systems are acceptable. For some businesses, hand-entry methods may require less time and involvement than accounting software.

One advantage of accounting software is that it puts more advanced forms of accounting at your fingertips. Financial reports that can take considerable time to create by hand are generated automatically, and the complexities of double-entry accounting take place behind the scenes. If your business is anything other than the simplest one-person service enterprise, odds are that accounting software will increase your accounting accuracy and provide you with more complete financial information. As a side note, software simplifies the process of maintaining inventory records; this can prompt you to begin reselling materials if you are not already. If you keep an inventory, you should strongly consider using accounting software.

The learning curve for most accounting software is relatively short. Some software comes with tutorials that simplify the learning process. Nevertheless, a basic familiarity with bookkeeping is necessary. For a fee, an accountant can help you set up the software to match your business and get you started on a bookkeeping regimen.

ment is due within 10 days from the date the client receives the invoice.

One way to set up an accounts receivable ledger is to list each client on a separate ledger page. Each time you leave an invoice for a client, you make an entry into the accounts receivable ledger. Each accounts receivable entry should have the client's contact information at the top and columns to record invoice and payment history.

Columns should include the invoice date, invoice number, the amount, and the terms (e.g., net 10). When you receive payment from a client, use additional columns to record the date payment was received, the amount of payment, and the balance owed by the client. This format makes it easy to see which clients are paid up and which have outstanding balances. Accounting software automatically makes an entry into an accounts receivable ledger when an invoice is created or when a payment is entered.

Mileage Logbook

The IRS gives you a choice of claiming your actual business vehicle expenses or of using the standard mileage rate deduction, which reimburses business mileage at a flat rate that changes each year. In 2018, the standard mileage rate is 54.5 cents per mile (though only 18 cents per mile for medical or moving purposes and 14 cents per mile in the service of charitable organizations). In 2019, the standard mileage rate is 58 cents per mile (though only 20 cents per mile for medical or moving purposes and

14 cents per mile in the service of charitable organizations). Search online each year for "IRS standard mileage rate" for the most current information.

Your first year in business you must decide which of these methods you will use to claim vehicle expenses related to your business. If, during the first year, you choose to claim your actual vehicle expenses on tax returns, you cannot later switch to using the standard mileage rate deduction for that vehicle. And if you own or lease more than five vehicles that are used for business at the same time, you cannot use the standard mileage rate deduction.

The advantages of the standard mileage rate deduction are that it is simple to use, and you can change to claiming actual expenses later if you choose to. It may be helpful to keep track of vehicle expenses the first year to determine which method allows you to deduct more. An accountant or tax preparer can help you make the right choice for your business.

The IRS requires you to keep a mileage logbook regardless of which deduction method you use. The logbook supports the mileage claims associated with the business use of your vehicle. To document your business mileage, write down the date you began using the vehicle for business and the starting odometer reading in a small notebook to be kept in your truck. Each time you use your vehicle for business, record the date, the destination (e.g., "state university"), the number of business miles driven that day, and the reason for the trip (e.g., "integrated pest management course").

For a maintenance route, don't count the miles it takes you to drive from your residence to the first job, and don't count the miles it takes you to drive from your last job home. The IRS considers these miles "non-deductible commuting expenses". (If the accounts are outside of your metropolitan area, the commuting mileage may be deductible. IRS Publication 463 has the details.) At the end of the year, write down the ending odometer, the total miles you drove for the year, and the total number of business miles you drove. For more information, see "Car and Truck Expenses" on page 225.

Tip: Paying an auto shop to perform routine maintenance (e.g., tune up or oil change) near the end of each year will provide you with independent verification of the vehicle's odometer reading. IRS auditors sometimes request this independent verification when actual vehicle expenses are claimed (Fujie 2009).

CHAPTER 15

Taxes

- Federal taxes
- Schedule C
- Home office deductions
- Schedule SE
- Form 1040-ES
- Tax professionals
- Audits
- The tax benefits of retirement plans

Business owners are required to file and pay federal taxes to the Internal Revenue Service (IRS), which is the government agency in charge of collecting federal taxes and enforcing internal revenue laws. The IRS abides by federal laws that govern what you can and cannot be taxed on. In addition to federal taxes, you may also need to pay state and local taxes. Many cities base small business taxes on gross income and collect at the time of business license renewal. You can find links to the websites of state tax agencies through the Small Business Administration website at http://www.sba.gov/content/learn-about-your-state-and-local-tax-obligations.

This chapter looks at some federal tax forms required by sole proprietors and explains a few ways to legally maximize your deductions. The tax forms mentioned here may not be the only ones sole proprietors are required to file, and coverage of topics is not intended to be complete. Note that this chapter does not cover taxes for businesses structured as partnerships, corporations, or LLCs; payroll taxes and sales tax are also not covered.

If you do your own taxes, you will need to read the pertinent IRS publications and the IRS instructions for the forms in question. Included below are a few IRS publications where you can find more comprehensive tax information. *Always consult the current year's IRS publications for the most up-to-date information.*

- Publication 583 *Starting a Business and Keeping Records*
- Publication 334 *Tax Guide for Small Business*
- Publication 535 *Business Expenses*
- Publication 463 *Travel, Entertainment, Gift, and Car Expenses*
- Publication 587 *Business Use of Your Home*
- Publication 946 *How to Depreciate Property*
- Publication 505 *Tax Withholding and Estimated Tax*
- Publication 4035 *Home-Based Business Tax Avoidance Schemes*
- Publication 560 *Retirement Plans for Small Business*
- Publication 590-A *Contributions to Individual Retirement Arrangements* (Publication 590-B covers distributions.)

IRS Publications can be downloaded from the IRS website at http://www.irs.gov or requested by calling the IRS at 1-800-TAX-FORM (1-800-829-3676). Note that books on small business taxes cover many of the topics presented in IRS publications, in a way that is often easier to understand. A few notable books are *Tax Savvy for Small Business* by Fred Daily (Nolo) and *Taxe$ For Dummie$* by Eric Tyson, Margaret Munro, and David Silverman. Questions about how to complete your tax return can be directed to the Internal Revenue Service at 1-800-829-1040.

The laws and rules surrounding taxes are complex and change regularly—you can spend a great deal of time keeping up with the changes. Later, we look at some of the benefits of hiring a professional tax preparer. Money spent on professional tax preparation will help to ensure that your tax returns are completed correctly and will spare you many hours scrutinizing IRS publications.

Even if you hire a tax professional, you still need to understand the basics of small business tax preparation so you can provide your tax preparer with accurate, organized information, and so you can take maximum advantage of the legal tax reduction strategies available.

Federal Taxes

Federal taxes account for the bulk of your income tax and tax-related bookwork. Through a series of IRS forms, you systematically assess your income and expenses for the year and calculate how much money you owe the IRS.

Who has to file a tax return?

According to IRS Publication 334, "You have to file an income tax return for 2018 if your net earnings from self-employment were $400 or more. If your net earnings from self-employment were less than $400, you still have to file an income tax return if you meet any other filing requirement listed in the Form 1040 instructions."

Form 1040

Form 1040 helps you calculate your total annual income, allows for deductions and tax credits to reduce your tax burden, and helps you calculate what you owe the IRS. The concept is simple. It is the quantity of deductions and credits, and the volume of laws surrounding them that can make tax preparation complicated. You should be somewhat familiar with this form if you have filed taxes in the past. We do not examine the details of Form 1040 here.

If you have ever worked for someone else, calculating your income may have been as simple as copying your W-2 information into the appropriate box on Form 1040. As a self-employed person, you must determine your business income using an additional form called Schedule C. If you work for someone else and run your own business, you will use both the W-2 information and Schedule C when calculating your federal income tax.

Schedule C

Schedule C, *Profit or Loss From Business* is an attachment to Form 1040 that is used by sole proprietors. Sole proprietors file both Form 1040 and Schedule C. Small sole proprietorships that meet certain requirements may use a simpler form called Schedule C-EZ instead of Schedule C. Schedule C is the tax form most sole proprietors use.

Note that single-member limited liability companies (LLCs) also file Schedule C. However, businesses structured as partnerships and multimember LLCs do not file Schedule C. Business with these structures must file Form 1065 *U.S. Partnership Return of Income,* an information-only return (Daily 2005). The individual members of a partnership or multi-member LLC must also file Schedule E *Supplemental Income and Loss* (Kamoroff 2005). All business owners must file Form 1040.

Important: Partial descriptions of Schedule C categories are presented here to familiarize you with how this form works. To fill out Schedule C, you will need complete explanations and instructions: These are available in the IRS publication

Instructions for Schedule C, which is downloaded separately from the Schedule C tax form. (When downloading tax forms or instructions from the IRS website, be sure the correct year is listed in the title.) Tax professionals and qualified IRS employees can also answer questions pertaining to Schedule C. A reduced-scale copy of Schedule C is shown on page 228.

Schedule C, Part I: Gross Sales, Gross Profit, Gross Income

Part I of Schedule C is where you report your business income. If you are using the cash method of accounting, *gross receipts or sales* refers to the total income you received during the year. If you are using the accrual method, *gross receipts or sales* refers to the total sales you billed clients for services completed during the year.

Gross profit refers to your total annual sales minus the cost of returns and allowances, and minus the cost of goods sold. If you don't resell materials or products—and don't have returns or allowances—your gross profit will be the same as your gross sales. Your *gross income* is your business income before any deductions. Barring any other obscure income (described in detail in the instructions for Schedule C), your gross income will be the same as your gross profit.

Schedule C, Part II: Expenses

The expense section of Schedule C is where you deduct the cost of business expenses. This is one of the places you get to reduce the amount of money you will be taxed on. Keep in mind that the IRS only sends out audit notices when it thinks you've underpaid your taxes. Failing to claim all of your business expenses may not generate an inquiry from the IRS, but it means paying more taxes than you have to. Note that the expenses you do claim need to be well-documented. If you are audited, the IRS may ask to see your financial records. Audits are covered on page 232.

If you maintained an expenditure ledger throughout the year, completing the expense section may be as simple as entering the yearly totals from the expense categories into the appropriate lines on

Schedule C. If you did not maintain an expenditure ledger, you will need to take out your business expense receipts for the year and categorize your expenses.

Expense Categories

Schedule C has roughly 20 business expense categories. Partial category descriptions are provided here to demonstrate how a small landscape management business might categorize common expenses. Consult the IRS publication *Instructions for Schedule C* for complete instructions. If you are not sure where to categorize an expense or what a category includes, accountants and tax preparers can be of assistance. Note that personal deductions are never claimed on Schedule C.

Advertising: Classified advertising, copies for fliers, holiday cards for clients, a phone book ad, and business cards are some of the advertising expenses that can be claimed in this category.

Car and Truck Expenses: As explained in the bookkeeping chapter, you can deduct expenses related to the business use of your vehicle either by claiming your actual vehicle expenses or by using the standard mileage rate deduction. If you claim your actual expenses, you are allowed to deduct the cost of registration fees, lease payments, garage rent, licenses, repairs, gas, oil, tires, insurance, parking fees, tolls, and so on (IRS Publication 463).

If you use your vehicle for both business and personal use, you must determine the percentage of total yearly miles you used the vehicle for business, and you may only claim that percentage of your vehicle expenses. For example, if you drove 10,000 miles in one year, and 7,000 of that was for business, you may claim 70 percent of the cost of vehicle expenses. Claiming actual vehicle expenses also allows you to depreciate the cost of the vehicle itself, which is done on a separate line on Schedule C. These topics are explained in detail in IRS Publication 463, *Travel, Entertainment, Gift, and Car Expenses*. If you claim your actual vehicle expenses, you may also need to file Form 4562. See the IRS publication *Instructions for Schedule C* for more information.

The standard mileage rate deduction is a simple alternative to keeping track of your actual vehicle expenses. With this method, you multiply the total business miles you drove during the year—as recorded in your mileage logbook—and multiply this by the current standard mileage rate. In 2018, the rate is 54.5 cents per mile. In 2019, the rate is 58 cents per mile. See the topic "mileage logbook" in the Bookkeeping chapter for more details. The rate changes annually; occasionally it changes twice in a single tax year. You can find the current standard mileage rate in IRS Publication 463 or through a search on the IRS website. If you use the standard mileage rate, the only additional vehicle expenses that are deductible are parking, tolls, interest, and state and local taxes (Kamoroff 2005).

If you want to use the standard mileage rate, you must choose this method of deduction the year you begin using your vehicle for business. You cannot claim your actual vehicle expenses the first year, then switch to using the standard mileage rate after a few years. However, you can claim the standard mileage rate deduction in the first year, then switch to claiming actual vehicle expenses in later years. For this reason, and for overall simplicity, it makes sense to use the standard mileage rate the first year.

Consider keeping track of your actual vehicle expenses the first year to determine which method allows you to deduct the most. For more information, see "Mileage Logbook" on page 221. For complete instructions, see IRS Publication 463, *Travel, Entertainment, Gift, and Car Expenses.* Note: When claiming car and truck expenses, you may need to complete Part IV of Schedule C.

Contract labor: The yearly total paid for contract labor can be deducted here. Don't use this category to claim salaries and wages paid to employees. Other exceptions exist; see the IRS publication *Instructions for Schedule C.*

Depreciation and Section 179: Business property that has a useful life of "substantially beyond the tax year" is called a capital expense and needs to be claimed in smaller amounts over several years. This "spread out" method of deduction is called depreciation. Depreciation is a complex subject, and the laws surrounding it change frequently. It is in your best interest to hire a professional tax preparer for this work to ensure that it is done correctly. The tax preparer will need to know the cost of each depreciable item and the date you began using the item for business. Depreciation is done with IRS Form 4562, *Depreciation and Amortization.*

Section 179 of the Internal Revenue Code allows you to deduct the full cost of many capital expenses in a single tax year (up to $1 million in 2018, adjusted for inflation thereafter; check Section 179 annually for the current figure). This will mean a larger expense deduction in that year than if you had depreciated the item. Note that the equipment must be placed in service the same tax year the deduction is taken.

You can choose to depreciate capital expenses or deduct them in full in a single tax year under Section 179. There are benefits to either method, depending on your financial circumstances. For example, if you buy a lot of equipment in the first year, but your income is modest, it might be in your best interest to depreciate at least some of the items to spread out your tax cuts over several years. An accountant or professional tax preparer can help with these types of decisions. In general, capital expenses over $500 (e.g., lawn mowers) are depreciated, and capital expenses under $500 (e.g., handheld power tools) are claimed under Section 179.

Special deduction rules apply to equipment that is not used strictly for business (e.g., a computer). See "Deducting Office Supplies and Equipment" on page 230 for more information. Note that some business expenses incurred before you start your business are considered capital expenses and are handled differently for tax purposes. See "Start-up Expenses" on the next page.

Employee benefit programs: If you have employees, you would deduct costs such as employee health or life insurance premiums here. You deduct the cost of your own health insurance on Form 1040. Note that the Self-Employed Health Insurance Deduction on Form 1040 may allow you to deduct 100 percent of the amount you paid for medical

Start-up Expenses

Business purchases made before starting your business are known as start-up expenses. In 2018, up to $5,000 worth of expenses that qualify as start-up expenses can be deducted in your first year in business. Start-up expenses exceeding $5,000 need to be spread out (amortized) over 15 years. You must attach a Section 195 statement to your tax return when claiming start-up expenses. IRS Publication 535 *Business Expenses* has more information. Note that certain business expenses (e.g., long-term assets, such as power equipment and computers) are not deducted as start-up expenses even if you purchase them before starting your business. Because of these and other complexities, it is a good idea to consult with a professional tax preparer when claiming start-up expenses.

and dental insurance for yourself, your spouse, and your dependents (Publication 535).

Insurance (other than health): This category is used to deduct the cost of your business insurance, such as general liability.

Interest: Use this category to deduct the interest on business mortgages and loans. Interest paid on credit cards for business purchases can also be claimed here. If you receive a Form 1098 (or similar) from the lending institution, enter the interest on line 16a. Other interest is entered on line 16b. IRS Publication 535 explains business interest expenses in detail.

Legal and Professional Services: This category is used to deduct business-related professional fees, such as legal fees, accounting fees, and professional tax preparation fees related to your business.

Office Expense: This category is used for business-related office expenses, such as invoice pads, ledger notebooks, envelopes, and paper.

Pension and profit-sharing plans: Contributions to a pension, annuity, or other plan for employees can be claimed here.

Rent or Lease: On line 20a you can claim equipment rental expenses such as the cost of renting a lawn aerator. The cost of business vehicle leases or rentals can also be deducted here. (Different rules apply to vehicles rented or leased for more than 30 days.) On line 20b you can claim the cost to rent or lease property, such as a work space or storage unit.

Repairs and Maintenance: Equipment repairs, such as new air filters, spark plugs, and blades for lawn mowers, can go here. If you do your own repairs, do not deduct the value of your own labor. Note that repairs that add value or increase the life of a piece of equipment are considered improvements and must be depreciated or deducted under Section 179, which was described previously.

Supplies: This category is for supplies, such as gas for equipment, two-cycle mix, trimmer line, burlap tarps, PVC cement, and so on. Generally, for an item to be included in this category, it should be used up in the tax year it is claimed. You can also use this category to deduct the cost of purchases made for clients during the year. For example, if you purchased several plants and a bag of potting soil for a client, and the client reimbursed you, the cost for these materials would be included here. If you don't include the cost of these purchases, you will wind up paying income tax on the amount. If you keep an inventory, do not include items that you sold that were part of your inventory; these are accounted for under "cost of goods sold" in Part I of Schedule C, not here.

SCHEDULE C (Form 1040)	**Profit or Loss From Business** (Sole Proprietorship)	OMB No. 1545-0074
Department of the Treasury Internal Revenue Service (99)	▶ Go to *www.irs.gov/ScheduleC* for instructions and the latest information. ▶ Attach to Form 1040, 1040NR, or 1041; partnerships generally must file Form 1065.	**2018** Attachment Sequence No. **09**

Name of proprietor	Social security number (SSN)

A Principal business or profession, including product or service (see instructions)   **B** Enter code from instructions ▶

C Business name. If no separate business name, leave blank.   **D** Employer ID number (EIN) (see instr.)

E Business address (including suite or room no.) ▶ ....
City, town or post office, state, and ZIP code

F Accounting method: **(1)** ☐ Cash **(2)** ☐ Accrual **(3)** ☐ Other (specify) ▶ ....

G Did you "materially participate" in the operation of this business during 2018? If "No," see instructions for limit on losses . ☐ Yes ☐ No

H If you started or acquired this business during 2018, check here . . . . ▶ ☐

I Did you make any payments in 2018 that would require you to file Form(s) 1099? (see instructions) . . . . ☐ Yes ☐ No

J If "Yes," did you or will you file required Forms 1099? . . . . ☐ Yes ☐ No

Part I   Income

1	Gross receipts or sales. See instructions for line 1 and check the box if this income was reported to you on Form W-2 and the "Statutory employee" box on that form was checked . . . . ▶ ☐	1	
2	Returns and allowances	2	
3	Subtract line 2 from line 1	3	
4	Cost of goods sold (from line 42)	4	
5	**Gross profit.** Subtract line 4 from line 3	5	
6	Other income, including federal and state gasoline or fuel tax credit or refund (see instructions)	6	
7	**Gross income.** Add lines 5 and 6 . . . . ▶	7	

Part II   Expenses. Enter expenses for business use of your home **only** on line 30.

8	Advertising	8		18	Office expense (see instructions)	18
9	Car and truck expenses (see instructions)	9		19	Pension and profit-sharing plans .	19
10	Commissions and fees .	10		20	Rent or lease (see instructions):	
11	Contract labor (see instructions)	11		a	Vehicles, machinery, and equipment	20a
12	Depletion	12		b	Other business property . . .	20b
13	Depreciation and section 179 expense deduction (not included in Part III) (see instructions).	13		21	Repairs and maintenance . . .	21
				22	Supplies (not included in Part III)	22
				23	Taxes and licenses	23
				24	Travel and meals:	
14	Employee benefit programs (other than on line 19) . .	14		a	Travel	24a
15	Insurance (other than health)	15		b	Deductible meals (see instructions)	24b
16	Interest (see instructions):			25	Utilities	25
a	Mortgage (paid to banks, etc.)	16a		26	Wages (less employment credits) .	26
b	Other	16b		27a	Other expenses (from line 48) . .	27a
17	Legal and professional services	17		b	**Reserved for future use** . . .	27b

28	**Total expenses** before expenses for business use of home. Add lines 8 through 27a . . . . . . ▶	28	
29	Tentative profit or (loss). Subtract line 28 from line 7	29	
30	Expenses for business use of your home. Do not report these expenses elsewhere. Attach Form 8829 unless using the simplified method (see instructions). **Simplified method filers only:** enter the total square footage of: (a) your home: _____ and (b) the part of your home used for business: _____ . Use the Simplified Method Worksheet in the instructions to figure the amount to enter on line 30	30	
31	**Net profit or (loss).** Subtract line 30 from line 29. • If a profit, enter on both **Schedule 1 (Form 1040), line 12** (or **Form 1040NR, line 13**) and on **Schedule SE, line 2**. (If you checked the box on line 1, see instructions). Estates and trusts, enter on **Form 1041, line 3.** • If a loss, you **must** go to line 32.	31	
32	If you have a loss, check the box that describes your investment in this activity (see instructions). • If you checked 32a, enter the loss on both **Schedule 1 (Form 1040), line 12** (or **Form 1040NR, line 13**) and on **Schedule SE, line 2**. (If you checked the box on line 1, see the line 31 instructions.) Estates and trusts, enter on **Form 1041, line 3.** • If you checked 32b, you **must** attach Form 6198. Your loss may be limited.	32a ☐ All investment is at risk. 32b ☐ Some investment is not at risk.

For Paperwork Reduction Act Notice, see the separate instructions.   Cat. No. 11334P   Schedule C (Form 1040) 2018

This is a reduced-scale copy of IRS 2018 Schedule C, Profit or Loss From Business; page 1 of 2. Page 2 is not included here. Reproduced for instructional purposes only.

Taxes and Licenses: If you have employees, you would use this category to deduct what you pay for their Social Security, Medicare, and federal unemployment taxes. These deductions must be reduced according to rules spelled out in *Instructions for Schedule C.* You can also use this category to deduct certain sales taxes, as well as license fees, such as business license renewal fees and certified pest control applicator's licensing fees. Of course, you cannot claim state or federal taxes as an expense. However, one-half of your self-employment tax (see "Schedule SE", next page) can be deducted on Form 1040.

Travel, Meals, and Entertainment: The IRS examines these business expenses closely because some small business owners attempt to categorize personal expenses here. As a landscape gardener, you probably won't have many expenses in this category, and the IRS is aware of this. If you have legitimate travel, meal, or entertainment expenses related to your business, of course claim them, but have records to back up your claims.

Utilities: If you have utilities costs (e.g., water, gas, electricity) associated with a rented office or warehouse space for your business, you would deduct these costs here. If you claim a home office, don't deduct home-office utilities here; these are claimed on Form 8829 and entered on line 30 of Schedule C.

Wages: This category is used to claim the total salaries and wages paid to employees during the tax year. Salaries paid to yourself are not included.

Other Expenses: This category can be used to claim expenses you are unable to categorize elsewhere. Deductions for this line are itemized in Part V of Schedule C. For example, you might deduct the cost of trade magazines or this book under the heading "publications". An accountant or professional tax preparer can offer advice on what expenses to categorize here and how to name them. If you use the accrual method of accounting, this category can also be used to claim bad debts.

Table 19. Home-Office Deduction Requirements

Your use of the business part of your home must be:

- Exclusive,

- Regular, and

- For your trade or business,

AND The business part of your home must be one of the following:

- Your principal place of business,

- A place where you meet and deal with customers in the normal course of your trade or business, or

- A separate structure you use in connection with your trade or business.

Adapted from IRS Publication 4035, "Home-Based Business Tax Avoidance Schemes".

Home Office Deductions

A home office deduction is a special deduction that allows you to deduct a portion of the mortgage interest, insurance, depreciation (or rent), real estate taxes, utilities, painting, and repairs related to the business use of your home. Many of these expenses you would not otherwise be able to deduct. The home office deduction is calculated on IRS Form 8829, *Expenses for Business Use of Your Home* and the amount is entered on line 30 of Schedule C.

Home office deductions are based on the percentage of your total living space used exclusively for business. To illustrate: if the electricity bill for your home comes to $1200 for the year, and you use 10 percent of your home exclusively for business, you can claim 10 percent of $1200 ($120) for electricity costs. Homeowners or renters can claim a home office deduction if the requirements in table 19 are met.

According to the *Instructions for Form 8829*, your home office qualifies as your principal place of business if the following requirements are met:

- You use it exclusively and regularly for administrative or management activities of your trade or business. (Continued, next page.)

- You have no other fixed location where you conduct substantial administrative or management activities of your trade or business.

The instructions for Form 8829 go on to give a few examples of administrative or management activities. They are:

- Billing customers, clients, or patients.
- Keeping books and records.
- Ordering supplies.
- Setting up appointments.
- Forwarding orders or writing reports.

Conclusion: The rules suggest that if you set up an area of your home to be used exclusively for business-related bookwork and managerial tasks and use that area regularly, you can claim the home office deduction. If you are still in doubt, Publication 587 *Business Use of Your Home* provides several examples that clear the issue up considerably.

You must also properly set up your home office to qualify for the home office deduction—the IRS has strict rules on this matter. For example, the space must only be used for business; personal use of the space is not allowed. It is a good idea to consult with a tax professional to ensure you qualify for the home office deduction and to learn how to properly set up your home office. For additional information, consult IRS Publication *Instructions for Form 8829* or IRS Publication 587 *Business Use of Your Home*.

Deducting Office Supplies and Equipment

You do not need to meet the requirements of the home office deduction to deduct office-related business expenses (e.g., office supplies, postage) or to depreciate (or claim under Section 179) the cost of office equipment designated for business use (e.g., computer, printer, fax machine, office

furniture) (Steingold 2005). Since computers are an integral part of most small businesses today, you may be able to deduct a percentage of the cost of a computer even if it is not used strictly for business. The deduction is based on the percentage of time the computer is used for business. Consult with an accountant for specifics.

Schedule SE

Schedule SE is an attachment to Form 1040 that is used to calculate self-employment tax. You must file Schedule SE (or short Schedule SE, if you qualify) if your business has net earnings of $400 or more in a given year, as calculated on Schedule SE. Self-employment tax goes to Social Security and Medicare. When you worked for someone else, your employer deducted Social Security and Medicare taxes from your paycheck and matched those deductions. In other words, you paid half and your employer paid the other half. When you are self-employed, you must pay the entire amount yourself. This comes to 15.3 percent (12.4% to Social Security and 2.9% to Medicare) of your net self-employment income for the first $128,400 for 2018; other rules apply if your net income is greater. As you can see, this is a significant addition to your tax burden. A small consolation is that you get to deduct one-half of your self-employment tax on Form 1040.

Form 1040-ES

When you work for someone else, your employer withdraws taxes from your paycheck and deposits them with the IRS on a regular basis. As a business owner, you are required to make estimated tax payments during the year if you expect to owe at least $1000 in federal taxes that year (as of 2018; see the most current IRS Form 1040-ES for details).

Form 1040-ES *Estimated Tax for Individuals* includes instructions and an estimated tax worksheet to help you calculate the payment amounts. It also includes the payment vouchers that need to be filled out and mailed to the IRS with your estimated tax payments. Payments can also be made by credit card over the phone, by electronic funds withdrawal, or online through the Electronic Federal Tax Payment System (EFTPS; http://www.eftps.

gov). Payments are due four times a year, explaining why they are sometimes called "quarterlies". The payment deadlines are approximately April 15, June 15, September 15, and January 15. April 15 is the first payment, and January 15 is the fourth payment. See the current Form 1040-ES for exact deadline dates.

Your estimated tax payments must be a minimum of 90 percent of your current year's taxes (see Form 1040-ES for exceptions). If what you pay in estimated tax payments turns out to be less than 90 percent of what you end up owing in taxes for the year, you will need to pay the extra taxes and a penalty. You can calculate this penalty using Form 2210 *Underpayment of Estimated Tax by Individuals, Estates, and Trusts,* or you can let the IRS calculate the penalty for you, which it recommends. Form 2210 also lets you request a penalty waiver.

You can avoid the risk of penalties by basing your estimated tax payments on 100 percent of the previous year's tax total (see Form 1040-ES for exceptions). For example, if you paid $8,000 in taxes the previous year, you can avoid the risk of penalties by making four estimated tax payments of $2000 each. By paying 100 percent of last year's tax total in the current year's estimated payments, you cannot be charged a penalty for underpayment of estimated taxes, even if your current year's taxes turn out to be more than the previous year's. You can use this method even if you were not in business the previous year (Kamoroff 2005).

A professional tax preparer can calculate your estimated tax payments for the upcoming year and provide you with payment vouchers. If you overpay in estimated taxes, you will get a refund.

Tax Professionals

It takes significant time and effort to stay on top of the complex and ever-changing tax laws and requirements. To lighten the work load, many small business owners hire a tax professional to complete their tax returns. A tax professional can help you claim all the deductions you are entitled to and ensure that your tax returns are completed correctly. The latter point is particularly important because the IRS audits small businesses more frequently than wage earners.

The four categories of tax professionals are tax preparers, enrolled agents (EAs), certified public accountants (CPAs), and tax attorneys. Tax attorneys are the most expensive and don't usually prepare taxes for small, service-based businesses. Of the three other types of tax professionals, CPAs have the most relevant training and education. Some preparers and EAs are knowledgeable enough to handle small business taxes. Small business taxes are routine for CPAs.

Many CPAs charge approximately $100 per hour, some charge more. CPA tax preparation for a simple small business can be less than $200. Considering the importance of tax preparation, this is reasonable. Friends or family may be able to refer you to an experienced CPA, or you can search in the phone book. When you contact a tax professional, inquire about hourly rates and tax-related services. How much experience does the person have working with small businesses? Is the person willing to answer questions by phone and email? How much of the work is performed by assistants? Is the person available to represent you in an audit?

Once you select a tax professional, ask the person about any procedures you must follow, such as completing questionnaires or emailing PDF files of financial reports generated by your accounting software. Once you learn your tax advisor's system, tax preparation can be a simple year-end procedure requiring minimal time. In general, it will save your preparer time if you provide the information required on Schedule C. This includes categorizing your business expenses and providing a total for each expense category.

Tax Software

Tax preparation software simplifies filling out federal and state tax forms by providing you with questionnaires and step-by-step instructions that walk you through the completion of your returns. Some tax preparation software companies have begun to offer web-based tax preparation, sometimes for free. A number of these online services

Length of Time to Keep Records

Generally, you must keep a tax return—or a record that substantiates an item on a tax return, such as an income or expense receipt—until the period of limitations runs out. The period of limitations is the length of time you have to amend the tax return to claim a credit or refund, or the length of time the IRS has to audit the tax return. IRS Publication 583, *Starting a Business and Keeping Records* gives the period of limitations for a number of circumstances.

In general, if you owe additional tax on a tax return, the period of limitations is three years; if you underreport your gross income on a return by more than 25 percent, the period is six years; and if you file a fraudulent return or did not file a return, the period is not limited. Regardless, it is prudent to keep your tax returns indefinitely and to keep supporting documents at least six years after you file a return—or indefinitely if you file a fraudulent return (Fishman 2005). See IRS Publication 583, *Starting a Business and Keeping Records* for more details.

can complete returns for small businesses. Check to see that the software supports Schedule C and any other IRS forms you must file. The company should be an authorized IRS e-file provider. A web search for "free federal and state return preparation", or similar, will turn up companies providing this service.

Audits

An audit is a procedure the IRS uses to investigate your business and the accuracy of your tax return. Most audits involve a specific area of your tax return that the IRS wants to see supporting documentation for. Small business owners have a greater chance of being audited by the IRS than the average wage-earner. That is because we are allowed more discretion when claiming income and deductions. Still, the IRS only audits 3 to 5 percent of all sole proprietors (Kamoroff 2005). Being selected for an audit does not necessarily mean that you have made an error on your return or that you are being accused of dishonesty. However, in the majority of audits, the taxpayer ends up owing more money.

The IRS uses a several methods to select tax returns for audit. In one method, a computer program called the Discriminant Inventory Function system (DIF) gives each return a numeric score, rating the return for its potential for unreported income. The returns with the highest scores get screened by IRS personnel, who then select some for audit.

Discrepancies between reported income and 1099 forms filed about income you received can also result in an audit. Even simple errors on your return can increase your chance of being audited. This is another reason to hire a tax professional to prepare your tax return. Professionals have the experience and knowledge to spot items on your return that might raise a red flag with the IRS, and they are less likely to make simple errors when completing your return.

Audits can take place at an IRS office (office audit), at your place of business (field audit), or by mail (correspondence audits). The audit notification will say what documentation the IRS agent will want to see. You are not required to discuss areas of your return that are not mentioned in the audit letter.

You can choose to have a tax advisor (an EA, CPA, or attorney) represent you in an audit, and it is probably a good idea to do so. Some tax professionals suggest that it is acceptable to represent yourself in an office audit (though, probably not a field audit) if you have kept good records and have nothing to hide (Daily 2005). Note that you can request representation in the middle of an audit. This is an important option to know about if you find yourself confused while representing yourself. The IRS has to stop asking you questions until you get representation.

Good records are your best resource in an audit. Keep all documentation pertaining to income and expenditures: insurance statements, mileage logbooks, ledgers, receipts, canceled checks, bank statements, and old tax returns, to name a few. If it is related to your taxes, hang onto it for a minimum of three years—six years to be safe. This is the usual amount of time the IRS has to audit you, though exceptions exist. See the sidebar for details on how long to keep tax returns and records. If the IRS ever requests documentation, send a copy and hang on to the original.

Besides audits, the IRS frequently sends out notices about such things as math errors, short payment amounts, penalties, or even a missing signature on a tax return. *Taxe$ For Dummie$* by Eric Tyson, Margaret Munro, and David Silverman has several detailed chapters on IRS notices and audits. It includes sample response letters and strategies for dealing with the IRS. *Tax Savvy for Small Business* by tax attorney Frederick Dailey includes several chapters on dealing with audits. Both of these books are available at many public libraries.

The Tax Benefits of Retirement Plans

Retirement plans provide small business owners and their employees a way to invest money tax-deferred for retirement. Contributions to a retirement plan are tax-deductible, and your investment appreciates tax-free until it is withdrawn. You pay taxes on the original contributions and any gains when you withdraw the money in retirement.

Assuming your income is lower in retirement than it is now, the money will be taxed at a lower rate when you withdraw it. Even if your tax rate is higher in retirement than it is now, you are still likely to come out ahead because of the compounding effect of the tax-deferred gains (Tyson and Silverman

1997). Unlike other investments, money cannot be withdrawn from a retirement plan before the age of 59 1/2 without facing early withdrawal penalties. Some exceptions exist.

While disciplined contributions to a retirement plan can result in a comfortable retirement, they can also help you reduce your taxes. By making contributions to your plan, it may be possible to reduce your tax bill by hundreds, if not thousands of dollars each year. For instance, if your taxes amount to approximately 30 percent of your earnings, a $2000 contribution to a retirement plan might save you $600 in taxes that year. Obviously, this is a simplified example, and tax computation is not this straightforward, but the point is that retirement plans afford you the opportunity to take large tax deductions.

Small business owners have the option of investing in various retirement plans, including employee pension plans (SEP), savings incentive match plan for employees (SIMPLE), qualified plans such as 401(k) plans and Keogh plans, and individual retirement arrangements (IRAs).

Plans commonly differ in their annual contribution limits, rules regarding employees, and withdrawal rules. For example, the annual contribution limit for an IRA in 2018 is $5500 ($6500 if you will be 50 or older by the end of the year). For 2019, the annual contribution limit for an IRA is $6000 ($7000 if you will be 50 or older by the end of the year). See the current year's IRS Publication 590-A for the latest figures. You can set up an IRA for yourself even if you have employees. There is a 10 percent penalty for early withdrawal. The Roth IRA is different from most retirement plans in that contributions are not tax-deductible. However, the money in a Roth IRA appreciates tax-free and *withdrawals* are not taxable so long as they are made after the age of 59 1/2. Contributions to IRAs are covered in IRS Publication 590-A, *Contributions to Individual Retirement Arrangements*.

Other retirement plans have significantly higher contribution limits. For example, in 2018, SEP IRAs allow contributions of up to 25 percent of your net earnings from self-employment a year, not to exceed $55,000 ($56,000 in 2019). Note that special rules apply when figuring the maximum deductible contribution when you are self-employed. IRS Publication 560 has the details. SEPs, SIMPLE, and qualified plans are explained in IRS Publication 560, *Retirement Plans for Small Business.* Granted, reading about retirement plan rules is not all that enjoyable, but tax savings are available, and professional consultants can provide guidance.

The annual contribution deadline for traditional and Roth IRAs is April 15—the due date of your tax return. (In general, the contribution deadline for non-IRA plans is the due date of the return, including any valid filing extensions.) In other words, contributions to your retirement plan for 2018 can be made throughout 2018 and up to April 15 of 2019, provided you don't exceed your plan's contribution limit. This gives you a few extra months to raise money to contribute to your plan, and it is a rare way to reduce your tax bill once the tax year is over.

In addition to choosing a plan, you also need to decide what to invest in. Stocks, bonds, CDs, and mutual funds are some of the choices. Once you set up a retirement plan, it is not difficult to change your investments. However, changing your retirement plan itself can prove more complicated. A professional consultant can help you choose a retirement plan and investments that will meet your criteria. Select an advisor who will provide you with objective information and guidance that is in your best interest. This usually means paying an independent consultant on an hourly flat-fee basis, not on commission for investments sold (Daily 2005). Your accountant may be able to recommend someone.

Use caution and common sense in the arena of financial advice and investing. Know where your money is going, how to monitor it, how to access it if you need to, and what the risks are. Finally, consult with your financial advisor before withdrawing money from a retirement plan.

Part IV

Appendixes

Appendix A: Resources

There are many good resources in landscaping and small business. Here is a partial list of books, trade publications, and trade associations. Many of these books can be found at public or university libraries.

Landscape Management Books

The American Horticultural Society (publisher Dorling Kindersley) has a number of high-quality gardening books. *The American Horticultural Society, Pests and Diseases* includes an A to Z plant guide listing common problems and treatments for each plant. *The American Horticultural Society A to Z Encyclopedia of Garden Plants* is a reference book containing over 15,000 ornamental plants and 6000 color photos.

Arboriculture: Integrated Management of Landscape Trees, Shrubs, and Vines, by Harris, Clark, and Matheny (Prentice Hall). This text is detailed while remaining readable.

Drip Irrigation For Every Landscape And All Climates, by Robert Kourik (Metamorphic Press). Kourik's book provides instruction on drip irrigation, and includes discussions of soil types and plant water requirements.

Ecological Golf Course Management, by Paul Sachs and Richard Luff (Wiley). A wealth of information on ecological turfgrass management.

Edaphos: Dynamics of a Natural Soil System, by Paul Sachs (The Edaphic Press) is an interesting introduction to soil, particularly the role of organic matter in soils.

Fundamentals of Turfgrass Management, by Nick Christians (Wiley). A popular textbook for many introductory turfgrass management courses.

Landscape Plants for California Gardens, by Bob Perry (Land Design Publishing). A detailed plant selection guide for California.

Manual of Woody Landscape Plants: Their Identification, Ornamental Characteristics, Culture, Propagation and Uses, by Michael A. Dirr (Stipes).

Professional Landscape Management, by David L. Hensley (Stipes). Coverage of many landscape management practices. Includes in-depth coverage of specifications and contracts suitable for commercial maintenance.

Sunset Western Garden Book, by the editors of Sunset Books and Sunset Magazine. This book provides detailed information on the climate zones in the west. It contains an encyclopedia of plants and a section on plant selection. Sunset has also published *Sunset National Garden Book* and *Sunset Northeastern Garden Book.*

Pruning Books

The American Horticultural Society Pruning & Training; A Fully Illustrated Plant-by-Plant Manual, by Christopher Brickell and David Joyce (Dorling Kindersley). This book includes instructive photographs and diagrams.

The Home Orchard: Growing Your Own Deciduous Fruit and Nut Trees (ANR Pub. 3485), by Ingels, Geisel, and Norton (University of California Agriculture & Natural Resources).

An Illustrated Guide to Pruning, by Edward F. Gilman (Delmar). Includes detailed coverage of the pruning and training of landscape trees.

Small-Business Books

The Employer's Legal Handbook, by Fred S. Steingold and Amy Delpo. This book provides in-depth coverage of many aspects of being an employer.

How To Price Landscape & Irrigation Projects by James R. Huston MBA, CPE (J. R. Huston Enterprises, Inc. 2003). Described in the chapter "Calculating an Accurate Hourly Rate", this 600-page book is an authoritative text on job pricing for the green industry. It includes detailed instruction on a broad range of bidding situations. The book includes numerous worksheets, forms, and sample bids.

Keeping the Books: Basic Recordkeeping and Accounting for the Successful Small Business, by Linda Pinson (Kaplan Business). An introduction to bookkeeping and accounting. Includes ledger forms that can be photocopied.

Legal Guide for Starting & Running a Small Business Volume 1, by attorney Fred S. Steingold. This is one among many law and business books produced by Nolo Press. Steingold explains the legal side of what small business owners need to know. The book covers licensing, employer matters, tax requirements, insurance, and more.

Small Time Operator: How to Start Your Own Business, Keep Your Books, Pay Your Taxes & Stay Out of Trouble, by Bernard Kamoroff, CPA (Bell Springs). A popular small business book that covers many bookkeeping and tax-related topics. Includes ledger forms that can be photocopied.

Tax Books and Publications

Deduct It! Lower Your Small Business Taxes, by Stephen Fishman (Nolo) details the many tax deductions available to small business owners.

Tax Savvy for Small Business, by Fred Daily (Nolo). A readable overview of tax fundamentals for small businesses. Includes coverage of business entities and chapters on dealing with audits.

Taxe$ For Dummie$, by Eric Tyson, MBA and David Silverman, EA (For Dummies). Explains the myriad of tax forms and procedures. Tax forms, including Schedule C, are explained line for line. Includes sections on dealing with IRS notices and audits.

Some free IRS publications are listed on page 213 and page 223. IRS publications can be requested by phone at 1-800-829-3676. Publications are also available through the IRS website at http://www.irs.gov.

Scheduling and Billing Software

Scheduling and billing software streamlines common business management tasks including route designation, job costing assistance, crew assignment, invoice creation, estimate creation, accounts receivable, client history, sales tax reports, scheduling/tracking chemical applications, and more. A few of the products available are Groundskeeper Pro (Adkad Technologies, Inc., http://www.adkad.com), Gopher Billing and Scheduling Software (Ditech, http://www.gophersoftware.com), LawnPro (http://www.lawnprosoftware.com), Clip (Sensible Software, Inc., http://www.clip.com), and LM Software (Alocet, Inc., http://www.alocet.com. Alocet also makes QXpress, a QuickBooks add on).

Online Landscaping Forums

A few of the many online forums are LawnSite.com, LawnCafe.com, GroundTradesXchange.com, LawnForums.com, Lawnserviceforum.com, and iVillage GardenWeb (http://forums.gardenweb.com/forums/).

Trade Publications

"Landscape Management" (http://www.landscape-management.net). Phone: 1-800-736-3665; see their practical research journal "Turfgrass Trends" at http://www.turfgrasstrends.com.

"Turf" (published by Moose River Media) is a magazine for landscape and lawn care professionals. The website is http://www.turfmagazine.com. Phone 802-748-8908.

"Grounds Maintenance" is a trade magazine for landscape professionals. Practical coverage of pest control, equipment, irrigation, and more: http://grounds-mag.com.

"Lawn & Landscape Magazine". Subscriptions can be obtained online along with access to their website: http://www.lawnandlandscape.com.

The Lawn Institute at http://www.lawninstitute.com has turf management tips. Phone: 1-800-405-8873 or 847-705-9898.

Professional Associations

PLANET, the Professional Landcare Network, is a large trade association serving the green industry. PLANET emerged in 2005 when the Associated Landscape Contractors of America (ALCA) joined forces with the Professional Lawn Care Association of America (PLCAA). PLANET can be found online at http://www.landcarenetwork.org or contacted by phone at 703-736-9666 or 1-800-395-2522.

Professional Grounds Management Society (PGMS) is a non-profit that provides its members with leading grounds management skills. This organization focuses on the needs of professionals responsible for the high-end grounds management of colleges, school districts, and more. Phone: 1-800-609-PGMS; http://www.pgms.org.

International Society of Arboriculture has information on becoming a certified arborist or tree worker. Phone: 1-888-472-8733; http://www.isa-arbor.com.

The Tree Care Industry Association (formerly the National Arborist Association). TCIA develops safety and education programs, standards of tree care practice, and management information for arboriculture firms worldwide. TCIA developed the ANSI A300 pruning and fertilization standards; http://www.tcia.org. Phone: 603-314-5380; 1-800-733-2622.

American Landscape Maintenance Association. In existence since 1988. http://www.almanow.com.

American Nursery & Landscape Association (ANLA). Phone: 202-789-2900; http://www.anla.org.

American Horticultural Society. Phone: 703-768-5700 or 1-800-777-7931; http://www.ahs.org.

The Irrigation Association. 6540 Arlington Blvd. Falls Church, VA 22042-6638. Phone: 703-536-7080.

American Water Works Association: http://www.awwa.org. Includes water conservation guidelines.

National Association for the Self Employed (NASE). This not-for-profit organization provides affordable health and other insurance packages to members. Phone:1-800-232-6273; http://www.nase.org.

Small Business Administration (SBA). The SBA partners with SCORE, Small Business Development Centers, and Women's Business Centers. You can find a regional SBA office in the phone book under the heading: United States Government Offices, or online at http://www.sba.gov.

Miscellaneous

Don Shor, owner of Redwood Barn Nursery, provides many informative horticulture articles on his website http://www.redwoodbarn.com.

The website of J.R. Huston Enterprises, Inc. sells books, CDs, and estimating software, and provides information on consulting and training by James Huston; http://www.jrhuston.biz.

Jess Stryker's Irrigation Tutorials contains an abundance of free irrigation information; http://www.irrigationtutorials.com.

Oregon, Blount's *Saw Chain, Guide Bar and Drive Sprocket Maintenance and Safety Manual* can be downloaded at http://www.oregonproducts.com/pro/pdf/maintenance_manual/ms_manual.

An excellent website for integrated pest management guidelines is UC IPM Online at http://www.ipm.ucdavis.edu.

Appendix B: Maintenance Package Rate Worksheet

Make photocopies of this worksheet to rework your maintenance package rates as needed. Estimates of hourly equipment costs are included in table 17 on page 186. For information on determining a monthly rate for maintenance accounts and to learn about staying profitable, see page 195. See chapter 11 beginning on page 181 for complete instruction.

Phase I: Production Costs

Phase I: Labor

Crew average wage or CAW: (total of all hourly wages paid divided by # of crew members): $_____

Overtime factor: _____ (as percent). Change to decimal and multiply by CAW: $_____

Risk factor: _____ (as percent). Change to decimal and multiply by CAW: $_____

Loaded crew average wage (loaded CAW; this is the CAW + overtime factor + risk factor): $_____

Production labor total: labor hours (hours spent at job sites per day) x loaded CAW = $_____

Phase I: Equipment

Add or subtract equipment to match daily equipment use in your business.

21" mower $_____/hr. x _____ hours = $_____

36" mower $_____/hr. x _____ hours = $_____

Clipper, edger, blower, etc. $_____/hr. x _____ hours (for all tools) = $_____

Production equipment total = $_____

Phase II: General Conditions

Phase II: Labor

Load/unload time per day _____ hours x _____ crew members = _____ x loaded CAW = $_____ load/unload cost per day.

Drive time per day _____ hours x _____ crew members = _____ x loaded CAW = $_____ drive time cost per day.

Break time per day _____ hours x _____ crew members = _____ x loaded CAW = $_____ break time cost per day.

Haul debris (labor) time per day _____ hours x _____ crew members = _____ x loaded CAW = $_____ haul debris cost per day.

General conditions labor total: (load/unload + drive time + break time + haul debris [labor]) = $_____

Phase II: Equipment

Haul debris (truck + trailer) $_____/hr. (combined) x _____ hours = $_____

Truck costs = $_____/hr. x _____ hours in workday = $_____

Trailer costs = $_____/hr. x _____ hours in workday = $_____

Materials, if applicable (e.g., average daily transfer station fee) = $_____

General conditions equipment total: (Haul debris + truck + trailer + materials) = $_____

Phase III: Markups and Margins

Labor total: (production labor total + general conditions labor total) = $_____

Labor burden: labor total x 30% = $_____

Equipment total: (production equipment total + general conditions equipment total) = $_____

Total direct costs or TDC: (labor total + labor burden + equipment total) = $_____

G&A Overhead

Overhead per year (see "G&A Overhead" on page 241): $_____

Projected billable field labor hours for the upcoming year (use average labor hours per week x weeks in work year [assume 4.33 wks/month]): _____

Overhead per hour (OPH; yearly overhead divided by projected yearly field labor hours) = $_____

Overhead for generic day = OPH x field labor hours in a generic day = $_____

Break even point or BEP: (add overhead for generic day to total direct costs to get BEP) = $_____

Net profit margin (NPM) percentage (see page 194): _____

Add the NPM: (BEP divided by 1.0 - NPM [as decimal]; see page 194) = _____

Final Price for generic day: $_____

Curb Time Rate

The curb time rate is the *final price* divided by production labor hours in the generic day. The curb time rate is your hourly rate for maintenance.

Curb time rate: $_____/hr.

Crew curb time rate: (curb time rate x number of crew members) $_____/hr.

Appendix C: Forms

Included here are two business forms that can be photocopied.

Invoice sheet: The invoice sheet can be personalized with a rubber stamp or letterhead and photocopied at two per an 8.5" x 11" sheet of paper. For maintenance contracts, circle the maintenance month just completed. Fill out a copy of the invoice for yourself each time, and keep it for your records. Alternatively, you can use carbonless invoices. Note that it is illegal to place invoices in a client's mail box. Leave invoices half-way under a doormat or in another location where the client will easily find it.

Call Sheet: To record clients' contact information during the initial call. Photocopy at greater than 100 percent to fill an 8.5" x 11" sheet of paper.

STATEMENT

Date _____

_____

_____

Maintenance: Jan Feb Mar Apr May Jun Jul Aug Sep Oct Nov Dec

Total:		

Name	Phone	Address	Date	Notes	Bid	Paid

Appendix D: Equivalents and Metric Conversion Tables

Measurement Equivalents (U.S.)

3 teaspoons (tsp) = 1 tablespoon (tbsp)

2 tablespoons = 1 fluid ounce (fl oz)

16 tablespoons = 1 cup

1 cup = 8 fluid ounces (fl oz)

2 cups = 1 pint* (pt)

2 pints = 1 quart (qt)

4 quarts = 1 gallon (gal)

*U.K. pint = 20 fluid ounces.

Conversion Factors for U.S. Customary Units to SI (International System) Units.*

SYMBOL	WHEN YOU KNOW	MULTIPLY BY	TO FIND	SYMBOL
in	inches	25.4	millimeters	mm
ft	feet	0.305	meters	m
yd	yards	0.914	meters	m
mi	miles	1.61	kilometers	km
in^2	square inches	645.2	square millimeters	mm^2
ft^2	square feet	0.093	square meters	m^2
yd^2	square yards	0.836	square meters	m^2
ac	acres	0.405	hectares	ha
mi^2	square miles	2.59	square kilometers	km^2
fl oz	fluid ounces	29.57	milliliters	mL
gal	gallons	3.785	liters	L
ft^3	cubic feet	0.028	cubic meters	m^3
yd^3	cubic yards	0.765	cubic meters	m^3
oz	ounces	28.35	grams	g
lb	pounds	0.454	kilograms	kg
T	tons (2000 lb)	0.907	metric ton	Mg ("t")
°F	Fahrenheit	(F-32)/1.8	Celsius	°C

*These conversion factors are approximate and suitable for measuring most landscape materials.

Appendix E: IFAS Extension Copyright

Included below are the footnotes and copyright information for the University of Florida IFAS Extension article *Considerations for Developing a Lawn and Landscape Maintenance Contract,* by Sydney Park Brown and Michael Holsinger, included in the Sample Maintenance Contract chapter.

Footnotes 1. This document is SS-ENH-09, which replaces Fact Sheet OHC-10, a series of the Environmental Horticulture Department, Florida Cooperative Extension Service, Institute of Food and Agricultural Sciences, University of Florida. First published: May 1994. Reviewed: January 1995. Revised: February 2001. Please visit the EDIS website at http://edis.ifas.ufl.edu. 2. Sydney Park Brown, extension agent, Environmental Horticulture, Hillsborough County; Michael J. Holsinger, extension agent, Environmental Horticulture, Sarasota County, Cooperative Extension Service, Institute of Food and Agricultural Sciences, University of Florida, Gainesville FL 32611. The use of trade names in this publication is solely for the purpose of providing specific information. UF/IFAS does not guarantee or warranty the products named, and references to them in this publication does not signify our approval to the exclusion of other products of suitable composition. The Institute of Food and Agricultural Sciences (IFAS) is an Equal Opportunity Institution authorized to provide research,educational information and other services only to individuals and institutions that function with non-discrimination with respect to race, creed, color, religion, age, disability, sex, sexual orientation, marital status, national origin, political opinions or affiliations. For more information on obtaining other extension publications, contact your county Cooperative Extension service. U.S. Department of Agriculture, Cooperative Extension Service, University of Florida, IFAS, Florida A. & M. University Cooperative Extension Program, and Boards of County Commissioners Cooperating. Larry Arrington, Dean.

References

Most of the internet addresses for online articles have changed since they were first accessed. For this reason, the internet addresses listed have been limited to the main domain.

Chapter 1: Starting a Landscape Management Business

"Do You Need a California Seller's Permit?" California State Board of Equalization Publication 107. March, 2005.

Pakroo, Peri. *The Small Business Start-Up Kit.* California: Nolo Press, 2004.

Steingold, Fred. *Legal Guide for Starting & Running a Small Business.* 8th ed. California: Nolo Press, 2005.

West Brittin, Jocelyn. "Selecting the Legal Structure of Your Business." U.S. Small Business Administration: Management and Planning Series, Document MP-25.

Chapter 2: Equipment and Supplies

Donahue, Sean. "Winterize Your Warm-Weather Power Equipment." Smart HomeOwner. Nov/Dec 2002. http://www.smart-homeowner.com.

Kerkhoff, Karen L. "How To: Store Equipment For Winter." Grounds Maintenance. November, 2005. http://www.grounds-mag.com.

Oredson, Jennifer. "Understanding Emissions Regulations." Grounds Maintenance. March, 2006. http://www.grounds-mag.com.

"Shindaiwa C4 Technology." Shindaiwa, Inc., 2006. http://www.shindaiwa.com.

"What Should I Do if I Won't Be Using My Unit For a Long Period of Time?" Echo FAQs. http://www.echo-usa.com.

Chapter 3: Safety

Berkow, Robert, M.D. ed. *The Merck Manual of Medical Information; Home Edition.* New Jersey: Merck Research Laboratories, 1997.

"Best Practices Guide: Fundamentals of a Workplace First-Aid Program." OSHA, 2006. http://www.osha.gov.

"Chainsaw Maintenance." Grounds Maintenance. April, 2001. http://www.grounds-mag.com.

"Definition of Hand-arm Vibration Syndrome." MedicineNet.com. September, 2006. http://www.medicinenet.com.

Eke, Tom, Sahar Al-Husainy, and Mathew K. Raynor, "The Spectrum of Ocular Inflammation Caused by Euphorbia Plant Sap." Arch Ophthalmol. 2000; 118: 13-16. http://archopht.ama-assn.org.

Eldridge, Bruce. "How to Manage Pests: Pests of Homes, Structures, People, and Pets: Mosquitoes." University of California Integrated Pest Management Online, 1998. http://www.axp.ipm.ucdavis.edu.

"Handle With Care." Grounds Maintenance. March, 2002. http://www.grounds-mag.com.

Kemper, Donald, and The Healthwise Staff. *Kaiser Permanente Healthwise Handbook; A Self-Care Guide For You And Your Family.* Idaho: Healthwise Publications, 1994.

"Kickback." Oregon Cutting Systems, 2009. http://www.oregonchain.com/kickback.htm.

"Leaf Blowers: A Guide to Safe And Courteous Use." OPEI, 2003. http://www.opei.org.

"Medical researchers: 80,000 injuries a year attributed to mower accidents." Landscape Management. November, 2006. http://www.landscapemanagement.net.

Mussen, E.C. "Yellowjackets And Other Social Wasps." University of California Integrated Pest Management Online. August, 2001. http://www.ipm.ucdavis.edu.

"OPEI Safety Manual: Think Safety and Environment with Power in Your Hands." Outdoor Power Equipment Institute, 2004. http://www.opei.org.

"OSHA Quick Card: Chainsaw Safety Tips." OSHA. http://www.osha.gov.

"OSHA Quick Card: Electrical Safety." OSHA. http://www.osha.gov.

"OSHA Quick Card: Respirators." OSHA. http://www.osha.gov.

"OSHA Quick Card: Rodents, Snakes and Insects." OSHA. http://www.osha.gov.

"OSHA Quick Card: Tree Trimming & Removal." OSHA. http://www.osha.gov.

"OSHA Quick Card: West Nile Virus." OSHA. http://www.osha.gov.

"OSHA Quick Card: Work Zone Traffic Safety." OSHA. http://www.osha.gov.

"Pesticide Safety." University of Illinois Extension. http://web.extension.uiuc.edu.

"Private Pesticide Applicator Training Manual." University of Minnesota Extension Service. http://www.extension.umn.

Ratcliff, Cindy. "Safety In Numbers." Grounds Maintenance. July, 2005. http://grounds-mag.com.

"Raynaud's Disease." Mayo Clinic. http://www.mayoclinic.com.

"Safety Meeting Topics: Portable Fire Extinguishers." State Compensation Insurance Fund, 2006. http://www.scif.com.

"Staying Safe At The Pump." API. September, 2006. http://www.api.org.

"The Straight Dope: Why Does Gasoline Go Stale So Quickly?" August, 2006. http://www.straightdope.com/columns/060825.html.

"Ticks." Northwest Mosquito And Vector Control District. http://www.northwestmosquitovector.org.

"Vibration White Finger." BBC News. January, 1999. http://news.bbc.co.uk/.

"Vibration White Finger." Repetitive Strain Injury Association. http://www.rsi.org.uk.

"West Nile Virus." U.S. Food and Drug Administration. August, 2007. http://www.fda.gov.

Chapter 4: Turfgrass Management

Adams, Nancy E. "Does Your Lawn Measure Up? Proper Application of Lawn Fertilizers." University of New Hampshire Cooperative Extension, 2003. http://ceinfo.unh.edu.

Allen, Phil S. and Donald B. White. "Lawn Clipping Management." University of Minnesota Extension Service. http://www.extension.umn.edu.

Anderson, Scott. "Area Calculations: Title Fertilizer and Lime Calculations." Spectrum Analytic Inc. http://www.spectrumanalytic.com.

Aveni, Marc and David Chalmers. "Aerating Your Lawn." Virginia Cooperative Extension. June, 2001. http://www.ext.vt.edu.

Brophy, Bob. "Perfect Timing." Grounds Maintenance. March, 2004. http://www.grounds-mag.com.

Broschat, Timothy, "Fertilization of Field-grown and Landscape Palms in Florida." (Publication #ENH1009). University of Florida IFAS Extension, 2008. http://edis.ifas.ufl.edu/ep261.

Christians, Nick. *Fundamentals of Turfgrass Management, Second Edition.* New Jersey: John Wiley and Sons, 2004.

Christians, Nick. *Fundamentals of Turfgrass Management, Third Edition.* New Jersey: John Wiley and Sons, 2007.

Costello, L.R., J.R. Clark, N.P. Matheny, K.S. Jones, "A Guide to Estimating Irrigation Water Needs of Landscape Plantings in California: The Landscape Coefficient Method and WUCOLS III." California Sate Department of Water Resources. http://www.water.ca.gov/wateruseefficiency/publications.

"Creating lawn mower stripes." Lawn and Mower, 2005. http://www.lawnandmower.com.

Delahaut, Karen. "Gardening and IPM." University of Wisconsin Horticultural Website: Landscape. http://wihort.uwex.edu.

DeOreo, William, Paul W. Lander, Russell J. Qualls Ph.D., and Joshua M. Scott. "Soil Moisture Sensors: Are They A Neglected Tool?" California Urban Water Conservation Council. http://www.cuwcc.org.

Duble, Richard L. "Water Management on Turfgrasses." Texas Cooperative Extension. http://texasextension.tamu.edu.

Dukes, Michael D. and Dorota Z. Haman. "Residential Irrigation System Rainfall Shutoff Devices." University of Florida IFAS Extension. http://edis.ifas.ufl.edu.

Ervin, Erik H. and Brad S. Fresenburg, and John H. Dunn. "Home Lawn Watering Guide." University of Missouri Extension, 1993. http://muextension.missouri.edu.

"Estimating Soil Moisture by Feel and Appearance Estimating Soil Moisture by Feel and Appearance." USDA. http://www.usda.gov.

Fishel, Fred. "Integrated Pest Management in Missouri's Green Industries." University of Missouri Extension, 1993. http://muextension.missouri.edu.

Gaussoin, Roch E. and Robert (Bob) Shearman. "Thatch Prevention and Control." University of Nebraska Lincoln, 1985. http://www.unl.edu.

Gelernter, Wendy and Larry Stowell. "Keeping an Eye On Nitrogen." Grounds Maintenance. April, 2006. http://grounds-mag.com.

"Getting A Handle On Debris." Grounds Maintenance. June, 2005. http://grounds-mag.com.

"Grass Growth and Regrowth for Improved Management." Oregon State. http://forages.oregonstate.edu.

Hale, Trent C. "Aerating Lawns." Clemson Extension. http://hgic.clemson.edu.

Haman, Dorota Z., Gary A. Clark, and Allen G. Smajstrla. "Irrigation of Lawns and Gardens." University of Florida IFAS Extension. http://edis.ifas.ufl.edu.

Harivandi, Ali and Victor A. Gibeault. "Mowing Your Lawn and 'Grasscycling'." UC Division of Agriculture and Natural Resources, 1999. http://danrcs.ucdavis.edu.

Huang, Bingru. "Grass Roots." Grounds Maintenance. April, 2006. http://grounds-mag.com.

Huck, Mike. "Irrigation Uniformity." Irrigation and Turfgrass Services. http://www.turf.msu.edu.

"Irrigation Notes: Scheduling Irrigation." Hunter Industries. June, 2005. http://www.hunterindustries.com.

"Irrigation Notes: Slope Irrigation." Hunter Industries. http://www.hunterindustries.com.

"Irrigation Notes: The Basics of Matched Precipitation." Hunter Industries. http://www.hunterindustries.com.

"IPM For Turfgrass in Schools." Bio-Integral Resource Center. http://www.birc.org.

"Keeping your lawn healthy and well-groomed." American-Lawns, 2001. http://www.american-lawns.com.

Kerkhoff, Karen L. "How To: Irrigate Slopes." Grounds Maintenance. June, 2005. http://grounds-mag.com.

Klocke, Norman L., Kenneth G. Hubbard, William L. Kranz, and Darrell G. Watts. "Evapotranspiration (ET) or Crop Water Use." University of Nebraska Lincoln. October, 1996. http://www.unl.edu.

Kussow, Wayne R. "Contributions of Nitrogen and Phosphorus to Surface and Groundwater from a Kentucky Bluegrass Lawn." University of Wisconsin-Madison. http://www.soils.wisc.edu.

Landry, Gil. "The Basics of Turfgrass Fertilization." Cooperative Extension Service: The University of Georgia College of Agricultural and Environmental Sciences. March, 2000. http://www.caes.uga.edu.

"Landscape Irrigation Scheduling and Water Management." Water Management Committee of The Irrigation Association. March, 2005.

Landschoot, Peter and Grady Miller. "Feast or Famine Fertility." Grounds Maintenance. April, 2003. http://grounds-mag.com.

Landschoot, Peter. "Turfgrass Fertilization: A Basic Guide for Professional Turfgrass Managers." Pennsylvania State University, 2003. http://turfgrassmanagement.psu.edu.

"Lawn Fertilization." Texas Cooperative Extension Horticulture. March, 2004. http://www.plantanswers.com.

Luff, Richard and Paul D. Sachs. *Ecological Golf Course Management.* New Jersey: John Wiley and Sons, 2002.

"L.R. Nelson Introduces Soil Moisture Sensor Irrigation Control." L.R. Nelson Press Releases. March, 2005. http://www.nelsonturf.com.

McCarty, L.B. "Integrated Pest Management Strategies." University of Florida IFAS Extension. http://edis.ifas.ufl.edu.

McCarty, L.B. and Jerry B. Sartain. "How to Calibrate Your Fertilizer Spreader." University of Florida IFAS Extension. http://edis.ifas.ufl.edu.

Mugaas, Robert J. "Lawn Care Practices to Reduce the Need for Fertilizers and Pesticides." University of Minnesota Extension Service, 1999. http://www.extension.umn.edu.

Mugaas, Robert J. "Responsible Fertilizer Practices for Lawns." University of Minnesota Extension Service, 1995. http://www.extension.umn.

Murphy, Tim R. "Maximize your pre-emergence herbicide performance." Athletic Turf. April, 2006. http://www.athleticturf.net.

Nees, Allen. "Enhancing Efficiency." Grounds Maintenance. April, 2004. http://grounds-mag.com.

"Nutrient Mgt. Recommendations for Turfgrass." Maryland Department of Agriculture. http://www.mda.state.md.us.

"Overview of IPM: Strategies." Texas IPM. May, 2006. http://ipm.tamu.edu.

"Overview of IPM: The Role of Pesticides in IPM." Texas IPM. May, 2006. http://ipm.tamu.edu.

"Professional Turf Manager's Guide to Efficient Irrigation Practices and Equipment." Hunter Industries, 2004. http://www.hunterindustries.com.

"Rainbird Distribution Uniformity For Sprinkler Irrigation." Rain Bird Corporation, 1996. http://www.rainbird.com.

Ratcliff, Cindy. "Healthy to the core." Grounds Maintenance. July, 2001. http://www.grounds-mag.com.

"Research Update: N Losses to Urban Runoff and Leaching." Grounds Maintenance. May, 2002. http://grounds-mag.com.

Reicher, Zac. "Don't raise the mowing height during drought." Purdue. June, 2007. http://www.agry.purdue.edu.

Rieke, Paul E. "Cool-season turf benefits from fall fertilization." Grounds Maintenance. August, 1998. http://grounds-mag.com.

Rose, Forrest. "Autumn is the best time to 'open up' your lawn." University of Missouri Extension. September, 2002. http://agebb.missouri.edu.

Rosen, C.J., and B. P. Horgan. "Preventing Pollution Problems from Lawn and Garden Fertilizers." University of Minnesota Extension, 2005. http://www.extension.umn.edu.

Rosen, C.J., B. P. Horgan, and R. J. Mugaas. "Fertilizing Lawns." University of Minnesota Extension, 2006. http://www.extension.umn.

Rosen, Carl and Ron Struss. "New phosphorus lawn fertilizer law now in effect." University of Minnesota Extension Service. April, 2005. http://www.extension.umn.

Sartain, J.B. "Food for turf: Slow-release nitrogen." Grounds Maintenance. April, 2002. http://grounds-mag.com.

Sartain, J.B. and J. K. Kruse. "Selected Fertilizers Used in Turfgrass Fertilization." University of Florida IFAS Extension. http://edis.ifas.ufl.edu.

"Scheduling Irrigation Using Evapotranspiration Data." Irrigation and Green Industry. http://www.igin.com.

Scherer, C.W. and P. G. Koehler and D. E. Short. "Landscape Integrated Pest Management." University of Florida IFAS Extension. http://edis.ifas.ufl.edu.

"Spring and Summer Lawn Management Considerations for Warm-Season Turfgrasses." Virginia Cooperative Extension. August, 2005. http://www.ext.vt.edu.

Starbuck, Chris. "Grass Clippings, Compost and Mulch, Frequently Asked Questions." University of Missouri Extension, 1993. http://extension.missouri.edu.

Stier, John C. "Lawn aeration and topdressing." University of Wisconsin Extension, 2000. http://cecommerce.uwex.edu.

Swift Ph.D, Curtis E. "Characteristics of Nitrogen (N) Fertilizers." Colorado State Cooperative Extension. October, 1996. http://www.coopext.colostate.edu.

Taylor, D.H., C. J. Rosen, and D. B. White. "Fertilizing Lawns." University of Minnesota Extension Service, 1990. http://www.extension.umn.edu.

Taylor, Gene. "Integrated Pest Management for the Turfgrass Manager." Texas Agriculture Extension Service. February, 2000. http://aggie-horticulture.tamu.edu.

"Technical Information: Using Evapotranspiration Data." Austin Lawn Sprinklers Association. http://www.alsaustin.org.

Tichenor, Jack. "Smarter Lawn Watering – Automatically." University of Florida IFAS Extension. http://edis.ifas.ufl.edu.

Torello, William A. and Haim B. Gunner. "Exploring the Role of Nitrogen in Integrated Pest Management Strategies." Turfgrass Trends. September, 2003. http://www.turfgrasstrends.com.

"Toxic Substances Hydrology Program: Eutrophication." USGS. April, 2006. http://toxics.usgs.gov/definitions/eutrophication.html.

Trenholm, L.E., J. Bryan Unruh, and J.L. Cisa. "How to Calibrate Your Sprinkler System." University of Florida IFAS Extension. http://edis.ifas.ufl.edu.

Trenholm, L.E. and J. Bryan Unruh. "Let Your Lawn Tell You When To Water." University of Florida IFAS Extension. http://edis.ifas.ufl.edu-EP054.

Trenhold, Cisar, and Unruh, "St. Augustine Grass for Florida Lawns." Publication ENH5, University of Florida IFAS Extension, 2006. http://edis.ifas.ufl.edu/lh010.

"Turfgrass Tips." Illinois Turfgrass Foundation, 2002. http://www.illinoisturfgrassfoundation.org.

Turgeon, A.J. *Turfgrass Management.* 5th ed. New Jersey: Prentice Hall, 1999.

"UC Pest Management Guidelines: Turfgrass General Information." UC IPM. June, 2003. http://www.ipm.ucdavis.edu.

"Using Monitoring as a Key Component of IPM." Gempler's. http://www.gemplers.com.

Voigt, Tom. "Turfgrass Irrigation." Turfgrass Extension and Outreach. http://www.turf.uiuc.edu.

Voigt, Tom. "Turfgrass Mowing." Turfgrass Extension and Outreach. http://turf.uiuc.edu.

Voigt, Tom, and Tom Fermanian. "Integrated Pest Management for Turf Managers." Turfgrass Extension and Outreach. http://www.turf.uiuc.edu.

Voigt, Tom, and Tom Fermanian. "Turfgrass Cultivation and Thatch Control." Turfgrass Extension and Outreach. http://www.turf.uiuc.edu.

Voigt, Tom, Tom Fermanian, and David Wehner. "Turfgrass Fertilization." Turfgrass Extension and Outreach. http://www.turf.uiuc.edu.

"Water Holding Capacity: Sponge Model." West Texas A & M University. http://www.wtamu.

Watschke, Thomas L. "Proper use of fertilizers minimizes environmental effects." Grounds Maintenance. March, 1998. http://grounds-mag.com.

Whiting, D., R. Tolan, B. Mecham, and M. Bauer. "Soil Water Holding Capacity and Irrigation Management." Colorado State University Cooperative Extension. March, 2005. http://www.ext.colostate.edu.

Wilson, Carl. "Aerate, Don't Power Rake to Remove Lawn Thatch. " Colorado State University Cooperative Extension. http://www.coopext.colostate.edu.

Chapter 5: Landscape Plant Management

"American National Standard for Tree Care Operations–Tree, Shrub, and Other Woody Plant Maintenance–Standard Practices (Fertilization)." ANSI A300, Part 2. American National Standards Institute, 2004.

Appleton, Bonnie and Kathy Kauffman. "Fertilizing Landscape Trees And Shrubs." Virginia Cooperative Extension. June, 1999. http://www.ext.vt.edu.

Benham, Brian and Blake Ross. "Filtration, Treatment, and Maintenance Considerations for Micro-Irrigation Systems." Virginia Cooperative Extension. March, 2002. http://www.ext.vt.edu.

Black, Robert J., Edward F. Gilman, Gary W. Knox, Kathleen C. Ruppert. "Mulches for the Landscape." University of Florida IFAS Extension. http://edis.ifas.ufl.edu.

Bomberger, Kim. "Staking and Guying Landscape Trees." Kansas Forest Service At Kansas State University. September, 2005. http://www.oznet.ksu.edu.

Bosmans, Raymond V. "Fertilizing Landscape Trees And Shrubs." Maryland Cooperative Extension Home And Garden. http://www.hgic.umd.edu.

Boulden, Steve. "Plant Selection Choosing The Right Plants." Landscape Design Do It Yourself. http://www.the-landscape-design-site.com.

Broschat, Timothy, "Fertilization of Field-grown and Landscape Palms in Florida." (Publication #ENH1009). University of Florida IFAS Extension, 2008. http://edis.ifas.ufl.edu/ep261.

Carlson, Dennis W. ""Fertilizing Trees." Kansas Forest Service At Kansas State University. May, 2001. http://www.oznet.ksu.edu.

Chalker-Scott, Linda. "Wood chip mulch: Landscape boon or bane?" Washington State University, 2007. http://www.puyallup.wsu.edu.

Conlon, Hubert P. and Wayne K. Clatterbuck. "Fertilizing Landscape Trees." University of Tennessee Agricultural Extension Service. http:// utextension.tennessee.edu.

Costello, L.R., J.R. Clark, N.P. Matheny, K.S. Jones, "A Guide to Estimating Irrigation Water Needs of Landscape Plantings in California: The Landscape Coefficient Method and WUCOLS III." California Sate Department of Water Resources. http://www.water.ca.gov/wateruseefficiency/publications.

DeWald, Scott J., Steven D. Rasmussen, Charles A. Shapiro, and Scott J. Josiah. "Determining the Need to Fertilize Landscape Trees and Shrubs." University of Nebraska Lincoln. March, 2004. http://www.ianrpubs.unl.edu.

"Fertilizer Recommendations for Landscape Plants." University of Florida IFAS Extension. http://edis.ifas.ufl.edu.

"Fertilizing Landscape Trees And Shrubs." Washington State University Extension. October, 1991. http://cru.cahe.wsu.edu.

"Frequently Asked Questions About ANSI Standards." Tree Care Industry Association. http://www.treecareindustry.com.

Gill, Stanton. "What's New–Fertilization of Trees and Shrubs in the Landscape." University of Maryland Cooperative Extension. http://www.agnr.umd.edu.

Gill, Stanton, Raymond Bosmans, and Wanda MacLachlan. "Fertilizer Recommendations for Landscape Trees & Shrubs (For Professional Grounds Managers and Landscape Contractors)." University of Maryland Cooperative Extension. http://www.agnr.umd.edu.

Gillman, Jeff and Carl Rosen. "Tree Fertilization: A Guide for Fertilizing New And Established Trees In The Landscape." University of Minnesota Extension Service. http://www.extension.umn.edu.

Gilman, Edward F. *An Illustrated Guide to Pruning, Second Edition.* Delmar/Thompson Learning Inc. 2002.

Gilman, Edward F. "Irrigating Landscape Plants During Establishment." University of Florida IFAS Extension. Publication ENH857, 2002. http://edis.ifas.ufl.edu.

Gilman, Edward F. "Where Are Tree Roots?" University of Florida IFAS Extension. Publication ENH137, 2009. http://edis.ifas.ufl.edu.

"Guideline Specifications for Nursery Tree Quality." http://urbantree.org.

Ham, Donald L. and Larry R. Nelson. "Newly Planted Trees." Clemson University Extension. http://www.state.sc.us.

Hanzely, Thomas. "Fertilizing Trees and Shrubs in Accordance with the New ANSI A300 Standard." http:// www.mortonarboretumphc.org.

Hensley, David L. *Professional Landscape Management.* Illinois: Stipes Publishing. 2004.

Hillock, David and Mike Schnelle. "Winter Protection for Landscape Plants." Oklahoma Cooperative Extension. http://www.osuextra.com.

Hla, Aung K. and Thomas F. Scherer. "Introduction to Micro-irrigation." North Dakota State University Extension Service. March, 2003. http://www.ext.nodak.edu.

Iles, Jeff. "1998 Iowa Turfgrass Research Report." Iowa State University. http://turfgrass.hort.iastate.edu.

Johnson, Tim A. "New Tree Fertilization Standards." Tree Care Industry. February, 1999. http://www.treecareindustry.org.

Jones, K.S., and L.R. Costello. "Irrigating the Home Landscape." University of California Cooperative Extension. August, 2003. http://ucanr.org.

Kerkhof, Karen L. "How To: Fertilize Trees." Grounds Maintenance. April, 2005. http://www.grounds-mag.com.

Kerkhof, Karen L. "How To: Transplant Trees." Grounds Maintenance. September, 2005. http://www.grounds-mag.com.

Klett, J. "Home Landscape Watering During Drought." Colorado State University Cooperative Extension. http://www.ext.colostate.edu.

Koetter, Rebecca and Gary R. Johnson. "Will Fill Kill?" DNR Forestry: Forest Health Unit. http:// files.dnr.state.mn.us.

Konjoian, Peter. "Have algae met their match?" http://www.greenbeam.com.

Konjoian, Peter. "Maintenance Tips For Drip Irrigation." Konjoian's Floriculture Education Services. http://www.horticulture.com.

Kujawski, Ronald F., and H. Dennis Ryan. "Fertilizing Trees and Shrubs." U Mass Extension, 2000. http://www.umass-greeninfo.org.

Muntean, Dirk. "Tree and Shrub Decline in the Landscape." Soil and Plant Laboratory, Inc. http://www.soilandplant-laboratory.com/pdf/articles/TreeShrubDeclineInLand.pdf.

Panter, Karen L. "Landscaping: Fertilizing Trees and Shrubs." University of Wyoming Department of Plant Sciences, 2006. http://www.uwyo.edu.

Perry, E. J. "Phytophthora Root and Crown Rot in the Garden." UC IPM Online, 2008. http://www.ipm.ucdavis.edu.

Perry, Leonard. "Fertilizing Landscape Plants." University of Vermont Extension. December, 1997. http://www.uvm.edu.

Powell, Kim. "Watering Landscape Plants 101." NC State University. http://www.bae.ncsu.edu.

"Proper Mulching Techniques." International Society of Arboriculture, 1995. http://www.treesaregood.com.

Rose, Mary Ann and Elton Smith. "Ohio State University Fact Sheet: Fertilizing Landscape Plants." Ohio State University Extension. http://ohioline.osu.edu.

Rosen, Carl, Peter Bierman, Roger Eliason, "Soil Test Interpretations and Fertilizer Management for Lawns, Turf, Gardens, and Landscape Plants." University of Minnesota, 2008. http://conservancy.umn.edu.

Schrock, Denny. "Water-Efficient Gardening and Landscaping." University of Missouri Extension. http://extension.missouri.edu.

Smiley, E. Thomas, and A.M. Shirazi. "Fall Fertilization And Cold Hardiness In Landscape Trees." Journal of Arboriculture. November, 2003. http://www.treelink.org.

"Soil Test Interpretations and Fertilizer Management for Lawns, Turf, Gardens, and Landscape Plants: Trees, Shrubs and Fruits." University of Minnesota Extension Service, 2004. http://www.extension.umn.edu.

Starbuck, Christopher J. "Irrigating Trees and Shrubs During Summer Drought." University of Missouri Extension. http://extension.missouri.edu.

Sunset Western Garden Book. 5th ed. Joseph Williamson, ed. dir. California: Sunset Publishing Corporation, 1991.

Sunset Western Garden Book; Completely Revised and Updated. Kathleen Norris Brenzel, ed. California: Sunset Publishing Corporation, 2007.

"To Stake or Not to Stake." ISU Forestry Extension. January, 2005. http://www.forestry.iastate.edu.

"Tree and shrub irrigation water requirements in Northern Arizona." University of Arizona Agricultural and Biosystems Engineering. http://ag.arizona.edu.

Trenholm, L.E., E.F. Gilman, G.W. Knox, and R.J. Black. "Fertilization and Irrigation for Florida Lawns and Landscapes." University of Florida IFAS Extension. http://edis.ifas.ufl.edu.

Warren, Stuart. "Fertilize woody ornamentals the right way." Grounds Maintenance. September, 1999. http://www.grounds mag.com.

"Water Conservation Factsheet: Trickle Irrigation Scheduling Using Evapotranspiration Data." British Columbia Ministry of Agriculture, Food, and Fisheries. May, 2004. http://www.gov.bc.ca.

"Watering Home Gardens and Landscape Plants." Washington State University Extension. http://gardening.wsu.edu.

Watson, Gary W. and E. B. Himelick. *Principles and Practice of Planting Trees and Shrubs.* International Society of Arboriculture, 1997.

Wilson, C. and M.Bauer. "Drip Irrigation for Home Gardens." Colorado State University Cooperative Extension. March, 2006. http://www.ext.colostate.edu.

Zoldoske, David F. and Kenneth H. Solomon. "Micro-Irrigation Scheduling and Management." Center for Irrigation Technology. June, 1990. http://cati.csufresno.edu.

Chapter 6: Soil

Anderson, Scott. "To lime or not to lime." Athletic Turf News. November, 2002. http://www.athleticturf.net.

Brown, R.B. "Soil Texture." University of Florida IFAS Extension. http://edis.ifas.ufl.edu.

Brundrett, Mark. "Introduction to Mycorrhizas." CSIRO Forestry and Forest Products. http://www.ffp.csiro.au.

Buchholz, Daryl D. "Missouri Limestone Quality: What is ENM?" University of Missouri Extension. June, 2007. http://extension.missouri.edu.

Buchholz, Daryl D., J.R. Brown, and Roger G. Hanson. "Using Your Soil Test Results." University of Missouri Extension. June, 2005. http://muextension.missouri.edu.

Clement, David L. Ph.D., and Jon H. Traunfeld. "Soil Test Basics." University of Maryland Cooperative Extension. http://extension.umd.edu.

Darlington, William. "Compost: A Guide for Evaluating and Using Compost Materials as Soil Amendments." Soil & Plant Laboratory, Inc., Orange Office. http://www.soilandplant-laboratory.com.

Davis, J.G. and C.R. Wilson. "Choosing a Soil Amendment." Colorado State University Cooperative Extension. June, 2005. http://www.ext.colostate.edu.

Delahaut, Karen and C.F. Koval, "Earthworms: Beneficials or Pests?" University of Wisconsin Urban Horticulture. http://www.uwex.edu.

Diver, Steve. "Alternative Soil Testing Laboratories." National Center for Appropriate Technology. October, 2002. http://attra.ncat.org.

Edwards, Clive A. "The Soil Biology Primer: Chapter 8: Earthworms." Natural Resources Conservation Service. http://soils.usda.gov.

Feucht, J.R. "Soil: The Key to Successful Gardening." Colorado State University Cooperative Extension. August, 2004. http://www.ext.colostate.edu.

Gao, Gary, Joe Boggs, and Jim Chatfield. "Soil Testing is an Excellent Investment for Garden Plants and Commmercial Crops." Ohio State University. http://ohioline.osu.edu.

Gardner, E. Hugh, Michael Robotham, and John Hart. "Soil Sampling for Home Gardens and Small Acreages." Oregon State University Extension Service. April, 2003. http:// extension.oregonstate.edu.

"GreenShare Factsheets: Lime and pH." University of Rhode Island Department of Horticulture Program, 2000. http://www.uri.edu.

Hart, J. "Fertilizer and Lime Materials." Oregon State University Extension Service. May, 1998. http://extension.oregonstate.edu.

Herrera, Esteban. "Soil Test Interpretations." New Mexico State University. June, 2000. http://www.cahe.nmsu.edu.

"How to Sample: Homeowners." University of Minnesota College of Agricultural, Food, and Environmental Sciences, Department of Soil, Water, and Climate. http://soiltest.coafes.umn.edu.

Ingham, Elaine R. "The Soil Biology Primer: Chapter 3: Bacteria." USDA Natural Resources Conservation Service. http://www.urbanext.uiuc.edu.

Ingham, Elaine R. "The Soil Biology Primer: Chapter 4: Soil Fungi." USDA Natural Resources Conservation Service. http://www.urbanext.uiuc.edu.

Klocke, Norman L., and Gary W.Hergert. "How Soil Holds Water." University of Nebraska-Lincoln Institute of Agriculture and Natural Resources Cooperative Extension. http://ianrhome.unl.edu.

Knudsen, Delno and K.D. Frank. "Understand Your Soil Test: Calcium, Magnesium, Boron, Copper, Chlorine, Molybdenum." University of Nebraska-Lincoln. October, 1996. http://ianrpubs.unl.edu.

Knudsen, Delno and K.D. Frank. "Understand Your Soil Test: pH-Excess Lime-Lime Needs." University of Nebraska-Lincoln. January, 2001. http://ianrpubs.unl.edu.

Landschoot, Peter J. "Liming Turfgrass Areas." Penn State Department of Crop and Soil Sciences–Cooperative Extension. http://turfgrassmanagement.psu.edu.

Landschoot, Peter. "Managing soil pH in turf." Grounds Maintenance. February, 1998. http://grounds-mag.com.

Lee, Ed. "MG Lime Application Calculator." Tulsa Master Gardeners. http://www.tulsamastergardeners.org.

Lickacz, J., and D. Penny. "Soil Organic Matter." Alberta Government Agriculture, Food, and Rural Development. May, 2001. http://www.agric.gov.ab.ca.

Mamo, Martha, Charles Wortmann, and Charles Shapiro. "Lime Use for Soil Acidity Management." University of Nebraska-Lincoln Institute of Agriculture and Natural Resources Cooperative Extension. March, 2009. http://ianrpubs.unl.edu.

Marx, E.S., J. Hart, and R.G. Stevens. "Soil Test Interpretation Guide." Oregon State University Extension Service. August, 1999. http://extension.oregonstate.edu.

Mason, Sandra. "Soil Conditioners Are Explained." University of Illinois Extension The Homeowner's Column. http://www.extension.uiuc.edu.

Muntean, Dirk W. "Beneficial Soil Microorganisms." Soil and Plant Laboratory. www.soilandplantlaboratory.com.

Muntean, Dirk W. "Don't Freak Out! It is Only pH." Soil and Plant Laboratory. http://www.soilandplantlaboratory.com.

Muntean, Dirk W. "Herbicide Detection in Landscape Soils." Soil and Plant Laboratory. http://www.soilandplantlaboratory.com.

Muntean, Dirk. "Tree and Shrub Decline in the Landscape." Soil and Plant Laboratory. http://www.soilandplantlaboratory.com.

"Organic Matter In Soil." USDA Natural Resources Conservation Service. http://www.nrcs.usda.gov.

"Organic Matter Management." University of Minnesota Extension Service, 2002. http://www.extension.umn.edu.

Peacock, Bill. "The Use of Soil and Water Analysis." University of California Cooperative Extension: Tulare County. March, 1998. http://cetulare.ucdavis.edu.

"Recommended Chemical Soil Test Procedures for the North Central Region." Missouri Agricultural Experiment Station. January, 1998. http://extension.missouri.edu.

Reid, Greg and Percy Wong. "Soil biology basics: Soil Bacteria." State of New South Wales Department of Primary Industries, 2005. http://www.dpi.nsw.gov.au.

Sachs, Paul D. *Edaphos: Dynamics of a Natural Soil System.* 2nd ed. Vermont: The Edaphic Press, 1999.

Self, J.R. "Soil Testing." Colorado State University Cooperative Extension. June, 2005. http://www.ext.colostate.edu.

Simmons, Joel. "A Re-evaluation: Biological Soil Management." EarthWorks and Turf Grass Trends. November, 1994. http://www.soilfirst.com.

"Soil Creatures." Environmental Literacy Council. June, 2005. http://www.enviroliteracy.org.

"Soil Sampling." Soil and Plant Laboratory, Inc., 2003. http://www.soilandplantlab.com.

"Soil Test Interpretations and Fertilizer Management for Lawns, Turf, Gardens, and Landscape Plants: Raising Soil pH." University of Minnesota Extension Service, 2004. http://www.extension.umn.edu/.

"Soil Test Interpretations and Fertilizer Management for Lawns, Turf, Gardens, and Landscape Plants: Soil Acidification." University of Minnesota Extension Service, 2004. http://www.extension.umn.edu.

"Soil Test Interpretations and Fertilizer Management for Lawns, Turf, Gardens, and Landscape Plants: Soil pH Modification." University of Minnesota Extension Service, 2004. http://www.extension.umn.edu.

"Soil Testing." North Carolina Department of Agriculture And Consumer Services. http://www.agr.state.nc.us.

"Soil: The importance and protection of a living soil." Soil Association. http://www.soilassociation.org.

"Soil Quality Indicators: pH." USDA Natural Resources Conservation Service. January, 1998. http://soils.usda.gov.

"Soil Sampling Instructions." Soil and Plant Laboratory. http://www.soilandplantlaboratory.com.

St. John, Ted. "Never treat soil like dirt: how to tell the difference, and how to turn each into the other." BioNet, LLC.

Street, John R., and Susan K. White. "Lime And The Home Lawn." HYG-4026-90. Ohio State University Extension. http://ohioline.osu.edu.

Struss, Ron. "Lawn Soil Testing." University of Minnesota Extension Service. http://www.extension.umn.edu.

"Submitting a soil sample." Cornell Soil Labs. http://www.css.cornell.edu.

Swift, Curtis E. "Alkaline Soils and the Buffering Effect of Calcium Carbonate." Colorado State University Cooperative Extension Tri River Area. March, 2005. http://www.colostate.edu.

Swift, Curtis E. "The Soil Testing Procedure." Colorado State University Cooperative Extension Tri River Area. April, 2004. http://www.coopext.colostate.edu.

Townsend, Lee, Dan Potter, and A. J. Powell. "Earthworms: Thatch-busters." University of Kentucky Entomology. January, 1994. http://www.uky.edu.

Tucker, M. Ray and J. Kent Messick. "Lime: Essential for Nursery Crops." North Carolina Department of Agriculture & Consumer Services. May, 1995. http://www.ncagr.com.

"Urban Soil Primer." USDA Natural Resources Conservation Service, 2005. http://soils.usda.gov.

Watson, Maurice E. "Guidelines for Choosing a Soil-Testing Laboratory." Ohio State University Extension. http://ohioline.osu.edu.

Watson, Maurice. "Testing Compost". Ohio State University Extension Fact Sheet ANR-15-03.

Werner, Peter. "Mycorrhizal Symbiosis." Mycena News and MykoWeb. May, 2005. http://www.mykoweb.com.

Whiting, D., C.Wilson, and A. Card. "Soil pH," Colorado State University Cooperative Extension. January, 2005. http://www.ext.colostate.edu.

Williams, Sara. "Soil Texture: From Sand to Clay." University of Saskatchewan Extension Division. http://gardenline.usask.ca.

Wortmann, Charles S. and Paul J. Jasa. "Management to Minimize and Reduce Soil Compaction." University of Nebraska-Lincoln Institute of Agriculture and Natural Resources Cooperative Extension. May, 2004. http://www.ianrpubs.unl.edu.

Wysong, David S., Mark O. Harrell, and Donald H. Steinegger, "Iron Chlorosis of Trees and Shrub." University of Nebraska-Lincoln Institute of Agriculture and Natural Resources Cooperative Extension. January, 1996. http://ianrpubs.unl.edu.

Chapter 7: Pruning

"American National Standard for Tree Care Operations–Tree, Shrub, and Other Woody Plant Management–Standard Practices (Pruning)." ANSI A300, Part 1. American National Standards Institute, 2008.

"Care of California's Native Oaks; Bulletin of the California Oak Foundation." California Oak Foundation. http://www.californiaoaks.org.

Colt, W.M. R.R. Tripepi, and R.L. Mahoney. "How to Prune Deciduous Landscape Trees." University of Idaho Cooperative Extension System. http://www.uidaho.edu/extension.

Costello, Larry, *Training Young Trees for Structure and Form,* (video). UC Television. http://www.uctv.tv/search-details.aspx?showID=5598.

"Garden Hedges." Royal Horticultural Society. November, 2002. http://www.rhs.org.uk.

Gilman, Edward F. *An Illustrated Guide to Pruning, Second Edition.* Delmar/Thompson Learning Inc. 2002.

"Horticultural Report MF650: Hedges in the Home Landscape." Kansas State University, 1982. http://www.oznet.ksu.edu.

"HOW to Prune Trees." National Forest Service. http://www.na.fs.fed.us.

Mitchell, Paul J. "Training Young Shade and Ornamental Trees." Oklahoma Cooperative Extension Service. February, 1999. http://www.okstate.edu.

Sunset Pruning Handbook. John McClements, ed. and Philip Edinger. California: Lane Publishing Co., 1988.

Schalau, Jeff. "Killing Woody Plant Stumps." Arizona Cooperative Extension. April, 2006. http://ag.arizona.edu.

Smith, Curtis W. "Tree Pruning Techniques." New Mexico State University Cooperative Extension Service. September, 2005. http://www.cahe.nmsu.edu.

"Structural Strength." Urban Tree Foundation. http://www.urbantree.org.

"Sudden Oak Death and Care of Native Oaks." County of Los Angeles; Agricultural Commissioner/Weights & Measures, 2004. http://acwm.lacounty.gov.

Tatum, David. "Pruning Landscape Plants." Mississippi State University Extension Service. http://msucares.com.

"Training Young Trees." Urban Tree Foundation. http://www.urbantree.org.

"Training Young Trees." Vermont Urban And Community Forestry Program. http://www.vtcommunityforestry.org.

"Type of Pruning Depends on Age of Tree." Tree Care Industry Association. http://www.treecareindustry.org.

Whiting, D., J. Bousselot, R. Cox, and C. O'Meara. "Structural Training of Trees with a Central Leader." Colorado State University Cooperative Extension. http://www.ext.colostate.edu.

Whiting, D., J. Bousselot, R. Cox, and C. O'Meara. "Structural Training of Trees with Multiple Scaffold Branches." Colorado State University Cooperative Extension. December, 2005. http://www.ext.colostate.edu.

Worf, G.L. and J.E. Kuntz. "Deciduous trees disorder: Miscellaneous causes of decline." University of Wisconsin Extension, 1986. http:// www.uwex.edu.

Chapter 8: Pruning Roses

Chute, Angelina P. "Winter Protection for Roses: Everything You Need to Know." Rhode Island Federation of Garden Clubs, Inc. November, 2005. http://www.gardencentral.org.

Justice, Connie. "Winter Protection for Roses." Garden Central. http://www.gardencentral.org.

Kuze, Hugo. "Pruning Your Roses." Central Florida Rose Society. http://CentralFloridaRoseSociety.org.

Pawlikowski, Marty. "Basic Pruning Guidelines." Central Florida Rose Society. http://CentralFloridaRoseSociety.org.

Villegas, Baldo. "Rose Pruning Winter Care For the Sacramento Area!" Sierra Foothills Rose Society. http://www.geocities.com/rainforest/vines/4825/horticulture/84sac-wintercaretips.html.

Chapter 9: Pruning Fruit Trees

"Apple Coddling Moth." University of California Agriculture and Natural Resources. August, 2002. http://axp.ipm.ucdavis.edu.

"Backyard Orchard Culture: Growing Fruit Trees in Limited Space." Dave Wilson Nursery, 1994. http://www.crfg.org.

Bennet, Jennifer. *The Harrowsmith Book of Fruit Trees.* Ontario, Canada: Camden House Publishing, 1991.

Boyd, J.E., and W.R. Jacobi. "Fire Blight." Colorado State University Cooperative Extension. April, 2005. http://www.ext.colostate.edu.

Brickell, Christopher and David Joyce. *The American Horticultural Society Pruning & Training; A Fully Illustrated Plant-by-Plant Manual.* New York: DK Publishing, Inc., 1996.

Byrne, David H. and Terry Bacon. "Chilling Accumulation: its Importance and Estimation." TAMU Stone Fruit Breeding Texas A&M University Dept. Horticultural Sci. http://aggie-horticulture.tamu.edu.

Caprile, J. and P. Vossen. "Codling Moth." University of California Agriculture and Natural Resources. December, 2005. http://www.ipm.ucdavis.edu.

"Citrus Ants." University of California Agriculture and Natural Resources. November, 2003. http://www.ipm.ucdavis.edu.

"Citrus Brown Rot." University of California Agriculture and Natural Resources. July, 2003. http://www.ipm.ucdavis.edu.

"Codling Moth." University of California Agriculture and Natural Resources, 2006. http://www.ipm.ucdavis.edu.

Erb, Alan. "Pruning Fruit Trees." Kansas State University Agricultural Experiment Station And Cooperative Extension Service. November, 1998. http://www.oznet.ksu.edu.

Farnham, D.S. "Why Do We Prune Fruit and Nut Trees." UC Davis. http://ceamador.ucdavis.edu.

"Fruit Tree Pruning." Wegman's Nursery. January, 2006. http://www.WegmansNursery.com.

Funt, Richard C., David C. Ferree, and Robert G. Hill, Jr. "Training and Pruning Fruit Trees." Purdue University Cooperative Extension Service. http://www.hort.purdue.edu.

Grove, Dr. Gary. "Brown Rot of Stone Fruits." Washington State University Tree Fruit Extension Team. February, 2001. http://fruit.wsu.edu.

Hale, Frank A. and Mark A. Halcomb. "Common Tree Borers in Tennessee." University of Tennessee Agricultural Extension Service. http://www.utextension.utk.edu.

Herrera, Esteban. "Summer Pruning of Apple Trees." New Mexico State University. July, 2001. http://www.ams.usda.gov.

"Horticultural Advice." Royal Horticultural Society, 2006. http://extension.oregonstate.edu.

"Horticultural Spray Adjuvants." Penn State College of Agricultural Sciences Cooperative Extension, 1998. http://pubs.cas.psu.edu.

Ingels, Chuck and Eleanor Dong. "Training and Pruning Fruit Trees." University of California, Sacramento County Cooperative Extension. January, 2000. http://ucce.ucdavis.edu.

Ingels, Chuck, Pamela M. Geisel, and Carolyn L. Unruh. "Fruit Trees: Training and Pruning Deciduous Trees." ANR Pub. 8057. University of California Division of Agriculture and Natural Resources, 2002. http://anrcatalog.ucdavis.edu.

Jauron, Richard. "Pruning Neglected Apple Trees." Department of Horticulture Iowa State University. February, 2001. http://www.ipm.iastate.edu.

Laivo, Ed. "Planting Backyard Orchards." Dave Wilson Nursery, Inc., 2006. http:// www.davewilson.com.

Laivo, Ed. "Tame that Big & Old tree!" Dave Wilson Nursery. http://www.davewilson.com.

Marini, Richard P. "Physiology of Pruning Fruit Trees." Virginia Cooperative Extension. November, 2003. http://www.ext.vt.edu.

Micke, Warren, Allen Hewitt, Jack Kelly Clark and Marvin Gerdts. *Pruning Fruit and Nut Trees; Leaflet 21171.* California: University of California Division of Agriculture and Natural Resources.

"National List: Regulatory Text." The National Organic Program. http://www.ams.usda.gov.

Ohlendorf, Barbara, senior writer. *Integrated Pest Management For Apples & Pears; Publication 3340.* California: University of California Division of Agriculture and Natural Resources, 1991.

Parker, Michael L. "Growing Apple Trees In The Home Garden." North Carolina Cooperative Extension Service. May, 1997. http://www.ces.ncsu.edu.

Parker, Michael L. "Training and Pruning Fruit Trees." North Carolina Cooperative Extension Service. http://www.ces.ncsu.edu.

"Pruning Apple Trees." Ricker Hill Orchards. http://www.rickerhill.com.

Relf, Diane. "Tree Fruit in the Home Garden." Virginia Cooperative Extension. August, 2000. http://www.ext.vt.edu.

Renquist, Steve. "Restore those old fruit trees." Oregon State University Extension Service. http://extension.oregonstate.edu.

Sauls, Julian W. "Citrus Pruning." Texas Cooperative Extension. August, 2002. http://aggie-horticulture.tamu.edu.

Schupp, James R. "Renovating Old Apple Trees." University of Maine Cooperative Extension. March, 2006. http://www.umext.maine.edu.

Shor, Don. "Dormant Spraying: Fruit Trees and Ornamentals." Redwood Barn Nursery, 2008. http://www.redwoodbarn.com.

Shor, Don. Email correspondence with the author, 2008.

Stebbins, Robert L. "Training and Pruning Sweet Cherry Trees for Mechanical Harvesting." Oregon State University Extension Service. October, 1999. http://extension.oregonstate.edu.

Steinegger, Donald H. "Pruning Fruit Trees." University of Nebraska Cooperative Extension. http://ianrpubs.unl.edu.

"Sunscald of Trees." Colorado State University Cooperative Extension. March, 2007. http://www.ext.colostate.edu.

Swift, Curtis E. "Sunscald." Colorado State University Cooperative Extension Tri River Area. http://www.coopext.colostate.edu.

"Tree Fruit IPM Advisory." Utah State University Extension. April, 2006. http://extension.usu.edu.

"Using Refined Horticultural Oils on Fruit Trees." University of New Hampshire Cooperative Extension. September, 2000. http://extension.unh.edu.

Vaden, Mario. "Sunburn and Sunscald: Trees." 2006. http://www.mdvaden.com.

Wasner, Ronald H., Wilford A. Wright, and Alvin R. Hamson. "Pruning the Orchard." Utah State University Extension. March, 1994. http://extension.usu.edu.

"What Is Backyard Orchard Culture? Summer Pruning For Size Control." Dave Wilson Nursery, 2007. http://www.davewilson.com.

"What's Said in Ed's Head: Dwarf." Dave Wilson Nursery, 2003. http://www.davewilson.com.

Wheaton, T.A. "Alternate Bearing of Citrus in Florida." University of Florida Citrus Research and Education Center. http://www.lal.ufl.edu.

Chapter 10: Irrigation System Repair

Carowitz, Jeff. "Troubleshooting irrigation controls." Grounds Maintenance. August, 2001. http://grounds-mag.com.

Charlot, Micah. Conversation with author, 2007.

"Consumer Products Catalog." Rain Bird Corporation, 2004. http://www.rainbird.com.

Crosby, George. "High-voltage advice on irrigation wiring." Grounds Maintenance. August, 1997. http://www.grounds-mag.com.

Crosby, George. "Test irrigation wiring with a multimeter." Grounds Maintenance. June, 1999. http://grounds-mag.com.

"Cross-Connection Control Manual." Environmental Protection Agency Office of Water. February, 2003. http://www.epa.gov/safewater.

Drip Irrigation Guidelines. California: East Bay Municipal Utilities District, Administration Department.

"Electrical Troubleshooting With the Volt/Ohm Meter." *Ewing News*; Summer 1999, No. 48.

"Fault Finding Equipment; Progressive Electronics." *Ewing News*. Fall 1999, No. 49.

Higgins, Mike. "Winterization Sprinkler Systems." Colorado State University Cooperative Extension Tri River Area. October, 1998. http://www.coopext.colostate.edu.

"Homeowner's Guide to Winterization." Rain Bird Corporation. http://www.rainbird.com.

"Impact Sprinkler Troubleshooting Guide." Rain Bird Sprinkler Mfg. Corp., 1991. http://www.rainbird.com.

"Irrigation System Freeze Protection." Hunter Industries. http://www.hunterIndustries.com.

"Irrigation System Hydraulics: Interpreting Catalog Data." *Ewing Irrigation Products p.186-187* (catalog). Phoenix, Arizona: Ewing.

"Irrigation Troubleshooting Guide." *Harmony Farm Supply p. 53-57* (catalog). Sebastapool, California.

"Irrigation Troubleshooting Guide." Rain Bird Corporation. http://www.rainbird.com/pdf/diy/IrrigationTroubleshootingGuide.pdf.

Kourik, Robert. *Drip Irrigation For Every Landscape And All Climates.* California: Metamorphic Press, 1992.

"Landscape Irrigation Design Manual." Rain Bird Corporation, 2001. http://www.rainbird.com.

Martin, William T. "Mr. Fix-it: Diagnosing problems with landscape irrigation systems." Turf & Landscape Irrigation. April, 2002. http://www.irrigation.org.

Mugaas, Bob. "Winterizing your lawn starts now." University of Minnesota Extension Service. August, 2005. http://www.extension.umn.edu.

Muir, John. *How To Keep Your Volkswagen Alive; A Manual Of Step-By-Step Procedures For The Comleat Idiot.* New Mexico: John Muir Publications, 1974.

"Professional Turf Manager's Guide to Efficient Irrigation Practices and Equipment." Hunter Industries Incorporated. http://www.hunterIndustries.com.

"Rain Bird: Landscape Irrigation Products: 1800 PCS Pressure Compensating Screens." Rain Bird Corporation, 2007. http://www.rainbird.com.

"Solenoid Valve Function, Troubleshooting and Repair." *Ewing Irrigation Products p.188-192* (catalog). Phoenix, Arizona: Ewing.

Stryker, Jess. "Irrigation FAQs: Smart Controllers for Irrigation Systems." Jess Stryker's Irrigation Tutorials, 2006. http://irrigationtutorials.com.

Stryker, Jess. "Landscape Sprinkler Design Tutorial Step #2: Valves." Jess Stryker's Irrigation Tutorials, 2001. http://www.irrigationtutorials.com/sprinkler10.htm.

Stryker, Jess. "Sprinkler Spacing." Jess Stryker's Irrigation Tutorials, 2003. http://www.irrigationtutorials.com.

Stryker, Jess. "Winterizing Your Irrigation System." Jess Stryker's Irrigation Tutorials, 2001. http://www.irrigationtutorials.com.

"The Basics of Matched Precipitation." Hunter Industries. http://www.hunterIndustries.com.

"The Handbook of Technical Irrigation Information." Hunter Industries, 2006. http://www.hunterIndustries.com.

"Turf and Landscape Irrigation Best Management Practices." Water Management Committee of The Irrigation Association. April, 2005. http://www.irrigation.org.

"Using your volt/ohm meter to analyze irrigation system electrical wiring." The Urban Farmer Store, 2003. http://urbanfarmerstore.com.

"Valve troubleshooting." The Urban Farmer Store. http://urbanfarmerstore.com.

Wilson, Tim. "Choosing the Right Meter: Troubleshooting Irrigation Control Electrical Problems." H2O Stewardship Solutions. March, 2004. http://www.igin.com.

Wilson, Tim and David F. Zodolske. "Evaluating Sprinkler irrigation Uniformity." Center for Irrigation Technology. July, 1997. http://www.wateright.org.

"Winterizing." The Drip Store. September, 2006. http://www.dripirrigation.com.

"Winterizing Your Irrigation System." Hunter Industries Incorporated. http://www.hunterindustries.com.

Woodford, Katherine. "This Is A Test For Your Irrigation System." October, 2001. http://www.igin.com.

Zazueta, Fedro S., Allen G. Smajstrla, and Gary A. Clark. "Irrigation System Controllers." University of Florida IFAS Extension. http://edis.ifas.ufl.edu.

Chapter 11: Calculating an Accurate Hourly Rate

Budzynski, Jim. "How To: Increase Your Business." Grounds Maintenance. October, 2001. http://www.grounds-mag.com.

Chaltas, Jeff. "Gauging Your Business." Grounds Maintenance. April, 2004. http://www.grounds-mag.com.

Greenwald, Steve. "Don't let lowballers bite into your profits." Landscape Management. April, 2002. http://www.landscape-management.net.

Hall, Ron. "Making the cut." Landscape Management. September, 2005. http://www.landscapemanagement.net.

Huston, James. "Pricing it Right." Grounds Maintenance. July, 2005. http://www.grounds-mag.com.

Huston, Jim. "Better Bids." Grounds Maintenance. July, 2004. http://www.grounds-mag.com.

Huston, Jim. "Don't sell yourself short." Grounds Maintenance. June, 2002. http://www.grounds-mag.com.

Huston, Jim. "Job Costing: Why it is Critical and What to Look For." Hunter: The Irrigation Innovators, 2006. http://www.hunterindustries.com.

Huston, Jim. "Pricing it Right." Snow & Ice Manager. October, 2002. http://snow.grounds-mag.com.

Kay, Michael. "Financial terms 101: Confusing markup with margin causes profit slippage." Landscape Management. January, 2006. http://www.landscapemanagement.net.

Kay, Mike. "Pricing vs. estimating." Landscape Management. October, 2005. http://www.landscapemanagement.net.

Liskey, Eric. "Calculate areas." Grounds Maintenance. October, 1997. http://www.grounds-mag.com.

Nilsson, Phil. "Cutting Yourself Short?" Grounds Maintenance. November, 2003. http://grounds-mag.

Nilsson, Phil. "Numbers you should track: Keeping an eye on daily sales and labor hours will allow you to make in-season adjustments to meet your company's goals." Landscape Management. October, 2004. http://www.landscapemanagement.net.

Porter, Susan. "Learn the basics of landscape estimating." Landscape Management. April, 2006. http://www.landscape-management.net.

Schellhammmer, Lance. "Estimate labor costs." Grounds Maintenance. October, 1998. http://grounds-mag.com.

Taylor, Ken. "The Equipment Equation." Grounds Maintenance. November, 2005. http://www.grounds-mag.com.

Trusty, Steve and Suz Trusty. "Value vs. Volume." Februrary, 2005. http://grounds-mag.com.

Volz, Wayne. "Key factors for profitable mowing." Landscape Management. September, 2005. http://www.landscapemanagement.net.

Volz, Wayne. "Mow For More $$: Use these strategies and build your own system to price work for profit." Landscape Management. March, 2002. http://www.landscapemanagement.net.

Welterlen, Mark. "The Price Is Right." Grounds Maintenance. November, 2003. http://www.grounds-mag.com.

Chapter 12: Maintenance Contracts

Brown, Sydney Park and Michael J. Holsinger. "Considerations for Developing a Lawn and Landscape Maintenance Contract." University of Florida IFAS Extension, 2001. http://edis.ifas.ufl.edu/pdffiles/LH/LH03100.pdf.

Chapter 13: Employer Requirements

"Basic Employer Requirements." Montana's Official State Website. http://wsd.dli.mt.gov.

"Independent Contractors vs. Employees." Internal Revenue Service. http://www.irs.gov.

Form DE 542, *Report of Independent Contractors*. State of California Empoyment Development Department. 2005. http://www.edd.ca.gov/pdf_pub_ctr/de542.pdf.

Fujie, Ronald, CPA. Email correspondence with the author, 2009.

"Poster Page: Workplace Poster Requirements for Small Businesses and Other Employers." U.S. Department of Labor Office of Small Business Programs. September, 2006. http://www.dol.gov.

"Publication 15: (Circular E) Employer's Tax Guide." Internal Revenue Service. January, 2006. http://www.irs.gov.

"Publication 15a: Employer's Supplemental Tax Guide." Internal Revenue Service. January, 2006. http://www.irs.gov.

"Publication 1179: Independent Contract or Employee." Internal Revenue Service. http://www.irs.gov.

"Publication 509: Tax Calendars for 2006." Internal Revenue Service. December, 2005. http://www.irs.gov.

"Recordkeeping." U.S. Department of Labor Occupational Safety and Health Administration, 2001. http://www.osha.gov/.

"Ten Steps to Hiring Your First Employee". Small Business Administration, 2010. http://business.sba.gov/business-law/employment/hiring/first-employee.html.

Steingold, Fred. *The Employer's Legal Handbook*. 7th ed. California: Nolo Press, 2005.

Chapter 14: Bookkeeping

Coleman, Mary-Alice and Richard Elbrecht. *Using The Small Claims Court; A Handbook for Plaintiffs and Defendants*. California: California Department of Consumer Affairs, 1992.

Fujie, Ronald, CPA. Email correspondence with the author, 2009.

Kamoroff, Bernard. *Small Time Operator: How to Start Your Own Business, Keep Your Books, Pay Your Taxes, and Stay Out of Trouble!* 8th ed. California: Bell Springs, 2004.

Pinson, Linda. *Keeping The Books: Basic Recordkeeping and Accounting for the Successful Small Business*. 6th ed. Kaplan Business, 2004.

"Publication 535: Business Expenses." Internal Revenue Service, 2005. http://www.irs.gov.

"Publication 583: Starting A Business And Keeping Records." Internal Revenue Service. March, 2006. http://www.irs.gov.

"Recordkeeping in Small Business." U.S. Small Business Administration. http://www.sba.gov.

Chapter 15: Taxes

"2005 Instructions for Form 1065:U.S. Return of Partnership Income." Internal Revenue Service, 2005. http://www.irs.gov.

"2005 Instructions for Forms 1099, 1098, 5498, and W-2G." Internal Revenue Service, 2005. http://www.irs.gov.

"2005 Instructions for Forms 1120 and 1120-A." Internal Revenue Service, 2005. http://www.irs.gov.

"2005 Instructions for Form 2210." Internal Revenue Service, 2005. http://www.irs.gov.

"2005 Instructions for Schedule C: Profit or Loss From Business." Internal Revenue Service, 2005. http://www.irs.gov.

"2005 Instructions for Schedule SE (Form 1040): Self Employment Tax." Internal Revenue Service, 2005. http://www.irs.gov.

"2006 Instructions for Form 1099-MISC." Internal Revenue Service, 2006. http://www.irs.gov.

"2006 Instructions for Schedule C: Profit or Loss From Business." Internal Revenue Service, 2006. http://www.irs.gov.

Daily, Frederick W. *Tax Savvy for Small Business*. 9th ed. California: Nolo, 2005.

Fishman, Stephen. *Deduct It! Lower Your Small Business Taxes*. 2nd ed. California: Nolo Press, 2005.

"Form 1040-ES: Estimated Tax For Individuals." Internal Revenue Service, 2007. http://www.irs.gov.

"Form 1040: Schedule C: Profit or Loss From Business." Internal Revenue Service, 2005. http://www.irs.gov.

"Form 1040: Schedule C-EZ:Net Profit from Business." Internal Revenue Service, 2005. http://www.irs.gov.

"Form 1040: Schedule C-EZ: Net Profit from Business." Internal Revenue Service, 2005. http://www.irs.gov.

"Form 1040: Schedule E: Supplemental Income and Loss." Internal Revenue Service, 2005. http://www.irs.gov.

"Form 1040: Schedule SE:Self Employment Tax." Internal Revenue Service, 2006. http://www.irs.gov.

"Form 1040X: Amended U.S. Individual Tax Return." Internal Revenue Service. http://www.irs.gov.

"Form 1065: U.S. Return of Partnership Income." Internal Revenue Service, 2005. http://www.irs.gov.

"Form 1099-MISC." Internal Revenue Service, 2007. http://www.irs.gov.

"Form 2210: Underpayment of Estimated Tax by Individuals, Estates, and Trusts." Internal Revenue Service, 2005. http://www.irs.gov.

"Form 3115:Application for Change in Accounting Method." Internal Revenue Service, 2005. http://www.irs.gov.

"Form 8822:Change of Address." Internal Revenue Service. http://www.irs.gov.

"Form 8829:Expensese for Business Use of Your Home." Internal Revenue Service, 2006. http://www.irs.gov.

"Form 8832:Entity Classification Election." Internal Revenue Service. http://www.irs.gov.

"Form 8846: Credit for Employer Social Security and Medicare Taxes Paid on Certain Employee Tips." Internal Revenue Service, 2005. http://www.irs.gov.

"Form 8881: Credit for Small Employer Pension Plan Startup Costs." Internal Revenue Service, 2005. http://www.irs.gov.

"Form SS-4: Application for Employer Identification Number." Internal Revenue Service. February, 2006. http://www.irs.gov.

"Form SS-8: Determination of Worker Status for Purpose of Federal Employment Taxes and Income Tax Withholding." Internal Revenue Service. November, 2006. http://www.irs.gov.

"Home-Based Business Tax Avoidance Schemes." Internal Revenue Service. http://www.irs.gov.

"Instructions for Form 3115." Internal Revenue Service, 2006. http://www.irs.gov.

"Instructions for Form 4562." Internal Revenue Service, 2005. http://www.irs.gov.

"Instructions for Form 8829." Internal Revenue Service, 2005. http://www.irs.gov.

Daily, Frederick W. *Tax Savvy for Small Business.* 9th ed. California: Nolo, 2005.

Kamoroff, Bernard. *Small Time Operator: How to Start Your Own Business, Keep Your Books, Pay Your Taxes, and Stay Out of Trouble!* 8th ed. California: Bell Springs 2004.

"Publication 15-A: Employer's Supplemental Tax Guide." Internal Revenue Service. January, 2007. http://www.irs.gov.

"Publication 334:Tax Guide for Small Business." Internal Revenue Service, 2005. http://www.irs.gov.

"Publication 463: Travel, Entertainment, Gift, and Car Expenses." Internal Revenue Service, 2006. http://www.irs.gov.

"Publication 535: Business Expenses." Internal Revenue Service, 2006. http://www.irs.gov.

"Publication 538: Accounting Periods and Methods." Internal Revenue Service. March, 2004. http://www.irs.gov.

"Publication 553: Highlights of 2005 Tax Changes." Internal Revenue Service. March, 2006. http://www.irs.gov.

"Publication 560: Retirement Plans for Small Business." Internal Revenue Service, 2005. http://www.irs.gov.

"Publication 583: Starting a Business and Keeping Records." Internal Revenue Service. January, 2007. http://www.irs.gov.

"Publication 587: Business Use of Your Home." Internal Revenue Service, 2006. http://www.irs.gov.

"Publication 590-A: Contributions to Individual Retirement Arrangements." Internal Revenue Service, 2017. http://www.irs.gov.

"Publication 600: State and Local General Sales Taxes." Internal Revenue Service, 2006. http://www.irs.gov.

"Publication 946: How To Depreciate Property." Internal Revenue Service, 2005. http://www.irs.gov.

Tyson, Eric and David Silverman. *Taxe$ For Dummie$.* 1997 ed. California: IDG Books Worldwide, Inc., 1997.

"The Examination (Audit) Process." Internal Revenue Service. January, 2006. http://www.irs.gov.

"What You Should Know About The Audit Reconsideration Process." Internal Revenue Service. http://www.irs.gov.

Index

fruit trees; *see also* pruning
    biennial bearing/alternate bearing, 137
    chill factor, 137
    chill hour, 137
    genetic dwarfs, 133, 137
    pests, 147–149
    physiology, 135
    rootstocks, 136–137
    size control, 139–140
    spurs, 135–136, 140, 141
FUTA, 189

G

gasoline containers, 19, 25, 29, 33–34
gasoline stabilizer, 17
gate valve, *see* irrigation systems
gear-driven sprinklers, *see* irrigation systems
general and administrative overhead (G&A overhead), 189–193
general conditions, 183, 187–188, 189, 193
general liability, *see* insurance
genetic dwarfs, *see* fruit trees
grandifloras, *see* pruning: roses
grass trimmers, 14, 15, 16, 18, 39, 40, 186
    safety, 26, 29, 40
greensand, 47
gross income, gross profit, gross sales, 223, 225
ground fault circuit interrupter (GFCI), 170
guesstimation, 181–182
gypsum, 104

H

hand-arm vibration syndrome (HAVS), 35
hand tools, 18–20, 29, 145, 146
    and estimating, 192
Harivandi, Ali, 50
haul debris (equipment), 188
haul debris (labor), 188
heading back, *see* pruning
head-to-head coverage, *see* irrigation systems
hearing protection, 20, 25–26, 28
hearing protectors, 16, 20, 28, 35, 192
heat exhaustion and heatstroke, 34
heavenly bamboo (*Nandina domestica*), 120
hedge clippers, 14, 15, 111, 120, 185
hedges, 15, 199–121

hemlock (*Tsuga*), 114
herbicides, 8, 11, 20, 31, 67, 201, 204; *see also* pesticides
    and turf cutting height, 43
    as mulch alternative, 40
    organic alternatives, 204
    and suckers, 117
    weed and feed, 54, 83
home-office, 191, 193, 229–230
honeydew, 147
horticultural oil, 70, 131, 146–149, 201
hourly equipment costs, 185–187
humus, 97, 98, 100, 101, 103, 108
Huston, James R., 182, 183, 184, 185, 187, 189, 190, 191, 192, 193, 194, 195, 197
hybrid tea roses, 125, 129, 130; *see also* pruning
hydrangeas, 108

I

impact drive sprinklers, 39, 153, 155–156
income, 213, 214, 215, 216, 217, 219, 223, 224, 225, 226, 232, 233
included bark, 74, 115, 123
income ledger, *see* ledgers
independent contractor, 209, 211–212
Individual Retirement Arrangements (IRAs), 223, 233
inlet port, *see* irrigation systems
insects
    common fruit tree pests, 147–149
    and dormant sprays, 146
    and IPM, 68–70, 147, 201, 202, 239
    overwintering on roses, 131
    and safety, 32–33
    and soil structure, 97–98
    and sunlight protection for trees, 148
    and thatch, 66–67
insurance
    agents, 11
    business, 9–10
    coverage B (employer liability), 207
    deducting employee health insurance, 226
    deducting business insurance, 225, 227
    disability, 208, 209
    general liability, 11, 189, 227
    health, 9
    and home office deduction, 229

U

undercut nozzles, 155
underground feeder (UF) wire, 172
underground utilities, 30
Underwriters Laboratories (UL), 172
unemployment taxes, 189, 211, 229
Uniform Partnership Act (UPA), 6
urea, *see* nitrogen

V

valve seat/seat assembly, *see* irrigation systems
valves, *see* irrigation systems
vehicle expenses, 216, 222, 225, 226
vehicle insurance, 9, 11
vertical spacing, 123, 134; *see also* training
verticutting, 68, 202
vibration reduction, 14, 36
vibration white finger, 35
volatilization, *see* nitrogen
voltage, 168
volt/ohm meter (VOM), 19, 168–169, 170, 171, 172, 173, 174; *see also* digital multimeter (DMM)

W

warm-season grasses, *see* turfgrass
wasps, 32, 69
water hammer, 163, 177,
water-insoluble nitrogen (WIN), *see* nitrogen
water main shut off, 166, 174
watersprouts, 114, 117, 119, 138, 139, 140, 141, 143; *see also* suckers
weed and feed, *see* herbicides
weeds, 31, 37, 147, 205
    and herbicides, 54, 67
    and IPM, 68, 69, 201
    and irrigation, 55, 56
    in lawn gaps, 39, 40
    minimizing spread in turf, 44
    and mowing, 41, 42–43
    and mulch, 79, 88
    seed germination, 40, 47, 50, 67, 68, 71, 103
    tools for removing, 15, 18, 19, 69
weed whackers, *see* grass trimmers
West Nile Virus, 33

whip, 74
wildland-urban interface (WUI), 29
winterizing
    irrigation systems, 177
    roses, 131–132
    power equipment, 17–18
wire splice, 19, 171, 172, 174, 175
workers' compensation insurance, 9, 11, 189, 203, 207–208, 211
WUCOLS guide, 88, 89

X Y Z

Xylosma, 121
yew, 113, 119
zoning ordinances, 8–9
Zoysia, 37
    cutting height, 43
    nitrogen requirement, 51
    root depth potential, 60

020050619

Made in the USA
Columbia, SC
31 May 2020